Mental Illness, Human Rights and the Law

This book is dedicated to Regina, Eoin and Isabel

Mental Illness, Human Rights and the Law

Brendan D. Kelly

RCPsych Publications

RCPsych Publications is an imprint of the Royal College of Psychiatrists, 21 Prescot Street, London E1 8BB
http://www.rcpsych.ac.uk

British Library Cataloguing-in-Publication Data.
A catalogue record for this book is available from the British Library.
ISBN 978 1 909726 51 2

Distributed in North America by Publishers Storage and Shipping Company.

The views presented in this book do not necessarily reflect those of the Royal College of Psychiatrists, and the publishers are not responsible for any error of omission or fact.

Some of the material in Chapter 4 is adapted from:
  Kelly, B. D. (2015) Revising, reforming, reframing: Report of the Expert Group on the Review of the Mental Health Act 2001 (2015). *Irish Journal of Psychological Medicine*, **32**, 161–166, with permission of Cambridge University Press and the College of Psychiatrists of Ireland.

Some of the material in Chapter 6 is adapted from:
  Kelly, B. D. (2005) Structural violence and schizophrenia. *Social Science and Medicine*, 61, 721–730. ©(2005), with permission from Elsevier.

  Kelly, B. D. (2006) The power gap: freedom, power and mental illness. *Social Science and Medicine*, **63**, 2118–2128. ©(2006), with permission from Elsevier.

  Kelly, B. D. (2014) Voting and mental Illness: the silent constituency. *Irish Journal of Psychological Medicine*, **31**, 225–227, with permission of Cambridge University Press and the College of Psychiatrists of Ireland.

Some of the material in Chapter 7 is adapted from:
  Kelly, B. D. (2015) Human rights in psychiatric practice: an overview for clinicians. *BJPsych Advances*, **21**, 54–62.

This book contains public sector information licensed under the Open Government Licence v1.0 and Open Government Licence v2.0, and Scottish Parliamentary information licensed under the Open Scottish Parliament Licence v1.0.

Quotations from *The Irish Times* are used by kind permission of *The Irish Times*.

Printed by Bell & Bain Limited, Glasgow, UK.

Contents

Foreword

Tom Burns

Professor Brendan Kelly has given us three books for the price of one. In the Preface and Chapter 1 we get a brilliant, crystal-clear overview of the international legislation that has driven mental health law since the Second World War. The alphabet soup of all the various conventions (the UDHR, ECHR, CRPD and more) is clarified for us, with their key features and differences laid out and explained. In Chapters 2–5 he presents the key features of the mental health legislations that clinicians need to understand. He does this in a separate chapter for each of the three UK jurisdictions (England and Wales, Scotland and Northern Ireland) and also for Ireland. These chapters chart how each of these jurisdictions has followed its own individual route to protect the human rights of people with mental illness. What are essentially universal and timeless challenges have been approached using the same basic set of tools but with different priorities. One jurisdiction emphasises advance statements, another advocacy, one emphasises best interests, another is concerned more with risk, whereas another attempts to integrate mental health law entirely with capacity legislation. Last, in Chapters 6 and 7 we are lifted from the mechanics of mental health legislation to consider the broader social context in which the positive human rights of the mentally ill are so clearly compromised and neglected. Why, despite all the rhetoric, is this group of individuals still denied a voice and social inclusion?

Readers will get more from this book than perhaps they expect. Presumably, the most thumbed pages will be your local legislation. Kelly's style of tracing the changes across the reviews and amendments of the individual Acts makes sense of how each jurisdiction has come to its current set of principles and practices. It also highlights those things we have probably become aware of in our peripheral vision. How many of us registered, for instance, that the Mental Health Act 1983 gave mental health review tribunals powers beyond simply upholding or discharging sections? I thought they had just drifted into doing it more and more and we had gone along with it.

How important, in reality, are these differences in emphasis between the jurisdictions? As Kelly points out, the level of ambition in revising legislation varies enormously, from tidying-up operations through to radical reform; the tone and emphasis also vary considerably. Yet we know that the Acts are concerned with the same practical procedures that we carry out all the time, wherever on these islands we work. How different would the detention and tribunal review of an individual with psychosis appear to an informed observer in Ireland, Scotland or England? Is it all just words or will the differences in emphasis lead to differences in practice? For a health services researcher like me this is the greatest lost opportunity in these legislative revisions.

What a pity, in this era of evidence-based medicine, that we could not get our legislators to require a full engagement in rigorous evaluations of these changes. And by this I mean rigorous, research-informed and hypothesis-driven evaluations, not just the voluminous annual reports of routinely collected figures. Imagine if we had been able to ask each of the drafting groups (who will have spent hundreds of hours on their tasks – this is no minor undertaking) to attach a clear hypothesis to each proposed change. Even going one stage back and asking them, before fixing a change into law, to state explicitly what was wrong with the current practice. Similarly to record how that could be demonstrated. What would be the anticipated change, and how would the outcome be demonstrated? What would they anticipate to be the change in outcome by legislating for the mental health review tribunal to be able to stipulate a treatment that is not in the current care plan? What will be the effect in Scotland of increased attention to previously expressed preferences and prioritising advance directives? Perhaps most important, how would you measure its effects? How would you decide if the change had been effective and worthwhile? What finding would be enough to make them rethink their changes? Does abandoning the distinction between mental illness and personality disorder and the associated treatability requirement in England and Wales result in more frequent compulsory admissions of individuals with personality disorder? Chapters 2–5 throw up an endless series of such questions and reading across them should stimulate several comparative research projects.

In Chapters 6 and 7, where Kelly concentrates on the forces that continue to disadvantage the mentally ill, he is at his most passionate and powerful. In our current technological phase of medicine it is easy to forget that our profession has a long history of political engagement (not always benign or successful). However, the point is made with some force that the major determinants of a decent life, with dignity, with social inclusion and rights protected as much as possible, lie outside the direct therapeutic encounter. This overlap between the macro-political, what Kelly refers to as 'structural violence', and the technicalities of the treaties influencing mental health legislation provides much of the most thought-provoking and emergent quality of this book.

Kelly praises the 1950 European Convention on Human Rights (ECHR) and its adoption in 1998 as the UK's Human Rights Act. It has provided an intuitively accessible framework for clear thinking about many tricky problems and highlighted unrecognised errors. We are now all familiar with Articles 2, 5 and 8 (protection of life and of family life and the prohibition of arbitrary detention).

But what are we to make of the 2006 United Nations Convention on the Rights of Persons with Disabilities (CRPD)? Kelly welcomes its unequivocal support for an active campaign to ensure the social rights of marginalised individuals, not just a careful eye to avoid entrenching or strengthening discrimination. However, its statement that no disability should contribute to a decision to deprive an individual of their liberty appears to totally undercut the basis of any mental health law. Mental health law is predicated on the understanding that there are conditions which, by their nature, deserve and require special consideration. Indeed, the whole justification for our profession rests on this!

In the Northern Ireland 'fusion' legislation, we see the most pronounced attempt to bring mental healthcare in line with the CRPD. Whether this drive to base compulsion entirely on capacity and thereby treat the mentally and physically ill equally is convincing you will have to decide yourself. I found it tortuous and unconvincing – in particular the introduction of 'appreciation' as a way of smuggling psychiatric thinking (and presumably diagnosis) back into the process without actually naming it. Surely this would be an example of where sophisticated research could really teach us something?

The CRPD question brings up an even bigger issue that Kelly seems well aware of, but (probably sensibly) leaves out of this book. This is whether mental health law thinking has become too dominated by an Anglophone (mainly US) over-preoccupation with autonomy as the overriding (sometimes, it seems, the only) principle of medical ethics. An invariable feature of ethical principles is that they are several and they are often at variance with each other and have to be weighed up in each individual case. That, of course, is why they remain principles, not laws. Few textbooks of medical ethics get away with less than four (beneficence, non-malfeasance, autonomy, dignity) and many have several more. In most of the world the autonomous individual is not the obvious ideal. People strive to be good members of families, clans, groups and so on. Obligations are as sacred as rights.

When Isaiah Berlin delivered his 1958 inaugural lecture in Oxford on 'Two Concepts of Liberty' he distinguished 'freedom from' and 'freedom to'. He identified then the hollow boast of prizing autonomy for individuals who were left to remain diseased or hungry. Thirty years later, in the wake of the successes of their human rights initiatives in mental health, US psychiatrists were writing of the shame of patients with psychosis being left to 'die with their rights on'. Feminist sociologists, with their 'ethics of care', have consistently and cogently critiqued this overemphasis of legalism and autonomy. Psychiatrists in our daily work are confronted with its limitations, people exist in and through relationships – they are not an optional add-on. Being careful about protecting autonomy is clearly a good start (our history gives no room for complacency), but it is not really enough. In this excellent book Brendan Kelly has given us the tools and the initiative to move forward the thinking about mental health law and mental healthcare.

Tom Burns
Emeritus Professor of Social Psychiatry,
Department of Psychiatry, University of Oxford

Preface

This is a book about psychiatry, mental illness and human rights. It is also, unashamedly, a manifesto for change, urging reconsideration of the ways in which the human rights of people with mental illness are protected and promoted, and urging social activism in addition to enhanced psychiatric care.

As is both traditional and necessary, much of this book explores legislative provisions relating to the right to liberty among people with mental illness. In the complicated, contested setting of mental healthcare, it is clearly essential that involuntary detention and treatment are appropriately regulated and monitored, so as to preserve this fundamental right. The opening chapters of this book duly examine legislation relating to these matters in some detail, in England and Wales, Northern Ireland, the Republic of Ireland and Scotland.

An exclusive focus on the right to liberty alone, however, fails to address or even acknowledge a range of broader social injustices and denials of rights commonly experienced by people with enduring mental illness (Kelly, 2007a). This book takes this broader perspective strongly to heart, especially in the closing chapters, which are devoted to achieving social justice for the mentally ill and practical steps towards effecting change.

Chapter 1 sets the scene by considering the emergence of the idea of human rights in the first instance and the relationship between human rights and mental illness. This chapter also explores the United Nations (UN) Universal Declaration of Human Rights (UN, 1948) and eventual recognition of the particular importance of human rights in the context of mental illness in the late 20th century. Key provisions of the legally binding European Convention on Human Rights (ECHR) (Council of Europe, 1950) are outlined next, along with measures to incorporate the ECHR into national law in the UK (Human Rights Act 1998) and Ireland (European Convention on Human Rights Act 2003).

It is the ECHR that has produced the greatest shift in thinking in this area, with a series of judgments that strongly re-emphasised various protections for the rights of the detained mentally ill, especially in relation to humane conditions in therapeutic settings and prompt, effective reviews. As is the case throughout this book, the examination of case law in this chapter is thematic rather than exhaustive; more detailed accounts of case law are available elsewhere (e.g. Bartlett & Sandland, 2014). Instead, this chapter explores cases selected thematically to demonstrate key ECHR principles that are likely to be applicable across all countries within the remit of the ECHR, and, possibly, beyond. Chapter 1 concludes with a consideration of the UN Principles for the Protection of Persons with Mental Illness and the Improvement of Mental Health Care (1991) and the UN Convention on the Rights of Persons with Disabilities (CRPD) (2006), with particular focus on the rights of people with mental illness.

The next four chapters of the book examine legislative provisions relating to mental illness and human rights, with particular focus on involuntary admission and treatment, in England and Wales (Chapter 2), Northern Ireland (Chapter 3), Ireland (Chapter 4) and Scotland (Chapter 5).

Chapter 2 examines the Mental Health Acts of 1983 and 2007 in England and Wales, with particular emphasis on human rights. A detailed and excellent 'how to' guide for users of the legislation is already available from Zigmond (2016), so this chapter focuses instead on specific human rights issues that arose following the Mental Health Act 1983, relating to public safety, the burden of proof in mental health tribunals, the right to 'respect for private and family life' (ECHR, Article 8) and powers of tribunals to release patients. This chapter then explores key features of the Mental Health Act 2007 from a human rights perspective, including its definition of mental disorder, criteria for detention, expansion of professional roles, supervised community treatment and mental health tribunals. As with the other chapters, this chapter examines civil rather than criminal mental health legislation, provisions relating to adults rather than children, and mental health legislation rather than mental capacity legislation, although the latter is considered from time to time insofar as it relates directly to mental health legislation.

Chapter 3 examines current mental health legislative reform in Northern Ireland, commencing with the 'comprehensive legislative framework' presented by the Bamford Review of Mental Health and Learning Disability (2007a). This chapter then examines Northern Ireland's Mental Capacity Bill 2015, which seeks to fuse mental health legislation and mental capacity legislation, in apparently improved compliance with the CRPD and along lines similar to those proposed by Dawson & Szmukler (2006) and Szmukler et al (2014). This is one of the most challenging and possibly progressive innovations in European mental health legislation in several decades and merits close attention.

Chapter 4 examines mental health legislation in Ireland from a human rights perspective, exploring legislation prior to Ireland's Mental Health Act 2001 as well as key provisions of the 2001 Act. Specific human rights issues are then examined, pertaining to, among other matters, mental health tribunals for detained patients, civil proceedings in the courts, mental health tribunals for discharged patients, issues of capacity among 'voluntary' patients, the speedy introduction of the Mental Health Act 2008, and alleged paternalism in the interpretation of the 2001 Act by the Irish courts. Particular attention is paid to the implications of these matters for the human rights of the mentally ill and the likely direction of future reforms in Ireland, based on the report of the Expert Group on the Review of the Mental Health Act 2001 (2015).

Chapter 5 moves to Scotland, and focuses on reform of mental health legislation there, commencing with an overview of the Mental Health (Care and Treatment) (Scotland) Act 2003. Again, this is not an exhaustive analysis of the content of the 2003 Act or a 'how-to' manual for practitioners, but rather a basis for exploring the process of reform in Scotland, with particular emphasis on human rights. Rather than assuming an approach primarily rooted in case law, this chapter focuses on the process of reform and examines the Limited Review of the Mental Health (Care and Treatment) (Scotland) Act 2003 (Scottish Government Review Group, 2009) ('McManus Review') and subsequent Mental Health (Scotland) Act 2015. The chapter concludes with a consideration of the challenges inherent to reform of mental health legislation not only in Scotland but in other jurisdictions too.

Chapter 6 moves beyond issues directly related to mental health legislation and uses as its starting point the provisions of the CRPD, especially in relation to economic and social rights, and avoidance of discrimination and stigma. The concept of 'structural violence' (Farmer, 2003) is invoked to describe the cumulative effects of adverse social, economic and societal forces which, along with the social stigma of mental illness, impair access to psychiatric and social services among people with mental illness, impinge on rights, and amplify the effects of illness in the lives of sufferers and their families (Kelly, 2005). As a result of these overarching social and economic factors, many of the mentally ill are systematically excluded from full participation in civic and social life, and are constrained to live lives shaped by stigma, isolation, homelessness and denial of rights.

Rights-based mental health legislation is not necessarily the only or even the best way to address key aspects of this situation, which relates in large part to broader social injustice and denial of rights, rather than just denial of liberty. This chapter argues that the enhancement of individual agency is central to efforts to address the 'power gap' experienced by people with mental illness. This can be achieved, at least in part, through a combination of (a) rights-based approaches, (b) approaches based on enhancing direct political participation (e.g. voter registration, formation of more effective interest groups) and (c) additional approaches, including increasing accountability throughout services, recognising the effects of sociopolitical change on the context of care and adapting the concept of 'soft power' to strengthen advocacy programmes.

Chapter 7 concludes by summarising and synthesising key themes and arguments from earlier chapters and outlining ways in which mental health workers can protect and promote human rights and social justice in day-to-day clinical practice, as well as fight for social justice for the mentally ill at local, national and international levels (Callard *et al*, 2012). In this chapter, as is the case throughout the book, there is a strong emphasis on not only the protection of specific human rights, but also the enhancement of societal circumstances that shape the landscape in which mental illness develops and is treated, in which rights are observed or violated and in which recovery takes place.

Acknowledgements

I wish to acknowledge the educational influences of my colleagues in clinical and academic psychiatry, the doctors, nurses, social workers, occupational therapists, psychologists, lecturers, administrators and students with whom I work. I also wish to express my appreciation to Dr John Sheehan, Professor Patricia Casey, Dr Eugene Breen, Dr John Bruzzi, Dr Larkin Feeney, Dr Gavin Davidson, Mr David Jago, Ms Lynnette Maddock, two anonymous reviewers, Dr Michelle Ramage, Dr Alastair Hull and Ms Úna Fowler. In addition, I have benefited enormously from my contact with mental health patients and their families, carers, advocates and legal advisors. I am very grateful to Professor Tom Burns for writing the Foreword for this book.

This book is based, in part, on my PhD thesis at the School of Law, University of Leicester, England, titled *Human Rights Protection for the Mentally Ill through Mental Health Law in England and Ireland* (2013). I am very grateful for the support of my supervisors, Professor José Miola and Professor Elizabeth Wicks at the School of Law, University of Leicester. I am also grateful for the earlier supervision of Professor Jean V. McHale (now at Birmingham Law School, University of Birmingham) and the assistance of Ms Jane Sowler, Postgraduate Research Administrator at the School of Law, University of Leicester.

I greatly appreciate the teaching and guidance of my teachers at Scoil Chaitríona, Renmore, Galway, Ireland; St Joseph's Patrician College, Nun's Island, Galway; and the School of Medicine at the National University of Ireland (NUI) Galway.

Most of all, I appreciate deeply the support of my wife (Regina), children (Eoin and Isabel), parents (Mary and Desmond), sisters (Sinéad and Niamh) and nieces (Aoife and Aisling) throughout my various endeavours.

The contents of this book do not represent legal advice. Neither the author nor the publisher accepts any responsibility for the use of this book's contents as legal advice. In clinical and legal practice, readers are advised to seek formal legal advice in relation to matters discussed in this book, rather than relying on the overviews, analyses and opinions presented here.

Boxes

Legislation, treaties and conventions

European Union

Treaty on European Union ['Maastricht Treaty'], 1992

Treaty of Amsterdam amending the Treaty of the European Union, the Treaties establishing the European Communities and certain related acts, 1997

Charter of Fundamental Rights of the European Union, 2000

Consolidated versions of the Treaty on European Union and the Treaty on the Functioning of the European Union ['Treaty of Lisbon' or 'Reform Treaty'], 2008

UK

Habeas Corpus Act 1679

Bill of Rights 1689

Vagrancy Act 1744

Mental Treatment Act 1930

Human Rights Act 1998

Domestic Violence, Crime and Victims Act 2004

England and Wales

Mental Health Act 1959

Mental Health (Amendment) Act 1982

Mental Health Act 1983

Mental Health Act 1983 (Remedial) Order 2001

Mental Capacity Act 2005

Mental Health Act 2007

Scotland

Mental Health (Scotland) Act 1984

Criminal Procedure (Scotland) Act 1995

Adults with Incapacity (Scotland) Act 2000

Mental Health (Care and Treatment) (Scotland) Act 2003

Mental Health (Scotland) Bill 2014

Mental Health (Scotland) Bill 2015

Mental Health (Scotland) Act 2015

Northern Ireland

Mental Health (Northern Ireland) Order 1986

Enduring Power of Attorney (Northern Ireland) Order 1987

Mental Capacity Bill 2015

Ireland

Criminal Lunatics (Ireland) Act 1838

Constitution of Ireland (Bunreacht na hÉireann) 1937

Mental Treatment Act 1945

Public Authorities Judicial Proceedings Act 1954

Mental Health Bill 1999

Human Rights Commission Act 2000

Mental Health Act 2001

Mental Health Act 2008

European Convention on Human Rights Act 2003

Assisted Decision-Making (Capacity) Bill 2013

Mental Health (Amendment) Act 2015

Cases

UK

P v Cheshire West and Chester Council and Anor, and P and Q v Surrey County Council [2014] UKSC 19.

R v Deputy Governor of Parkhurst Prison, ex parte Hague and Weldon [1992] 1 AC 58.

R (C) v London South and West Region Mental Health Review Tribunal [2001] EWCA Civ 1110, [2002] 1 WLR 176.

R (D) v Secretary of State for the Home Department [2002] EWHC 2805 (Admin), [2003] 1 WLR 1315.

R (H) v Mental Health Review Tribunal [2002] EWHC 1522 (Admin), [2002] QB 1.

R (H) v Secretary of State for Health [2005] UKHL 60, [2006] 1 AC 441.

R (KB) v Mental Health Review Tribunal [2003] EWHC 193 (Admin), [2004] QB 936.

R (M) v Secretary of State for Health [2003] EWHC 1094 (Admin), [2003] 1 MHLR 88.

R (Munjaz) v Mersey Care NHS Trust [2003] EWCA Civ 1036, [2004] QB 395.

R (Munjaz) v Mersey Care NHS Trust [2005] UKHL 58, [2006] 2 AC 148.

R (N) v Ashworth Special Hospital Authority [2001] EWHC 339 (Admin), [2001] HRLR 46.

R (PS) v Responsible Medical Officer [2003] EWHC 2335 (Admin).

Rabone and Anor v Pennine Care NHS Trust [2012] UKSC 2.

Savage v South Essex Partnership NHS Foundation Trust [2008] UKHL 74.

Savage v South Essex Partnership NHS Foundation Trust [2010] EWHC 865 (QB).

Ireland

AMC v St Lukes Hospital, Clonmel [2007] IEHC 65.

Croke v Smith [1994] 3 IR 529.

Croke v Smith (No. 2) [1998] 1 IR 101.

D Han v The President of the Circuit Court and Doctor Malcolm Garland and Doctor Richard Blennerhassett and Doctor Conor Farren and Professor Patrick McKeon and the Mental Health Commission and the Mental Health Tribunal [2008] IEHC 160.

EH v Clinical Director of St. Vincent's Hospital and Ors [2009] IEHC 69.

EH v St. Vincent's Hospital and Ors [2009] IESC 46.

FW v Dept. of Psychiatry James Connolly Memorial Hospital [2008] IEHC 283.

FX v Clinical Director of the Central Mental Hospital [2015] IEHC 190.

JB v The Director of the Central Mental Hospital and Dr. Ronan Hearne and the Mental Health Commission and the Mental Health Tribunal [2007] IEHC 201.

JF v DPP [2005] 2 IR 174.

JH v Vincent Russell, Clinical Director of Cavan General Hospital [2007] unreported High Court judgment.

MD v Clinical Director of St Brendan's Hospital & Anor [2007] IEHC 183.

MM v Clinical Director Central Mental Hospital [2008] IESC 31.

MR v Cathy Byrne, administrator, and Dr. Fidelma Flynn, clinical director, Sligo Mental Health Services, Ballytivnan, Co. Sligo [2007] IEHC 73.

Patrick McCreevy v The Medical Director of the Mater Misericordiae Hospital in the City of Dublin, and the Clinical Director of St. Aloysius Ward Psychiatric Unit of the Mater Misericordiae Hospital in the City of Dublin and the Health Service Executive and, by order, the Mental Health Tribunal [2007] SS 1413.

PL v Clinical Director of St. Patricks University Hospital and Dr. Séamus Ó Ceallaigh [2012] IEHC 15.

Q v St Patrick's Hospital [2006] O'Higgins J, *ex tempore*, 21 December 2006.

SM v The Mental Health Commissioner, The Mental Health Tribunal, The Clinical Director of St Patrick's Hospital, Dublin, Attorney General and the Human Rights Commission [2008] JR 749.

TH v DPP [2006] 3 IR 520.

T O'D. v Harry Kennedy and Ors [2007] IEHC 129.

TS v Mental Health Tribunal, Ireland, The Attorney General, The Minister for Health and Children, The Mental Health Commission, Bola Oluwole and Ciaran Power [2007] JR 1562.

WQ v Mental Health Commission [2007] IEHC 154.

Z v Khattak and Anor [2008] IEHC 262.

European Court of Human Rights

CHAPTER 1

Human rights and mental illness

On 17 December 1991, the United Nations (UN) General Assembly formally adopted Resolution 46/119, which contains the Principles for the Protection of Persons with Mental Illness and the Improvement of Mental Health Care (United Nations, 1991). These principles articulate a range of rights to which individuals with mental illness are entitled, including the right to receive the best available mental healthcare, to live, work and receive treatment in the community, and to access appropriately structured and resourced mental health facilities. Furthermore, mental healthcare should be based on internationally accepted ethical standards and an impartial review body should, in consultation with mental health practitioners, review the cases of involuntary patients.

Although these principles do not have the status of 'hard law' and nation states are not obliged to adhere to them, they nonetheless represent an important recognition of the idea that individuals with mental illness require specific protection of human rights for the reason that they are mentally ill, with all of the challenges, difficulties and discrimination that this can bring (Goldman, 2000; Harding, 2000; Kelly, 2001). This chapter begins by describing the gradual emergence of this idea, commencing with the development of the concept of human rights and the emergent relationship between mental illness and the language of human rights during the 19th century. This is followed by a consideration of the UN's Universal Declaration of Human Rights (adopted in 1948) and subsequent expressions of human rights values in international legislative forms, including the Council of Europe's European Convention on Human Rights (ECHR) (drafted in 1950) (Council of Europe, 1950). The ECHR was given further effect in the UK through the Human Rights Act 1998 and in Ireland through the European Convention on Human Rights Act 2003.

The purpose of this discussion is to describe one element of the legislative background (i.e. the human rights element) against which new mental health legislation has been or is being developed in England and Wales (Mental Health Act 2007), Ireland (Mental Health Act 2001), Scotland (Mental Health (Scotland) Act 2015) and Northern Ireland

(Mental Capacity Bill 2015). Finally, this chapter presents and examines relevant provisions of the UN Principles for the Protection of Persons with Mental Illness and the Improvement of Mental Health Care (United Nations, 1991) and the UN Convention on the Rights of Persons with Disabilities (United Nations, 2006).

What are human rights?

Early philosophies of human rights

A right is an entitlement, a thing that one may legally or morally claim (Pearsall & Trumble, 1996: p. 1240). The term 'human rights' refers specifically to rights that a human being possesses by virtue of the fact that he or she is a human being (Edmundson, 2004; Ishay, 2004; Hunt, 2007). Human rights do not need to be earned or granted; they are the birthright of all human beings simply because they are human beings – no other qualification is required. The best way to understand the key philosophies of human rights is through a brief examination of the evolution of contemporary conceptualisations of human rights and the philosophies underpinning key developments in the field.

One of the earliest secular statements of human rights was issued by Cyrus the Great, King of the Achaemenid Persian Empire in the 6th century BC, and contained references to entitlements to security, liberty, freedom of movement, property ownership, and certain social and economic rights (O'Sullivan, 1998). Although it is unclear to what extent these principles were observed in practice, and whether they applied to all individuals, this statement of entitlements was nonetheless conceptually significant, and many of its principles were later reflected in both the Universal Declaration of Human Rights and the Universal Islamic Declaration of Human Rights (Islamic Council, 1981). As a result, these concepts remain central to the key philosophies of human rights today. There is also now a specific tradition of mental health law in Islamic psychiatric and legal tradition (Dols, 1987; Pridmore & Pasha, 2004; Dols, 2007).

At around the same time that Cyrus the Great issued his statement of entitlements, the Chinese philosopher Confucius (551–479 BC) outlined a philosophy that encompassed certain aspects of what are now described as human rights, including the idea that all people should have access to education and that government should take specific steps to ensure the social and moral welfare of its people (Chang, 1998). Consistent with this, Greek philosophers Socrates (469–399 BC) and Plato (428–347 BC) postulated the existence of a universal view of human goodness, forming the basis for an early version of human rights (Ishay, 2004). Aristotle (384–322 BC) believed that virtue lay at the heart of a good human life and placed strong emphasis on the individual's psychological and behavioural commitment to engage with the world in a virtuous fashion that promoted the common good.

Marcus Tullius Cicero (106–43 BC), a Roman statesman and legal scholar, also accorded substantial importance to the actions and reasoning of the individual in respect of the common good. Cicero postulated the existence of a natural law that was applicable to all men, in accordance with nature and unchanging over time (Cicero, 54–51 BC). This conception of natural law confirmed the uniqueness and dignity of each individual, and emphasised the need for individuals to act in the service of others and of society in general.

From a philosophical perspective, the idea of 'natural rights' is one of the key theories of rights that remains both relevant and contested today (Freeman, 2002: pp. 18–22). Cicero's conception of universal justice was consistent with the foundation texts of many philosophical, religious and spiritual traditions, most of which contain teachings about individuals' entitlements and responsibilities which could now be interpreted as reflecting concepts and values that correspond to contemporary human rights.

René Cassin, one of the key architects of the Universal Declaration of Human Rights, noted the particular relevance of Jewish principles of justice (Ishay, 2004), which echo earlier concepts outlined in Hammurabi's Code, the oldest body of laws still in existence, but broaden the application of these principles to include both Jews and gentiles. Similarly, in Islamic tradition, the Qur'an outlined analogous principles of respect, solidarity and justice, and literature based on Buddhist philosophy in India contains myriad expressions of similar philosophical principles (Ali, 1989).

The Enlightenment: the philosophy of secular human rights

The more immediate philosophical roots of the secular human rights movement lie in the 18th-century Enlightenment, which saw a decline in the influence of the Roman Catholic Church in Europe and the birth of new attitudes with ostensibly greater roots in secular rationality. Thomas Hobbes (1588–1679) believed that every individual had the right to life and that entering into a form of social contract with other people could deepen the protection of this basic, natural right.

From a philosophical perspective, this idea of the 'social contract' remains one of the key underpinnings of human rights thought today (Hunt, 2007: p. 285) and can be traced clearly to England's Habeas Corpus Act 1679, which aimed to protect the individual from violations of personal liberty by the state (e.g. wrongful imprisonment) (Adams, 1912). The Habeas Corpus Act 1679 built on the provisions of both the Petition of Right 1628, which confirmed 'the diverse rights and liberties of the subjects', and, to a lesser extent, the Magna Carta (1215), which guaranteed the right to a free trial for freemen.

The English Bill of Rights 1689 further endorsed the rule of law and underlined the importance of 'the true, ancient and indubitable rights and liberties of the people of this kingdom'. It placed particular emphasis on the need to protect the individual from unduly harsh treatment by the state, with a specific prohibition of 'cruel or unusual punishments'. In 1689–1690, John Locke (1632–1704) published his *Letter Concerning Toleration*, which asserted the individual's right to freedom of religion (Locke, 1689), and his *Second Treatise of Government*, which balanced the individual's natural right to preserve their own life with their duty to preserve the lives of others (Locke, 1690).

According to Locke, the state had the right to make and enforce laws provided that it acted in a fashion consistent with the trust placed in it: this was the 'social contract'. Seven decades later, Jean-Jacques Rousseau (1712–1778), a Swiss-French philosopher and social critic, published *The Social Contract* (1762), in which he argued that while an individual's private interests may differ from the social interest, the individual still benefitted from entering a social contract that protected civil rights, such as the right to legally own property. With Rousseau, the 'social contract' became a key iconic feature of philosophies of human rights.

The USA and France: a political philosophy of individual rights

In 1776, Thomas Paine (1737–1809), an English writer and revolutionary, produced an influential pamphlet entitled *Common Sense*, in which he called for equal rights for all citizens. A political philosophy of individual rights was further endorsed by the US Declaration of Independence in July 1776. This Declaration had, in turn, a substantial influence on the drafting of the US Constitution of 1787 and, in particular, the first ten amendments, known collectively as the Bill of Rights (1791). Despite the conceptual and rhetorical advances represented by the Constitution and Bill of Rights, however, it is apparent that these rights and principles were not necessarily universal, as, for example, the Constitution still left the issue of slavery at the discretion of individual states.

Moreover, the framers of the Declaration of Independence, by stating that certain 'truths' were 'self-evident', presupposed the existence of self-evident, natural rights which, by implication, stemmed from Cicero's philosophy of natural law, applicable everywhere and to all. The philosophy of natural law was strongly opposed by the English philosopher and jurist Jeremy Bentham (1748–1832), who argued that natural law was entirely without basis and proposed adapting the principle of utility (or net benefit) when assessing human laws and actions (Welch, 1984). Over a century later, writing in the context of the Universal Declaration of Human Rights, Macdonald (1963) similarly suggested that natural rights had no apparent basis in nature, were essentially the product of human choices and provided no 'natural' basis for theories of human rights. Nonetheless, the idea of 'natural rights' is still a key element of the philosophy of human rights in practice in many countries.

Another, later philosophy of human rights stems from the idea that they are rooted human nature, i.e. a combination of shared observations about the state of being human, including, for example, the existence of human needs and an individual sense of human dignity. On the basis of considerations such as these, Nussbaum (1992, 2000) developed a theory of human 'capabilities' in which, for example, the ability of the individual to reason suggests the existence of a right to protect the individual's freedom of conscience. As a general basis for governing human conduct, however, this theory presents significant difficulties, including its minimal guidance on (i) making difficult moral distinctions between what is 'good' and 'bad' (Freeman, 2002) and (ii) reaching resolution when the needs of one person are incompatible with those of another (Gray, 1986).

Notwithstanding these philosophical controversies over concepts of 'natural' rights, which emerged in the 18th century and persist to this day, the French Revolution of 1789–1799 was to prove an important step forward for the formal recognition of individual human rights in Europe, culminating in the adoption of the *Déclaration des droits de l'homme et du citoyen* (Declaration of the Rights of Man and of the Citizen) by the Assemblée Nationale Constituante (National Constituent Assembly) in August 1789.

The French Declaration transformed the language of human rights, and while its text did not win universal approval, criticisms such as that launched by Edmund Burke (1729–1797) in 1790 tended to generate swift and emphatic defences from writers such as Mary Wollstonecraft (1759–1797) and Thomas Paine, in his celebrated *Rights of Man* (1791). Notwithstanding these defences, however, there was still clear room for expansion of the principle of universalism, and in 1791 the French writer Olympe de Gouges (born Marie Gouze, 1748–1793) wrote an outspoken *Déclaration des droits de la femme et de la citoyenne* (Declaration of the Rights of Woman and of the Citizen), and the English writer Mary Wollstonecraft followed suit in 1792 with *A Vindication of the Rights of Woman*.

As both de Gouges and Wollstonecraft warned, the exclusion of women and other groups from these declarations of rights was to prove a particularly problematic legacy of 18th-century rights movements. In the UK, the exclusion of certain groups from voting rights came to particular prominence in the early 1800s, as William Lovett (1800–1877), a London political activist, published *The People's Charter* (1838), which recommended that every person over 21 years of age should be entitled to vote (Thompson, 1971). These developments highlight another of the key features of many philosophies underlying human rights that remains highly relevant today: equality (Freeman, 2002: pp. 107–108).

Despite the popularity of the Chartist and similar movements, voting rights were not extended to all male citizens until the end of the 19th century and the struggle for votes for women was to continue into the 20th century. Gradually, however, the suffragette movement attained voting rights for women in various countries around the world, including New Zealand (1893) and Norway (1913) and, eventually, the UK (1918) and USA (1920). In the USA, the exclusion of slaves from the new language of rights had already led to the American Civil War (1861–1865), resulting in three

5

new amendments to the US Constitution, abolishing slavery (Thirteenth Amendment), extending federal legal protections to all citizens regardless of race (Fourteenth Amendment) and abolishing racial restrictions on voting (Fifteenth Amendment).

Overall, then, the key philosophies of human rights underpinning the emergence of contemporary ideas of rights included natural law, the idea of a social contract, the principle of equality, and some of the philosophies informing recurring critiques of human rights, such as those laid out by Burke and Bentham. Many of these philosophical debates continue today and are unlikely ever to be resolved definitively. This, arguably, is an essential feature of human rights discourse: a diversity of philosophies is necessary to ensure that concepts of human rights remain relevant and applicable as societies evolve and change over time.

Mental illness and human rights in the 19th century

One of the groups not specifically mentioned in these declarations of rights were those with mental illness. Historical evidence suggests that throughout the course of the 18th and 19th centuries, individuals with mental illness in much of Europe tended to live lives of poverty and destitution, generally untouched by changing trends in political thought (Psychiatrist, 1944; Shorter, 1997). In 1817, the House of Commons of the United Kingdom of Great Britain and Ireland set up a Select Committee to examine the state of 'the lunatic poor in Ireland' (Reynolds, 1992). The Right Honourable Denis Browne (a Mayo Member of Parliament) gave evidence about the fate of people with mental illness in rural Ireland:

> 'There is nothing so shocking as madness in the cabin of the peasant, where the man is out labouring in the fields for his bread, and the care of the woman of the house is scarcely sufficient for the attendance on the children. When a strong young man or woman gets the complaint, the only way they have to manage is by making a hole in the floor of the cabin not high enough for the person to stand up in, with a crib over it to prevent his getting up, the hole is about five feet deep, and they give the wretched being his food there, and there he generally dies. Of all human calamity, I know of none equal to this, in the country parts of Ireland which I am acquainted with' (Select Committee on the Lunatic Poor in Ireland, 1817: p. 23).

In Ireland, which was a predominantly Catholic country, the Catholic Church played little role in providing for the mentally ill during this period, although there is evidence that it did not support witch hunts against individuals with mental illness in Ireland (such as occurred in many European countries) (Robins, 1986). In England and Wales, by contrast, there is greater evidence of proactive involvement of religious groups in providing for the mentally ill. In 1792, for example, following the death of a Quaker woman in the York Lunatic Asylum, William Tuke, himself a Quaker, founded the Retreat, a private hospital for individuals with mental illness (Torrey & Miller, 2001). Fifty years later, the Anglican Church played a pivotal role in establishing the list of subscribers for the North Wales Lunatic Asylum in Denbeigh (in the 1840s), when members of the Bible Society were also recruited for door-to-door collections (Michael & Hirst, 1999; Andrews & Scull, 2002).

Consistent with this difference between the attitudes of the Catholic Church in Ireland and those of religious groups in various parts of Great Britain, there is evidence that differences between Catholic and Protestant groups in Ireland had significant impacts on both asylum life and interpretations of mental illness. Up until 1904, for example, all of the physicians and staff at Ballinasloe Asylum (in the west of Ireland) were Protestant, whereas over 90% of patients were Catholic (Walsh, 1999). Irish Protestants tended to attribute mental illness resulting from 'religious excitement' to certain features of Roman Catholicism, although records from Ballinasloe Asylum would appear to suggest that 'religious excitement' was, in fact, more common among Protestants than among Catholics at this time.

Notwithstanding the varying responses of religious groups to the problems presented by the large numbers of mentally ill persons in need of medical and social care, philanthropic and governmental responses were remarkably consistent across Europe and the USA, as public authorities moved swiftly to establish large institutions dedicated to accommodating this 'hurried weight of human calamity' (Hallaran, 1810), providing shelter, food and (later) various forms of 'treatment'.

The expansion in asylum populations was particularly notable in England and Ireland: in 1859, there were 1.6 asylum inmates per 1000 population in England, and by 1909 this had risen to 3.7 per 1000 (Shorter, 1997). In Ireland, there were 3234 individuals in asylums in 1851, and by 1914 this had risen to 16 941 (Williamson, 1970; Walsh & Daly, 2004; Kelly, 2008a). This expansion in asylum populations was attributable to both governmental concern about the social problems presented by the mentally ill and the philanthropic impulses of 19th-century social activists.

The relative absence of mental illness from human rights discourse throughout this period is probably related to a number of factors, including the absence of clear definitions of 'lunacy' or mental illness, the paucity of effective treatments, stigma associated with mental illness, and the resultant exclusion of individuals with mental illness from most forms of political and societal discourse (Shorter, 1997; Kelly, 2005, 2006a; Scull, 2005). Ironically, it is likely that the era of institutionalisation in the late 19th century represented a time when there was a particular need to focus on the human rights of the mentally ill, especially given the close relationship between mental health policy and the exercise of governmental power in the form of involuntary detention and treatment (Gostin & Gable, 2004).

The dramatic increase in numbers of patients detained in asylums in the 19th century certainly represented a significant exercise of governmental power, and while generally motivated by humanitarian concerns, this

7

development was to bring myriad problems chiefly related to involuntary admission processes that often resulted in lengthy periods of detention in large public asylums, at least some of which were severely overcrowded and poorly therapeutic.

In addition, admission to asylums was, in both England and Ireland, generally possible only on an involuntary basis, and the most common pathways into asylums involved criminal as opposed to civil processes in the courts: in Ireland, for example, the Criminal Lunatics (Ireland) Act 1838 provided that individuals who were considered to be dangerous could be detained indefinitely at the behest of two justices of the peace, who had the option of using medical evidence to inform their decision (but did not have to). As the 19th century progressed, it was readily apparent that the 'dangerous lunacy' procedures were commonly misused, resulting in lengthy, inappropriate detentions in ill-suited institutions (Kelly, 2008b). The situation in England was similar, with an emphasis on involuntary as opposed to voluntary admission and a strong trend towards increased rates of detention (Torrey & Miller, 2001).

In theory, the emerging interest in the protection of the civil and political rights of all human beings throughout the 18th and 19th centuries should, automatically and without discrimination, have included the protection of the civil and political rights of individuals with mental illness. The historical experiences of the mentally ill, however, and especially their increased rates of incarceration, highlight the need for proactive consideration of the human rights of this group, especially when they may lack capacity, opportunity or facility adequately to assert these rights for themselves. The need to provide dedicated safeguards for the rights of the mentally ill was not to be substantively recognised in the 19th century, however, as formal declarations of human rights did not include specific consideration of increased risks to the civil and political rights of people with mental illness until well into the 20th century.

Human rights in the early 20th century

The tumultuous events of the early decades of the 20th century resulted in significant political change throughout Europe and directed increased attention to the concept of human rights. Following the end of the First World War (1914–1918), the League of Nations (an international organisation founded to prevent further war) oversaw the establishment of several newly independent states in Europe and there was, in at least some countries, recognition of a need for particular protections for the rights of specific groups. The 1918 Russian Declaration of the Rights of the Working and Exploited People (*Deklaratsia prav trudyashchegosya i ekspluatiruemogo naroda*), for example, focused on workers' rights and aimed 'to abolish all exploitation of man by man, to completely eliminate the division of society into classes, to mercilessly crush the resistance of the exploiters' (Lenin, 1918; quotation from 1964 reprint: p. 423). Typically, this document blended the general language of human rights with the more specific and occasionally colourful language of the political values its authors sought to promote (i.e. communism).

Two decades later, the advent of the Second World War (1939–1945), commencing with the German invasion of Poland in September 1939, highlighted the fragility of the uneasy world order that was established after the First World War and demonstrated the need for stronger international mechanisms to prevent the emergence of conflict between nations, resolve disputes as they arise, and protect individual human rights both within and across national borders. In 1941, in the midst of the Second World War, Franklin D. Roosevelt, President of the United States, outlined 'four essential human freedoms' in an influential address to the US Congress; these were: 'freedom of speech and expression', 'freedom of every person to worship God in his own way', 'freedom from want' and 'freedom from fear' (Roosevelt, 1941; quotation from 2005 reprint: p. 359).

In light of the unprecedented destruction and atrocities of the Second World War, a new international body was founded to replace the League of Nations, promote international peace and security, and reduce the possibility of further world wars. The United Nations was formally established on 24 October 1945 with the ratification of the Charter of the United Nations by the five permanent members of the UN Security Council: the USA, UK, Republic of China, Union of Soviet Socialist Republics (USSR) and France. The Charter built on previous dialogue and agreements reached in the 1942 Declaration by United Nations and at the 1944 Dumbarton Oaks Conference in Washington, DC. One of the primary aims of the new organisation was to articulate an intellectual and legal framework to support the observance of human rights among member states and promote a culture of human rights in the world.

The Universal Declaration of Human Rights

The Declaration

To promote its goals through an international bill of rights, the UN created the UN Commission on Human Rights in 1946, and a final draft of the Universal Declaration of Human Rights was adopted by the UN General Assembly at Palais de Chaillot in Paris on 10 December 1948 (Morsink, 1999; Ishay, 2004). The Declaration was presented as a non-binding statement of rights and ratified by 50 of the 58 UN member states; the Byelorussian SSR, Czechoslovakia, Poland, Saudi Arabia, South Africa, the Ukrainian SSR, the USSR and Yugoslavia abstained.

The Universal Declaration of Human Rights comprises 30 articles, preceded by a short preamble stating that 'recognition of the inherent dignity and of the equal and inalienable rights of all members of the human family is the foundation of freedom, justice and peace in the world' and that 'it is essential, if man is not to be compelled to have recourse, as a last resort, to rebellion against tyranny and oppression, that human rights should be protected by the rule of law'. Article 1 states that 'all human beings are born free and equal in dignity and rights' and Article 2 establishes the universal nature of these rights: 'Everyone is entitled to all the rights and freedoms set forth in this Declaration, without distinction of any kind, such as race, colour, sex, language, religion, political or other opinion, national or social origin, property, birth or other status'.

This emphasis on universality was both useful and necessary, not least because previous declarations of rights had commonly been interpreted in such a way as to exclude certain groups (e.g. women). The UN Declaration provided a list of factors that explicitly were not to form the basis of discrimination in relation to rights. Although mental illness was not specifically mentioned in this list, the universal spirit of the Declaration was beyond doubt and its exhortation against discrimination on the basis of 'other status' can reasonably be interpreted as including discrimination on the basis of mental illness. In 1991, the UN made this more explicit in its Principles for the Protection of Persons with Mental Illness and the Improvement of Mental Health Care (see pp. 28–29 below).

Articles 3 to 19 of the Universal Declaration of Human Rights articulate a range of rights fundamentally rooted in the principle of liberty, including 'the right to life, liberty and security of person'. The explicit articulation of this right, especially in the context of universal rights, is particularly relevant to people with mental illness, not least because of their increased risk of lengthy involuntary detention in various institutions. Again, the need to respect the right to liberty, along with the other rights outlined in the Universal Declaration of Human Rights, was strongly re-emphasised in 1991 in the UN's Principles for the Protection of Persons with Mental Illness and the Improvement of Mental Health Care.

Articles 20 to 26 of the Universal Declaration of Human Rights outline rights related to equality and political participation: Article 23 provides for the individual's 'right to work'; Article 25 states that 'everyone has the right to a standard of living adequate for the health and well-being of himself and of his family'; and Article 26 provides 'the right to education' which 'shall be free, at least in the elementary and fundamental stages'.

Articles 27 and 28 outline social and cultural rights 'to participate in the cultural life of the community, to enjoy the arts and to share in scientific advancement and its benefits' within the context of 'a social and international order in which the rights and freedoms set forth in this Declaration can be fully realized'. Finally, Articles 29 and 30 outline the overall principles governing the observance of these human rights, including the provision that these rights 'shall be subject only to such limitations as are determined by law solely for the purpose of securing due recognition and respect for the rights and freedoms of others and of meeting the just requirements of morality, public order and the general welfare in a democratic society'.

Controversies relating to the Universal Declaration of Human Rights

In the seven decades since its adoption, the Universal Declaration of Human Rights has proven both an influential and a controversial document. In terms of controversy, the eight countries that abstained from ratifying the Declaration at the outset in 1948 expressed immediate concerns about both specific rights (e.g. freedom of movement) and the possibility that the non-binding Declaration might challenge domestic jurisdictions (Ishay, 2004).

This concern was compounded by the perceived Western bias of the Declaration (Cassese, 1992), with some commentators seeing the Declaration as a reinforcement of the political values of the USA and Western Europe, with limited applicability to other areas of the world (Pollis & Schwab, 1980). More specifically, some Islamic commentators were concerned that the Declaration failed adequately to reflect Islamic culture, religion and tradition; as a result, on 5 August 1990, representatives of 45 Islamic countries in the Organization of the Islamic Conference adopted an alternative declaration of rights, the Cairo Declaration on Human Rights in Islam (Organization of the Islamic Conference, 1990).

The Universal Declaration of Human Rights also generated controversy owing to the exclusion of certain rights, such as an explicit right to conscientious objection. The Irish politician and Nobel Peace Prize winner Seán MacBride (1904–1988) emphasised this omission in his 1974 Nobel lecture and suggested that 'the right to refuse to kill' be added to the Declaration (MacBride, 1997). Various other rights that were not accorded prominence in the Universal Declaration of Human Rights have also become the subjects of increasing concern over the years. These include the right to a clean environment (Tomuschat, 2008) and the rights of specific groups such as gay, lesbian and transgender individuals (Smith, 2007). Some of these criticisms can be addressed, at least in part, through appeal to other rights in the original Declaration (such as rights to life or to freedom of opinion and expression), but they also reflect the ongoing and legitimate evolution of concepts of rights since the Declaration was agreed.

Other controversies have focused on the inclusion of certain rights, especially economic and social rights, in the Declaration. Whereas civil and political rights are primarily concerned with protection of the individual from undue interference by the state and facilitation of participation in civil and political life without repression or discrimination, economic and social rights are primarily concerned with socioeconomic matters as they relate to the individual, such as rights to food, housing and health.

There is considerable controversy over just how justiciable such rights truly are, given their inevitable relationship with a state's political and economic situations (Freeman, 2002; Neier, 2006). Their inclusion in the Universal Declaration of Human Rights was the subject of considerable debate during the initial drafting process (Morsink, 1999) and this

11

persistent concern (Puta-Chekwe & Flood, 2001) resulted in the adoption of two separate covenants by the UN General Assembly in 1966: the International Covenant on Civil and Political Rights and the International Covenant on Economic, Social and Cultural Rights.

One of the key differences between these covenants was the immediacy with which these two categories of rights were to be observed: civil and political rights were to be implemented immediately, whereas social and cultural rights were to be implemented progressively, consistent with other national programmes. In other words, the realisation of social and cultural rights was explicitly dependent on a range of other factors, such as policy programmes in specific states, economic plans, processes of national development, and broader programmes of political action and development.

The importance of political context in the implementation of human rights was immediately apparent following the adoption of the Universal Declaration of Human Rights. The Cold War between the USA and the USSR (1940s to 1990s) presented immediate and substantial problems as both sides failed meaningfully to engage with binding human rights treaties, but did not hesitate to use the rhetoric of human rights for their own political purposes (Forsythe, 1995; Freeman, 2002; Ishay, 2004).

Notwithstanding these difficulties, there were some developments throughout the 1960s and 1970s, including, in 1967, the adoption of Resolution 1235 of the Economic and Social Council (permitting discussion of human rights violations in specific countries) and, in 1976, the establishment of the Human Rights Committee. There was also significant growth in non-governmental human rights activity in various countries during this period (e.g. Charter 77 in Czechoslovakia) (Bugajski, 1987; Havel, 2008), some of which contributed to the decline of communist political systems in Europe and elsewhere (Donnelly, 1998; Forsythe, 2000).

Following the end of the Cold War in the early 1990s, there was further expansion of public and academic human rights discourse, but also some notable failures on the part of the international community, and the UN in particular, to act to protect basic human rights in several settings (e.g. Yugoslavia in the late 1990s) (Power, 2002, 2008). The ongoing importance of political contexts in the observance of human rights was further underlined following the terrorist attacks of 11 September 2001 in the USA, when governmental responses resulted in significant restrictions on civil liberties and, arguably, a certain erosion of legal culture in the USA among other places (Tomuschat, 2008).

Mental illness and human rights in the 20th century

Notwithstanding the various challenges to the emergence of human rights discourse during the 20th century, this period saw the first signs that the new language of human rights might have some positive implications for individuals with mental illness, if only by drawing greater attention to the ever-increasing numbers detained indefinitely in large psychiatric institutions, many of which lacked appropriate, non-restrictive, therapeutic facilities (Walsh & Daly, 2004). The subsequent increase in governmental and public concern about mental illness was accompanied by a renewed emphasis on the search for new treatments and management strategies, rather than simple, interminable institutionalisation.

This therapeutic enthusiasm found its roots in the work of 19th-century psychiatrists such as Wilhelm Griesinger (1817–1868) and Emil Kraepelin (1856–1926), who precipitated a revolution in psychiatric taxonomy by differentiating between the syndromes of dementia praecox (schizophrenia) and manic depression (bipolar affective disorder). As a result of these and other developments, the early decades of the 20th century saw the emergence of novel, often controversial treatments such as insulin coma therapy and electroconvulsive therapy. Not all of these treatments have stood the test of time and some, such as lobotomy, were undoubtedly used with unjustified enthusiasm and tragic results (Shorter, 1997; El-Hai, 2005). This was, nonetheless, a period of distinct therapeutic enthusiasm that also saw the emergence of psychoanalysis, pioneered by Sigmund Freud (1856–1939) in Vienna and London, and readily adaoted by psychiatrists and psychologists throughout Europe and, especially, the USA (Shorter, 1997; Torrey & Miller, 2001; Porter, 2002).

As the 20th century progressed, there were also significant developments in relation to mental health legislation. In Ireland, for example, the Mental Treatment Act 1945 introduced several important reforms by (a) establishing a process of voluntary admission to psychiatric facilities; (b) underlining and strengthening the mandatory role of medical practitioners in certifying involuntary admissions; (c) reforming the processes whereby individuals could be transferred to in-patient forensic psychiatric care; and (d) making myriad changes to the administration and governance of psychiatric facilities (Kelly, 2008c).

By this time, Great Britain (1930) and Northern Ireland (1932) had already introduced novel mental health legislation, which, among other measures, established new procedures for voluntary admission to psychiatric in-patient facilities (O'Neill, 2005). Consistent with these relatively enlightened reforms, the therapeutic enthusiasm of the 20th century reached a peak in the early 1950s, when Jean Delay and Pierre Deniker published clinical data supporting the usefulness of chlorpromazine for the treatment of psychosis, thus establishing it as the first effective medication for the treatment of schizophrenia (Shorter, 1997).

Notwithstanding these developments, many countries saw the number of people detained in asylums continue to increase as the 20th century progressed. In Ireland, the number of psychiatric in-patients peaked in 1958, but was still notably slow to decline after that: even in 1961, one in every 70 Irish people above the age of 24 was resident in a psychiatric hospital (Lyons, 1985; Healy, 1996). In the UK, the 1957 Royal Commission on the Law Relating to Mental Illness and Mental Deficiency (the 'Percy

Commission') attempted to open a new era of 'community care' by declaring that:

> 'No patient shall be retained as a hospital in-patient when he has reached the stage at which he could return home if he had a reasonably good home to go to. At that stage the provision of residential care becomes the responsibility of the local authority' (Royal Commission on the Law Relating to Mental Illness and Mental Deficiency, 1957).

Over the following decades, considerable progress was made dismantling traditional institutional and residential care structures in the UK, although the development of community-based alternatives was criticised as being too slow and inadequate (Fadden *et al*, 1987; Dyer, 1996). In Ireland, a similar process of deinstitutionalisation also commenced, with a substantial reduction in the number of in-patient beds and renewed emphasis on the development of community facilities. As in the UK and USA, however, concern has been consistently expressed about the adequacy of social and community provision, especially for individuals with enduring illnesses such as schizophrenia (Mollica, 1983; Fadden *et al*, 1987; Dyer, 1996; Kelly, 2004*a*, 2005).

Notwithstanding these generally positive developments, the first half of the 20th century did not see the emergence of any explicit, systematic or binding recognition of a need for specific protections for the human rights of individuals with mental illness. Indeed, for much of the early 20th century, large numbers of individuals remained detained in psychiatric institutions; certain treatment initiatives appear to have been deployed excessively or inappropriately (El-Hai, 2005); there was little evidence of social reintegration or political empowerment of individuals released from asylums; and – to this day – there remain large parts of the world in which psychiatric practices are largely untouched by any of these legislative and therapeutic developments (Bloch & Reddaway, 1977, 1985; Munro, 2000, 2002, 2006; Callard *et al*, 2012).

Ultimately, clear recognition of the need to provide specific protections for the rights of the mentally ill was not to take shape until the latter half of the 20th century and, when it occurred, this development largely found its roots in international declarations of rights, including the Universal Declaration of Human Rights (1948), the European Convention on Human Rights (1950) and, eventually, the UN's Principles for the Protection of Persons with Mental Illness and the Improvement of Mental Health Care (1991).

The European Convention on Human Rights

The Convention

In 1950, the Council of Europe adopted the Convention for the Protection of Human Rights and Fundamental Freedoms (also known as the European

Convention on Human Rights (ECHR)), which aims to protect human rights and the fundamental freedoms 'which are the foundation of justice and peace in the world and are best maintained on the one hand by an effective political democracy and on the other by a common understanding and observance of the human rights upon which they depend' (Council of Europe, 1950: Preamble).

Consistent with the Universal Declaration of Human Rights, section I of the EHCR outlines a range of individual rights, including rights to life (Article 2) and to liberty, security and a fair trial (Article 5); respect for private and family life (Article 8); freedom of thought, conscience, religion (Article 9), expression (Article 10), assembly and association (Article 11); the right to marry (Article 12); and the right to 'an effective remedy before a national authority notwithstanding that the violation has been committed by persons acting in an official capacity' (Article 13). There are also prohibitions on torture (Article 3), slavery, forced labour (Article 4), discrimination (Article 14) and abuse of rights (Article 17).

Unlike the Universal Declaration of Human Rights, the ECHR established a binding legal mechanism for the enforcement of these rights, the European Court of Human Rights (Article 19), which was founded in January 1959 and by December 2007 held jurisdiction over 47 states. The number of applications to the Court has increased steadily since the 1970s, and in 2007 there were 49 750 applications, of which approximately 26 000 were dealt with judicially: over 24 000 applications were declared inadmissible or struck off the list and 1649 judgments were delivered (Tomuschat, 2008).

Notwithstanding these various challenges, the European Court of Human Rights has become the international front-runner in legislating for human rights and a model for similar initiatives elsewhere. There are, however, significant problems related not only to the limitations on financial and institutional resources for the Court, but also to enforcement of judgments, especially when findings may be attributable to deficits in domestic legal order in relevant states (Tomuschat, 2008). In addition, many of the rights outlined in the ECHR are subject to various limitations and qualifications, all of which require interpretation (Wadham et al, 2007).

Overall, there is some evidence that the ECHR has provided enhanced protection of basic human rights in ratifying states (Smith, 2007) and, more specifically, helped emphasise certain important legal principles, such as the positive obligation of public bodies to take reasonable operational measures to prevent violations of ECHR rights (Wadham et al, 2007). On this basis, Smith (2007) contends that the ECHR has matured to become the most effective and sophisticated human rights treaty in the world, and has generated the most comprehensive jurisprudence on human rights. This positive assessment is not universally agreed (Letsas, 2007) and the ECHR is, moreover, a victim of its own popularity, as demands on the Court continue to increase, resulting in delays and inefficiencies (Helfer, 2008).

The solution to these problems may lie, at least in part, in efforts to 'embed' the principles of the ECHR more deeply in national political and judicial decision-making, thus reducing the need for individuals to apply to the European Court of Human Rights with their complaints (Helfer, 2008). This kind of enhanced recognition of the ECHR at national level might be achieved in a number of ways, not least through the implementation of national legislation, such as the Human Rights Act 1998 in the UK, which clearly reflect the principles of the ECHR (see pp. 22–24 below).

The ECHR in relation to mental illness

There is now a significant body of jurisprudence in relation to mental illness and the ECHR (Perlin *et al*, 2006a,b; Bartlett *et al*, 2007). The European Court of Human Rights delivered its first significant decision in relation to mental disability in 1979 and has remained active in this area ever since: between 2000 and 2004 the Court delivered over 40 judgments relating to mental disability and various issues related to psychiatric detention (Bartlett *et al*, 2007). A wide range of issues has been addressed by the Court over this period, many of which concern (a) involuntary detention owing to mental illness, (b) conditions while detained and (c) review of involuntary detention.

Involuntary detention owing to mental illness

A number of cases before the European Court of Human Rights have centred on alleged breaches of Article 5(1) of the ECHR which states:

> 'Everyone has the right to liberty and security of person. No one shall be deprived of his liberty save in the following cases and in accordance with a procedure prescribed by law [including] (e) the lawful detention of persons for the prevention of the spreading of infectious diseases, of persons of unsound mind, alcoholics or drug addicts or vagrants'.

One of the most widely cited cases to have come before the court on this matter was *HL v UK (Bournewood)* [2004], which centred on an individual with severe intellectual disability who was compliant while in hospital but was not detained under mental health legislation; i.e. HL was an 'informal' patient, but had he tried to leave, he would have been detained.[1] HL lacked capacity to make decisions regarding treatment, so the clinical team made decisions that it believed were in HL's best interest. The European Court of Human Rights concluded that there was a breach of Article 5(1) of the ECHR when HL was an informal patient, on the basis that, although the clinical team acted in what it believed to be HL's best interests, there was no protection against arbitrary detention under these circumstances, as there would have been if HL had been legally detained (Eastman & Peay, 1998; Morris, 1999; Bartlett & McHale, 2003; Laing, 2003; Robinson & Scott-Moncrieff, 2005).

When considering whether or not there has been a breach of Article 5(1) in relation to any admission (voluntary or involuntary), the Court acknowledges a need to take account of a range of factors surrounding the admission:

'In order to determine whether someone has been "deprived of liberty" within the meaning of Article 5, the starting point must be his concrete situation and account must be taken of a whole range of criteria such as the type, duration, effects and manner of implementation of the measure in question'.[2]

The provisions of Article 5(1) may be applied not only to 'persons of unsound mind' who are physically detained in a psychiatric institution 'in accordance with a procedure prescribed by law', but also to individuals who are not physically detained in a psychiatric institution but are subject to other forms of control, such as living at home but under conditions determined by psychiatric 'community treatment orders' (Kelly, 2009a).

In relation to deciding who is and who is not of 'unsound mind', the European Court of Human Rights has made it clear that a diagnosis of mental disorder cannot be based solely on the individual holding views that differ from societal norms: according to the Court, a diagnosis of 'mental disorder' must be based on 'objective medical expertise'.[3] If an individual is to be deprived of liberty, 'the mental disorder must be of a kind or degree warranting compulsory confinement' and 'the validity of continued confinement depends upon the persistence of such a disorder'. In addition, 'it is essential that the person concerned should have access to a court and the opportunity to be heard either in person or, where necessary, through some form of representation [...]. Mental illness may entail restricting or modifying the manner of the exercise of such a right, but it cannot justify impairing the very essence of the right. Indeed, special procedural safeguards may prove called for in order to protect the interests of persons who, on account of their mental disabilities, are not fully capable of acting for themselves'.

The *Winterwerp* judgment strengthened greatly the requirement that detention on the grounds of mental illness required objective medical expertise to support such a detention in the first instance (the so-called admission order). It did not, however, specify such a requirement for renewal of such detention orders. This matter is now of increased relevance in relation to the amendments to the Mental Health Act 1983 brought about by the Mental Health Act 2007 in England and Wales: under the unamended 1983 Act, the making of a renewal order, like an admission order, required an examination and report by the 'responsible medical officer' (sections 20(3) and (4)), but following the amendments introduced by the 2007 Act, the 'responsible clinician' (who may or may not be a medical doctor) can make out a renewal order, although they must consult with another 'professional' involved before doing so (Mental Health Act 2007, section 9(4)(b); amending Mental Health Act 1983, section 20(5A)). This may not meet the *Winterwerp* criteria for 'objective medical expertise' to support detention.

The *Winterwerp* judgment also emphasised that an individual detained on grounds of mental illness should have access to a 'court' to determine the appropriateness of detention, even if the mental illness required modifications in the manner of exercising this right. The Court was especially emphatic that if an individual is detained, 'the mental disorder must be of a kind or degree warranting compulsory confinement' and 'the validity of continued confinement depends upon the persistence of such a disorder'.

In emergencies, it may be difficult to obtain 'objective medical expertise' and the Court has determined that in such situations the protections of Article 5 are reduced; i.e. it may be neither feasible nor necessary to obtain 'objective medical expertise' prior to such a detention, although such detentions still must be in accordance with domestic law.[4] The rights to review of emergency detention, under Article 5(4), are also reduced,[5] although it appears likely that the duration of the emergency detention should be minimised, and non-emergency detention instigated in a timely fashion, if indicated.[6]

The determination of whether or not an individual's mental disorder is 'of a kind or degree warranting compulsory confinement' may be based on the individual's need for treatment and/or apparent dangerousness; i.e. apparent dangerousness may be sufficient to warrant detention of an individual with mental disorder.[7] In either case, individuals who are detained pursuant to the ECHR Article 5(1)(e) have the right to be informed promptly of the reasons for their 'arrest', as outlined in Article 5(2): 'Everyone who is arrested shall be informed promptly, in a language which he understands, of the reasons for his arrest and of any charge against him'.[8]

Conditions while detained

The European Court of Human Rights has articulated a need for detention to occur in a location that bears some relation to the reason for detention. For example, if an individual is detained because they are deemed to be of 'unsound mind', detention must occur in a therapeutic environment such as a hospital; the hospital wing of a prison would not suffice.[9] In such locations, once a specific treatment is based on medical necessity and shown to be in the best interests of the patient, procedures such as force-feeding or placing in isolation might not constitute breaches of Article 3 of the ECHR.[10]

A number of cases relating to detained individuals have referred to Article 8 of the ECHR, which outlines a right to 'private and family life' and states that any interference with this right must be 'in accordance with the law' and 'necessary in a democratic society in the interests of national security, public safety or the economic well-being of the country, for the prevention of disorder or crime, for the protection of health or morals, or for the protection of the rights and freedoms of others'.

From a psychiatric perspective, it is conceivable that the psychiatric condition of certain individuals with mental disorder might deteriorate as a result of stimulation stemming from visits to them by family or friends. This is supported by observations that violent incidents among in-patients may be associated with recent contact with staff members, other patients and visitors. Although this evidence is somewhat inconsistent, this inconsistency is likely attributable to the small size, limited statistical power and low number of relevant studies (Bernstein *et al*, 1980; Phillips & Nasr, 1983; Powell *et al*, 1994). Notwithstanding these limitations, this literature at the very least suggests that there may, in certain cases, be a reasonable medical rationale for placing limits on visits for certain periods of time, for the 'protection of health'. From a human rights perspective, however, any such 'interference' must be proportionate to demonstrated need: in *Nowicka v Poland* [2003], for example, the European Court of Human Rights ruled that restricting family visits to once a month was not proportionate to, and did not pursue, any legitimate aim and was a breach of Article 8 of the ECHR.[11]

Regarding duration of detention necessitated by mental disorder, the Court has ruled that 'the validity of continued confinement depends upon the persistence of such a disorder'.[12] This is not an absolute requirement, however, as the Court recognises that it may not be appropriate to 'order the immediate and absolute discharge of a person who is no longer suffering from the mental disorder which led to his confinement' but that such discharge might best occur in a phased fashion, subject to conditions.[13]

In addition, if a patient remains detained for longer than necessary owing to the absence of community treatment resources that would facilitate discharge, the Court has not ruled against such detentions, consistent with its general reluctance to generate rulings that have might have substantial resource implications in various countries with differing models and levels of mental health services.[14] In the event, however, that a tribunal authorises discharge subject to certain conditions, and such a discharge does not occur (e.g. for resource reasons), that individual's continued detention is regarded by the Court as a fresh detention which must then be reviewed with 'requisite promptness'.[15]

Review of involuntary detention

Article 5(4) of the ECHR states that 'everyone who is deprived of his liberty by arrest or detention' shall be entitled to 'take proceedings by which the lawfulness of his detention shall be decided speedily by a court'. In the case of detention in mental health institutions, the meaning of 'court' is relatively wide, provided that the 'court' is independent of the executive and parties to the case, and is of judicial character (Bartlett *et al*, 2007).[16]

The European Court of Human Rights regards this requirement for review under Article 5(4) as separate to the question of the legality of detention under Article 5(1); i.e. there can be a violation of Article 5(4) as well as a violation of Article 5(1).[17] For example, the Court declared a breach of Article 5(4) in *HL v UK (Bournewood)* [2004],[18] on the grounds that, since HL was an informal patient, there was no adequate procedure for him to challenge his *de facto* detention.

The Court has placed particular emphasis on the necessity for mental health review tribunals (or similar bodies) to have the power to discharge formally detained patients, if they see fit. In the case of forensic patients in the UK, for example, such tribunals had, under the Mental Health Act 1983, the power to recommend release but could not discharge patients themselves; the European Court of Human Rights ruled that these powers were insufficient and the tribunals were subsequently given the power to discharge forensic patients.[19]

In 1981, the European Court of Human Rights delivered its judgment relating to section 65 of the Mental Health Act 1959, which gave the Home Secretary exclusive authority to discharge patients detained under hospital orders and impose restrictions on the discharge. The Court found that habeas corpus, the only form of review open to a patient recalled following apparent non-compliance with restrictions, did not constitute a form of judicial review sufficiently wide substantively to examine the justification of detention.[20] Following this ruling, the government enacted the Mental Health (Amendment) Act 1982, giving restricted patients the right to a binding mental health review tribunal (Gostin & Gable, 2004).

The European Court of Human Rights has specified that certain procedural safeguards are necessary to ensure that reviews of detention are effective (e.g. there may need to be a lawyer involved, even if the patient does not want one).[21] The Court has, in addition, provided guidance on the ECHR's requirement that 'the lawfulness of [...] detention shall be decided speedily' (Article 5(4)). The Court has found that delays of 55 days[22] and 24 days[23] are not sufficiently speedy, suggesting that a maximum delay of approximately 2 or 3 weeks is likely to be acceptable, in the absence of specific requests by the patient for deferral (e.g. in order to seek independent medical opinion) (Bartlett et al, 2007).

Notwithstanding this range of mental disability-related topics dealt with by the European Court of Human Rights since its foundation, issues related to mental disability and mental disorder still seem underrepresented in the Court's activities as a whole (Bartlett et al, 2007; Prior, 2007). This apparent paucity of cases may stem, at least in part, from the absence of assertive legal advocacy for individuals with mental disability and the complexities involved in accessing European courts. The issue of advocacy could be addressed, at least in part, through the proactive provision of greater legal aid and advocacy services for individuals with mental illness, which would be consistent with the ECHR's positive obligation on states in respect of protecting human rights (Feldman, 2002). Problems related to the complexities of accessing European courts may also be addressed, at least in part, through the incorporation of the principles of the ECHR into domestic law in the UK (Human Rights Act 1998) and Ireland (European Convention on Human Rights Act 2003).

The European Union

The ECHR and the European Court of Human Rights are not the sole mechanisms dedicated to the promotion and protection of human rights at European level: in 1952 the European Court of Justice was founded in

Luxembourg. This is the highest court of the European Union (EU) and has the primary aims of ensuring equitable application of EU law across member states and reconciling provisions of EU law with national law within member states. Despite an initial reluctance to become involved in human rights issues, the European Court of Justice has now developed a significant body of jurisprudence in relation to human rights (Smith, 2007).

This EU commitment to human rights and the consequent importance of the European Court of Justice in terms of human rights, were enhanced in 1992 in the Treaty on European Union 1992 ('Maastricht Treaty'), which stated that 'the Union shall respect fundamental rights, as guaranteed by the European Convention for the Protection of Human Rights and Fundamental Freedoms' (European Union, 1992). Again, in 1997, the Treaty of Amsterdam further extended the role of the European Court of Justice in relation to human rights by bringing more provisions of the Treaty on European Union under the jurisdiction of the European Court of Justice (European Union, 1997; Smith, 2007).

In 2000, at the EU Summit in Nice, the Charter of Fundamental Rights of the European Union was adopted in order to 'strengthen the protection of fundamental rights in the light of changes in society, social progress and scientific and technological developments by making those rights more visible in a Charter' (European Union, 2000). De Búrca (2001) notes that the Charter emerged from an EU drafting process that was relatively open and experimental, in contrast with more usual, rather secretive processes associated with the EU. The contents of the Charter demonstrate a number of different influences throughout its drafting, including the Council of Europe's Convention on Human Rights and Biomedicine and the revised version of the European Social Charter, which came into effect in 1999 (Hervey, 2005).

The rights and prohibitions outlined in the Charter of Fundamental Rights of the European Union are generally consistent with those outlined in other, comparable documents, most notably the ECHR. Chapter 1, devoted to dignity, for example, outlines rights to 'human dignity', life and 'integrity of the person'; it also includes prohibitions on 'torture and inhuman or degrading treatment or punishment' and 'slavery and forced labour'. Chapter 2, devoted to freedoms, outlines rights to 'liberty and security', 'respect for private and family life', 'protection of personal data' and 'freedom of thought, conscience and religion', among others. Chapters 3 to 6 outline further rights on the themes of equality, solidarity, citizens' rights and justice, consistent with the provisions of the ECHR.

The implications of the Charter in terms of healthcare law and policy are not yet fully clear. In particular, although it is apparent that the Charter may raise awareness of issues related to rights and provide a context for subsequent debate, it is not at all clear whether it will drive or facilitate the development of solutions in various areas of healthcare policy in the EU (McHale, 2009). Conceivably, the very existence of the Charter may exert pressure on policy makers at both transnational and national levels to devise and implement policies that reflect the content and spirit of the Charter.

Consistent with this, Menéndez (2002) argues that the Charter has both symbolic and legal value in the EU despite the fact that it has not been incorporated into Union law but rather consolidates existing law. Lord Goldsmith (2001) highlights the Charter's intention to protect human rights by limiting the powers of EU institutions and emphasising that they cannot trample on the fundamental rights of citizens.

In Article 52, the Charter attempts explicitly to optimise consistency with the ECHR:

> 'In so far as this Charter contains rights which correspond to rights guaranteed by the Convention for the Protection of Human Rights and Fundamental Freedoms, the meaning and scope of those rights shall be the same as those laid down by the said Convention. This provision shall not prevent Union law providing more extensive protection'.

The issue of consistency is an important one. Although the European Court of Justice is part of the EU and the European Court of Human Rights is part of the Council of Europe, the European Court of Justice may, nonetheless, refer to case law derived from the European Court of Human Rights. While all EU member states have ratified the ECHR and are therefore under the jurisdictions of both the European Court of Justice and the European Court of Human Rights, the Treaty of Lisbon ('Reform Treaty') (European Union, 2008) provided that the EU itself would become a signatory to the ECHR and, as a result, the European Court of Justice would be formally subject to the rulings of the European Court of Human Rights. This would have the merit of possibly improving consistency in human rights case law in Europe, but the demerit of constricting and homogenising avenues of redress following alleged violations of human rights. The effects of an EU constitution may be similar, although its precise implications would depend on the text and the extent to which its provisions applied to all member states and were, in due course, interpreted by the European courts.

Human rights in national legislative form

The Human Rights Act 1998 in the UK

The Human Rights Act 1998 was introduced in the UK to 'give further effect to rights and freedoms guaranteed under the European Convention on Human Rights; to make provision with respect to holders of certain judicial offices who become judges of the European Court of Human Rights; and for connected purposes' (Preamble). The Act makes a remedy for breach of the ECHR available in UK courts (section 8); abolishes the death penalty (section 21); requires judges in the UK to take account of decisions of the European Court of Human Rights (section 2); and makes it unlawful for public bodies in the UK to act in a way that is incompatible with the ECHR (section 3), unless an act of Parliament dictates otherwise, in which case a 'declaration of incompatibility' can be made by a higher court (section 4).

The Preamble to the Human Rights Act defines 'Convention rights' to include all ECHR rights except for Articles 1 (requiring states to 'secure' ECHR rights to 'everyone within their jurisdiction') and 13 (right to 'an effective remedy before a national authority notwithstanding that the violation has been committed by persons acting in an official capacity'). Section 2 requires that a UK 'court or tribunal determining a question which has arisen in connection with a Convention right must take into account' the jurisprudence of the European Court and Commission on Human Rights and the Committee of Ministers (of the Council of Europe) in 'so far as, in the opinion of the court or tribunal, it is relevant to the proceedings'. Section 3 requires that national legislation be interpreted in accordance with the ECHR as far as possible. This requirement applies not only to courts and tribunals, but to all parties interpreting legislation and is, arguably, one of the strongest provisions of the Act (Wadham *et al*, 2007).

Section 4 of the Human Rights Act states that if a higher court 'is satisfied that [a provision of primary legislation] is incompatible with a Convention right, it may make a declaration of that incompatibility', although such a declaration 'does not affect the validity, continuing operation or enforcement of the provision' and 'is not binding on the parties to the proceedings in which it is made'. Section 19 attempts to reduce the likelihood of such 'declarations of incompatibility' being made by requiring that a 'Minister of the Crown in charge of a Bill in either House of Parliament must, before Second Reading of the Bill' either make a 'statement of compatibility' with the ECHR or else explicitly acknowledge that 'he is unable' to do so but 'nevertheless wishes the House to proceed with the Bill'. In the event that a 'declaration of incompatibility' is ultimately made by a court, however, and 'if a Minister of the Crown considers that there are compelling reasons for proceeding under this section, he may by order make such amendments to the legislation as he considers necessary to remove the incompatibility' (section 10).

Overall, the Human Rights Act 1998 represents a significant recognition of the importance of human rights in the UK. Subsequent case law relating to the Act has involved a range of themes, including individual rights to privacy, objections against eviction from public lands by public authorities, and various issues related to immigration (Fenwick, 2007; Wadham *et al*, 2007). The Act has also been used extensively in the context of health and healthcare (McHale *et al*, 2007; Wicks, 2007) and provides an important mechanism for protecting rights in a variety of circumstances (Fenwick, 2007).

There are still, however, several important issues outstanding in relation the Human Rights Act. In a general sense, Wadham *et al* (2007) lament the perceived failure of the Act to create a culture of respect for human rights, and note that it is widely misunderstood and mistrusted by the public. Fenwick (2007) highlights another important issue by drawing attention to the extent to which the Act constitutes a bill of rights as opposed to simply being a means of giving 'further effect' to the ECHR; this matter is, as yet, unresolved.

The European Convention on Human Rights Act 2003 in Ireland

Irish law is rooted in the Constitution of Ireland (Bunreacht na hÉireann), which was enacted on 1 July 1937, came into operation on 29 December 1937, and has been amended more than 20 times since then (Government of Ireland, 1937; Hogan & Whyte, 2003). The Constitution establishes the principles of democratic government in Ireland and gives all citizens the right to vote (Article 16).

The central references to 'fundamental rights' are contained in Articles 40 to 44. Article 40 deals with 'personal rights' and states that 'all citizens shall, as human persons, be held equal before the law'. Further, 'the State guarantees in its laws to respect, and, as far as practicable, by its laws to defend and vindicate the personal rights of the citizen'. In addition, 'no citizen shall be deprived of his personal liberty save in accordance with law' and 'the State guarantees liberty for the exercise of the following rights, subject to public order and morality: [...] The right of the citizens to express freely their convictions and opinions [...]; to assemble peaceably and without arms [and] to form associations and unions'.

Article 42 deals with the 'right' to education: the state shall ensure that 'children receive a certain minimum education, moral, intellectual and social'. Article 43 outlines the right to 'private property' and notes that the exercise of this right 'ought, in civil society, to be regulated by the principles of social justice'. Article 44 outlines the right to religious expression, stating that 'freedom of conscience and the free profession and practice of religion are, subject to public order and morality, guaranteed to every citizen'.

Economic and social rights are not mentioned in the Constitution, but Article 45 deals with relevant issues as 'directive principles of social policy' and states that 'the State shall strive to promote the welfare of the whole people by securing and protecting as effectively as it may a social order in which justice and charity shall inform all the institutions of the national life'. More specifically, state policy shall be directed towards securing 'an adequate means of livelihood' for all citizens and ensuring that 'control of the material resources of the community' are distributed so as 'best to subserve the common good'; 'free competition shall not be allowed so to develop as to result in the concentration of the ownership or control of essential commodities in a few individuals to the common detriment'. In addition, 'the State pledges itself to safeguard with especial care the economic interests of the weaker sections of the community, and, where necessary, to contribute to the support of the infirm, the widow, the orphan, and the aged'.

The inclusion of these rights in the 1937 Constitution marked a notable departure from earlier drafts, which devoted little space to rights. Even when the 1937 Constitution was finally published, little attention was paid to the rights outlined in it, although, as Hogan & Whyte (2003: p. 1245) argue, these provisions have contributed significantly to the protection of the rights of the individual. Bacik (2001: p. 23), in contrast, notes it can be argued that the effects of constitutional rights in the lives of individuals in Ireland has been minimal, owing to both the belief system underpinning the Constitution and conservative interpretations by judges.

Relevant case law in relation to Irish Constitutional rights, however, demonstrates at least some evidence of growing judicial activism in this area throughout the 1970s. This trend was greatly strengthened by the increasing influence of the ECHR (1950) and Ireland's accession to the EU (1973), both of which, in large part, started to move Ireland towards a 'culture of human rights' by the 1990s (Bacik, 2001). This trend took a significant step forward in 2000 with the Human Rights Commission Act 2000. This Act found its roots not only in the slowly emerging emphasis on human rights in Irish and European courts, but also in the Northern Ireland Peace Agreement of 10 April 1998 (the 'Good Friday Agreement'), in which the Irish government agreed to 'take steps to further strengthen the protection of human rights in its jurisdiction'; 'establish a Human Rights Commission'; and 'introduce equal status legislation' (section 6, para. 9).

Consistent with this agreement, the Human Rights Commission Act (Preamble) aimed 'to provide further protection for human rights and, for that purpose, to establish a body to be known as 'an Coimisiún um Chearta an Duine' or, in the English language, the Human Rights Commission'. Section 2 defined 'human rights' as '(a) the rights, liberties and freedoms conferred on, or guaranteed to, persons by the Constitution, and (b) the rights, liberties or freedoms conferred on, or guaranteed to, persons by any agreement, treaty or convention to which the State is a party'.

The Irish Human Rights Commission was founded by the 2000 Act (sections 3 and 4) and its functions were to review state laws and practices relating to the protection of human rights; examine legislative proposals; make relevant recommendations to government; and promote understanding and awareness of human rights (section 5). It could also conduct enquiries (section 9), publish research and reports, apply to appear before the High Court or the Supreme Court as *amicus curiae* (or 'friend of the Court'), and, under certain circumstances, institute proceedings relating to 'any matter concerning the human rights of any person or class of persons'.

In 2006, 5 years after its establishment, the Irish Human Rights Commission had become active in a range of areas related to human rights, and, throughout 2006, received 242 communications from members of the public and 64 communications from organisations or in respect of legal proceedings (Irish Human Rights Commission, 2007). Almost one-third of communications related to the administration of justice (32.3%), whereas matters related to economic and cultural rights accounted for just 12%. During 2006, the Commission received 43 case notifications under the ECHR. The Commission's role in these cases was as *amicus curiae* and these cases involved a range of issues, including public housing, free legal aid assistance and various other matters. The Irish Human Rights Commission was merged with the Equality Authority to form the Irish Human Rights and Equality Commission in November 2014.

Consistent with this increased emphasis on human rights in Irish public life from the 1970s onwards, the ECHR was finally formally incorporated into Irish law in 2003, with the European Convention on Human Rights Act 2003. This Act aimed, primarily, 'to enable further effect to be given, subject to the Constitution, to certain provisions of the Convention for the Protection of Human Rights and Fundamental Freedoms' (Preamble). Using wording similar to the Human Rights Act 1998 in the UK, section 2 of Ireland's 2003 Act states that:

> 'In interpreting and applying any statutory provision or rule of law, a court shall, in so far as is possible, subject to the rules of law relating to such interpretation and application, do so in a manner compatible with the State's obligations under the Convention provisions'.

Section 3 outlines the duty of all public bodies to adhere to the ECHR, stating that 'every organ of the State shall perform its functions in a manner compatible with the State's obligations under the Convention provisions'. Section 4 states that 'judicial notice shall be taken of the Convention provisions' and of the jurisprudence of the European Court of Human Rights, European Commission of Human Rights and Council of Ministers, and that 'a court shall, when interpreting and applying the Convention provisions, take due account of the principles laid down by those declarations, decisions, advisory opinions, opinions and judgments'.

The High Court or Supreme Court may make a 'declaration of incompatibility' when 'a statutory provision or rule of law is incompatible with the State's obligations under the Convention provisions' (section 5). Following a declaration of incompatibility, a copy of the declaration will 'be laid before each House of the Oireachtas' (Irish parliament) and 'the Government may request an adviser appointed by them to advise them as to the amount of [...] compensation (if any)' (section 5).

The formal incorporation of the ECHR into Irish law represented a significant enhancement of the importance accorded to human rights in Irish law. It is notable that the European Convention on Human Rights Act 2003 has much in common with the Human Rights Act 1998 in the UK, especially in terms of its aim to give 'further effect' to the ECHR in domestic law (Preamble); the direction that interpretation of any 'statutory provision or rule of law' be consistent with the ECHR (section 2); the direction that 'every organ of the State' shall 'perform its functions' in a fashion consistent with the ECHR (section 3); the direction that national courts shall take 'judicial notice' of relevant ECHR jurisprudence (section 4); and the establishment of a procedure for a 'declaration of incompatibility' to be made by higher courts, when national legislation is incompatible with the ECHR (sections 5 and 6).

There are, however, also significant differences between the incorporation of the ECHR into national legislation in Ireland and the UK: whereas Ireland has a single, formal, written, unified constitution which guarantees various rights, there is no single, formal, written, unified constitution in the UK. In addition, in the UK, but not Ireland, there is a legislative requirement that ministers outline to Parliament whether or not proposed legislation is compatible with the ECHR; although this mechanism is unlikely to provide an absolute assurance of compatibility, bills in the UK can also be scrutinised by the Joint Committee on Human Rights in order to optimise compatibility.

More significantly, while the Human Rights Act 1998 in the UK presents a clear outline of the procedure to be followed in making a 'remedial order' following a 'declaration of incompatibility' (schedule 2), there are no similar guidelines or provisions in the European Convention on Human Rights Act 2003 in Ireland, apart from a procedure to award compensation to any 'injured party' (section 5). In addition, there is no provision for Irish courts to quash legislation that is found to be incompatible with the ECHR. Mullan (2008) argues that the reason given for such exclusions is that they help avoid a clash between the ECHR and the Irish Constitution, but this might have been prevented by stating that such powers must be exercised subject to the Constitution. In any case, it remains the position that if an Irish judge finds that a law is contrary to the ECHR but is without means to act upon this finding, it is likely that judges (of superior courts) will prefer to declare such a law to be contrary to the Constitution, with the usual consequent effect that it is struck down.

In Ireland, experience to date confirms that, while the principles of the ECHR are increasingly discussed in Irish courts, there is a tendency for cases to be decided by reference to the Constitution or domestic law rather than the ECHR or the European Convention on Human Rights Act 2003. In *TH v DPP*, for example, the applicant argued that a series of alleged irregularities during his trial had violated both his constitutional and ECHR rights, but when the High Court found that the delay violated his constitutional right to a reasonably expeditious trial, the court did not deem it necessary to proceed to consider arguments based on the ECHR.[24] Similarly, in *JF v DPP* the court found that there had been a breach of the constitutional right to a fair trial and went on to state that the ECHR did not provide additional rights above and beyond those already contained in domestic law in this matter.[25]

Overall, the passage of the European Convention on Human Rights Act 2003 has resulted in ECHR principles being discussed in an increasing number of cases in Irish courts; increased consideration of ECHR-related jurisprudence from other jurisdictions (e.g. UK) in Irish courts; and increased public awareness of the ECHR. Further experience is necessary to determine the precise interrelationship between ECHR rights and the Irish Constitution, and the extent to which the European Convention on Human Rights Act represents an effective incorporation of ECHR principles into Irish law, especially in relation to mental illness.

Human rights and mental illness: the United Nations and World Health Organization

United Nations Principles for the Protection of Persons with Mental Illness and the Improvement of Mental Health Care (1991)

The Universal Declaration of Human Rights (United Nations, 1948) and European Convention on Human Rights (Council of Europe, 1950) are general declarations of human rights. The most detailed declaration of rights in the specific context of mental illness is provided by the UN in its Principles for the Protection of Persons with Mental Illness and the Improvement of Mental Health Care (United Nations, 1991). These are summarised in Box 1.1 and emphasise that all people are entitled to receive the best mental healthcare available, be treated with humanity and respect, and receive mental healthcare based on internationally accepted ethical standards. In addition, mental health facilities should be appropriately structured and resourced, and an impartial review body should, in consultation with mental health practitioners, review the cases of involuntary patients.

Many of these principles were re-emphasised in 1996 in the World Health Organization's (WHO's) Ten Basic Principles of Mental Health Care Law (Division of Mental Health and Prevention of Substance Abuse, 1996) (Box 1.2), which require that all decisions should be in keeping with applicable law in the jurisdiction and not made on an arbitrary basis. Against this background, the WHO subsequently published the most detailed systematic set of human rights standards for national mental health legislation assembled to date, in the *WHO Resource Book on Mental Health, Human Rights and Legislation* (WHO, 2005).

In its *Resource Book*, the WHO sets out a 'Checklist for mental health legislation', detailing specific human rights standards which, according to the WHO, need to be met in each jurisdiction. These standards are clearly based on previous UN and WHO publications and centre on the provision of mental healthcare that is reasonable, equitable and in accordance with international standards. Mental health legislation in each jurisdiction has a key role in meeting these WHO standards, and in England and Wales civil mental health legislation meets 90 (54.2%) of the 166 relevant standards, while legislation in Ireland meets 80 (48.2%) (Kelly, 2011). Areas of relatively high compliance include definitions of mental disorder, procedures for involuntary admission and treatment, and clarity regarding offences and penalties. Areas of medium compliance relate to competence, capacity and consent; oversight and review (which exclude long-term voluntary patients);

Box 1.1 Key rights outlined in the Principles for the Protection of Persons with Mental Illness and the Improvement of Mental Health Care

- All people are entitled to receive the best mental healthcare available and to be treated with humanity and respect.
- There shall be no discrimination on the grounds of mental illness. All people with mental illness have the same rights to medical and social care as other ill people.
- All people with mental illness have the right to live, work and receive treatment in the community, as far as possible.
- Mental healthcare shall be based on internationally accepted ethical standards, and not on political, religious or cultural factors.
- The treatment plan shall be reviewed regularly with the patient.
- Mental health skills and knowledge shall not be misused.
- Medication shall meet the health needs of the patient and shall not be administered for the convenience of others or as a punishment.
- In the case of voluntary patients, no treatment shall be administered without their informed consent, subject to some exceptions (e.g. patients with personal representatives empowered by law to provide consent). In the case of involuntary patients, every effort shall be made to inform the patient about treatment.
- Physical restraint or involuntary seclusion shall be used only in accordance with official guidelines.
- Records shall be kept of all treatments.
- Mental health facilities shall be appropriately structured and resourced.
- An impartial review body shall, in consultation with mental health practitioners, review the cases of involuntary patients.

(Adapted from: United Nations, 1991)

---

and rules governing special treatments, seclusion and restraint. Areas of low compliance relate to promoting rights, voluntary patients (especially non-protesting, incapacitous patients), protection of vulnerable groups and emergency treatment. In both jurisdictions, however, mechanisms other than mental health law meet some of these WHO requirements. I explore issues relating to social justice (apart from dedicated mental health law) in Chapter 6, with particular emphasis on the UN Convention on the Rights of Persons with Disabilities (2006), the contents of which are outlined briefly next, by way of introduction to it.

United Nations Convention on the Rights of Persons with Disabilities (2006)

In 2006, the human rights landscape again changed significantly with the adoption of the UN Convention on the Rights of Persons with Disabilities (CRPD) by the UN General Assembly (United Nations, 2006; Bartlett *et al*, 2007). The CRPD commits signatory countries 'to promote, protect and ensure the full and equal enjoyment of all human rights and fundamental

> **Box 1.2** World Health Organization's Ten Basic Principles of Mental Health Care Law
>
> - Everyone should benefit from the best possible measures to promote mental well-being and prevent mental disorders.
> - Everyone who is in need should have access to basic mental healthcare.
> - Mental health assessments should be made in accordance with internationally accepted medical principles and instruments.
> - People with mental disorders should be provided with healthcare that is the least restrictive possible.
> - Consent is required before any type of interference with a person takes place.
> - If a patient has difficulty understanding the implications of a decision, they should benefit from the assistance of a knowledgeable third party of their choosing.
> - There should be a review procedure available for any decision made by official (e.g. a judge) or surrogate (e.g. a representative, guardian) decision makers, or by healthcare providers.
> - In the case of a decision affecting liberty (hospital admission) and/or integrity (treatment) with a long-lasting impact, there should be an automatic mechanism for periodic review.
> - Decision makers acting in official capacity (e.g. a judge) or surrogate (consent-giving) capacity (e.g. a guardian, friend, relative) must be appropriately qualified.
> - Decisions should be in keeping with applicable law in the jurisdiction and should not be made on an arbitrary basis.
>
> (Adapted from: Division of Mental Health and Prevention of Substance Abuse (WHO), 1996*b*)

freedoms by all persons with disabilities, and to promote respect for their inherent dignity' (Article 1). It goes on to specify that 'persons with disabilities include those who have long-term physical, mental, intellectual or sensory impairments which in interaction with various barriers may hinder their full and effective participation in society on an equal basis with others' (Article 1).

In the context of psychiatry, it seems clear that this definition of 'persons with disabilities' does not include all people with mental disorder, not least because many mental disorders (e.g. adjustment disorder) are not 'long-term' (Kelly, 2014*a*). The CRPD does not, however, present its definition of 'persons with disabilities' as a comprehensive one, but states that the term 'persons with disabilities' includes people with 'long-term' impairments; others, presumably, may also fit the definition. As a result, it is likely that some people with mental disorder meet the definition at least some of the time (e.g. an individual with an intellectual disability), but others do not (e.g. an individual with adjustment disorder). Moreover, the CRPD states that 'disability is an evolving concept and that disability results from the interaction between persons with impairments and attitudinal and environmental barriers that hinders their full and effective participation in society on an equal basis with others' (Preamble); this de-links the definition of 'persons with disabilities' from any specific diagnoses and moves it into a social context.

Both mental health legislation and mental capacity legislation in various jurisdictions appear to violate the CRPD. For example, the CRPD specifies that 'the existence of a disability shall in no case justify a deprivation of liberty' (Article 14). If certain persons with mental disorder (e.g. some people with chronic schizophrenia) fit the UN definition of 'persons with disabilities', then mental health legislation in England, Wales and Ireland (for example) is clearly inconsistent with this provision, given the clear links that legislation in these jurisdictions draws between mental disorder, risk and involuntary admission (Kelly 2014a).

In relation to mental capacity, the CRPD specifies that persons with disability 'enjoy legal capacity on an equal basis with others in all aspects of life' (Article 12 (2)) and this appears violated by the fact that the remit of decision-making supports is limited in several jurisdictions. For example, Ireland's Assisted Decision-Making (Capacity) Bill 2013 excludes areas such as marriage and voting from its decision-making supports (section 106) (Kelly 2015a); in England and Wales, family relationships (Mental Capacity Act 2005; section 27), Mental Health Act matters (section 28) and voting rights (section 29) are excluded; in Northern Ireland, the Mental Capacity Bill 2015 has exclusions for family relationships (section 273) and voting rights (section 274). In addition, it is not at all clear whether or not the CRPD is consistent with any form of substitute decision-making, although there is some evidence that it may be acceptable in certain circumstances (Bartlett, 2012; Szmukler et al, 2014).

The Committee on the Rights of Persons with Disabilities (2014),[26] however, in its 'General comment' on Article 12 of the CRPD ('equal recognition before the law') is clear that even a 'functional approach' to assessing mental capacity is not an acceptable means for denying a person legal capacity, and that decision-making supports rather than substitute decision-making are appropriate. The Committee also specifies that developing a model of supported decision-making alongside a model of substitute decision-making is not sufficient to meet the CRPD requirement for 'equal recognition before the law' (Article 12). Regrettably, the Committee's comments, like the CRPD itself, leave unaddressed the uncommon but not unknown situation in which it is not possible to identify in any form whatsoever the 'will and preferences' of the individual.

Minkowitz (2007), a chairperson of the World Network of Users and Survivors of Psychiatry and member of the UN Working Group that produced the first draft of the CRPD, argues that all forced psychiatric interventions are by their very nature violations of the CRPD, requiring that perpetrators (i.e. mental health professionals) be criminalised and victims receive reparations. Minkowitz bases this argument on alleged violations of CRPD Articles 12 ('equal recognition before the law'), 15 ('freedom from torture or cruel, inhuman or degrading treatment or punishment'), 17 ('protecting the integrity of the person') and 25 ('health', especially the requirement for 'free and informed consent' for care). Current mental health legislation may also violate Article 4 (no 'discrimination of any kind on the basis of disability') (Szmukler *et al*, 2014). In the UK jurisdictions and Ireland, however, there are national laws permitting involuntary psychiatric detention and treatment under certain circumstances and, once such laws are observed, it appears unlikely that mental health professionals can be labelled as criminal. Dawson (2015), in particular, argues persuasively for a more realistic approach to interpreting the CRPD in this and other regards.

Conclusions

Although the 1700s and 1800s saw significantly increased emphasis on, and restatements of, key ideas about justice and human rights, the experiences of many individuals with mental illness remained unremittingly bleak, characterised by chronic neglect, social exclusion and, in certain cases, denial of liberty and dignity in large, overcrowded institutions.

Notwithstanding this situation, the general observance of human rights for most individuals, although not the mentally ill, took an important step forward in 1948 with the UN Universal Declaration of Human Rights (United Nations, 1948), followed in 1950 by the European Convention on Human Rights (ECHR) (Council of Europe, 1950). The ECHR had greater legal impact than the Universal Declaration of Human Rights and was given further effect in the UK through the Human Rights Act 1998 and in Ireland through the European Convention on Human Rights Act 2003. The ECHR provisions regarding liberty and reviews of involuntary detention have proven particularly relevant to people with mental illness, with a series of judgments that strongly emphasise various protections for the rights of the detained mentally ill, especially in relation to humane conditions in therapeutic settings and prompt, effective reviews.

As regards declarations of rights specific to the mentally ill, the most detailed statement to date is found in the UN's Principles for the Protection of Persons with Mental Illness and the Improvement of Mental Health Care (United Nations, 1991), which articulate rights 'to receive the best mental health care available', 'live, work and receive treatment in the community' and access 'mental health facilities' that are 'appropriately structured and resourced'. In addition, 'mental health care will be based on internationally accepted ethical standards' and 'an impartial review body will, in consultation with mental health practitioners, review the cases of involuntary patients'.

The WHO's 'Checklist for mental health legislation' (WHO, 2005) details specific human rights standards that it believes should be met in each jurisdiction. Concerningly, mental health legislation in England,

Wales and Ireland fails to meet many of these standards, chiefly (but not exclusively) in areas relating to promoting rights, voluntary patients (especially non-protesting, incapacitous patients), protection of vulnerable groups and emergency treatment (Kelly, 2011). However, mechanisms other than mental health law (e.g. mental health policy) may meet some of the WHO requirements, and I explore issues relating to legal and non-legal mechanisms for promoting human rights and achieving social justice for the mentally ill in Chapters 6 and 7.

Most recently, the Convention on the Rights of Persons with Disabilities (CRPD) (United Nations, 2006) has presented the greatest challenges and opportunities for all who seek to build better protections for the rights of people with mental illness. The tone of the CRPD is typified by its stern requirement that 'the existence of a disability shall in no case justify a deprivation of liberty' (Article 14). While the potentially profound implications of this statement for mental health legislation are not yet clear (Kelly, 2014a), it is already apparent that this raises important issues about the primacy, enforceability and pragmatism of the CRPD (Dawson, 2015). This statement does not appear, for example, to permit any involuntary psychiatric treatment based on risk associated with mental disorder. This not only places all four jurisdictions that I examine in this book in clear violation of the CRPD, but also flies in the face of many centuries of history during which myriad democratically elected governments passed various mental health laws permitting involuntary care on the basis of mental disorder and associated risk to self and others.

From a clinical perspective, there are also concerning issues regarding the practical day-to-day application of some of the CRPD's provisions, including the position of the Committee on the Rights of Persons with Disabilities (2014) that developing a model of supported decision-making alongside a model of substitute decision-making is not sufficient to meet the CRPD requirement for 'equal recognition before the law'. This leaves unresolved the situation where it is not possible to identify in any form whatsoever the 'will and preferences' of a given individual. While the UN and the Committee on the Rights of Persons with Disabilities may not encounter these complex clinical dilemmas in their work, clinicians and families do encounter such cases, and the CRPD offers no useful guidance for these extreme situations. Indeed, the Committee creates additional obstacles by presenting critiques of 'functional' methods of assessing capacity, but not offering any alternative approaches and therefore not contributing to problem-solving in these extreme situations in any pragmatic way.

One possible result of this situation is that the CRPD may simply be ignored in practice or else deemed to be a campaigning document that overstates its case in order to correct the undeniable historical injustice against persons with impaired mental capacity. That would be regrettable, because there are many valuable, progressive and historically important aspects of the CRPD, such as the requirement that signatory countries 'promote, protect and ensure the full and equal enjoyment of all human rights and fundamental freedoms by all persons with disabilities' and 'promote respect for their inherent dignity' (Article 1). This requirement for strong, assertive action to promote rights (and not just avoid impinging on them) permeates the entire CRPD, and provides patients, advocates and carers with a fresh and solid basis for more assertive action for the protection of rights not only in the legal sphere, but also in the realms of social advocacy and political activism (Kelly, 2014b).

I explore these matters in greater depth in Chapters 6 and 7, with particular emphasis on non-legal mechanisms for protecting and promoting rights. First, however, the critical role of mental health law in relation to human rights and justice is explored in some detail as concerns England and Wales (Chapter 2), Northern Ireland (Chapter 3), Ireland (Chapter 4) and Scotland (Chapter 5). In particular, I focus on the implications of mental health and capacity legislation for human rights and social justice, as well as the unique opportunities offered by current processes of legal reform in Scotland and, especially, Northern Ireland, where the CRPD appears to have played a critical role in determining the shape of change.

CHAPTER 2

Mental Health Acts 1983 and 2007: England and Wales

Chapter 1 of this book provided a background to key concepts relating to mental illness and human rights, especially the growing application of the principles of human rights to the mentally ill throughout the late 20th century, and the emergence of the UN Principles for the Protection of Persons with Mental Illness and the Improvement of Mental Health Care (United Nations, 1991) and UN Convention on the Rights of Persons with Disabilities (CRPD) (United Nations, 2006).

This chapter moves this examination forward by focusing on mental health legislation in England and Wales. More specifically, this chapter examines the provisions of the Mental Health Act 1983, specific issues stemming from the 1983 Act, and the provisions and human rights implications of the Mental Health Act 2007, which substantially amended, but did not replace, the 1983 Act. The chapter concludes with an overall assessment of current mental health legislation in England and Wales in the context of human rights.

Background to current mental health legislation in England and Wales

Background to the Mental Health Act 1983

There has been some form of statutory control or regulation of individuals with mental illness since at least the 14th century, when the *De Praerogativa Regis* permitted the Crown to acquire the estates and lands of 'lunatics' and 'idiots' (Bowen, 2007: p. 10). The first substantial, specific legislative recognition of the need for dedicated in-patient psychiatric care was the Vagrancy Act 1744, which permitted the detention of individuals with mental illness on the order of two Justices of the Peace. The legislative framework underpinning asylum care evolved throughout the 1800s, with lunacy legislation of the early 1890s substantially revising admission criteria (Shorter, 1997: p. 231).

In 1926, the Royal Commission on Lunacy and Mental Disorder signalled a significant shift in emphasis by proposing a voluntary admission status and establishment of out-patient and aftercare services (Royal Commission, 1926). The Mental Treatment Act 1930 duly introduced voluntary admission status, a development that coincided with the introduction of out-patient psychiatric services throughout France, Germany, England and elsewhere (Shorter, 1997: p. 230).

In 1948 the National Health Service (NHS) was established, adding impetus to the move from institutional to community care (Mulholland, 2009). In 1957, the Royal Commission on the Law Relating to Mental Illness and Mental Deficiency (the Percy Commission) declared that when any hospital in-patient was at a point where they could be discharged if they had a reasonably good home to go to, provision of residential care became the responsibility of the local authority (Royal Commission on the Law Relating to Mental Illness and Mental Deficiency, 1957). The Commission recommended that psychiatric treatment should be provided with the minimum curtailment of liberty and as little legal formality as possible.

The Mental Health Act 1959 reinforced many key elements of the Mental Treatment Act 1930 and 1957 Commission, most notably by promoting voluntary as opposed to involuntary admission and changing the decision process regarding involuntary admission from a judicial to a clinical one (Unsworth, 1987; Moncrieff, 2003). Doctors and social workers were given discretionary powers to detain and treat individuals with mental illness where it was necessary for their health and safety or the protection of others.

Over the following decades, significant progress was made dismantling institutional care structures throughout England. Although this had the welcome effect of promoting treatment in non-restrictive settings, the development of community-based facilities was commonly criticised as inadequate (Fadden et al, 1987; Dyer, 1996). In 1975, a government White Paper, Better Services for the Mentally Ill, presented specific targets for improving community-based facilities (Department of Health and Social Security, 1975a). Despite various problems achieving those targets, the Department of Health published a further consultation document in 1981, Care in the Community: A Consultative Document on Moving Resources for Care in England, Outlining a Continued Commitment to Community Care (Department of Health and Social Security, 1981a).

Notwithstanding the emergence of community-based treatments for mental illness during the 1960s and 1970s, there was still a recognised need to strengthen safeguards for human rights in relation to admission, especially involuntary admission, to psychiatric hospitals (Gostin, 1975a,b). Acknowledgement of this need stemmed from specific human rights concerns (Bowen, 2007: p. 14)[27] as well as the broader growth of the civil rights movement and patient groups such as the National Association for Mental Health (Gostin, 1975a,b; Gunn, 1981; Bluglass, 1984). In 1978, the government published a White Paper proposing increased safeguards for the liberties of individuals with mental illness while also having regard for the safety of others (Department of Health and Social Security, 1975*b*). These concerns were again reflected in a further White Paper in 1981, *Reform of Mental Health Legislation* (Department of Health and Social Security, 1981*b*), which helped shape the Mental Health Act 1983.

The Mental Health Act 1983

The Mental Health Act 1983 introduced important reforms to mental health legislation, many of which had implications in terms of human rights. An understanding of key provisions of the Mental Health Act 1983 and issues stemming from it helps contextualise the Mental Health Act 2007, which amended, but did not replace, the 1983 legislation.

The Mental Health Act 1983 defined 'mental disorder' to include 'mental illness, arrested or incomplete development of mind, psychopathic disorder and any other disorder or disability of mind' (section 1(2)). Definitions were also provided for 'severe mental impairment', 'mental impairment' and 'psychopathic disorder', but there was no further definition of 'mental illness'. The Act stated that nobody was to be deemed to suffer from a mental disorder 'by reason only of promiscuity or other immoral conduct, sexual deviancy or dependence on alcohol or drugs' (section 1(3)). This slightly vague but intentionally restrictive statement clarified the emphasis to be placed on medical diagnosis rather than societal judgement in determining who could be detained.[28]

The 1983 Act permitted involuntary 'admission for assessment' for individuals with mental disorder for up to 28 days, provided admission was supported by medical opinion (section 2(3)). 'Admission for treatment' for up to 6 months (section 3(2)(a)) required two medical opinions, and assurance that 'in the case of psychopathic disorder or mental impairment, such treatment is likely to alleviate or prevent a deterioration of his condition' (section 3(2)(b)) and 'it is necessary for the health or safety of the patient or for the protection of other persons that he should receive such treatment' (section 3(2)(c)).

The legislation also contained provisions for 'guardianship' (section 7(2)(a)), based on 'the written recommendations in the prescribed form of two registered medical practitioners' (section 7(3)). Compared to involuntary admission, guardianship was more limited and gave the guardian (e.g. local authority) specific powers to determine where the individual shall live, that they shall have treatment and may be visited at home (Gunn, 1981).

Regarding treatment of individuals detained or under guardianship:

'The consent of a patient shall not be required for any medical treatment given to him for the mental disorder from which he is suffering, not being treatment falling within section 57 or 58 above, if the treatment is given by or under the direction of the responsible medical officer' (section 63).

Second opinions were required prior to administration of certain treatments (e.g. psychosurgery) to detained patients (section 57(1)–(2)). If an individual was detained for more than 3 months, they had to either consent to continued 'administration of medicine' (with the responsible medical officer documenting capacity) or be seen by another medical practitioner to certify 'that the patient is not capable of understanding the nature, purpose and likely effects of that treatment or has not consented to it but that, having regard to the likelihood of its alleviating or preventing a deterioration of his condition, the treatment should be given' (section 58(3)(b)). This requirement for consent for certain treatments recognised that the detained patient could retain capacity for certain matters and increased observance of patients' autonomy and dignity.

Detained patients could apply to the Mental Health Review Tribunal (now properly called the First-tier Tribunal (Mental Health) or, less formally, mental health tribunal) following admission for assessment (within 14 days), admission for treatment (within 6 months) or being received into guardianship (within 6 months), among other circumstances (section 66). The tribunal could direct the discharge of a patient detained for assessment if it was not satisfied that the patient had a 'mental disorder of a nature or degree which warrants his detention in a hospital for assessment' and 'that his detention as aforesaid is justified in the interests of his own health or safety or with a view to the protection of other persons' (section 72(1)(a)).

The tribunal could direct the discharge of a patient otherwise detained if not satisfied:

'(i)   that he is then suffering from mental illness, psychopathic disorder, severe mental impairment or mental impairment or from any of those forms of disorder of a nature or degree which makes it appropriate for him to be liable to be detained in a hospital for medical treatment; or

(ii)   that it is necessary for the health of safety of the patient or for the protection of other persons that he should receive such treatment; or

(iii)   in the case of an application by virtue of paragraph (g) of section 66(1) above, that the patient, if released, would be likely to act in a manner dangerous to other persons or to himself' (section 72(1)(b)).

While these provisions paternalistically permitted detention of individuals who 'if released, would be likely to act in a manner dangerous to other persons or to himself', the 1983 Act also provided more subtle, discretionary powers to tribunals: the tribunal could, for example, 'direct the discharge of a patient on a future date specified in the direction' or make recommendations that 'he be granted leave of absence or transferred to another hospital or into guardianship' (section 72(3)) or that 'the responsible medical officer consider whether to make a supervision application' (section 72(3A)). This reflected a modulated, nuanced and broadly realistic approach to cases that were likely to be complex and changeable over time. Overall, these tribunals reflected the European Convention on Human Rights (ECHR) (Article 5(4)) requirement that detention orders be independently reviewed by a 'court', although it was less clear whether the time frames involved were consistent with the ECHR requirement to hold reviews 'speedily'.

Finally, the Mental Health Act 1983 outlined a mechanism for 'aftercare under supervision' in the community, once certain conditions were met and it was supported by medical opinion (section 25B(5)–(6)). Compulsory treatment in the community is, however, a deeply controversial topic and its clinical usefulness far from established (Kisely & Campbell, 2014; Lawton-Smith *et al*, 2008). In addition, although community treatment orders may facilitate treatment in a setting less restrictive than hospital detention, they also support the idea that individuals who are not detained in an institution can be subject to restrictions and requirements that impinge significantly on their freedoms (Kelly, 2009*a*). The human rights implications of such orders are discussed in greater depth in 'Supervised community treatment' (pp. 53–58), after consideration of broader issues that arose following the 1983 Act.

Issues stemming from the Mental Health Act 1983

Owing to a long-acknowledged need for reform (Department of Health and Social Security, 1975*b*, 1981*b*), the Mental Health Act 1983 was met with varying levels of approval and enthusiasm (Bluglass, 1984). In the years between the 1983 and 2007 Acts, however, two key issues were to become the focus of concern: public safety and human rights.

Public safety

There has long been an association between mental disorder and dangerousness in the public mind, even in advance of any systematic studies of the matter (Shorter, 1997). Research over recent decades has confirmed that individuals with mental disorders such as schizophrenia are slightly more likely to engage in acts of violence than individuals without such illnesses (Torrey, 2001; Foley *et al*, 2005). At population level, however, the proportion of violent crime attributable to mental disorder is extremely low (Walsh *et al*, 2001) and much is attributable to co-occurring drug misuse, which increases the risk of violence in individuals with and without mental disorder (Steadman *et al*, 1998).

Despite this increased risk, violence remains a rare event in mental disorder and is therefore extremely difficult to predict: the most detailed predictive models, which include almost all known risk factors for violence in schizophrenia, can explain only 28.3% of the variation in violence between individuals with schizophrenia (Foley *et al*, 2005). Even if there was a predictive model that was 90% sensitive and 90% specific (both of which are unrealistically high levels in any field of medicine), the rarity of homicide by individuals with severe mental disorder means that such a model would generate at least 2000 false positives for every true positive, i.e. 2001 mentally ill individuals would need to be detained in order to prevent (or delay) a single homicide (Szmukler, 2000).

Notwithstanding these considerations, the issue of public safety has featured prominently in most considerations of mental health law in the UK in recent decades, especially as governments appear to have been substantially influenced by homicides by mentally disordered people, with resultant tensions between public safety and social inclusion in both mental health law and policy (Fennell, 2007: pp. 6–7; Bartlett & Sandland, 2014). As a result, public safety has remained a key consideration in the formulation of mental health legislation in England, even in an era of increased emphasis on human rights (Bowen, 2007: pp. 10–23).

The issue of public safety came to particular attention in 1992 when Christopher Clunis, a man with a history of mental disorder, killed Jonathan Zito, a musician, in London. Eight days earlier, Mr Clunis had been found wandering the streets and attacking people with a breadknife and screwdriver (Court, 1994). The subsequent enquiry was critical of the police, doctors, nurses and social workers and of the general lack of resources required to monitor and treat patients who appeared to present a high risk to the public (Coid, 1994; Ritchie *et al*, 1994). The enquiry recommended a national register of patients considered at high risk of violence, specialist services for their care and procedures for supervised discharge orders, to permit patients to be recalled if they did not adhere to treatment.

This concern with public safety became a key feature in the deliberations of an expert committee, chaired by Professor Genevra Richardson, charged with advising the government 'on the degree to which current legislation needs updating to support effective delivery of modern patterns of clinical and social care for people with mental disorder and to ensure that there is a proper balance between safety (both of individuals and the wider community) and the rights of individual patients' (Department of Health, 1999: p. 127).

The Richardson Committee noted that a 'small minority' believed that 'a Mental Health Act should authorise treatment in the absence of consent *only* for those who lack capacity' and 'if a person with a mental disorder who refused treatment was thought to pose a serious risk to others then he or she should be dealt with through the criminal justice system, not through a health provision' (p. 19, emphasis added). There was, however, 'a much larger body of opinion which was prepared to accept the overriding of a capable refusal in a health provision on grounds of public safety in certain circumstances' (p. 19).

The Committee inclined towards the latter view:

'The reasons given were in part pragmatic and in part driven by principle. Essentially most of those who commented accepted that the safety of the public must be allowed to outweigh individual autonomy where the risk is sufficiently great and, if the risk is related to the presence of a mental disorder for which a health intervention of likely benefit to the individual is available, then it is appropriate that such intervention should be authorised as part of a health provision. Mental disorder unlike most physical health problems may occasionally have wider consequences for the individual's family and carer, and very occasionally for unconnected members of the public affected by the individual's behaviour, acts and omissions. The Committee supports this reasoning and in what follows we seek to describe a framework which adequately reflects it' (p. 19).

This concern with public safety is evident throughout the recommend-ations of the Committee, including, for example, its suggestion that criteria for compulsory orders include not only that mental disorder is present, treatment is the least restrictive possible and treatment is in the patient's best interests, but also (for patients who lack capacity) that treatment 'is necessary for the health or safety of the patient or for the protection of others from serious harm' and (for patients with capacity) that 'there is a substantial risk of serious harm to the health or safety of the patient or to the safety of other persons if s/he remains untreated' (p. 70).

This concern with public safety was later reflected, at least to a certain extent, in the Mental Health Act 2007 in, for example, the Act's broadening of the definition of mental disorder (section 1(2)) and requirement that individuals with an intellectual disability (termed 'learning disability' in the legislation) 'shall not be considered by reason of that disability' to be suffering from mental disorder 'unless that disability is associated with abnormally aggressive or seriously irresponsible conduct on his part' (section 2(2)). By the time the Mental Health Act 2007 was published, however, another key concern had emerged: the human rights of detained patients (Richardson, 2005).

Human rights

Protecting the human rights of detained patients was the second key issue that became the focus of concern in relation to the Mental Health Act 1983, especially following the Human Rights Act 1998. This issue can be usefully explored by examining related case law since the Human Rights Act 1998 was implemented in 2000. Selected cases are considered here under four headings: the burden of proof in mental health tribunals; the ECHR right to respect for a private and family life (Article 8); powers of tribunals to release patients; and various other matters.

Burden of proof in mental health tribunals

The first declaration of incompatibility made under the Human Rights Act 1998 related to the Mental Health Act 1983. The 1983 Act outlined criteria to be used by mental health tribunals to make their decisions and indicated that a tribunal had to discharge the patient if satisfied that criteria for detention were not met, i.e. the patient had to show that the criteria were not met (sections 72 and 73). In R (H) v Mental Health Review Tribunal,[29] a man who was detained under section 3 of the Mental Health Act 1983 sought his release and argued that this provision of the Act violated his ECHR rights because it placed the burden of proof on the patient to demonstrate that criteria for detention were not met (Dyer, 2001).

41

The Court of Appeal concluded that this was indeed incompatible with Article 5(1) of the ECHR (specifically, that the 'reverse burden of proof' violated the right to liberty) and granted a declaration of incompatibility. As a result, the Mental Health Act 1983 (Remedial) Order 2001 (SI 2001/3712) amended the 1983 Act to the effect that, unless a tribunal finds that the criteria for detention are met, it must discharge the patient. This, broadly, shifts the burden of proof from patient to responsible authority and provides greater protection of the right to liberty, in accordance with the ECHR.

Right to respect for private and family life

A number of cases have centred on the ECHR right to respect for private and family life (Article 8). *R (M) v Secretary of State for Health*, for example, focused on the fact that the Mental Health Act 1983 did not allow the patient to change their 'nearest relative', as defined in section 26 of the Act.[30] The nearest relative has a range of important roles and the High Court ruled that the absence of a process by which the patient could apply to change their nearest relative constituted a breach of their right to respect for their private and family life. This breach was not rectified until the amendments introduced by the Mental Health Act 2007.

The ECHR right to respect for private and family life was also the focus of *R (N) v Ashworth Special Hospital Authority*, in which the High Court ruled that monitoring and recording of telephone calls in a high secure setting was not a breach of this right.[31] In *R (Munjaz) v Mersey Care NHS Trust*, however, the Court of Appeal found that there was a breach of this right when the seclusion policy of Ashworth Hospital failed to adhere to the Mental Health Act Code of Practice as regards seclusion and mechanical restraint (Department of Health, 2008).[32] However, this Code (now in a revised edition: Department of Health, 2015) is designed for 'guidance' purposes only (Mental Health Act 1983: section 118). While the Court of Appeal acknowledged that there could be good reasons to depart from the Code in particular cases, the Court did not agree that a hospital could depart from it as a matter of policy.

On appeal, a majority in the House of Lords did not agree that there had been a breach of this right.[33] The minority (Lords Steyn and Browne-Wilkinson), who supported the Court of Appeal decision, argued that, because the ECHR states that any interference with the right to respect for private and family life must be 'in accordance with the law' and there is no statutory framework governing seclusion in England and Wales, the Code of Practice should have the force of law. The majority (Lords Bingham, Hope and Scott), however, did not agree that the Code had the force of law, and noted that Ashworth Hospital was a high-security institution and, thus, significantly different from the majority of psychiatric institutions. Moreover, Ashworth Hospital had devoted considerable thought to devising its own seclusion policy to meet its particular clinical needs and although this placed Ashworth's policy at variance with the Code of Practice it was, nonetheless, permissible.

This case went on to the European Court of Human Rights, which stated that the practice of seclusion can indeed interfere with the right to respect for private and family life, but that in this case Ashworth Hospital's policy was sufficiently foreseeable to be in accordance with law and, as a result, the right had not been interfered with arbitrarily.[34] The European Court of Human Rights also ruled that there was no breach of Article 3 (relating to torture or inhuman or degrading treatment or punishment) or Article 5 (the right to liberty and security of person) in this case.[35]

Does this decision regarding seclusion undermine the role of the Code of Practice in relation to seclusion, a practice with serious implications for the dignity and rights of detained individuals? It is noteworthy that, although the majority in the House of Lords did not agree that the right to respect for private and family life had been violated in this case, they went to great lengths to emphasise the importance of the Code. They stated that, notwithstanding their decision in this case, the Code always carries substantial weight and should be considered with great care. Although the Code is not a binding instruction, it is more than mere advice. Departures from the Code should be rare and reasons for such departures should be spelled out clearly and logically in each case (Department of Health, 2015: p. 12).

Notwithstanding these caveats, does this decision still reflect an over-emphasis on control and paternalism at the expense of dignity and respect for private and family life? In the first instance, one of the key ways of maintaining the dignity of the mentally ill is through effective treatment of mental illness (Kelly, 2014c). However, certain measures that are used as part of such treatment (e.g. seclusion) may have the potential to undermine dignity in the short term. There is, then, a need for vigilance in order to ensure that such interventions are proportionate, linked to therapeutic aims, implemented with minimum erosion of dignity and performed in accordance with law. The *Munjaz* case, in its complex totality, demonstrates vividly the difficulties inherent in striking such a balance between tailoring interventions to meet the needs of individual patients and ensuring that interventions such as seclusion are subject to sufficient regulation to prevent unjustified erosion of dignity and rights.

A solution may lie in devising a legally binding code, such as that introduced in Ireland, where the Mental Health Act 2001 (section 69(1)) clearly states that seclusion and restraint can only be used in accordance with rules made by the Mental Health Commission (2009) under the Act, violation of which constitutes an offence. Although this approach has the demerit of possibly not tailoring the seclusion regime to the needs of the individual patient, it has the merits of ensuring accountability and equity of treatment for patients who are secluded and, arguably, minimising erosion of dignity and rights.

Powers of tribunals to release patients

A further declaration of incompatibility was granted in the case of *R (D) v Secretary of State for the Home Department*, which focused on a prisoner who was serving life imprisonment and transferred to a psychiatric hospital; a tribunal could not, however, release him, but only recommend release, because release of a life-sentence prisoner is a matter for the Parole Board.[36] However, a life-sentence prisoner could not, when transferred to hospital, make an application to the Parole Board and it was up to the Home Secretary to decide whether or not the Parole Board should hear such a case. D argued that this violated his right to apply for a court order to challenge the lawfulness of his detention (ECHR: Article 5(4)), and the High Court agreed, granting a declaration of incompatibility. This was followed by an amendment of the relevant statute so as to permit a patient to apply to the Parole Board once a recommendation for release from hospital had been made (Criminal Justice Act 2003: section 295). Again, this provides further protection for the right to liberty for detained individuals, in accordance with the ECHR.

Various other matters

Declarations of incompatibility have been granted in relation to procedural and resourcing issues in connection with mental health tribunals that were concluded to have significant implications for human rights. In *R (KB) v Mental Health Review Tribunal*[37] the High Court found that inadequate resourcing of tribunals resulted in delays to hearings and, in respect of the test cases brought before it, granted a declaration as to a breach of Article 5(4) (Richardson, 2005). It has also been determined[38] that the timing of tribunals must be flexible, in order to respond to individual patient's circumstances (Mandelstam, 2005). These judgments represented a clear articulation of the need for authorities to provide adequate resources for mental health tribunals in order to ensure appropriately timed hearings, consistent with the ECHR right to liberty.

Another case relating to tribunals focused on a woman with intellectual disability detained under the Mental Health Act 1983 (section 2) and in respect of whom an application was lodged with the county court to change the person named as her nearest relative.[39] Once such an application was made, a patient's detention was automatically extended until the matter was dealt with by the county court (section 29(4)). During this extension, the patient did not have the right to apply for a second time to a tribunal (section 66(2)(a)). In addition, for a patient detained under section 2 who lacked capacity, there was no facility for the patient to make their own application to a tribunal, and the Secretary of State for Health had to be asked to refer the matter to a tribunal (as occurred in this case).

The Court of Appeal granted two declarations of incompatibility, stating that (a) the absence of a system to ensure referral to a tribunal for individuals who lack capacity and are detained under section 2 was incompatible with the ECHR, and (b) the lack of a right to further challenge detention when it is extended owing to an application for displacement of the nearest relative was also incompatible. The House of Lords overturned both declarations on the grounds that: (a) Article 5(4) of the ECHR did not require a reference to capacity; the 1983 Act required the patient be made aware of their right to apply to a tribunal; and the test for capacity to make such an application is, in any case, low; and (b) the correct response following an extended detention owing to an application for displacement of the nearest relative is for the courts to deal with the application swiftly; i.e. the existing system could be operated in a fashion consistent with the ECHR and granting of declarations of incompatibility was, therefore, not proper.

The principles of the ECHR have also been evoked in relation to treatment, with rulings indicating that treatment, when provided, must be based on medical necessity and in the best interests of the patient,[40] although there is not an automatic right to treatment (e.g. for an individual with untreatable personality disorder who is detained on the basis of public protection).[41]

Finally, section 6(1) of the Human Rights Act 1998, which makes it 'unlawful for a public authority to act in a way which is incompatible with [an ECHR] right', has proven relevant in a number of cases, chiefly concerned with mental healthcare, as opposed to mental health legislation *per se*. The case of *Savage v South Essex Partnership NHS Foundation Trust*,[42] for example, involved the suicide of a detained psychiatric patient, and it was alleged that the NHS trust had failed to protect the patient's ECHR right to life (Article 2(1)). The House of Lords concluded that the trust had a duty to reasonably protect psychiatric patients from taking their own lives, under the Human Rights Act. The UK Supreme Court later declared that, under certain circumstances, this obligation can extend to voluntary patients, even when on home leave.[43]

Overall, these cases demonstrate that, first, ECHR rights are having a significant effect on mental health case law in England, especially since the Human Rights Act 1998. Second, courts are applying ECHR rights to the situation of the mentally ill in very detailed ways, recognising, for example, a need to balance the ECHR right to respect for private and family life (Article 8) with monitoring of communications for legitimate reasons in secure settings.[44] This suggests that the Human Rights Act has, at the very least, modified the ways in which mental health legislation affects the rights of people with mental illness, apparently serving to protect their ECHR rights and increase dignity. Third, by articulating strongly the relevance of human rights in mental disorder, these cases ensured that human rights were firmly on the agenda during the next reform of mental health legislation, which culminated in the Mental Health Act 2007. This process of reform is considered next.

Moving towards reform

Against this background of growing human rights concerns throughout the 1980s, 1990s and 2000s, the Richardson Committee was 'determined to include sufficient safeguards to ensure appropriate protection of the patient's individual dignity, autonomy and human rights' (Department of

Health, 1999: p. 44). In its final report, the Committee duly cited human rights considerations in relation to its conclusions on a range of issues, emphasising that 'it is now accepted, and indeed demanded by the Human Rights Act, that an individual subject to detention on the grounds of his or her mental disorder must have the right to test the legality of that detention before an independent "court"' (p. 120).

An emphasis on human rights was in clear evidence from other sources too, including psychiatrists, who stressed the implications not only of the ECHR and Human Rights Act 1998 (Bindman *et al*, 2003; Curtice, 2009), but also of the work of the Working Party on Human Rights in Psychiatry appointed by the European Council of Ministers in 1996 (Council of Europe, 2000a; Kingdon *et al*, 2004). The Working Party built on previous statements of the Council of Europe in relation to the legal protection of individuals with mental illness (Council of Europe, 1977), rules governing involuntary detention and judicial review (Council of Europe, 1983) and specific therapeutic issues, including electroconvulsive therapy, psychosurgery, isolation cells, mechanical restraint and matters related to research (Council of Europe, 1994). The Working Party included both psychiatric and legal experts, charged with formulating guidelines to further the protection of human rights in mental health settings owing to the exceptional situation of involuntary patients and thus the exceptional need for protection of their rights (Council of Europe, 2000b; Kingdon *et al*, 2004). The Working Party's final recommendations aimed to provide guidance in various areas, including national legislation, in order to harmonise and improve mental healthcare across Europe.

These recommendations were consistent with a range of other concerns regarding mental health legislation, many of which reflect and highlight specific human rights issues, including concern about high rates of psychiatric detention among Black compared with White patients in certain countries (Singh *et al*, 2007), different rates of appeal after detention among different ethnic groups (Nilforooshan *et al*, 2009), and relatively low levels of understanding among consultant psychiatrists regarding their roles at Mental Health Review Tribunal hearings (Nimmagadda & Jones, 2008) and among general hospital doctors regarding their roles assessing capacity under the Mental Health Act 1983 (Richards & Dale, 2009).

These concerns were underpinned and magnified by a continued increase in the number of patients involuntarily detained during the opening years of the new century: in 2003–2004 there were 45 691 formal detentions under the Mental Health Act 1983 in England; by 2005–2006 this had increased to 47 394; and by 2010–2011 it had risen again, to 49 365 (Information Centre, 2007: p. 4; NHS Information Centre for Health and Social Care, 2011: p. 9). In north-east London, the period between 1997 and 2007 saw not only a significant increase in the use of the Mental Health Act to detain patients, but also a substantial increase in the proportion of detentions that went to appeal (from 34% in 1997 to 81% in 2007), although the proportion upheld at appeal (66%) did not change (Singh & Moncrieff, 2009).

Overall, the years between 1983 and 2007 also saw greatly increased emphasis placed on public safety in the context of mental illness, driven largely by public and political responses to specific tragedies, and crystallised in the report of the Richardson Committee. This period also saw greatly increased emphasis placed on the human rights of the mentally ill, both in England (largely in response to the Human Rights Act 1998 and ECHR) and throughout Europe, as reflected by the work of the Council of Europe (2000b). At least some of the issues that emerged from these debates, and especially those related to public safety, human rights or both, were addressed, at least in part, by the Mental Health Act 2007.

Before considering the Mental Health Act 2007 further, however, it is worth pausing to note certain issues that did not appear to play substantial roles in shaping the new legislation. The issue of dignity, an absolutely key concept in human rights discourse, especially in relation to mental health (Kelly, 2014b), received just fleeting mention in the Richardson Committee report (Department of Health, 1999: pp. 2, 28, 35, 44). This is most likely because the report was largely centred on concerns about public safety and specific provisions of the Human Rights Act 1998, as opposed to broader conceptualisations of rights linked more clearly with dignity or capabilities.

During various other stages in the development of the 2007 Act, issues such as autonomy and paternalism were raised, albeit in varying levels of detail and by various groups. The Mental Health Alliance, a coalition of 75 organisations of service users and service providers, for example, articulated a need explicitly to balance rights to autonomy and non-discrimination with public protection and paternalism (Mental Health Alliance, 2006: p. 1). Notwithstanding such concerns, however, the Richardson Committee did not engage in a detailed consideration of the merits and demerits of paternalism, presumably owing to its strong concern with public safety, which supports rather than challenges traditional interpretations of paternalism.

Interestingly, even in its brief mentions of paternalism, the Richardson Committee did not dismiss it outright, simply noting that 'few if any would wish to return to *unchallenged* paternalism' (Department of Health, 1999: p. 20; emphasis added). The Committee did not take its explicit consideration of the matter appreciably further than that and focused instead on the concepts of dangerousness and public safety, as opposed to broader-based paternalism across mental health services. Key provisions of the subsequent legislation as they relate to human rights, which arguably reflect the Richardson Committee's position on this, are examined next.

The Mental Health Act 2007

The Mental Health Act 2007 is a piece of amending legislation that amends not only the Mental Health Act 1983, but also the Domestic Violence, Crime and Victims Act 2004 and the Mental Capacity Act 2005. A detailed and excellent account of the Mental Health Act 1983, as amended by the Mental Health Act 2007, is provided by Zigmond (2016). The present discussion focuses on the provisions of the 2007 Act of greatest relevance to human rights, which primarily relate to:

- definition of mental disorder
- criteria for detention
- expansion of professional roles
- definition of nearest relative
- supervised community treatment
- safeguards regarding electroconvulsive therapy
- timescales for Mental Health Review Tribunal hearings
- advocacy.

Definition of mental disorder

The Mental Health Act 2007 removed the four categories of mental illness outlined in the 1983 Act and redefined 'mental disorder' as 'any disorder or disability of the mind' (section 1(2)). Individuals with an intellectual ('learning') disability 'shall not be considered by reason of that disability' to be suffering from mental disorder 'unless that disability is associated with abnormally aggressive or seriously irresponsible conduct on [their] part' (section 2(2)).

These changes are in line with recommendations of the Richardson Committee (Department of Health, 1999) and the Mental Health Act Commission (2003: pp. 85–86), which noted that 'if there is widespread co-morbidity between personality disorders and mental illness irrespective of Mental Health Act classification, then the dichotomy imposed by legal classification is misleading and obscures the multiple problems shared by patients in the two categories. This would suggest that the Government is correct in seeking to abandon the legal classifications in the next Mental Health Act'.

The exclusion criteria in the Mental Health Act 1983 were also amended. The 1983 Act stated that nobody was to be deemed to suffer from a mental disorder 'by reason only of promiscuity or other immoral conduct, sexual deviancy or dependence on alcohol or drugs' (section 1(3)). The 2007 Act replaced these exclusion criteria by the following: 'Dependence on alcohol or drugs is not considered to be a disorder or disability of the mind' (section 1(3)). As a result, the exclusions for 'promiscuity or other immoral conduct, [or] sexual deviancy' were repealed.

While this change may reflect the current apparent unlikeliness of anyone being diagnosed as mentally ill owing to 'promiscuity or other immoral conduct [or] sexual deviancy', this amendment nonetheless means that it is no longer explicitly unlawful (under mental health legislation) to make such a diagnosis. The effects of these changes have yet to be seen in practice, as it remains the case that, regardless of whether or not an individual fulfils the criteria for a mental disorder, there is still considerable clinical discretion about whether or not any provisions of the legislation are applied in a particular case (Hall & Ali, 2009), i.e. not everyone with mental disorder is detained.

Criteria for detention

Prior to the Mental Health Act 2007, the processes of civil committal under the 1983 Act included the section 2 process for admission for assessment for up to 28 days, the section 3 process for admission for treatment for up to 6 months in the first instance and the section 4 process for admission 'in any case of urgent necessity'. The 2007 Act introduced significant amendments to certain elements of these processes.

In the first instance, the 1983 Act permitted civil committal of individuals with 'psychopathic disorder or mental impairment' under section 3 only if 'treatment is likely to alleviate or prevent a deterioration of his condition' (section 3(2)(b)), and the same criterion applied to renewal orders for all forms of mental disorder (section 20(4)(b)). If this condition was not met, a renewal order could still be made in respect of a patient with 'mental illness or severe mental impairment' if 'the patient, if discharged, is unlikely to be able to care for himself, to obtain the care which he needs or to guard himself against serious exploitation' (section 20(4)).

The 2007 Act replaced these notably paternalistic 'treatability and care tests' with an 'appropriate treatment test', which applies to all forms of mental disorder, and stated that orders (under sections 3, 37, 45A and 47) can be made or renewed only if 'appropriate medical treatment is available' (section 4). The 2007 Act also expands the areas of application of the new appropriate treatment test to include accused individuals on remand to hospital for treatment (section 5(2)), transfer directions for remand prisoners and other detainees (section 5(3)) and 'hospital orders' (section 5(4)).

Renewal orders must now also meet this condition (section 4(4)), and if it is not met, tribunals can discharge patients (section 5(8)). This criterion does not apply to those detained under sections 2 ('admission for assessment'), 35 ('remand to hospital for report on accused's mental condition'), 135 ('warrant to search for and remove patients') or 136 ('mentally disordered persons found in public places'). The provision to make a renewal order under section 20(4) of the 1983 Act (i.e. 'the patient, if discharged, is unlikely to be able to care for himself, to obtain the care which he needs or to guard himself against serious exploitation') was repealed (section 4(4)(c)).

The 2007 Act also amended the definition of 'medical treatment' to include, in addition to 'nursing' (section 145(1)), 'psychological intervention and specialist mental health habilitation, rehabilitation and care' (section 7(2)). 'Medical treatment' refers only to 'medical treatment the purpose of which is to alleviate, or prevent a worsening of, the disorder or one or more of its symptoms or manifestations' (section 7(3)) and, for each patient, such treatment must be 'appropriate in his case, taking into account the nature and degree of the mental disorder and all other circumstances of his case' (section 4(3)).

The implications of these changes are not yet fully clear. For example, the effects of the removal of the need for 'abnormally aggressive or seriously irresponsible conduct' for a diagnosis of 'psychopathic disorder' (section 1(2)) are unclear, not least because detention can still only occur when 'it is necessary for the health or safety of the patient or for the protection of other persons that he should receive such treatment' (section 3(2)(c)); a similar provision applies to 'admission for assessment' (section 2(2)(b)).

The 2007 Act's amendment of the 'treatability test' proved especially controversial during the Act's passage through Parliament (Bowen, 2007: p. 47). The resulting compromise removed the need to demonstrate that 'treatment is likely to alleviate or prevent a deterioration' of 'psychopathic disorder or mental impairment' (section 3(2)(b)) and replaced it with the need to demonstrate that 'appropriate medical treatment is available' (section 4(2)(b)), the 'purpose of which is to alleviate, or prevent a worsening of, the disorder or one or more of its symptoms or manifestations' (section 7(3)); this applies to detention orders under sections 3, 37, 45A and 47, and to all forms of mental disorder. Under these provisions, then, it is no longer necessary to demonstrate that treatment is 'likely' to help, but rather that it has the 'purpose' of helping, apparently regardless of likely efficacy. Notwithstanding this limitation, the introduction and expansion of the appropriate treatment test appears to go well beyond the requirements of the ECHR (section 5(1)(e)), which does not outline any treatability test for individuals of 'unsound mind' who are detained, once the detention is 'in accordance with a procedure prescribed by law'.

Bowen (2007: p. 55) argues that these amendments to the treatability test are unlikely to lead to 'preventive detention' because if the treatment is not benefitting the patient, the doctor is obliged to discharge the patient, regardless of other matters. It is possible, however, that widening the role of 'responsible clinician' to include other professionals (discussed in the next section) may result in greater decision-making by individuals trained in settings with different priorities, such as prisons, further complicating matters.

Notwithstanding this concern, it remains possible that the new appropriate treatment test may set the threshold for detention higher than previously, as it is now necessary that the proposed treatment is available to the patient. It is no longer acceptable that an individual be detained in the anticipation of such treatment becoming available in the future, as a result of expansion of resources or advances in therapeutics.

Expansion of professional roles

The Mental Health Act 2007 resulted in substantial expansions of the professional roles of a range of individuals in relation to involuntary admission and treatment. Under the 1983 Act (section 34(1)), each detained patient came under the care of a 'responsible medical officer' who had to be a 'registered medical practitioner' (section 55(1)). Under the 2007 Act (section 9(9)), references to 'responsible medical officer' were replaced by 'responsible clinician' who, in relation to a detained patient, is 'the approved clinician with overall responsibility for the case' (section 12(7)(a)) and, in relation to guardianship, is 'the approved clinician authorised by the responsible local social services authority to act (either generally or in any particular case or for any particular purpose) as the responsible clinician' (section 10).

The Mental Health Act 2007 Explanatory Notes point out that 'approval need not be restricted to medical practitioners, and may be extended to practitioners from other professions, such as nursing, psychology, occupational therapy and social work' (Department of Health and Social Security, 2007; paragraph 48). Under the 2007 Act, the responsible clinician will take over the roles previously performed by the responsible medical officer, as well as additional roles in relation to supervised community treatment.

The 2007 Act did not change the requirement of the 1983 Act that 'medical recommendations' for admission for assessment (section 2), treatment (section 3) or guardianship (section 7) be provided by 'registered medical practitioners' (section 12(2)). This remains consistent with the requirement, outlined by the European Court of Human Rights, that there must be objective medical evidence that an individual is of 'unsound mind' if they are to be deprived of their liberty (ECHR: Article 5(1)).[45]

The 2007 Act did, however, change the position regarding renewal orders. Under the 1983 Act, the making of a renewal order, like an admission order, required an examination and report by the responsible medical officer (sections 20(3)–(4)), but under the Mental Health Act 2007, the responsible clinician (who may or may not be a medical doctor) can make out a renewal order, although they must consult with another 'professional' involved in the case before doing so (section 9(4)(b)).

The other significant revision of professional roles introduced by the Mental Health Act 2007 concerns the 'approved social worker' who, under the 1983 Act, had a range of roles, most notably in making applications for detention for assessment (sections 2 and 11), treatment (sections 3 and 11) or guardianship (sections 7 and 11). The 2007 Act replaced the term 'approved social worker' with 'approved mental health professional' (section 18). Prior to approving someone as an approved mental health professional, the 'local social services authority shall be satisfied that he has appropriate competence in dealing with persons who are suffering from mental disorder', but the 'local social services authority may not approve a registered medical practitioner to act as an approved mental health professional' (section 18).

Overall, the expansion of professional roles in the Mental Health Act 2007, if implemented in practice, would represent a radical departure from the traditional dominance of psychiatrists in directing psychiatric care. The British Medical Association, which represents doctors (including psychiatrists), expressed strong concern about this dilution of the role played by psychiatrists and stated that there were no other countries in which the psychiatrist did not direct care of the patient (Bamrah *et al*, 2007; Hall & Ali, 2009).

Most notably, the Mental Health Act 2007 indicated that a renewal order can be made out by the responsible clinician (who is not necessarily a medical doctor), after consultation with another professional (who may not be a medical doctor either), possibly resulting in a renewal without any evidence from a medical doctor at any point (section 9(4)(b)). It is unclear whether or not this meets the requirement for objective medical evidence required by the ECHR, if liberty is lawfully to be denied on the grounds of 'unsound mind'; the issue is whether or not this ECHR requirement applies to renewal orders as well as admission orders.

Definition of nearest relative

The Mental Health Act 1983 provided definitions of 'relative' and 'nearest relative' (sections 26–30), with the results that patients did not have a choice in determining who was their nearest relative, and civil partners under the Civil Partnership Act 2004 were not included (Bowen, 2007: p. 62.) The Mental Health Act 2007 introduced several important reforms in this area, all of which appear to advance patient autonomy and help address the incompatibility between the 1983 Act and the ECHR right to respect for private and family life (Article 8).[46] The key changes include a right for the patient to apply to displace their nearest relative (section 23(2)) and, if the court decides to make an order on such an application, the following rules (section 23(3)) now apply:

> '(a) If a person is nominated in the application to act as the patient's nearest relative and that person is, in the opinion of the court, a suitable person to act as such and is willing to do so, the court shall specify that person (or, if there are two or more such persons, such one of them as the court thinks fit);
>
> (b) otherwise, the court shall specify such person as is, in its opinion, a suitable person to act as the patient's nearest relative and is willing to do so'.

The 2007 Act also expands the grounds on which such an application can be made (section 29(3)) to include 'that the nearest relative of the patient is otherwise not a suitable person to act as such' (section 23(5)(b)). Other amendments in relation to the nearest relative include a right for the patient to apply to discharge or vary an order appointing an acting nearest relative (section 24(2)) and inclusion of civil partners within the definition (section 26). These changes represent a significant advance on the 1983 Act in terms of patient autonomy and the right to respect for private and family life (ECHR: Article 8), although it is notably paternalistic that the patient's nominee for nearest relative must be, 'in the opinion of the court, a suitable person to act as such' (section 23(3)). In addition, it is not entirely clear to what extent the importance of the nearest relative is reflected in the courts; Bartlett & Sandland (2014: pp. 262–269) summarise some rather dispiriting evidence that little importance is accorded to the nearest relative, at least in certain circumstances.

Supervised community treatment

The Mental Health Act 1983 contained certain provisions for compulsory treatment in the community, including granting 'leave to be absent' (section 17(1)) for detained patients, subject to certain conditions (section 17(3)), and authorising the responsible medical officer to recall the patient if needed (section 17(4)). Alternatively, section 25 of the 1983 Act (amended in 1996) outlined a mechanism for 'after-care under supervision': this was subject to many conditions (section 25A(4)) and the process involved was complex to the point of virtual impenetrability (sections 25A–J).

The Mental Health Act 2007 repealed sections 25A–J of the 1983 Act and introduced a new 'supervised community treatment order', which can only be used when detained patients are leaving hospital, i.e. it cannot be used *de novo* in the community. Under the 2007 Act, 'the responsible clinician may by order in writing discharge a detained patient from hospital subject to his being liable to recall' under certain circumstances (section 32(2)). The agreement of an approved mental health professional (section 32(2)) is needed and various criteria must be met before such an order is made.

The five criteria are:

'(a) the patient is suffering from mental disorder of a nature or degree which makes it appropriate for him to receive medical treatment;
(b) it is necessary for his health or safety or for the protection of other persons that he should receive such treatment;
(c) subject to his being liable to be recalled as mentioned in paragraph (d) below, such treatment can be provided without his continuing to be detained in a hospital;
(d) it is necessary that the responsible clinician should be able to exercise the power under section 17E(1) below to recall the patient to hospital; and
(e) appropriate medical treatment is available for him' (section 32(2)).

In addition, the order 'shall specify conditions to which the patient is to be subject while the order remains in force' provided the responsible clinician and the approved mental health professional agree that such conditions are 'necessary or appropriate for one or more of the following purposes: (a) ensuring that the patient receives medical treatment; (b) preventing risk of harm to the patient's health or safety; (c) protecting other persons' (section 32(2)).

Patients can be recalled to hospital if they require in-patient treatment, present a risk to themselves or others that can be addressed by recalling them to hospital, or fail to comply with conditions in the order. If the patient is recalled, the community treatment order can be revoked by the responsible clinician, with the agreement of an approved mental health professional and the patient is again detained in hospital. If the community treatment order is not revoked, the patient can be treated as a detained patient in hospital for up to 72 hours and then released, but 'remains subject to the community treatment order' (section 32(2)).

A community treatment order remains in force for 6 months, but can be extended for a further 6 months, then for a year, 'and so on for periods of one year at a time' (section 32(3)). Within a 2-month period ending on the date of expiry of the order, the responsible clinician must examine the patient and provide a report to 'the managers of the responsible hospital' as to whether the conditions for renewal of the order are met (section 32(3)). If the order is not renewed, it expires: (a) 6 months after it was made; or (b) when the patient is discharged 'by the responsible clinician, by the managers of the responsible hospital, or by the nearest relative of the patient' (schedule 3, section 10(4)) or by a mental health tribunal (Schedule 3, section 20); or (c) when the initial application for admission for treatment ceases to have effect (section 32(3)); or (d) when the order is revoked following recall to hospital (section 32(2)).

Regarding the provision for 'leave of absence' in the 1983 Act (section 17(1)), the 2007 Act states that 'longer-term leave may not be granted to a patient unless the responsible clinician first considers whether the patient should be dealt with under section 17A instead' (i.e. community treatment order); for this purpose, 'longer-term leave of absence' is defined as 'a specified period of more than seven days' (section 33(2)).

Under the 2007 Act, a patient over the age of 16 years on a community treatment order can be given treatment if:

- the patient has capacity and consents to treatment;
- a donee (a representative appointed under a lasting power of attorney), court appointed deputy or the Court of Protection itself consents on the patient's behalf (section 35(1));
- treatment is authorised in accordance with section 64D ('adult community patients lacking capacity') or section 64G ('emergency treatment for patients lacking capacity or competence').

Some of these reforms to supervised community treatment procedures aroused significant concern among patient groups, who felt that they were excessively paternalistic and might lead to human rights abuses if used inappropriately or too widely, most notably through the imposition of involuntary treatment regimes on individuals well enough to live in the community (Butcher, 2007). On the day these changes came into effect, the Royal College of Psychiatrists and Department of Health moved swiftly to reassure the public that clinicians would use their powers fairly, for the benefit of mental health patients and their families (Bhugra & Appleby, 2008).

The European Court of Human Rights has already accepted the general principle that conditions may be placed on discharge from psychiatric facilities in certain cases.[47] There are still, however, specific human rights issues in relation to supervised community treatment, including the fact that community treatment orders can be revoked by the responsible clinician or, in the case of a recalled patient, by the responsible clinician once they have the agreement of an approved mental health professional, and none of these individuals need be a medical doctor.

In addition, mental health tribunals do not have the power to vary the conditions of a community treatment order, even though it is conceivable that such conditions could, under certain circumstances, contravene ECHR rights (Bowen, 2007: p. 92). As 'public authorities', tribunals have a duty to comply with ECHR rights under section 6(1) of the Human Rights Act 1998, but a tribunal has a defence if it is giving effect to an Act of Parliament, although it must first ensure that the legislation 'cannot be read or given effect in a way which is compatible with the Convention rights' (section 6(2)). While this affords tribunals a degree of responsibility in reading or giving effect to legislation, a tribunal may still be unable to prevent a contravention of ECHR rights, and the relevant legislation would then be subject to challenge.

These issues may not, however, represent violations of the ECHR in relation to supervised community treatment, because, notwithstanding the fact that tribunals cannot provide detailed guidance on which detained patients should be treated on community treatment orders and what the conditions on such orders should be, they still have the key power to revoke a patient's detention if it feels that is appropriate. In addition, the *Winterwerp* criteria indicate that objective medical expertise is one of the criteria for compulsory confinement,[48] and proposed amendments to the Mental Health Act 2007 which would have required the opinion of a medical doctor prior to revoking a community treatment order were explicitly rejected by the House of Commons during its consideration of the legislation.

Safeguards regarding electroconvulsive therapy

Under the Mental Health Act 1983, a detained patient could receive electroconvulsive therapy (ECT) if:

'(a) he has consented to that treatment and either the responsible medical officer or a registered medical practitioner appointed for the purposes of this Part of this Act by the Secretary of State has certified in writing that the patient is capable of understanding its nature, purpose and likely effects and has consented to it; or

(b) a registered medical practitioner appointed as aforesaid (not being the responsible medical officer) has certified in writing that the patient is not capable of understanding the nature, purpose and likely effects of that treatment or has not consented to it but that, having regard to the likelihood of its alleviating or preventing a deterioration of his condition, the treatment should be given' (section 58(3); see also: Department of Health and Social Security, 1983; regulation 16).'

Before making a certificate as outlined in section 58(3)(b), 'the registered medical practitioner concerned shall consult two other persons who have been professionally concerned with the patient's medical treatment, and of those persons one shall be a nurse and the other shall be neither a nurse nor a registered medical practitioner' (section 58(4)).

The Mental Health Act 2007 introduced a number of further provisions in relation to ECT for specific groups, including that detained patients who lack capacity can be administered ECT only when a 'second opinion appointed doctor' (Part 4) certifies that the patient lacks capacity, ECT is an appropriate treatment and (for an adult) does not conflict with a valid advance directive or decision made by a donee or deputy or by the Court of Protection (except in case of emergency) (section 27). Detained patients over the age of 18 years with capacity can be administered ECT only if they consent and a second opinion appointed doctor certifies capacity (except in case of emergency) (section 27). The 2007 Act also restricts the grounds for emergency ECT to circumstances in which '(a) it is immediately necessary to save the patient's life; or (b) it is immediately necessary to prevent a serious deterioration of the patient's condition and is not irreversible' (section 35(1)).

These amendments are consistent with the recommendations of the Richardson Committee, which suggested that 'certain forms of treatment [including ECT] should attract specific safeguards' (Department of Health, 1999: p. 5), but also 'heard argument to the effect that there may be occasions on which delay might endanger life and thus it would be unwise to remove ECT from the scope of the successor to section 62' (p. 85). The 2007 Act balances the retention of emergency ECT in certain cases with this new restriction on the circumstances in which it can be administered (Hall & Ali, 2009: p. 229), reflecting a delicate balance between the autonomy of the patient, the paternalism inherent in involuntary treatment and the right to medical care under the 1948 Universal Declaration of Human Rights, which states that 'everyone has the right to a standard of living adequate for the health and well-being of himself and of his family, including food, clothing, housing and medical care and necessary social services' (United Nations, 1948: Article 25(1)).

Timescales for Mental Health Review Tribunal hearings

Under the Mental Health Act 1983, detained patients could apply to the Mental Health Review Tribunal (now formally called the First-tier Tribunal (Mental Health) and informally a mental health tribunal) following admission for assessment (within 14 days), admission for treatment (within 6 months) or being received into guardianship (within 6 months), among other circumstances (section 66). The Mental Health Act 2007 altered some of these provisions to take account of various other changes in the legislation, including revised provisions for supervised community treatment (sections 32–36).

The 2007 Act also requires that hospital managers make referrals to a tribunal within 6 months of admission for:

'(a) a patient who is admitted to a hospital in pursuance of an application for admission for assessment;
(b) a patient who is admitted to a hospital in pursuance of an application for admission for treatment;
(c) a community patient;
(d) a patient whose community treatment order is revoked under section 17F above;
(e) a patient who is transferred from guardianship to a hospital in pursuance of regulations made under section 19 above' (section 37(3)).

Hospital managers must also refer all such cases to a tribunal 'if a period of more than three years (or, if the patient has not attained the age of 18 years, one year) has elapsed since his case was last considered by such a tribunal, whether on his own application or otherwise' (section 68(6)).

The 2007 Act, therefore, requires automatic referral to a tribunal for patients admitted for assessment, albeit after 6 months of detention (section 37); such patients are generally detained for only 28 days, but this period may be extended if there is an application to displace a nearest relative (section 29(4)), and during such an extended period there is no right of appeal to a tribunal (Bowen, 2007: p. 64).[49] The inclusion of an automatic referral to a tribunal after 6 months goes some of the way towards addressing the concerns articulated in *R (M) v Secretary of State for Health*,[50] although greater efficiency in processing requests to displace the nearest relative, as recommended by the House of Lords, would also help protect the ECHR right to respect for private and family life (Article 8).

Overall, the 2007 Act's changes in relation to mental health tribunals appear likely to result in greater involvement of clinicians in tribunal hearings, which may add to workloads but also, possibly, result in greater emphasis on the 'best' rather than 'medical' interests of patients, i.e. greater emphasis on autonomy and dignity, as opposed to a clinically constructed 'right' to treatment (Sarkar & Adshead, 2005). Interestingly, although ECHR principles have been evoked in relation to treatment, rulings indicate that treatment, when provided, must be based on medical necessity and in the patient's best interests,[51] but there is no automatic right to treatment (e.g. for an individual with untreatable personality disorder, detained on the basis of public protection).[52]

Advocacy

The Mental Health Act 2007 requires that the 'appropriate national authority shall make such arrangements as it considers reasonable to enable persons ("independent mental health advocates") to be available to help qualifying patients' (section 30(2)). Such help 'should, so far as practicable, be provided by a person who is independent of any person who is professionally concerned with the patient's medical treatment' and can relate to a range of matters, including details of the 2007 Act, medical treatment, 'rights which may be exercised under this Act by or in relation to [the patient and] help (by way of representation or otherwise) in exercising those rights'.

A patient is a 'qualifying patient' for advocacy services if he or she is: (a) liable to be detained under this Act (otherwise than by virtue of section 4 or 5(2) or (4) above or section 135 or 136 below);[53] (b) subject to guardianship under this Act; or (c) a community patient' (section 30(2)).

Patients are also qualifying patients even if they do not fulfil these criteria but they discuss 'with a registered medical practitioner or approved clinician the possibility of being given a form of treatment to which section 57 above applies' (section 30(2)), i.e. 'treatment requiring consent and a second opinion' including '(a) any surgical operation for destroying brain tissue or for destroying the functioning of brain tissue; and (b) such other forms of treatment as may be specified for the purposes of this section by regulations made by the Secretary of State'. Each qualifying patient is to be made aware of the advocacy services by a 'responsible person', who may be the hospital manager, responsible clinician, approved clinician, registered medical practitioner or responsible social services authority (section 30(2)).

Although this strengthening of advocacy services should help with the promotion of dignity and autonomous exercise of patients' capabilities, the new provisions do not specify the position of patients who lack capacity to make certain decisions (e.g. to consent to providing access to their records). This may present a significant problem because an advocate can access a patient's records only (a) 'where the patient has capacity or is competent to consent' and does consent, or (b) 'in any other case, [if] the production or inspection would not conflict with a decision made by a donee or deputy or the Court of Protection and the person holding the records' believes that the records are relevant to the advocate's work (section 30(2)).

Therefore, while patients capable of accessing advocacy services are likely to benefit from the enhanced provision of such services under the new legislation, patients incapable of accessing and engaging with advocates (ironically, those most in need of advocacy) may experience difficulty engaging effectively. Notwithstanding this caveat, the enhanced emphasis on advocacy in the 2007 Act is likely to assist in enhancing patient dignity and autonomy by providing at least some patients with a stronger voice and facilitating exercise of specific capabilities.

Overall assessment

In the field of mental health law, it is clear that the ECHR has had greater legal impact than the Universal Declaration of Human Rights, especially since the ECHR was given further effect through the Human Rights Act 1998. The ECHR provisions regarding liberty and reviews of involuntary detention (Article 5) have proven particularly relevant to people with mental illness, with judgments strongly re-emphasising the importance of various protections for the rights of the detained mentally ill, especially in relation to humane conditions, therapeutic settings and prompt, effective reviews.

Similar themes have recurred in cases since the implementation of the Human Rights Act, which have dealt with issues such as the burden of proof in hearings before mental health tribunals, respect for private and family life (ECHR: Article 8) and the power of tribunals to release patients, among other matters. The provision of the Human Rights Act that makes it 'unlawful for a public authority to act in a way which is incompatible with [an ECHR] right' (section 6(1)) appears to have particularly broad implications for mental health services, especially in relation to the prevention of suicide, although this has yet to be fully delineated and operationalised satisfactorily.

The Mental Health Act 2007 made a number of important changes with the potential to advance the dignity and human rights of detained patients. Key changes include revising and simplifying the definition of 'mental disorder' as 'any disorder or disability of the mind' (section 1(2)) (although this is a notably broad definition) and repealing the previous categorisations of mental disorder. The effects of these changes are not yet fully clear and it is noteworthy that the explicit exclusions for 'promiscuity or other immoral conduct, sexual deviancy' are now repealed (section 1(3)).

Most interestingly, the 2007 Act replaced the 'treatability test' of the 1983 Act with a requirement that 'appropriate medical treatment is available' (section 4(2)(b)), although it is no longer necessary to demonstrate that treatment is 'likely' to help, but rather that it has the 'purpose' of helping, apparently regardless of likely efficacy. In addition, widening the role of responsible clinician (sections 9–17) may result in greater decision-making by individuals trained in settings that prioritise public safety over patient well-being, for example prisons; the effects of this, if any, are not clear.

More broadly, the 2007 Act introduced a significant expansion of professional roles, potentially resulting in greater teamwork and sharing of responsibility among various members of multidisciplinary teams, although, again, it remains unclear whether renewal orders made out without the involvement of medical doctors will meet the requirement for objective medical evidence if liberty is lawfully to be denied on the grounds of 'unsound mind' (ECHR: Article 5(1)).[54] The 2007 Act also permits a patient's civil partner to be the nearest relative and allows a patient to apply to displace their nearest relative (which supports patient autonomy), although the court must be of the opinion that the patient's nominee is 'a suitable person to act as such' (section 23(3)) – a notably paternalistic caveat.

Regarding treatment, the 2007 Act revised and simplified supervised community treatment procedures (sections 32–36), although a tribunal's power over such orders is still limited: they may be revoked without the opinion of medical doctors. While treatment in the community as opposed to hospital is, at least in theory, supportive of patients' liberty, dignity and exercise of capabilities, the idea of compulsory treatment in the community is of unproven efficacy and may be subject to misuse (Lawton-Smith *et al*, 2008; Kisely & Campbell, 2014).

Regarding ECT, the 2007 Act introduced new safeguards for detained patients and further restricted the grounds on which emergency ECT can be administered, both of which are protective of patients' rights, including their right to treatment.

Finally, the 2007 Act introduced automatic referral to a tribunal for patients admitted for assessment (section 2), although referral will occur 6 months after admission on what was initially a 28-day order (this 28-day period may be extended if there is an application to displace a nearest relative). The legislation also requires that the 'appropriate national authority' introduce a system of independent mental health advocates (section 30(2)), a measure that has the potential to assist greatly with the protection of rights and exercise of capabilities, although not all patients qualify.

Overall, the changes introduced by the 2007 Act presented a mixture of increased protections for certain human rights, specific measures that support patient dignity and capabilities, and other measures that are clearly paternalistic or even regressive in nature, the last owing chiefly to the legislation's emphasis on public protection. One of the key effects of the legislation has been to increase the net for compulsory treatment by broadening the meaning of 'mental disorder' and making the imposition of a community treatment order somewhat simpler for clinicians. Eliminating the treatability requirement for people with a personality disorder also broadens the scope of compulsion. These aspects of the 2007 Act, along with the absence of an 'impaired decision-making criterion', weigh heavily against the positive human rights aspects of the legislation.

Notwithstanding these concerns, however, certain aspects of the 2007 Act do have significant potential to help advance rights. In particular, the effective use of advocacy could greatly increase opportunity for patients to voice their views and exercise their capabilities in relation to care, and thus enhance their dignity.

Against his background, the 2007 Act was welcomed by many groups, most of whom recognised a broad need for reform (Brindle, 2007). The Royal College of Psychiatrists and the Department of Health welcomed the Act warmly, noting that the legislation represented an important milestone in the reform of mental health services (Bhugra & Appleby, 2008). The King's Fund (2008), an independent charity focusing on health policy and practice, noted that the government had achieved many of its aims in amending the 1983 Act, even though the new measures did not represent a root-and-branch review of the legislation. The King's Fund welcomed measures relating to supervised community treatment on the grounds that it broke the link between involuntary treatment and hospital, and had the potential to reduce violent incidents in the community.

The King's Fund also highlighted the possibility of court challenges to the precise relevance of the Mental Health Act Code of Practice, the requirement to ensure an 'age-appropriate' setting in hospitals for children and renewal of detention orders by responsible clinicians who are not doctors. Overall, it appeared to see the legislation as striking a reasonable balance between autonomy and paternalism, although there was scant mention of the extent to which the legislation did or did not support patients' dignity or autonomous exercise of capabilities.

The Mental Health Alliance (2006) was concerned about many of the same issues as the King's Fund, including the renewal of detention orders by responsible clinicians who are not doctors; they recommended that at least two professionals of different disciplines should agree on the detention, with at least one of them providing the requisite 'objective medical expertise'.

From the perspective of mental health social workers, it was especially notable that the 2007 Act replaced the term 'approved social worker' with 'approved mental health professional' (section 18). Rapaport & Manthorpe (2008), writing in the *British Journal of Social Work*, argued that research demonstrated a difference in ethics between healthcare and social work in approaches to the use of compulsion and that the realistic possibility of nurses promoting the social model of care was far from clear. This change, nonetheless, appears to be a potentially positive one (Bartlett & Sandland, 2014), although the extent of implementation of this and other reforms to professional roles under the new legislation is unclear. In July 2012, the Department of Health's post-legislative assessment of the 2007 Act reported that:

> 'The Department does not collect information on how many approved clinicians there are who are not medical practitioners nor how many approved mental health professionals there are who are not social workers. However, the purpose of the change was not to require a different approach but to give flexibility to employers should they feel that the users of their services would benefit from a wider set of clinical expertise. A report in May 2012 of inspections of the 22 AMHP [approved mental health professional] training courses in England found that of the 936 candidates who had completed their training since November 2008, 84% were social workers and 15% nurses. The health professionals were found to be as equally competent in the role as social workers' (Department of Health, 2012: p. 7).

This passage suggests that the pace of change is slow, with a strong majority of approved mental health professionals still belonging to the social work profession. Clearly, for nurses to take up these roles, appropriate training is needed, along with a corresponding increase in resources (Laing, 2012).

The pace of change in relation to non-doctors becoming responsible clinicians is even less clear, although it appears that the first non-doctor responsible clinician in London, a consultant clinical psychologist, was approved in May 2013 (Oxleas NHS Foundation Trust, 2013).

61

More generally and more worryingly, the Mental Health Foundation, a mental health charity, expressed concern that the 2007 legislation increased the stigma associated with mental illness through its focus on risk of violence (Batty, 2008). This is, possibly, the most far-reaching criticism of the 2007 Act, as it may help explain why certain issues such as human dignity and capabilities were not substantively addressed by the legislation: by focusing on public safety, the legislation dealt largely with involuntary detention and treatment, leading to a general emphasis on paternalism that would have been less prominent had the legislation engaged more deeply with other issues, especially those that affect voluntary patients (e.g. standards of care, dignity), who constitute the majority of mental health patients.

Finally, both the Mental Health Alliance (2006) and the King's Fund (2008) noted that, by redefining mental disorder and removing the 'treatability' test, the provisions of the 2007 Act could permit clinicians to detain some patients who would not have been detained under the 1983 Act. Notwithstanding this concern, many of the changes in the new legislation, especially in relation to advocacy and definition of nearest relative, went at least some way to addressing the concerns of the Mental Health Foundation, Mental Health Alliance, King's Fund and others.

In the end, the precise extent to which these changes will advance or impede the protection of the human rights and dignity of detained patients is not yet clear, even some years after implementation. The ongoing impact of the amendments introduced by the 2007 Act will depend critically on (a) the responses of mental health service providers to the Act, (b) the attitude of the courts in interpreting them in the context of the Human Rights Act 1998 and ECHR and, increasingly, (c) legislative and policy developments at European level, including the Council of Europe, the EU and their various member states (Kelly, 2008d).

From the perspective of the UN, however, it is already clear that there are significant inconsistencies between the legislation in England and Wales, and the CRPD. Most strikingly, having 'mental disorder' remains a key element of detention criteria in England and Wales, and this appears to violate the CRPD, which specifies that 'the existence of a disability shall in no case justify a deprivation of liberty' (CRPD: Article 14(1)(b)) (see Chapter 1). If certain persons with mental disorder (e.g. some people with chronic schizophrenia) fit the UN definition of 'persons with disabilities', then the Mental Health Act 1983, as amended by the 2007 Act, clearly violates this provision, as does mental health legislation in Northern Ireland, Ireland and Scotland (Bennett, 2014; Kelly 2014a). These jurisdictions, and these issues, are considered next.

CHAPTER 3

Fusing mental health and capacity legislation: Northern Ireland

This chapter examines the process of reform of mental health and capacity legislation currently underway in Northern Ireland, a process that represents one of the most challenging and possibly progressive innovations in European mental health legislation in several decades. The chapter commences with an examination of the 'comprehensive legislative framework' presented by the Bamford Review of Mental Health and Learning Disability (2007*a*) and then examines the Mental Capacity Bill 2015, which is not implemented but seeks to fuse mental health legislation and mental capacity legislation into a single Bill, in apparently improved compliance with the United Nations Convention on the Rights of Persons with Disabilities (CRPD) (United Nations, 2006). The Bill, which reached its second stage in the Northern Ireland Assembly in June 2015, appears to be designed along lines similar to those proposed by Dawson & Szmukler (2006) and Szmukler *et al* (2014), and in this chapter it is duly examined in the context of this literature, and appropriate conclusions are drawn. As in other chapters of this book, this chapter examines civil rather than criminal provisions, and focuses on adults rather than children.

The Bamford Review of Mental Health and Learning Disability

The Bamford Review of Mental Health and Learning Disability (Northern Ireland) was established in 2002 and its main report, *A Comprehensive Legislative Framework*, published in August 2007 (Bamford Review of Mental Health and Learning Disability, 2007*a*). The terms of reference (p. 89) were quite broad:

'1. To carry out an independent review of the effectiveness of current policy and service provision relating to mental health and learning disability, and of the Mental Health (Northern Ireland) Order 1986.

2. To take into account:
   - The need to recognise, preserve, promote and enhance the personal dignity of people with mental health needs or a learning disability and their carers;

- The need to promote positive mental health in society;
- Relevant legislative and other requirements, particularly relating to human rights, discrimination and equality of opportunity;
- Evidence-based best practice developments in assessment, treatment and care regionally, nationally and internationally;
- The need for collaborative working among all relevant stakeholders both within and outside the health and personal social services sector;
- The need for comprehensive assessment, treatment and care for people with a mental health need or a learning disability who have offended or are at risk of offending; and
- Issues relating to incapacity.

3. To make recommendations regarding future policy, strategy, service priorities and legislation, to reflect the needs of users and carers'.

The perceived 'need for change' in Northern Irish mental health legislation stemmed not only from the fact that the 'current law' (the Mental Health (Northern Ireland) Order 1986) was 'rooted in nineteenth century legislation' (Bamford Review of Mental Health and Learning Disability, 2007a: p. 7), but also the views of users of mental health services and their carers (in favour of a 'capacity-based approach': p. 8), changes in society and professional practice (e.g. 'community-based care': p. 9), human rights requirements (e.g. the European Convention on Human Rights (ECHR)), changes in mental health law in other jurisdictions (e.g. Scotland, England and Wales, and Ireland) and the introduction of capacity legislation in other jurisdictions (e.g. Scotland). The implications of the 2000 Hague Convention on the International Protection of Adults and the 2006 CRPD were also relevant to the Review Group's work.

The Review Group summarised a number of concerns about the Mental Health (Northern Ireland) Order 1986:

'In formulating proposals for changes in legislation it has been essential to make a careful appraisal of the 1986 Order and its strengths and weaknesses. In doing this, account has been taken of the submissions made to the Review by users of services, carers and other stakeholders and the detailed analyses contained in the reports of committees and other commentaries relating to recent developments in Scotland, England and Wales, and in the Republic of Ireland.

While some elements of current legislation are considered to work well, it has become clear that aspects of the 1986 Order may not be human rights compliant. Neither is it in keeping with developments in good practice, which emphasise partnership between patients and professionals and a holistic approach to care and treatment. Nor is it based on the principles which the Review has identified as essential. The 1986 Order allows the individual's autonomy to be over-ridden in the interests of his own or other's safety, and the powers focus on compulsory assessment based on a relatively narrow definition of risk, rather than ensuring appropriate treatment for those who require it' (Bamford Review of Mental Health and Learning Disability, 2007b: pp. 2–3).

Human rights concerns identified by the Review Group related to a range of areas, including the fact that the 'use of compulsory powers was based on "substantial likelihood of serious physical harm" [section 2(4) of the 1986 Order], with narrower criteria than anywhere else in the United Kingdom, thereby excluding some people with severely deteriorating conditions by disregarding psychological harm' (Bamford Review of Mental Health and Learning Disability, 2007a: pp. 15–16). Other concerns centred on roles and criteria relating to compulsory admission to hospital, various aspects of admission procedures, guardianship (e.g. issues of compulsion), consent to treatment (especially relating to involuntary patients and electroconvulsive therapy (ECT)), mental health tribunals (chiefly operational issues) and various other matters (e.g. the relatively broad range of activities undertaken by the Office of Care and Protection).

The principles that the Review Group identified as 'essential', and with which it believed the 1986 Order did not comply, were stated clearly in its final report:

'i   Autonomy – respecting the person's capacity to decide and act on his own and his right not to be subject to restraint by others
ii   Justice –applying the law fairly and equally
iii   Benefit – promoting the health, welfare and safety of the person, while having regard to the safety of others
iv   Least Harm – acting in a way that minimises the likelihood of harm to the person' (p. 4).

The Review Group emphasised that:

'A principles base which respects the dignity of the person whose decision-making capacity is impaired will also respect the dignity and safety of others in the rare cases where that person's behaviour poses at risk. A balance must be struck between private rights and public safety.
[. . .]
Having a recognition and acceptance of principles does not provide a means of choosing between them. There remain fundamental tensions between autonomy and benefit, for example where emphasis on benefit can lead to paternalism. However, the need to have regard to all the principles provides a balance in the process' (pp. 4–5).

Against this background, the Review Group presented 18 key recommendations, including, most notably, that:

'There should be a single, comprehensive legislative framework for the reform of mental health legislation and for the introduction of capacity legislation in Northern Ireland. This should be through the introduction of provisions for all persons who require substitute decision-making. A framework is proposed for interventions in all aspects of the needs of persons who require substitute decision-making, including mental health, physical health, welfare or financial needs' (p. 84).

The various other 'overarching recommendations' were considerably less dramatic and are outlined in Box 3.1. The Review Group also presented 'specific recommendations' and 'recommendations on implementation'.

Following publication of the Bamford Review, the Royal College of Psychiatrists welcomed the announcement that Northern Ireland was to

Box 3.1 Summary of key overarching recommendations of the Bamford Review of Mental Health and Learning Disability (Northern Ireland)

- There should be a single, comprehensive legislative framework for the reform of mental health legislation and for the introduction of capacity legislation in Northern Ireland.
- The framework should be based on agreed principles, explicitly stated in legislation and supplemented, if necessary, in supporting Codes of Practice.
- The principles underpinning the new legislation should support the dignity of the individual and have regard to autonomy, justice, benefit and least harm.
- These principles should apply in a non-discriminatory and balanced way to all healthcare decisions, as well as to welfare and financial needs.
- Impairment of decision-making capacity is a mandatory prerequisite for any interference with a person's autonomy without their consent.
- The definition of capacity used in section 2 of the Mental Capacity Act 2005 (England and Wales) should be adopted in Northern Ireland; i.e. 'a person lacks capacity in relation to a matter if at the material time he is unable to make a decision for himself in relation to the matter because of an impairment of, or a disturbance in the functioning of, the mind or brain [...] It does not matter whether the impairment or disturbance is permanent or temporary'.
- Children and young people under the age of 18 who are affected by the proposed approach to substitute decision-making should be afforded special protections.
- A comprehensive legislative framework must take account of the particular needs and protections necessary for vulnerable adults, including compliant individuals with impaired decision-making capacity who are deprived of their liberty (Bournewood situations).[55]
- Individuals who are subject to the criminal justice system should have access to assessment, treatment and care which is equivalent to that available to all other people.
- Legislation must provide appropriate public and individual protection to the community against harm from individuals whose decision-making capacity is impaired and who present a risk to others. However, it must not discriminate unjustifiably against people who have mental health problems or an intellectual (learning) disability.

(Adapted from: Bamford Review of Mental Health and Learning Disability, 2007a: pp. 84–86)

introduce single mental health and capacity legislation, saying that this set a world lead in bringing equality for people with mental health problems.[56] Professor Dinesh Bhugra, then President of the College, said: 'This move to single legislation makes very good sense. We fundamentally consider that both mental health and capacity legislations are there to support others to intervene when mental disorder affects people's capacity to make decisions about their lives and treatment' (Royal College of Psychiatrists, 2009).

Dr Philip McGarry, Chair of the Royal College of Psychiatrists Northern Ireland Division, also welcomed the initiative:

'We are pleased that the Health Minister has listened, and we are pleased that the principle of autonomy integral in the Bamford Review has been maintained, so that individuals who have the mental capacity to make decisions for themselves will be allowed to do so.

The modernised legislation promises to be better for people with mental health problems, and better for society as a whole. Only a small proportion of people with mental health problems will ever need to be detained, usually because they want to harm themselves, and on some occasions because they are at risk of harming others. These people should have the same rights and protections as anyone else to whom capacity legislation applies.

Drafting a world-first piece of legislation will be challenging, but there will be considerable goodwill in the mental health and legal community in Northern Ireland, and the Royal College of Psychiatrists has pledged to work closely with the Department of Health to ensure that legislation will work in practice' (Royal College of Psychiatrists, 2009).

Five years later, in their Foreword to the Consultation Document published alongside the 2014 version of the Mental Capacity Bill, Edwin Poots MLA [Member of the Legislative Assembly] (Minister of the Department of Health, Social Services and Public Safety in Northern Ireland (DHSSPSNI)) and David Ford MLA (Minister of Justice, Northern Ireland Department of Justice (NIDoJ)) pointed to the centrality of the Bamford Review's report in shaping the Bill:

'The development of a single legislative framework for the reform of mental health legislation and for the introduction of mental capacity legislation in Northern Ireland was recommended by the Bamford Review in its report published in 2007 'A Comprehensive Legislative Framework'. This was one of a number of reports to come out of a review of mental health and learning disability services in Northern Ireland.

The new framework, the report concluded, would help reduce the stigma often associated with separate mental health legislation and provide an opportunity to strengthen protections for people who lack capacity to make decisions for themselves. The vision was also of a framework that would apply to everyone in society, including those subject to the criminal justice system.

In response to a public consultation on initial proposals by the Department of Health, Social Services and Public Safety in 2009, stakeholders were clear that the vision set out in the Bamford Review report was the right one. Since then, considerable time and effort has been applied to developing the new single legislative framework, which is now referred to as the draft Mental Capacity Bill' (DHSSPSNI & NIDoJ, 2014: p. i).

The Mental Capacity Bill 2015

Northern Ireland's Mental Capacity Bill 2015 is, in its own words, designed to 'make new provision relating to persons who lack capacity; to make provision about the powers of criminal courts in respect of persons with disorder; to disapply Part 2 of the Mental Health Order (Northern Ireland) 1986[56] in relation to persons aged 16 or over and make other amendments of that Order; to make provision in connection with the Convention on the International Protection of Adults signed at the Hague on 13th January

2000;[58] and for connected purposes' (Preamble). The relevant provisions can be usefully considered under the following key headings:

- principles
- future decision-making arrangements
- lack of capacity
- protection from liability and general safeguards
- additional safeguards for serious interventions
- second opinions
- authorisation for serious interventions
- independent advocate
- rights of review
- other decision-making mechanisms
- research
- other matters.

Principles

The Mental Capacity Bill 2015 outlines clear principles in section 1 and these are worth quoting in full:

'(1) The principles in subsections (2) to (5) must be complied with where for any purpose of this [Bill] a determination falls to be made of whether a person who is 16 or over lacks capacity in relation to a matter.

(2) The person is not to be treated as lacking that capacity unless it is established that the person lacks capacity in relation to the matter within the meaning given by section 3.

(3) Whether the person is, or is not, able to make a decision for himself or herself about the matter (a) is to be determined solely by reference to whether the person is or is not able to do the things mentioned in section 4(1)(a) to (d); and (b) accordingly, is not to be determined merely on the basis of any condition that the person has, or any other characteristic of the person, which might lead others to make unjustified assumptions about his or her ability to make a decision.

(4) The person is not to be treated as unable to make a decision for himself or herself about the matter unless all practicable help and support to enable the person to make a decision about the matter have been given without success (see section 5).

(5) The person is not to be treated as unable to make a decision for himself or herself about the matter merely because the person makes an unwise decision.

(6) Nothing in subsections (1) to (5) removes any obligation that a person may be under in a particular situation to take steps to establish whether another person has capacity in relation to a matter (section 1)'.

These principles have much in common with analogous legislation in other jurisdictions, including, for example, the Bill's presumption of capacity (section 1(2)) and the necessity to supply sufficient support to optimise the possibility of the person making their own decision (section 1(4) and section 5). There is a welcome requirement that relevant judgements are not based on 'any condition that the person has, or any other characteristic of the person, which might lead others to make unjustified assumptions' (section 1(3)).

The Bill goes on to specify that when 'an act is done [or] decision is made for or on behalf of a person who is 16 or over and lacks capacity' (section 2(1)), 'the act must be done, or the decision must be made, in the person's best interests' (section 2(2)).

This strong 'best interests' provision is consistent with Ireland's Mental Health Act 2001, which states that 'in making a decision under this Act concerning the care or treatment of a person (including a decision to make an admission order in relation to a person), the best interests of the person shall be the principal consideration with due regard being given to the interests of other persons who may be at risk of serious harm if the decision is not made' (section 4(1)). In England and Wales, the Mental Health Act 2007 (section 8) introduces 'patient wellbeing and safety' as a fundamental principle and the Mental Capacity Act 2005 states that 'an act done, or decision made, under this Act for or on behalf of a person who lacks capacity must be done, or made, in his best interests' (section 1(5)). In Scotland, the Mental Health (Care and Treatment) (Scotland) Act 2003 includes, as a principle, 'the importance of providing the maximum benefit to the patient' (section 1(3)(f)).

In Northern Ireland, the 2015 Bill specifies that determinations of what is in a person's (P's) 'best interests' should not be based on age, appearance or anything else that might lead to 'unjustified assumptions' (section 7(2)). The 'person making the determination' must:

- 'consider all the relevant circumstances (that is, all the circumstances of which that person is aware which it is reasonable to regard as relevant)' (section 7(3)(a));
- 'consider (a) whether it is likely that P will at some time have capacity in relation to the matter in question; and (b) if it appears likely that P will, when that is likely to be' (section 7(4));
- 'so far as practicable, encourage and help P to participate as fully as possible in the determination of what would be in P's best interests' (section 7(5));
- 'have special regard to (so far as they are reasonably ascertainable) (a) P's past and present wishes and feelings (and, in particular, any relevant written statement made by P when P had capacity); (b) the beliefs and values that would be likely to influence P's decision if P had capacity; and (c) the other factors that P would be likely to consider if able to do so' (section 7(6));
- 'so far as it is practicable and appropriate to do so, consult the relevant people about what would be in P's best interests and in particular about the matters mentioned in subsection (6); and (b) take into account the views of those people (so far as ascertained from that consultation or otherwise) about what would be in P's best interests and in particular about those matters' (section 7(7));

- 'have regard to whether the same purpose can be as effectively achieved in a way that is less restrictive of P's rights and freedom of action' (section 7(8));
- 'have regard to whether failure to do the act is likely to result in harm to other persons with resulting harm to P' (section 7(8)).

In addition, 'if the determination relates to life-sustaining treatment for P, the person making the determination must not, in considering whether the treatment is in the best interests of P, be motivated by a desire to bring about P's death' (section 7(10)).

The Consultation Document published alongside the 2014 version of the Bill specified that this 'best interests' principle, 'if applied correctly, is a significant safeguard that builds on the current common law by providing a checklist that must be followed when making a determination about what would be in a person's best interests' (DHSSPSNI & NIDoJ, 2014: pp. 8–9). In addition, 'this provision in the draft Bill has been drafted in such a way as to allow it to operate in a wide range of situations, including for example an emergency or what might generally be a routine intervention, such as washing or dressing someone. This has been achieved by conditioning some of the requirements set out above around what is reasonable, practicable or appropriate' (pp. 9–10).

Overall, this operational definition of 'best interests' is similar to that in the Mental Capacity Act 2005 (section 4) in England and Wales, and also similar to the steps to be taken when 'determining if an intervention is to be made' under the Mental Health (Care and Treatment) (Scotland) Act 2003 (section 1(4)) and the 'principles that apply before and during intervention in respect of relevant persons' under the Assisted Decision-Making (Capacity) Bill 2013 (Part 2) in Ireland. There is, then, substantial commonality across jurisdictions in relation to the operationalisation of these principles for persons with impaired capacity.

Future decision-making arrangements

The 2015 Bill contains quite detailed provisions regarding 'lasting powers of attorney' (Part 5), which means:

> 'power of attorney by which the donor confers on the attorney (or attorneys) authority to make decisions about (or about specified matters concerning) all or any of the following –
>
> (a) the donor's care, treatment and personal welfare,
> (b) the donor's property and affairs,
>
> and which includes authority to make such decisions in circumstances where the donor no longer has capacity' (section 95(1)).

This power is subject to certain restrictions (section 96). For example, if the lasting power of attorney authorises the attorney to make decisions about treatment, it 'authorises the giving or refusing of consent to the provision of life-sustaining treatment only if the instrument contains express provision to that effect' (section 96(2)(b)) and it does not authorise psychosurgery (section 96(7)).

Nor does the lasting power of attorney permit the attorney to deprive a person of their liberty (section 96(3)), and 'restraint' is authorised (section 96(4)) only if:

'the attorney reasonably believes:

(a) that the donor lacks capacity in relation to the matter in question;

(b) that there is a risk of harm to the donor if the attorney does not do or (as the case may be) authorise the act restraining the donor; and

(c) that doing or authorising that act is a proportionate response to
   (i) the likelihood of harm to the donor; and
   (ii) the seriousness of the harm concerned' (section 96(6)).

In addition,

'Any relevant decision to refuse the treatment made by the donor before the execution of the relevant instrument is to be treated as having been withdrawn by the execution of the relevant instrument (and accordingly is not an effective advance decision to refuse the treatment)' (section 97(3)).

The 2015 Bill also presents provisions relating to the scope of lasting powers of attorney (e.g. in relation to gifts) (section 98), appointment of attorneys (sections 99 and 100), appointment of replacement attorneys (sections 101–103), revocation (sections 104 and 105), protection of attorneys and others (sections 106 and 107) and 'powers of court' in relation to lasting powers of attorney (sections 108 and 109). Schedule 4 presents details of 'formalities', including making instruments (Part 1), registration (Part 2), cancellation of registration and notification of severance (Part 3) and records of alterations in registered powers (Part 4). The Enduring Powers of Attorney (Northern Ireland) Order 1987 would be repealed by the 2015 Bill (section 110), and Schedule 5 presents further operational details regarding 'existing enduring powers of attorney'.

Overall, as the Consultation Document notes, this system is 'modelled to some extent on the existing [enduring power of attorney] system but, importantly, allows a person (the "donor") to give someone else (the "attorney") the authority to make decisions on his/her behalf not just in relation to financial matters, but also health (mental and physical) and welfare matters' (DHSSPSNI & NIDoJ, 2014: p. 10). In addition, the lasting power of attorney 'must be registered with the new Office of Public Guardian [...]. This will allow the Public Guardian to investigate any complaints or fraudulent activity that might emerge' (pp. 10–11).

Lack of capacity

The 2015 Mental Capacity Bill specifies that,

'(1) For the purposes of this [Bill], a person who is 16 or over lacks capacity in relation to a matter if, at the material time, the person is unable to make a decision for himself or herself about the matter (within the meaning given by section 4) because of an impairment of, or a disturbance in the functioning of, the mind or brain.

(2) It does not matter –
(a) whether the impairment or disturbance is permanent or temporary;
(b) what the cause of the impairment or disturbance is.

(3) In particular, it does not matter whether the impairment or disturbance is caused by a disorder or disability or otherwise than by a disorder or disability' (sections 3(1)–(3)).

This passage appears to be a reasonably good effort to comply with the CRPD requirement that 'the existence of a disability shall in no case justify a deprivation of liberty' (Article 14(1)(b)), in light of the deprivation of liberty provisions elsewhere in the Bill (sections 24–27). The statement that the cause of the 'impairment or disturbance' is not relevant is certainly welcome, but, ultimately, it is still difficult to see how this meets the CRPD requirement because these provisions still clearly link decision-making capacity with 'an impairment of, or a disturbance in the functioning of, the mind or brain' (section 3(1)), which in effect often means an intellectual disability or mental disorder.

The 2015 Bill goes on to state that:

'a person is "unable to make a decision" for himself or herself about a matter if the person –
(a) is not able to understand the information relevant to the decision; or
(b) is not able to retain that information for the time required to make the decision; or
(c) is not able to appreciate the relevance of that information and to use and weigh that information as part of the process of making the decision; or
(d) is not able to communicate his or her decision (whether by talking, using sign language or any other means)' (section 4(1)).

This definition of incapacity is broadly similar to definitions in the Mental Capacity Act 2005 (section 3(1)) in England and Wales, the Adults with Incapacity (Scotland) Act 2000 (section 1(6)), and the Assisted Decision-Making (Capacity) Bill 2013 (section 3(2)) in Ireland. The Consultation Document, however, makes an interesting if contestable claim for the definition in Northern Ireland's Bill:

'This goes further than the equivalent statutory provision in England and Wales because of the inclusion of the appreciation element. Its inclusion means that, under the draft Bill, it will not be sufficient for a person to have a cognitive understanding of the information relevant to the decision if he/she is to be deemed to have capacity. A person whose insight is distorted by their illness or a person suffering from delusional thinking as a result of their illness, may not, therefore, meet this element of the test' (DHSSPSNI & NIDoJ, 2014: p. 13).

This is an extremely subtle purported difference between the definition in Northern Ireland and that in England and Wales. It is not at all clear just what the difference is between being just unable to 'use or weigh' the information (England and Wales) and being unable to 'use or weigh' and 'appreciate' the information (Northern Ireland) – is it possible that a person could 'use or weigh' the information but not 'appreciate' it? And how would one make this extraordinarily delicate distinction? The difference between the two positions appears vanishingly subtle in theory, let alone in clinical practice.

In any case, the 2015 Bill specifies that 'the "information relevant to the decision" includes information about the reasonably foreseeable consequences of – (a) deciding one way or another; or (b) failing to make the decision' (section 4(2)). Furthermore, 'the person is not to be regarded as "not able to understand the information relevant to the decision" if the person is able to understand an appropriate explanation of the information' (section 4(3)), i.e. 'an explanation of the information given to the person in a way appropriate to the person's circumstances (using simple language, visual aids or any other means)' (section 4(4)). 'All practicable help and support' must be given to enable the person to make their own decision, including provision of information under optimal decision-making circumstances (section 5).

Decisions about whether a person lacks capacity are to be made 'on the balance of probabilities' (section 6(1)), consistent the Mental Capacity Act 2005 (section 2(4)) in England and Wales and the Assisted Decision-Making (Capacity) Bill 2013 (section 3(6)) in Ireland.

Protection from liability and general safeguards

Part 2 of the 2015 Bill commences with provisions relating to 'protection from liability and general safeguards' and applies when an individual ('D') 'does an act in connection with the care, treatment or personal welfare of P' (section 9(1)(b)), before which D must take 'reasonable steps to establish whether P lacks capacity in relation to the matter' (section 9(1)(c)) and 'reasonably' believe 'that P lacks capacity in relation to the matter; and that it will be in P's best interests for the act to be done' (section 9(1)(d)); in addition, it must be the case that 'D would have been liable in relation to the act if P had had capacity in relation to the matter and D had done the act without P's consent' (section 9(1)(e)).

Under these circumstances, 'D does not incur any liability in relation to the act, apart from such liability, if any, as D would have incurred in relation to it even if P: (a) had had capacity to consent in relation to the matter; and (b) had consented to D's doing the act' (section 9(2)). This provision is, however, subject to specific limitations:

- it 'does not exclude – (a) civil liability for loss or damage resulting from a person's negligence in doing an act; or (b) criminal liability resulting from such negligence' (section 10(1));
- it 'does not apply in relation to an act which is, or is done in the course of, psychosurgery' (section 10(2));
- it 'does not apply in relation to an act that conflicts with a decision concerning the care, treatment or personal welfare [which] (a) is made

in accordance with this [Bill] by an attorney under a lasting power of attorney granted by P [...] or (b) is made in accordance with this [Bill] by a deputy appointed for P by the court' (section 10(3));

- nothing in the above 'prevents a person from – (a) providing life-sustaining treatment, or (b) doing an act which the person reasonably believes to be necessary to prevent a serious deterioration in P's condition, while a decision as respects any relevant issue is sought from the court' (section 10(4));
- the provision does not apply if it relates to 'carrying out or continuation of a treatment of P [which] conflicts with an effective advance decision to refuse treatment which has been made by P' (section 11(1)).

Further limitations relate to 'acts of restraint' (including 'use of force or a threat to use force') (section 12(4)(b)), for which D must 'reasonably' believe '(a) that failure to do the relevant act would create a risk of harm to P; and (b) that the relevant act is a proportionate response to – the likelihood of harm to P; and the seriousness of the harm concerned' (section 12(3)).

The Consultation Document published alongside the 2014 version of the Bill notes that this approach, based on 'protection from liability', puts 'into statute the common law doctrine of necessity' which is 'currently relied on by many people who work with, or care for, people who lack capacity to make decisions for themselves. In broad terms, it provides protection against civil and criminal liability (but not negligent acts) provided you act in the person's best interests' (DHSSPSNI & NIDoJ, 2014: pp. 13–14):

'Part 2 of the draft Bill, however, has a wider application than the existing common law because it applies to all acts in connection with a person's care, treatment and personal welfare. This includes acts that would currently be captured by the [Mental Health (Northern Ireland) Order 1986] (which will be revoked by the draft Bill in respect of persons aged 16 and over). In other words, any decisions regarding the detention or compulsory assessment or treatment of persons with mental disorder aged 16 or over will be governed by the provisions of the draft Bill not the Mental Health Order' (p. 14).

Additional safeguards for serious interventions

Chapter 2 of Part 2 of the 2015 Bill outlines 'additional safeguards for serious interventions' where a 'serious intervention' is:

'an intervention in connection with the care, treatment or personal welfare of P [which] –

(a) consists of or involves major surgery;
(b) causes P serious pain, serious distress, or serious side-effects;
(c) affects seriously the options that will be available to P in the future, or has a serious impact on P's day-to-day life; or
(d) in any other way has serious consequences for P, whether physical or non-physical' (section 60(1)).

This includes, but is not limited to,

'(a) any deprivation of liberty;
(b) the imposition of a requirement mentioned in section 28(1)(a) (requirements to attend at particular times or intervals for certain treatment);
(c) the imposition of a community residence requirement' (section 60(2)).

For these interventions, D is protected from liability (subject to the conditions outlined in Part 2) 'only if, before the act is done, a formal capacity
assessment is carried out' and a 'statement of incapacity' made (section
13(2)). A formal capacity assessment 'means an assessment carried out by a
suitably qualified person (who may be D if D is suitably qualified) of whether
P lacks capacity in relation to the matter in question' (section 14(2)).

This does not apply in an 'emergency' (section 13(4)), which is a situation
in which:

'(a) D knows that the safeguard [outlined for a specific intervention in other
areas of the Bill] is not met, but reasonably believes that to delay until
that safeguard is met would create an unacceptable risk of harm to P; or
(b) D does not know whether that safeguard is met, but reasonably believes
that to delay even until it is established whether it is met would create an
unacceptable risk of harm to P' (section 62(2)).

For D to be protected from liability (section 9(2)) for a 'serious
intervention', it is also necessary (in addition to requirements in section
9(1)(c) and (d) given on p. 73 above) that the 'nominated person conditions'
(section 15(2)) are satisfied, i.e. that '(a) a nominated person is in place for
P when D determines whether the act would be in P's best interests [and]
(b) D consults and takes into account the views of the nominated person to
the extent required' (section 15(3)), except in an emergency (section 15(4)).
There are various requirements in relation the nominated person (Part 3),
who must consent in writing to the role (section 68(2)(b)).

The Consultation Document published alongside the 2014 version of
the Bill emphasised that 'a Nominated Person must be in place when
determining what would be in the best interests of the person lacking
capacity' in relation to 'serious interventions'. Furthermore:

'The draft Bill sets out in Part 3 the process involved in appointing a
nominated person. In the first instance, as the name suggests, it will be
for the person concerned to determine who his/her nominated person is, if
he/she has the capacity to do so (capacity being decision specific). The Bill
does, however, provide for a default arrangement where the person lacks the
capacity to nominate someone, with the primary carer being at the top of the
list. Provisions are also included in Part 3 to enable an application to be made
to the [Mental Health Review] Tribunal to put in place a nominated person
or to displace a nominated person in certain circumstances' (DHSSPSNI &
NIDoJ, 2014: p. 19).

More specifically, a 'qualifying person' (e.g. an 'appropriate healthcare
professional') (section 78(5)(a)) may apply for the Tribunal to appoint a
nominated person if he or she 'reasonably believes' that 'P lacks capacity
to make decisions about who should be his or her nominated person'

(section 78(1)(a)) and either '(a) the person who is P's nominated person is not suitable to be so; (b) there is no-one who is P's nominated person; (c) it is not practicable to establish whether P has a nominated person [or] (d) someone is P's nominated person, but it is not practicable to establish who that is' (section 78(2)). If satisfied that relevant conditions are met, the Tribunal may make 'an order appointing as P's nominated person one person who is 16 or over' (section 79(3)). If and when P regains capacity, he or she can 'apply to the Tribunal for revocation of the appointment' (section 81(2)) and 'the Tribunal must make an order revoking the appointment under section 79 unless it is satisfied that P no longer has capacity to make decisions about who should be his or her nominated person' (section 81(3)).

Second opinions

Second opinions are required for certain treatments, except in emergencies (section 16(4)); these treatments include:

'(a) electro-convulsive therapy;
(b) any treatment with serious consequences which is also treatment of a description specified for the purposes of this paragraph by regulations;
(c) any treatment with serious consequences where, at the time of the act –
(i) the question whether it is in P's best interests for P to have the treatment is finely balanced; and
(ii) the circumstances are such as may be prescribed' (section 16(1)).

'Treatment with serious consequences' means treatment that:

'(a) causes the person to whom it is given serious pain, serious distress, or serious side-effects;
(b) is major surgery;
(c) affects seriously the options that will be available to that person in the future, or has a serious impact on his or her day-to-day life; or
(d) in any other way has serious consequences for that person, whether physical or non-physical' (section 20(1)).

For such treatments, as well as ECT, the 'second opinion must have been obtained recently enough before the act is done for it to be reasonable in all the circumstances to rely on it' (section 16(3)). A second opinion is also needed for the administration of regular medication for any condition (section 17(1)(a)) to a 'qualifying person' (section 17(1)(d)) if it is 'treatment with serious consequences' (section 17(1)(b)) and it is continued for 3 months or longer (section 17(1)(c) and 17(5)(b)). Here, a person is a 'qualifying person' if he or she 'is an in-patient or resident in a hospital, care home or place of a prescribed description; or is subject to a requirement to attend at a particular place and particular times or intervals for the purpose of being given treatment for the condition' (section 17(5)(a)).

The second opinion can be obtained from an 'appropriate medical practitioner' (section 18(1)(a)) and may be given 'only if the medical practitioner has consulted such person or persons as appear to him or her to be principally concerned with P's treatment' (section 18(3)). This process is to be overseen by the Regulation and Quality Improvement Authority (RQIA), which is Northern Ireland's independent health and social care regulator, and is similar, in certain respects, to second opinion provisions elsewhere (e.g. in Ireland's Mental Health Act 2001, Part 4).

Authorisation for serious interventions

Schedule 1 Authorisation of deprivation of liberty

Chapter 4 of Part 2 of the 2015 Bill concerns additional safeguards for certain interventions. The 2014 Consultation Document points out that authorisation, generally by a health and social care (HSC) trust panel, is required if:

- 'the act is, or is one of a number of acts that together, amount to a deprivation of liberty [...];
- the act is the imposition of an attendance requirement [...];
- the act is the imposition of a community residence requirement [...]; or
- the act is, or is done in the course of, the provision of treatment with serious consequences; and
  - the nominated person objects;
  - in prescribed circumstances, the person who lacks capacity resists; or
  - in prescribed circumstances, it is done while the person is being deprived of their liberty, or subject to either an attendance requirement or a community residence requirement' (DHSSPSNI & NIDoJ, 2014: p. 21).

In this context, the Consultation Document points to the difficulty establishing what is or is not a 'deprivation of liberty':

'There is no simple definition of a "deprivation of liberty". In fact, the European Court of Human Rights (ECtHR) has made it clear that the question whether someone has been deprived of their liberty depends on the particular circumstances of each case. The Code of Practice will provide guidance based on the sorts of circumstances that have to date been found by the courts to constitute a deprivation of liberty. However, each individual case will have to be assessed in its own right' (p. 22).[59]

Under the 2015 Bill, D is protected from liability for a deprivation of liberty if:

'(a) The deprivation of P's liberty consists of –
  (i) the detention of P, in circumstances amounting to a deprivation of liberty, in a place in which care or treatment is available for P; or
  (ii) related detention;
(b) the detention in question is authorised;[60] and
(c) the prevention of serious harm condition (as well as the conditions of section 9(1)(c) and (d),[61] and any other conditions that apply under this Part) is met' (section 24(2)).

The 'prevention of serious harm condition' is that at the time the act is done D reasonably believes:

'(a) that failure to detain P in circumstances amounting to a deprivation of liberty would create a risk of serious harm to P or of serious physical harm to other persons; and

(b) that the detention in question is a proportionate response to –
   (i) the likelihood of harm to P, or of physical harm to other persons; and
   (ii) the seriousness of the harm concerned' (section 25(5)).

Schedule 1 Authorisation by panel of certain serious interventions

There are two ways in which a deprivation of liberty can be authorised (section 25(3)):

> 'the criteria that must be met for such deprivations of liberty to be authorised are set out in Schedule 1 [...] except where it is the short term detention of a person for the examination of an illness (physical or mental). In that case, the criteria for authorisation are set out in Schedule 2' (DHSSPSNI & NIDoJ, 2014: p. 23).

The process for deprivation of liberty outlined in Schedule 1 involves an application to an HSC trust panel (see below) from a 'prescribed' person who 'is unconnected with P' (Schedule 1, paragraph 5(1)), i.e. is not a close relative, spouse, civil partner, or living with P, and has no interest in 'payments made on account of [P]'s maintenance' (paragraph 291(1)). This may be an 'approved social worker' or 'a person of a prescribed description who is designated by the managing authority of a hospital or care home in which P is an in-patient or resident as a person who may make applications under this Schedule' (Schedule 1, paragraph 5(2)).

The application must be on a 'prescribed form' (Schedule 1, paragraph 6(1)(a)) and include:

- a 'medical report' by a medical practitioner, who must be 'unconnected with P' and have 'examined P not more than two days' earlier, stating that 'the criteria for authorisation are met' (see below) (Schedule 1, paragraph 7);
- a 'care plan', which must include 'prescribed information about the measure or measures for which the application requests authorisation' and 'such other information relating to what is proposed as may be prescribed' (Schedule 1, paragraphs 8(a) and (b));
- 'prescribed information about the views, on prescribed matters, of P's nominated person and any prescribed person' (Schedule 1, paragraph 6(1)(d));
- 'any other prescribed information' (Schedule 1, paragraph 6(1)(e)).

The criteria for authorising 'detention of P in a place in circumstances amounting to a deprivation of liberty' are listed in Box 3.2. These are in addition to the 'prevention of serious harm condition', the conditions of paragraphs 9(1)(c) and (d), and any other conditions that apply under Part 2 of the Bill (section 24(2): see previous page).

The 2015 Bill also outlines procedures for 'taking [a] person to a place for deprivation of liberty' (section 26) and 'permission for absence' from that place (section 27). Overall, these conditions for deprivation of liberty are quite similar to those in other jurisdictions, although there appears to be a greater emphasis on 'harm' in Northern Ireland.

Box 3.2   Criteria for detention amounting to a deprivation of liberty under the Mental Capacity Bill (2015) (Northern Ireland)

'In relation to detention of P in a place in circumstances amounting to a deprivation of liberty, the criteria for authorisation are that:

(a) appropriate care or treatment is available for P in the place in question;

(b) failure to detain P in circumstances amounting to a deprivation of liberty in a place in which appropriate care or treatment is available for P would create a risk of serious harm to P or of serious physical harm to other persons;

(c) detaining P in the place in question in circumstances amounting to a deprivation of liberty would be a proportionate response to the likelihood of harm to P, or of physical harm to other persons; and the seriousness of the harm concerned;

(d) P lacks capacity in relation to whether he or she should be detained in the place in question; and

(e) it would be in P's best interests for P to be so detained.'

(Mental Capacity Bill (2015) (Northern Ireland): Schedule 1, paragraph 10)

Schedule 1 Authorisation of treatment, requirement to attend for treatment and community residence requirement

Authorisations of treatment (Box 3.3), requirement to attend for treatment (Box 3.4) and community residence requirement (Box 3.5) follow the same procedure as authorisation of deprivation of liberty, although specific criteria differ. Authorisations must be revoked when conditions are no longer met (sections 29 and 32).

In addition, if 'treatment with serious consequences' is to be administered despite 'a reasonable objection from P's nominated person' (section 19(1)(b)), D is protected from liability only if 'the provision of the treatment to P is authorised' (section 19(2)(a)), except in an emergency (section 19(3)), and 'the prevention of serious harm condition (as well as the conditions of section 9(1)(c) and (d), and any other conditions that apply under this Part) is met' (section 19(2)(b)). In addition, D is protected from liability if the act is resisted by P (section 22(1)(c)(i)) or P is subject to compulsion under the legislation (section 23) once the 'provision of the treatment to P is authorised' (section 22(2)), there is no objection from P's nominated person (section 22(1)(b)) and the requirements of section 9(1)(c) and (d) are met (section 22(2)).[62]

For a requirement to attend for treatment, in addition to the authorisation criteria (Box 3.4), it is necessary (section 28(2)(b)) that 'before doing the act, D takes reasonable steps to establish whether P lacks capacity in relation to the matter' (section 9(1)(c)) and 'when doing the act, D reasonably believes: that P lacks capacity in relation to the matter; and that it will be in P's best interests for the act to be done' (section 9(1)(d)). In addition, D must 'reasonably' believe 'that (a) failure to impose the requirement, or (b)

Box 3.3 Criteria for authorisation of treatment under the Mental Capacity Bill (2015) (Northern Ireland)

Schedule 1, paragraph 9(1)

'In relation to the provision to P of particular treatment, the criteria for authorisation are:

(a) that P lacks capacity in relation to the treatment;
(b) that it would be in P's best interests to have the treatment; and
(c) if P's nominated person has reasonably objected to the proposal to provide the treatment and has not withdrawn that objection, that the prevention of serious harm condition is met.'

Schedule 1, paragraph 9(2)

The prevention of serious harm condition is:

(a) that failure to provide the treatment to P would create a risk of serious harm to P or of serious physical harm to other persons; and
(b) that carrying out the treatment would be a proportionate response to:
    (i) the likelihood of harm to P, or of physical harm to other persons; and
    (ii) the seriousness of the harm concerned.'

(Mental Capacity Bill (2015) (Northern Ireland): Schedule 1, paragraphs 9(1) and (2))

---

where the requirement is already imposed, failure to ensure that P complies with the requirement, would be more likely than not to result in P's not receiving the treatment' (section 28(5)).

For the community residence requirement, in addition to the authorisation criteria (Box 3.5), it is again necessary (section 30(2)(b)) that 'before doing the act, D takes reasonable steps to establish whether P lacks capacity in relation to the matter' (section 9(1)(c)) and 'when doing

---

Box 3.4 Criteria for authorisation of requirement to attend for treatment under the Mental Capacity Bill (2015) (Northern Ireland)

'In relation to the imposition on P of a requirement to attend at a particular place at particular times or intervals for the purpose of being given particular treatment which would be likely to be treatment with serious consequences, the criteria for authorisation are that:

(a) failure to impose such a requirement would be more likely than not to result in P's not receiving the treatment;
(b) P lacks capacity in relation to whether he or she should attend for the purpose of being given the treatment at the place and times or intervals concerned; and
(c) a requirement to attend for that purpose at the place and times or intervals concerned would be in P's best interests.'

(Mental Capacity Bill (2015) (Northern Ireland): Schedule 1, paragraph 11)

Box 3.5 Criteria for authorisation of community residence requirement under the Mental Capacity Bill (2015) (Northern Ireland)

'In relation to the imposition on P of a community residence requirement, the criteria for authorisation are that:

(a) failure to impose a community residence requirement would create a risk of harm to P;
(b) imposing such a requirement would be a proportionate response to:
    (i) the likelihood of harm to P; and
    (ii) the seriousness of the harm concerned;
(c) P lacks capacity in relation to the matters covered by the community residence requirement;
(d) any services which, under regulations under section 33 [Duties in relation to people subject to community residence requirements], are required to be available to people subject to community residence requirements are available in the area in which P would be required by the community residence requirement to live; and
(e) The community residence requirement would be in P's best interests.'

(Mental Capacity Bill (2015) (Northern Ireland): Schedule 1, paragraph 12)

---

the act, D reasonably believes: that P lacks capacity in relation to the matter; and that it will be in P's best interests for the act to be done' (section 9(1)(d)). In addition, D must 'reasonably' believe '(a) that failure to do the act would create a risk of harm to P; and (b) that the act is a proportionate response to: the likelihood of harm to P; and the seriousness of the harm concerned' (section 30(4)). If implemented, the community residence requirement means a requirement 'for P to live at a particular place' (section 31(1)) and may also include '(a) a requirement for P to allow a healthcare professional access to P at a place where P is living' and '(b) a requirement (or requirements) for P to attend at particular places and times or intervals for the purpose of training, education, occupation or treatment' (section 31(2)), although not 'treatment which is likely to be treatment with serious consequences' (section 31(4)) (see section 28).

Schedule 1 The Health and Social Care (HSC) Trust panel

On receiving an application for any of these interventions, the relevant HSC trust must 'as soon as practicable: (a) give prescribed information to P and any prescribed person; and (b) constitute a panel to consider the application' (Schedule 1, paragraph 14(1)). The panel will comprise three members (yet to be determined) (section 283(2)) and must meet 'as soon as practicable' and, in any case, within 7 working days (Schedule 1, paragraph 19). If the panel feels that a decision is not possible within that period and 'it is more likely than not that the criteria for authorisation are met, the panel may grant an interim authorisation' for 28 days (Schedule 1, paragraph 20).

Regulations may make further recommendations governing panel membership (section 283(3)) and procedures, including:

'(a) provision requiring the panel to afford prescribed persons the opportunity to make representations;
(b) provision enabling the panel to request prescribed persons to provide information to the panel or attend before the panel to give oral evidence;
(c) provision about steps that the panel is, or is not, to be regarded as required by section 7 ['best interests'] to take where it has to make a determination of what would be in a person's best interests;
(d) provision for cases where the panel cannot reach a unanimous decision' (section 283(4)).

The 2014 Consultation Document emphasises that 'in making its decision, the panel may conduct an oral hearing at which those making the application, the person lacking capacity, the nominated person and the independent advocate [...] may give evidence. The panel will however be required to give its decision within 7 working days of being constituted' (DHSSPSNI & NIDoJ, 2014: p. 27).

Following its consideration of the matter, the panel may authorise or refuse to authorise the measure(s) requested in the application (Schedule 1, paragraph 15(1)). Intriguingly, if the authorised measure is a 'treatment', the panel may also include authorisation of another measure (relating to deprivation of liberty, requirement to attend for treatment or community residence) even though it was not requested in the application (Schedule 1, paragraphs 15(2) and 15(3)), once the panel 'considers that the criteria for authorisation are met in relation to that measure' (Schedule 1, paragraph 15(5)). Authorisation lasts for 6 months unless it is revoked (Schedule 1, paragraph 15(6)(b)) or extended.[63] Finally, an authorisation for treatment authorises not only the provision of treatment specified in the application, but also 'such modifications as the medical practitioner in charge of P's treatment may reasonably consider to be in P's best interests' (Schedule 1, paragraph 21(2)(b)).

Schedule 2 Authorisation of short-term detention in hospital for examination etc.

Schedule 2 of the 2015 Bill outlines a second authorisation procedure specifically for 'short-term detention in hospital for examination etc'. Under this procedure, 'the detention of a person in a hospital in circumstances amounting to a deprivation of liberty, for the purposes of examination (or of examination followed by other treatment or care), may be authorised by the making of a report' (Schedule 2, paragraph 2(1)) by an appropriate healthcare professional where 'in the opinion of the appropriate healthcare professional, the criteria for authorisation are met' (Schedule 2, paragraph 2(2)). Box 3.6 outlines the relevant criteria and required contents of the report, which is to be made out by 'an appropriate healthcare professional' such as 'an approved social worker' (Schedule 2, paragraph 3).

The Consultation Document published alongside the 2014 version of the Bill highlights the fact that this Schedule 2 process, unlike the Schedule 1 process, does not require authorisation by an HSC trust panel:

> 'This does not involve an application to an HSC Trust panel as there simply would not be time to do this given that there is often a need to assess the person's condition urgently. Authority is instead derived from the making of a report which must include a medical report stating that the criteria

---

Box 3.6 Authorisation of short-term detention in hospital for examination etc. under the Mental Capacity Bill (2015) (Northern Ireland)

Criteria for authorisation (Schedule 2, paragraph 2(3))

'The criteria for authorisation are that:

(a) P has an illness or there is reason to suspect that P has an illness;
(b) failure to detain P in a hospital in circumstances amounting to a deprivation of liberty, for the purposes of examination or of examination followed by other treatment or care, would create a risk of serious harm to P or of serious physical harm to other persons;
(c) Detaining P in the hospital in circumstances amounting to a deprivation of liberty, for those purposes, would be a proportionate response to:
   (i) the likelihood of harm to P, or
   (ii) of physical harm to other persons; and the seriousness of the harm concerned;
(d) P lacks capacity in relation to whether he or she should be so detained; and
(e) it would be in P's best interests for him or her to be so detained.'

Requirements for the authorising report (Schedule 2, paragraph 2(4))

'A report under this paragraph must be in the prescribed form and must:

(a) include a medical report [made by a medical practitioner who is unconnected with P and has examined P within the previous two days, stating that criteria for authorisation are met (Schedule 2, paragraph 4)];
(b) include a statement by the appropriate healthcare professional that in his or her opinion the criteria for authorisation [above] are met;
(c) include prescribed information about the views, on prescribed matters, of P's nominated person and any prescribed person;
(d) include any other prescribed information; and
(e) state that the report authorises the detention, in circumstances amounting to a deprivation of liberty, of P in a specified hospital for the purposes of examination or of examination followed by other treatment or care.'

Regarding P's capacity (Schedule 2, paragraph 2(5))

'If the appropriate healthcare professional is of the opinion that P is likely to lack capacity in relation to whether an application under section 45 (applications to Tribunal) should be made in respect of the authorisation granted by the making of the report under this paragraph, the report must contain a statement of that opinion.'

(Mental Capacity Bill (2015) (Northern Ireland): Schedule 2, paragraphs 2(3)–2(5))

---

for authorisation are met. Where the nominated person objects to the making of a report, an approved social worker must be consulted, even if it is an approved social worker making the report [Schedule 2, paragraph 6]' (DHSSPSNI & NIDoJ, 2014: p. 28).

If P was not a patient in hospital when the authorisation was made, the authorisation expires 2 days after the medical report was made, unless P is admitted to hospital in the meantime (Schedule 2, paragraph 9(1)); this may be extended by certain medical practitioners for up to 14 days 'because of exceptional circumstances' (Schedule 2, paragraph 9(2)(b)). The authorisation also expires if there is a 'failure to give P certain information' (Schedule 2, paragraph 10(2)) or an appropriate 'medical practitioner' (Schedule 2, paragraph 11(4)) has not examined P and prepared a report as soon as practicable (Schedule 2, paragraphs 11(2) and (3)). The 'admission report' must be completed by a medical practitioner other than the one who provided the initial report (Schedule 2, paragraph 11(5)) and must specify whether or not the condition in Box 3.7 is met (Schedule 2, paragraph 11(7)).

The authorisation expires 48 hours after the admission report was made if there is no examination and report by a 'suitable medical practitioner' within that time (Schedule 2, paragraphs 13(1) and (2)). This means that an admission report can detain P for 48 hours (e.g. over a weekend), during which time a more senior doctor will likely make a report. The authorisation also expires 14 days after admission if 'a suitable medical practitioner has not examined P and made a further report' (Schedule 2, paragraph 14(2)). There is also a provision for rectifying reports that are 'found to be in any respect incorrect or defective' (Schedule 2, paragraph 20(1)(a)), subject to certain guidelines (Schedule 2, paragraph 20(2)).

Box 3.7 The condition to be met for short-term detention in hospital for examination etc. under the Mental Capacity Bill (2015) (Northern Ireland)

'The condition [...] is that:

(a) failure to detain P in the hospital in circumstances amounting to a deprivation of liberty, for the purposes of further care, would create a risk of serious harm to P or of serious physical harm to other persons;

(b) detaining P in the hospital in circumstances amounting to a deprivation of liberty, for those purposes, is a proportionate response to the likelihood of harm to P, or of physical harm to other persons; and the seriousness of the harm concerned;

(c) P lacks capacity in relation to whether he or she should be so detained; and

(d) it would be in P's best interests for him or her to be so detained.'

(Mental Capacity Bill (2015) (Northern Ireland): Schedule 2, paragraph 12(2))

Independent advocates

The Consultation Document published alongside the 2014 version of the Bill noted that an 'independent advocate' must be in place 'where Part 2 of the Bill requires an act to be authorised or where, although not requiring authorisation, an act is a serious compulsory intervention' (DHSSPSNI & NIDoJ, 2014: p. 28). More specifically, D is protected from liability for a 'relevant act' 'only if the independent advocate conditions (as well as the conditions of section 9(1)(c) and (d) [see above], and any other conditions that apply under this Part) are met' (section 35(2)). The 'independent advocate conditions' are that:

'(a) at the time when D determines whether the act would be in P's best interests, there is an independent advocate who is instructed under section 89 ['Instruction of independent advocate'] to represent and provide support to P; and

(b) in determining whether the act would be in P's best interests, D consults and takes into account the views of the independent advocate to the extent required by section 7(7) (duty to consult where practicable and appropriate and to take views into account)' (section 35(3)).

A 'relevant act' means any of the following:

'(a) an act which amounts to a deprivation of P's liberty, or one of a number of acts that together amount to such a deprivation;

(b) the imposition on P of a requirement to attend at a particular place at particular times or intervals for the purpose of being given treatment which is likely to be treatment with serious consequences;

(c) the imposition on P of a community residence requirement;

(d) the provision of serious compulsory treatment; or

(e) a serious compulsory intervention not falling within paragraphs (a) to (d)' (section 36(1)).

An act is 'the provision of serious compulsory treatment' if '(a) it is, or is done in the course of, the provision to P of treatment with serious consequences; and (b) the treatment is carried out despite a reasonable objection[64] from P's nominated person' (section 36(2)) or 'is resisted by P (see section 66);[65] or is done while P is subject to an additional measure (see section 23)'[66] (section 36(4)). An act is a 'serious compulsory intervention' if '(a) it is, or is part of, a serious intervention; and (b) the intervention is carried out despite a reasonable objection from P's nominated person' (section 36(3)) or 'is resisted by P (see section 66); or is done while P is subject to an additional measure (see section 23)' (section 36(4)).

The requirement for an independent advocate does not apply when the situation is an emergency or if P 'has made a declaration under section 88 or 91 (declarations declining services of an independent advocate) in relation to the matter in question' (section 35(4)).

The 2015 Bill presents detailed provisions about the appointment and functions of independent advocates. Each relevant HSC trust has a duty to ensure that independent advocates are available (section 84) and regulations may prescribe steps to be taken by independent advocates, including steps for the purpose of:

'(a) providing support to P so that P may participate as fully as possible in any relevant decision;

(b) obtaining and evaluating relevant information;

(c) ascertaining P's past and present wishes and feelings and the beliefs and values that would be likely to influence P's decision if P had capacity;

(d) ascertaining what alternative courses of action are available in relation to P;

(e) informing persons responsible for determining what would be in P's best interests of the independent advocate's conclusions;

(f) informing P's nominated person (if any) of matters relevant to the nominated person' (section 85(3)).'

Regulations may also set out 'circumstances in which an independent advocate may challenge, or provide assistance for the purposes of challenging, any relevant decision' (section 85(4)).

An 'appropriate healthcare professional may request the relevant trust to instruct an independent advocate' (section 86(2)), but, if practicable, before this occurs, 'P must be given prescribed information relating to independent advocates' (section 87(2)) (including that information about P may be disclosed to the independent advocate) (section 87(6)), and an opportunity to decide whether to refuse an advocate (section 87(3)), if P has capacity to do so (section 87(5)). P may decline to have an independent advocate instructed (section 88) or discontinue involvement with the independent advocate (section 91), although the HSC trust does not have a duty to appoint a replacement independent advocate if the patient discontinues involvement with a specific independent advocate (section 92(2)(a)).

This system of independent advocates is similar to that introduced by the Mental Health Act 2007 in England and Wales, which requires that the 'appropriate national authority shall make such arrangements as it considers reasonable to enable persons ("independent mental health advocates") to be available to help qualifying patients' (section 30(2)), although, as in Northern Ireland, not all patients qualify (although patients subject to compulsion do) (section 30(2)).

Overall, these measures in the Northern Irish Bill seem likely to assist in protecting the rights of the patient not least because, in the words of the 2014 Consultation Document, 'the primary role of the independent advocate under the Bill is to support and represent the person who lacks capacity in the determination of whether a proposed act is in his/her best interests' (DHSSPSNI & NIDoJ, 2014: p. 29) – and the principle of best interests is, clearly, central to the 2015 Bill (section 2(2)).

Rights of review

The Consultation Document points out that the 2015 Bill (section 263) provides for the renaming of the Mental Health Review Tribunal: 'It will be known as the "Review Tribunal" in recognition of the wider scope of the applications (beyond detention for the assessment/treatment of mental disorder) that will be considered by it under the Bill' (DHSSPSNI & NIDoJ, 2014: p. 29). The 2015 Bill presents a useful table outlining the 'right to apply to Tribunal' (section 45(1)) and this is shown in Box 3.8.

For the purpose of such an application, a 'qualifying person' means (a) 'the person to whom the authorisation relates ("P")' or (b) 'a person who is P's nominated person' (section 45(2)), although 'if P has capacity in relation to whether an application under this section should be made, P's nominated person may make an application only with P's consent' (section 45(3)).

Such an application cannot be made if the authorisation is no longer in force (section 45(4)); this contrasts with the Mental Health Act 2001 in Ireland, which permits a mental health tribunal to review an order that is no longer in force, if the 'patient indicates by notice in writing addressed to the [Mental Health] Commission within 14 days of his or her discharge that he or she wishes such a review to be held' (section 28(5)(b)).

Box 3.8 Right to apply to the Mental Health Review Tribunal under the Mental Capacity Bill (2015) (Northern Ireland)

Where an event mentioned in the first column of the following table occurs, a qualifying person may apply to the Tribunal within the period mentioned in the corresponding entry of the second column of the table.

Event	Period for making application
The grant of an authorisation under paragraph 15 of Schedule 1 ['Authorisation by panel of certain serious interventions']	The period of 6 months beginning with the date the authorisation is granted
The grant of an interim authorisation under paragraph 20 of that Schedule	The period of 28 days beginning with the date the interim authorisation is granted
The grant of an authorisation under Schedule 2 ['Authorisation of short-term detention in hospital for examination etc.']	The period of 28 days beginning with the date of admission (as defined by paragraph 14(3) of Schedule 2)
The extension under Chapter 6 of the period of an authorisation under paragraph 15 of Schedule 1	The period: (a) beginning with the date when the period of the authorisation is extended; and (b) ending with the end of the period for which the authorisation is extended

(Mental Capacity Bill (2015) (Northern Ireland): section 45(1))

To advise whether an application to the Review Tribunal should be made or provide 'information as to the condition of P for the purposes of an application' (section 46(2)), a medical practitioner who is authorised by or on behalf of P, or by P's nominated person (section 46(1)), 'may, at any reasonable time, visit the person and examine him or her in private' (section 264(2)) and examine relevant records (section 264(3)) with P's consent (if P has capacity) (section 264(4)).

Others may also make applications to the Tribunal:

'There is also a provision in the Bill [section 47] that gives the Attorney General, the Department [of Health, Social Services and Public Safety] (DHSSPS) or the High Court Master (Care and Protection) the power to refer a case to the Tribunal. A duty is also placed on HSC Trusts to refer cases to the Tribunal for review where the original authorisation has been extended under the provisions of Part 2 of the Bill and the case has not already been considered by the Tribunal within one year in the case of 16 and 17 year olds, or two years for those aged 18 and over [section 48].[67] The Tribunal will have the power to revoke or confirm the authorisation. It will also be able to vary it by cancelling one measure where the authorisation covered more than one measure' (DHSSPSNI & NIDoJ, 2014: pp. 29–30).

More specifically, following an application or reference to the Tribunal in respect of an authorisation under Schedule 1 (i.e. 'certain serious interventions'), the Tribunal may '(a) revoke the authorisation; (b) if the authorisation authorises more than one measure [...], vary the authorisation by cancelling any provision of it which authorises a measure;' or '(c) decide to take no action in respect of the authorisation' (section 50(1)). Following an application or reference to the Tribunal in respect of an authorisation under Schedule 2 (i.e. 'short-term detention in hospital for examination etc.'), the Tribunal may '(a) revoke the authorisation; or (b) decide to take no action in respect of the authorisation' (section 51(1)).

Other decision-making mechanisms

In addition to the system of 'lasting powers of attorney' (Part 5), the 2015 Bill provides for another decision-making mechanism in the form of High Court powers and deputies (Part 6). More specifically, the High Court may make declarations (section 111) or decisions, and may appoint deputies (section 112). In terms of declarations, the Court may 'make declarations in relation to a person who is 16 or over as to: (a) whether the person has or lacks capacity to make a decision specified in the declaration; (b) whether the person has or lacks capacity to make decisions on a matter described in the declaration; [and] (c) the lawfulness or otherwise of any act done, or yet to be done, in relation to the person' (section 111(1)).

If P lacks capacity in relation to a matter concerning 'P's care, treatment or personal welfare, or P's property and affairs' (section 112(1)(a)), 'the Court may: (a) by making an order, make on P's behalf a decision or decisions that P lacks capacity to make in relation to the matter or matters; or (b) appoint a person (a 'deputy') to make decisions on P's behalf in relation to the matter or matters' (section 112(2)). This power is 'subject to the provisions of this [Bill] and, in particular, to sections 1, 2, 5 and 7 (principles, best interests)' (section 112(3)).

The Court thus has the option of appointing a deputy, but 'when deciding whether it would be in P's best interests to appoint a deputy, the Court must (in addition to complying with section 7) ['best interests'] have regard to the principles that: (a) a decision by the court is to be preferred to the appointment of a deputy to make a decision; and (b) the powers conferred on a deputy should be as limited in scope and duration as is practicable in the circumstances' (section 112(4)). 'The court may: (a) make such further orders, (b) give such directions, and (c) confer on a deputy such powers or impose on a deputy such duties, as it considers appropriate for giving effect to, or otherwise in connection with, an order or appointment made by it' (section 112(5)). These powers may concern 'P's care, treatment and personal welfare' (section 113) and 'P's property and affairs' (section 114) and are both extensive and subject to specified restrictions (section 116) (Box 3.9).

Further provisions relate to procedures for 'appointment of deputies' (section 115), 'reliance on authority of deputy in relation to treatment etc' (section 117), 'interim orders and directions' (section 118), 'power to call for reports' (e.g. from an employee of an HSC trust) (section 119 and 120) and 'applications to the court' (sections 121 and 122).

Box 3.9 Possible powers and restrictions relating to decisions by the High Court and deputies appointed by the High Court under the Mental Capacity Bill (2015) (Northern Ireland)

Possible powers in respect of care, treatment and personal welfare (section 113(1)):

(a) deciding where P is to live;
(b) deciding what contact, if any, P is to have with any specified persons;
(c) making an order prohibiting a specified person from having contact with P;
(d) giving or refusing consent to the provision of a treatment by a person providing healthcare for P;
(e) giving a direction that a person responsible for P's healthcare allow a different person to take over that responsibility.

Possible powers in respect of property and affairs (section 114(1); see also Schedule 6):

(a) the control and management of P's property;
(b) the sale, exchange, charging, gift or other disposition of P's property;
(c) the acquisition of property in P's name or on P's behalf;
(d) the carrying on, on P's behalf, of any profession, trade or business;

(continued)

(Box 3.9 continued)

(e) the taking of a decision that will have the effect of dissolving a partnership of which P is a member;

(f) the carrying out of any contract entered into by P;

(g) the discharge of P's debts and of any of P's obligations, whether legally enforceable or not;

(h) the settlement of any of P's property, whether for P's benefit or for the benefit of others;

(i) the execution for P of a will;

(j) the exercise of any power (including a power to consent) vested in P whether beneficially or as trustee or otherwise;

(k) the conduct of legal proceedings in P's name or on P's behalf.

Restrictions on deputies (section 116):

(1) A deputy does not have power to make a decision on behalf of P in relation to a matter unless P lacks capacity, or the deputy reasonably believes that P lacks capacity, in relation to that matter.

(2) The authority conferred on a deputy is subject to the provisions of this [Bill] and, in particular, sections 1, 2, 5 and 7 (principles, best interests).

(3) Nothing in section 112 or 113 permits a deputy to be given power: (a) to prohibit a specified person from having contact with P; (b) to direct a person responsible for P's healthcare to allow a different person to take over that responsibility.

(4) Nothing in section 112 or 114 permits a deputy to be given powers with respect to: (a) the settlement of any of P's property, whether for P's benefit or for the benefit of others; (b) the execution for P of a will; or (c) the exercise of any power (including a power to consent) vested in P whether beneficially or as trustee or otherwise.

(5) A deputy may not be given power to make a decision on behalf of P that is inconsistent with a decision that: (a) is made in accordance with this Act by an attorney under a lasting power of attorney granted by P; and (b) is within the scope of the attorney's authority.

(6) A deputy may not refuse consent to the provision of life-sustaining treatment to P.

(7) A deputy may not deprive P of his or her liberty or authorise another person to do so.

(8) A deputy may not do, or authorise another person to do, an act restraining P unless in doing so the deputy is acting within the scope of an authority expressly conferred on the deputy by the Court and the deputy reasonably believes: (a) that P lacks capacity in relation to the matter in question; (b) that there is a risk of harm to P if the deputy does not do or authorise the act restraining P; and (c) that doing or authorising that act is a proportionate response to: (i) the likelihood of harm to P; and (ii) the seriousness of the harm concerned.

(9) In this section an 'act restraining P' means an act (other than a deprivation of P's liberty) which: (a) is intended to restrict P's liberty of movement, whether or not P resists; or (b) is a use of force or a threat to use force and is done with the intention of securing the doing of an act that P resists.

(10) A deputy may not give consent to psychosurgery in respect of P.

(11) The Department may by regulations amend subsection (10) so as to extend the descriptions of treatment to which a deputy may not give consent.

(Adapted from: Mental Capacity Bill (2015) (Northern Ireland))

Overall, these provisions accord considerable power to the High Court:

'Unlike in England and Wales, it is not proposed to set up a separate Court of Protection in Northern Ireland. As concluded by the Bamford Review, the size of the jurisdiction does not warrant it. Instead Part 6 of the Bill sets out the declaratory and decision making powers of the High Court (the Court) in relation to determining a person's capacity and in relation to the care, treatment or personal welfare of a person who lacks capacity. These are broadly similar to those of the Court of Protection' (DHSSPSNI & NIDoJ, 2014: pp. 30–31).

These provisions, however, appear non-compliant with the CRPD, which states that 'persons with disabilities have the right to recognition everywhere as persons before the law' (Article 12(1)) and must 'enjoy legal capacity on an equal basis with others in all aspects of life' (Article 12(2)), and does not endorse substitute decision-making. On the other hand, in Northern Ireland, 'the authority conferred on a deputy is subject to the provisions of this Act and, in particular, sections 1, 2, 5 and 7 (principles, best interests)' (section 116(2)), and this requires that the deputy 'have special regard to (so far as they are reasonably ascertainable): (a) P's past and present wishes and feelings (and, in particular, any relevant written statement made by P when P had capacity); (b) the beliefs and values that would be likely to influence P's decision if P had capacity; and (c) the other factors that P would be likely to consider if able to do so' (section 7(6)).

Despite this requirement to take account of P's wishes, this entire section of the 2015 Bill accords poorly, if at all, with the view of the Committee on the Rights of Persons with Disabilities (2014), which is clear that supported decision-making rather than substitute decision-making is appropriate, and that developing a model of supported decision-making alongside a model of substitute decision-making is not sufficient to meet the CRPD requirement for 'equal recognition before the law' (Article 12).

Research

Part 8 of the 2015 Bill states that 'intrusive research carried out on, or in relation to, a person who is 16 or over and lacks capacity to consent to it is unlawful unless it is carried out: (a) as part of an approved research project (see subsection (3)); and (b) in accordance with sections 133 to 135' (section 130 (1)). 'Intrusive' research is research 'of a kind that would be unlawful if it were carried out: (a) on or in relation to a person who had capacity to consent to it; but (b) without that person's consent' (section 130(2)). For the purpose of section 130, 'a clinical trial which is subject to the provisions of clinical trials regulations is not to be treated as research' (section 131(2)).

For relevant research to be approved, the 'appropriate body' must be satisfied that the following requirements (section 132(2)–(7)) are met:

'(2) The research must be connected with:
  (a) an impairing condition affecting P;[68] or
  (b) its treatment

(3) There must be reasonable grounds for believing that research of comparable effectiveness cannot be carried out if the project has to be confined to, or relate only to, persons who have capacity to consent to taking part in it.

(4) The research must:
   (a) have the potential to benefit P without imposing on P a burden that is disproportionate to the potential benefit to P; or
   (b) be intended to provide knowledge of the causes or treatment of, or of the care of persons affected by, the same or a similar condition.

(5) If the research falls within paragraph (b) of subsection (4) but not within paragraph (a), there must be reasonable grounds for believing:
   (a) that the risk to P from taking part in the project is likely to be negligible; and
   (b) that nothing done to, or in relation to, P as part of the project will:
      (i) interfere with P's freedom of action or privacy in a significant way; or
      (ii) be unduly invasive or restrictive.

(6) Without prejudice to subsection (5), there must be reasonable grounds for believing that no serious intervention will be carried out in respect of P as part of the project unless the intervention is one that could lawfully be carried out in respect of P if it were not part of the project (for example, because the conditions of Part 2 are met).

(7) There must be reasonable arrangements in place for ensuring that the requirements of sections 133 to 135 will be met'.

Section 133 outlines a 'requirement to consult [the] nominated person, carer etc'; section 134 outlines an 'exception for urgent treatment'; and section 135(2)–(4) outlines 'additional safeguards', including:

'(2) Nothing may be done to, or in relation to, P in the course of the research:
   (a) to which P appears to object (whether by showing signs of resistance or otherwise) except where what is being done is intended to protect P from harm or to reduce or prevent pain or discomfort; or
   (b) which is the carrying out or continuation of treatment of P and would be contrary to:
      (i) an effective advance decision to refuse treatment which has been made by P, or
      (ii) any other form of statement made by P and not subsequently withdrawn, of which the person conducting the research project ("R") is aware.

(3) The interests of P must be assumed to outweigh those of science and society.

(4) If P indicates (in any way) a wish to be withdrawn from the project P must be withdrawn without delay'.

Comparison with legislation on research in England and Wales, in Scotland and in Ireland

These provisions are similar to those outlined in the Mental Capacity Act 2005 in England and Wales, which states that 'intrusive research carried out on, or in relation to, a person who lacks capacity to consent to it is unlawful unless it is carried out: (a) as part of a research project which is for the time being approved by the appropriate body for the purposes of this Act in accordance with section 31, and (b) in accordance with sections 32 and 33' (section 30(1)).

In England and Wales, research is 'intrusive' if 'it is of a kind that would be unlawful if it was carried out: (a) on or in relation to a person who had capacity to consent to it, but (b) without his consent' (section 30(2)). As in Northern Ireland, 'appropriate body' means 'the person, committee or other body specified in regulations made by the appropriate authority as the appropriate body in relation to a project of the kind in question' (section 30(4)), and 'a clinical trial which is subject to the provisions of clinical trials regulations is not to be treated as research for the purposes of this section' (section 30(3)).

For any research project to be 'approved' within the meaning of the 2005 Act, the 'research must be connected with: (a) an impairing condition affecting P, or (b) its treatment' (section 31(2)). In addition, 'there must be reasonable grounds for believing that research of comparable effectiveness cannot be carried out if the project has to be confined to, or relate only to, persons who have capacity to consent to taking part in it' (section 31(4)). 'The research must: (a) have the potential to benefit P without imposing on P a burden that is disproportionate to the potential benefit to P, or (b) be intended to provide knowledge of the causes or treatment of, or of the care of persons affected by, the same or a similar condition' (section 31(5)(b)).

As in Northern Ireland, there are regulations in England and Wales relating to 'consulting carers' (section 32) and 'loss of capacity during research project' (section 34). There are also 'additional safeguards' for any relevant research participant, including a stipulation that 'nothing may be done to, or in relation to, him in the course of the research (a) to which he appears to object (whether by showing signs of resistance or otherwise) except where what is being done is intended to protect him from harm or to reduce or prevent pain or discomfort, or (b) which would be contrary to an advance decision of his which has effect, or any other form of statement made by him and not subsequently withdrawn' (section 33(2)). In Scotland, the Adults with Incapacity (Scotland) Act 2000 contains similar provisions for research (section 51) which, like those in England, Wales and Northern Ireland, are detailed and explicit.

All of these provisions implicitly acknowledge that research is important among individuals with reduced capacity to consent – and this is especially true if more evidence-based treatments are to be developed for this population. In addition, these provisions show that it is eminently possible to formulate rules that both permit research and respect the rights and dignity of those who participate in it, even if their mental capacity is impaired. Both the 2015 Bill in Northern Ireland (section 135(3)) and the 2005 Act in England and Wales (section 33(3)) set this out very plainly when they state that 'the interests of [P/the person] must be assumed to outweigh those of science and society'.

These provisions in Northern Ireland, England, Wales and Scotland contrast sharply with the position in Ireland, where neither the Mental

Health Act 2001 nor the Assisted Decision-Making (Capacity) Bill 2013 address research in any depth. Ireland's 2001 Act simply states that 'a person suffering from a mental disorder who has been admitted to an approved centre under this Act shall not be a participant in a clinical trial' (section 70). The 2001 Act is silent on research in other circumstances. In a similar vein, Ireland's Assisted Decision-Making (Capacity) Bill 2013 states that 'nothing in this [Bill] shall be construed as authorising any person to give consent on behalf of a person who lacks capacity to be a participant in a clinical trial' (section 103). This is a missed opportunity to address this important topic in Ireland, along lines similar to those in Northern Ireland, England, Wales and Scotland (Kelly, 2014d).

Other matters

Northern Ireland's 2015 Bill contains various further provisions relating to 'provision of information' (sections 55 and 56), 'failure by [a] person other than D to take certain steps' (section 57), 'transfer between jurisdictions' (i.e. Northern Ireland, England, Wales or Scotland) (Part 11), offences (e.g. 'ill-treatment or neglect', 'unlawful detention of persons lacking capacity' and 'offences by bodies corporate') (Part 13), 'expenditure etc' (sections 265–268), various 'miscellaneous functions of HSC trusts' (sections 269 and 270) and 'direct payments in place of provision of care services' (section 271).

The Bill also provides a definition of 'mental disorder', taking it to mean 'any disorder or disability of the mind' (section 292(1)). This definition is the same as that introduced by the Mental Health Act 2007 (section 1(2)) in England and Wales, but contrasts with the positions in both Scotland and Ireland. In Scotland, the Mental Health (Care and Treatment) (Scotland) Act 2003 defines 'mental disorder' as 'any (a) mental illness; (b) personality disorder; or (c) learning disability, however caused or manifested' (section 328(1)) and specifies that 'a person is not mentally disordered by reason only of [...] dependence on, or use of, alcohol or drugs', among other conditions (section 328(2)). In Ireland, the Mental Health Act 2001 defines 'mental illness' as:

> 'a state of mind of a person which affects the person's thinking, perceiving, emotion or judgment and which seriously impairs the mental function of the person to the extent that he or she requires care or medical treatment in his or her own interest or in the interest of other persons' (section 3(2)).

In Ireland, mental illness is one of the three categories of 'mental disorder', although other criteria also need to be met for an individual to have 'mental disorder', chiefly because having 'mental disorder' under the 2001 Act means fulfilling criteria for involuntary admission and treatment (sections 3(1) and 8(1)). Ireland's 2001 Act specifies, however, that a person cannot be so admitted solely on the grounds that the person '(a) is suffering from a personality disorder, (b) is socially deviant, or (c) is addicted to drugs or intoxicants' (section 8(2)). In Northern Ireland, the 2015 Bill is notably subtle on this topic, as it specifies that 'dependence on alcohol or drugs is not to be considered a disorder or disability of the mind for the purposes of subsection (1) (but this does not prevent a disorder or disability of the mind that is related to alcohol or drugs, but is not dependence, from being so considered)' (section 292(2)). The caveat in this provision is interesting and appears to reflect the clinical reality that many cases of, for example, depression may be related in part to alcohol misuse (Joska & Stein, 2008); such misuse may not reach the threshold for 'dependence', but may contribute significantly to depression, with depression as the primary diagnosis.

The 2015 Bill has detailed provisions governing the 'power of police to remove [a] person to [a] place of safety' (Part 9)[69] and also makes provision for warrants 'authorising any constable accompanied by a medical practitioner to enter the premises, if need be by force, and remove [a] person' (section 278(2)) if 'it appears to a justice of the peace, on complaint on oath made by an officer of an HSC trust or a constable (a) that there is reasonable cause to believe that a person who by virtue of this [Bill] is liable to be taken to a relevant place is to be found on any premises; (b) that admission to the premises has been refused or that a refusal of such admission is apprehended; and (c) that it is reasonable in the circumstances to issue a warrant' (section 278(1)).

The 2015 Bill also:

'provides for a new officer to be known as the Public Guardian (PG) [Part 7]. This officer will be supported in the exercise of his functions by the Office of Public Guardian (OPG), which will be established within the Northern Ireland Courts and Tribunals Service. The role of the PG will be to establish and maintain a register of LPAs [lasting powers of attorney] and Court appointed deputies, supervise the work of the deputies, report to the Court on this and to investigate complaints in respect of the activities of attorneys acting under an LPA or an EPA [enduring power of attorney] and of deputies. In effect, the OPG will take over the current case management functions of the Office of Care and Protection. In addition, [section 126] places a duty on the HSC Board and trusts along with the RQIA to report to the OPG cases where there is concern about a person who lacks capacity and where the powers of the court may be exercised' (DHSSPSNI & NIDoJ, 2014: pp. 31–32).

There are certain limitations to the provisions of the 2015 Bill and, in particular, 'nothing in this [Bill] permits a decision on any of the following matters to be made on behalf of a person', including certain aspects of family relationships (e.g. consenting to marriage or a civil partnership or sexual relations) (section 273(1)) and voting rights, i.e. 'nothing in this [Bill] permits a decision on voting at an election for any public office, or at a referendum, to be made on behalf of a person' (section 274(1)). These exclusions are similar, although not identical, to those in other jurisdictions: Ireland's Assisted Decision-Making (Capacity) Bill 2013 excludes areas such as marriage, sexual relations and voting from its decision-making supports (section 106), and exclusions from the Mental Capacity Act 2005 in England and Wales relate to family relationships (section 27),

Mental Health Act matters (section 28) and voting rights (section 29). The Consultation Document published alongside the 2014 version of Northern Ireland's Bill highlights a key difference between exclusions in Northern Ireland and those in England and Wales:

> 'Unlike the equivalent legislation elsewhere, there is no exclusion in relation to matters covered by mental health legislation given that the Bill will revoke the Mental Health Order as it applies to persons aged 16 and over. This is the key difference between the Bill and, for example, the Mental Capacity Act 2005 in England and Wales and is why it is such a ground-breaking piece of legislation' (DHSSPSNI & NIDoJ, 2014: p. 35).

'Ground-breaking' as the 2015 Bill may or may not be, it is still the case that these exclusions appear to violate Article 12 of the CRPD (Minkowitz, 2007), which requires that persons with disabilities 'enjoy legal capacity on an equal basis with others in all aspects of life' (Article 12(2)). While it is difficult to see how any form of supported or substitute decision-making would be appropriate for decisions about marriage, sexual relations or even voting, the CRPD nonetheless requires that persons with disabilities 'enjoy legal capacity on an equal basis with others in *all* aspects of life' (emphasis added); exclusions, it seems, are not to be countenanced.

Finally, the 2015 Bill states that the DHSSPSNI 'must prepare and issue one or more Codes of Practice' in relation to a range of matters (section 276) (Box 3.10).

Box 3.10 Matters that must be covered by codes of practice under the Mental Capacity Bill (2015) (Northern Ireland)

'The Department [of Health, Social Services and Public Safety] must prepare and issue one or more codes of practice:

(a) for the guidance of persons assessing whether a person who is 16 or over has capacity in relation to any matter;
(b) for the guidance of persons acting in connection with the care, treatment or personal welfare of another person who is 16 or over;
(c) for the guidance of nominated persons;
(d) for the guidance of independent advocates;
(e) for the guidance of panels constituted under Part 2 of this [Bill];
(f) for the guidance of persons appointed as attorneys, or as replacements for attorneys, by a lasting power of attorney or an instrument executed with a view to creating such a power;
(g) for the guidance of deputies appointed by the court;
(h) for the guidance of persons carrying out research in reliance on any provision made by or under this [Bill] (and otherwise with respect to Part 8);
(i) with respect to such other matters concerned with this [Bill] as the Department considers appropriate.'

(Mental Capacity Bill (2015) (Northern Ireland): section 276(1))

These Codes of Practice are not strictly legally binding, but they cannot be ignored:

'(1) A person acting in any of the ways mentioned in subsection (2) in relation to a person who is 16 or over and lacks capacity must have regard to any relevant code of practice.

(2) The ways of acting are:
   (a) in a professional capacity;
   (b) for remuneration;
   (c) as an independent advocate;
   (d) as an attorney under a lasting power of attorney;
   (e) as a deputy appointed by the court;
   (f) as a person carrying out research in reliance on any provision made by or under this [Bill] (see Part 8).

(3) If it appears to a court or tribunal conducting any criminal or civil proceedings that (a) a provision of a code of practice or (b) a failure to comply with a code of practice, is relevant to a question arising in the proceedings, the provision or failure must be taken into account in deciding the question' (section 277(1)–(3)).

Summary

Northern Ireland's Mental Capacity Bill 2015 presents a range of interesting and occasionally progressive provisions relating to the treatment of persons whose mental capacity is impaired. Although its overarching principles have much in common with other jurisdictions (e.g. a presumption of capacity), the Bill is notable for its welcome, pragmatic emphasis on best interests and its clear enunciation that the precise cause of impaired mental capacity (e.g. disability) is irrelevant. Nevertheless, the Bill still links impaired mental capacity with 'an impairment of, or a disturbance in the functioning of, the mind or brain' (section 3(1)), which, in the context of involuntary admission, complies poorly with the CRPD requirement that 'the existence of a disability shall in no case justify a deprivation of liberty' (Article 14(1)(b)), chiefly because 'an impairment of, or a disturbance in the functioning of, the mind or brain' very often means an intellectual disability or mental illness.

The 2015 Bill presents rather elaborate criteria whereby someone who takes actions in relation to a person who lacks capacity is protected from liability, with additional safeguards for 'serious interventions'. There are also specific processes and requirements for authorising deprivation of liberty and involuntary treatment, requirements to attend for treatment and community residence requirements by HSC trust panels (Boxes 3.2–3.5). As a result, the powers of these panels are substantial and wide-ranging. These powers and provisions will provide welcome transparency in circumstances where the use of compulsion may already occur in dubious legal circumstances (e.g. nursing homes) and the capacity-based approach of these measures will assist with empowering patients and enhancing autonomy.

These authorisation provisions also present some especially intriguing features, including the fact that, if the authorised measure is a 'treatment', the HSC trust panel may include authorisation of another measure even though it was not requested in the application (Schedule 1, paragraph 15). In this and various other ways, the 2015 Bill accords substantial power to HSC trust panels, and, indeed, to the Mental Health Review Tribunal for Northern Ireland, which is to be renamed 'the Review Tribunal' (section 263). It is, however, regrettable that the person (P) cannot apply to the Tribunal if an authorisation is no longer in force (section 45(4)); Ireland's provisions, permitting a tribunal hearing if requested within 14 days of revocation, seem more just (Mental Health Act 2001: section 28(5)).

The 2015 Bill also presents detailed provisions regarding lasting powers of attorney and useful regulations relating to the providing of information, second opinions in certain circumstances (e.g. ECT), High Court decisions and appointment of deputies, research, the Office of Public Guardian, independent advocates and various other matters. Again, there are interesting subtleties, including, for example, that an independent advocate may examine medical records 'that the person holding the record considers may be relevant' (section 90(4)); the fact that it is the 'person holding the record' (and not the independent advocate or P) who determines which records are relevant seems potentially to undermine the independence of the advocacy process. Also, if P discontinues work with a specific independent advocate (possibly for very legitimate reasons), there is no requirement for a replacement to be found (section 92(2)(a)).

Ultimately, the extent to which these measures protect and promote the rights of the mentally ill will depend, in large part, on how they are structured, funded and operated in practice. This, in turn, will be highly dependent on Codes of Practice (promised in section 276) and the extent to which they are observed. These Codes will not be strictly legally binding, but relevant persons 'must have regard to any relevant code of practice' (section 277(1)). It is to be hoped that these Codes will be accorded at least the same importance as in England and Wales, where the House of Lords, although it tolerated a specific violation of a specific Code,[70] strongly emphasised the importance of the Code, stating that Codes carry substantial weight and should be considered with great care. Although a Code of Practice is not a binding instruction, it is more than mere advice; departures from it should be rare and their reasons should be spelled out in each case (see Chapter 2).

The report of the Bamford Review of Mental Health and Learning Disability (2007a: p. 5) emphasised this point strongly:

> 'Principles underpinning legislation will only have effect if they are translated into clear provisions, if there are adequate services to provide good quality treatment and care to allow them to act as intended and when all those operating the legislation have adequate education and training. The impact of the principles in the Code of Practice for the 1986 Order

was reduced because of delay in publication and a failure to deliver an associated training programme. Principles must be incorporated into the new law and elaborated upon in Codes of Practice. The new legislation, the Codes of Practice and related training programmes must be introduced at the same time'.

Overall, most of the measures presented in the 2015 Bill hold modest but significant potential to protect and promote the human rights of persons with impaired capacity, and there are several potentially quite progressive measures, including the elimination of distinction between those who are mentally ill and those who have reduced capacity for other reasons, inclusion of clear overarching principles (including best interests), the robust lasting powers of attorney system, revised rights of review, clear criteria for deciding who lacks capacity and how compulsion is to be authorised, and strong measures relating to nominated persons, independent advocates and second opinions. In addition, the Bill specifies that 'the fact that a person who has been subject to short-term detention has been subject to the relevant detention, or any failure to disclose that fact, is not a proper ground for dismissing or excluding the person from any office, profession, occupation or employment, or for prejudicing the person in any way in any occupation or employment' (section 59(5)); this is an important, necessary measure.

There are, however, also certain human rights concerns, most notably that linking deprivation of liberty with 'an impairment of, or a disturbance in the functioning of, the mind or brain' (section 3(1)) complies poorly with the CRPD requirement that 'the existence of a disability shall in no case justify a deprivation of liberty' (Article 14(1)(b)) – although it is, admittedly, difficult to see how this requirement of the CRPD can ever be met while mental health or capacity legislation permits any form of detention (Kelly, 2014a). In addition, the 2015 Bill states that 'nothing in this [Bill] permits a decision on any of the following matters to be made on behalf of a person', including family relationships (section 273) and 'voting rights' (section 274), and these exclusions, while pragmatic and similar to those in other jurisdictions, comply poorly with the CRPD requirement that persons with disabilities 'enjoy legal capacity on an equal basis with others in *all* aspects of life' (Article 12(2)) (emphasis added).

Notwithstanding these matters, Minister Edwin Poots MLA and Minister David Ford MLA point to the 'ground-breaking' nature of the 2014 version of the Bill:

'The core provisions of the draft Mental Capacity Bill are now being published for consultation. They are ground-breaking and, therefore, eagerly awaited. For the first time anywhere, there will be a single statutory framework governing all decision making in relation to the care, treatment (for a physical or mental illness) or personal welfare of a person aged 16 or over, who lacks capacity to make a specific decision for him/herself. This means that the current Mental Health (NI) Order 1986 will no longer apply to a person aged 16 or over' (DHSSPSNI & NIDoJ, 2014: p. i).

99

In the final analysis, the Bill may be genuinely 'ground-breaking' in one way only: it fuses mental health legislation and mental capacity legislation into a single Bill. But since none of the more detailed, specific measures presented in the Bill appears especially ground-breaking in itself, does integrating mental health and capacity legislation into a single document really reflect a ground-breaking step in its own right? Or is an integrated Bill just a different way of presenting some fairly traditional, if occasionally modestly progressive, measures relating to the mentally ill, and, possibly, extending them to additional sectors of the population not previously subject to this level of explicit legal regulation? Is such a development liberal or illiberal, and precisely whose interests does it serve most?

Fusion, confusion and extending the reach of law

Northern Ireland's 2015 Bill is the most striking example to date of the 'fusion proposal', based on merging mental health legislation with mental capacity legislation. This idea has received significant attention over a number of years, and has been considered several times in the past. In 2006, Dawson & Szmukler presented a detailed and especially compelling argument in favour of such a fusion law, noting that it could shift the focus away from risk of harm as the central criterion for involuntary treatment and thus facilitate earlier intervention and uniform application of criminal law. They argued that such a law would reduce discrimination and apply consistent ethical principles across medical law. They also identified potential limitations, including the absence of research on the reliability of emergency capacity assessments and the possibility that more people with personality disorders who retain capacity might be imprisoned rather than receiving forensic mental healthcare. In addition, Madden (2007) argued that repeatedly treating individuals to the point where they regain capacity and then leaving them to fend for themselves could have negative outcomes, although Dawson & Szmukler (2007) argued that their proposal was likely to reduce violence overall.

In 2014, Szmukler *et al* (2014) presented a further proposal for a fusion law, noting that conventional mental health legislation (e.g. in England and Wales) appeared to violate the CRPD in several respects and that the fusion proposal was more CRPD compliant. Specifically, they proposed that such a law would cover all persons regardless of whether they had a 'mental' or 'physical' illness, and would allow involuntary treatment only when the person's decision-making capability for a specific treatment decision was impaired (regardless of the health setting or the cause of the impairment) and where supported decision-making had failed. They proposed that, in addition to an impairment of decision-making capability, involuntary treatment would require an assessment of whether or not the proposed treatment gave the person's values and perspective paramount importance, i.e. a revised version of 'best interests' that takes account of multiple factors, including, most importantly, the person's past and present wishes.

While acknowledging the potentially non-discriminatory nature of the fusion proposal, Bartlett & Sandland (2014) note unclearness about what decisions are being considered (e.g. decisions regarding admission or decisions regarding treatment, or both) and argue that the fusion proposal thus moves away from the decision-specific model of capacity. They also argue that mixing capacity to consent to admission and capacity to consent to treatment creates problems in the context of international law (which tends to seek to separate the two) and in the context of the CRPD, which, they argue, precludes crisp distinctions between those who have capacity and those who do not (as the fusion proposal appears to require).

In the particular case of Northern Ireland's Bill, one of the other concerns, in addition to those expressed by Bartlett & Sandland, is that the 2015 Bill explicitly extends mental health-style legislation into areas and circumstances where the use of compulsion may already occur in dubious legal circumstances (e.g. nursing homes), but where the extraordinarily extensive measures outlined in the Bill are likely to be relatively new. These measures include powers to force individuals to accept treatment not only in psychiatric hospitals, but also in other establishments and community settings, even to the point of determining where a person may or may not live. Although increased transparency is certainly to be welcomed, the evidence base for the effectiveness of such provisions is decidedly unclear. Compulsory treatment in the community, for example, is a deeply controversial topic and its clinical usefulness far from established (Kisely & Campbell, 2014; Lawton-Smith *et al*, 2008). In addition, while such measures may facilitate treatment in a setting less restrictive than hospital detention, they also support the idea that individuals who are not detained in an institution can be subject to extensive restrictions and requirements that impinge significantly on their freedoms (Kelly, 2009*a*).

Consequently, although the 2015 Bill may indeed be, as claimed, ground-breaking (owing to its fusion of capacity and mental health legislation), it still potentially authorises a range of involuntary interventions in a broader portion of the population than was previously the case, to an extent that is astonishingly illiberal compared with, for example, Ireland, where compulsion in the community is not explicitly endorsed at all (see Chapter 4).

It is also noteworthy that Northern Ireland's 2015 Bill implicitly states that impairment of decision-making capacity is a mandatory prerequisite for any compulsory intervention in relation to any person, including a person with mental illness. In this context, it is interesting that the Richardson Committee, charged with advising the government on revising the Mental Health Act 1983 in England and Wales, found that only a 'small minority' of those consulted believed that 'a mental health act should authorise treatment in the absence of consent only for those who lack capacity' and that 'if a person with a mental disorder who refused treatment was thought to pose a serious risk to others then he or she should be dealt with through the criminal justice system, not through a health provision' (Department of

Health, 1999: p. 19). There was 'a much larger body of opinion which was prepared to accept the overriding of a capable refusal in a health provision on grounds of public safety in certain circumstances' and the Committee was strongly inclined to the latter view (Kelly, 2014a) (see Chapter 2). Notwithstanding such concerns, Northern Ireland's 2015 Bill authorises compulsory intervention only for those who lack capacity.

Finally, it is readily apparent that implementing the measures outlined in the 2015 Bill will present a real challenge to public services, and the report of the Bamford Review strongly emphasised the cross-cutting nature of the reforms that such a Bill would involve:

'The inter-departmental approach to the process of implementing the Bamford Review reports will be central to the successful development of legislative reform, which must be given a high priority by Government. It will be essential to have co-ordination between DHSSPS and other Departments, for example on risk management, on the particular needs of children and young people and on the need for a joint approach to effective monitoring and evaluation of the agreed framework' (Bamford Review of Mental Health and Learning Disability, 2007b: p. 10).

Conclusions

At the start of the Consultation Document published alongside the 2014 version of the Mental Capacity Bill for Northern Ireland, Minister Edwin Poots MLA and Minister David Ford MLA describe the Bill as 'not only a once in a generation opportunity to reform this important area of law but also an opportunity to be world leaders in doing so' (DHSSPSNI & NIDoJ, 2014: p. ii). Consistent with this, the 2014 Consultation Document concludes on a decidedly positive note:

'It is widely acknowledged that the draft Bill is a significant and progressive piece of legislation in human rights terms. In line with the recommendations of the Bamford Review, it is underpinned by principles that aim to protect and promote, on an equal basis, the dignity and autonomy of those who fall within its scope' (p. 67).

Certainly, the 2015 Bill is an intensely interesting and, in certain respects, potentially quite progressive development that will hopefully reduce the stigma associated with mental illness in general, and involuntary treatment in particular, by fusing mental health legislation with mental capacity legislation. The detailed measures outlined in the Bill, however, appear, at best, only modestly progressive and the vast powers of compulsion (in psychiatric hospitals, general hospitals, nursing homes, community residences, etc.) are, notwithstanding their increased transparency, strikingly illiberal, appearing to be driven by public safety more than patient need.

These are, however, complex proposals. On the one hand, it is to be welcomed that the Bill explicitly extends clear criteria for compulsion and rights of review into certain areas where compulsion may already occur in dubious legal circumstances. In this respect, the relevant provisions of the 2015 Bill are somewhat reminiscent of the Deprivation of Liberty Safeguards (DoLS) system in England and Wales, which, although unwieldy, at least attempts to regulate and protect rights in an important area of clinical and social care (Welsh & Keeling, 2013). On other hand, the powers of HSC trust panels in Northern Ireland to direct that people attend for treatment and live at certain addresses represent substantial interferences in liberty, and the evidence base for such supervised community interventions is very limited. This is especially ironic as the terms of reference for the Bamford Review explicitly required that the Review Group 'take into account [...] evidence-based best practice developments in assessment, treatment and care regionally, nationally and internationally' (Bamford Review of Mental Health and Learning Disability, 2007a: p. 89). Regrettably, the 2015 Bill patently fails to reflect the poor evidence base for compulsory community interventions, with the result that it is difficult to state that the demonstrated benefits of such intrusive measures are sufficient to justify the curtailment of liberty involved, even when the criteria and review processes are as clear and apparently reasonable as those outlined in the Bill.

Ultimately, the 2015 Bill, apart from the headline fusion of mental health legislation with mental capacity legislation, and despite the inclusion of certain modestly progressive measures, is a curiously illiberal document, mandating substantial interventions for existing and new groups within the population, and significantly extending the reach of coercive mental capacity law. The ultimate merits and demerits of this approach will not be entirely clear until the final measures are implemented in practice.

At this point, the 2015 Bill, as presently drafted, represents an intriguing experiment in mental health law – a very worthwhile and potentially useful experiment, but an experiment nonetheless.

Mental Health Act 2001: Ireland

In Ireland, there was scant provision for people with mental illnesses throughout the 17th and 18th centuries (Psychiatrist, 1944; Robins, 1986; Kelly, 2004b). The 19th century was, however, a time of intensive legislative activity, resulting in the establishment of a large network of public asylums (Hallaran, 1810; Finnane, 1981): in 1851 there were 3234 individuals in Irish asylums and by 1891 this number had increased to 11 265 (Inspectors of Lunatics, 1893). This trend continued well into the 20th century: by 1961, 1 in every 70 Irish people above the age of 24 was resident in a psychiatric hospital (Lyons, 1985). Although there were similar problems with high committal rates in other countries, including France, England and the USA (US Bureau of the Census, 1975; Shorter, 1997), Ireland's admission rates were especially high at their peak and especially slow to decline (Kelly, 2008b).

Against this background, Ireland introduced a significant reform of mental health legislation in the form of the Mental Treatment Act 1945. This Act was to remain the cornerstone of Irish mental health law until the Mental Health Act 2001 was fully implemented in November 2006. This chapter examines key issues in Irish mental health law and human rights prior to the Mental Health Act 2001. It then outlines provisions of the 2001 Act, explores human rights implications of the Act and summarises the report of the Expert Group on the Review of the Mental Health Act 2001 (2015). It concludes with an overall assessment of mental health law and human rights in Ireland today.

Irish mental health law prior to the Mental Health Act 2001

Ireland's Mental Treatment Act 1945 brought about several important reforms in mental health services. These included, most notably, the introduction of a voluntary admission status (section 1), a reform that had already been implemented in Great Britain (1930) and Northern Ireland (1932) (O'Neill, 2005; Kelly, 2008c). Ireland's 1945 Act also introduced two new procedures for involuntary admission, one for 'persons of unsound mind' and the other for 'temporary chargeable patients'. Both procedures required that a family member, relative or other person make an 'application' for involuntary admission (section 14(1)) and that an 'authorised medical officer' (e.g. general practitioner) examine the individual, who was then transported to a psychiatric hospital (by the police, if necessary), where a detention order could be completed by a doctor, following psychiatric examination.

The key difference between the 'person of unsound mind' procedure and the 'temporary chargeable patient' procedure was that the former resulted in detention and involuntary treatment for an indefinite period, whereas the latter resulted in detention and involuntary treatment for up to 6 months (although the period could be extended if clinically indicated). Neither form of detention involved automatic review by a mental health tribunal, although any detention order could be revoked at any time by the treating psychiatrist (section 14(3)). If patients wished to challenge their detention, they had either to write to the Inspector of Mental Hospitals (section 18; the Inspector could look into the matter and report to the Minister for Health, who could order discharge) or selected other parties (section 266: e.g. the Minister for Health or the President of the High Court) (Cooney & O'Neill, 1996), or to instigate legal action under the Constitution of Ireland 1937 (Article 40). Consequently, the 'person of unsound mind' procedure resulted in indefinite, potentially lifelong detention, without automatic review, which was a particular problem for individuals who lacked the mental capacity or financial resources to access the courts.

Even when a detained patient accessed legal representation in the High Court in order to challenge their detention, the 1945 Act, as amended by section 2(3) of the Public Authorities Judicial Proceedings Act 1954, stated:

> 'No civil proceedings shall be instituted in respect of an act purporting to have been done in pursuance of this Act save by leave of the High Court and such leave shall not be granted unless the High Court is satisfied that there are substantial grounds for contending that the person against whom the proceedings are to be brought acted in bad faith or without reasonable care' (section 260(1); see also: Spellman, 1998).

In 2008, after the Mental Treatment Act 1945 had been replaced by the Mental Health Act 2001, the Irish Supreme Court found that this section of the 1945 Act had been unconstitutional, as it restricted the grounds for challenging detention to just two: acting in 'bad faith' and proceeding 'without reasonable care' (Madden, 2009a). The Supreme Court stated that this was a disproportionate restriction on the detained patient's right to access the courts when a fundamental right, liberty, had been restricted, and was thus contrary to the Constitution of Ireland (Article 6).

Almost a decade earlier, in 1999, the Irish Law Society had already highlighted this problem, among others, in a report titled *Mental Health: The Case for Reform* (Law Reform Committee, 1999). The Law Society reviewed case law and international human rights standards, and suggested that: criteria for involuntary commitment be more clearly defined; a 'least restrictive alternative' principle be introduced; a right to a minimum level of psychiatric service be introduced by statute; formal safeguards be extended to voluntary patients; and measures be introduced to enable the proposed 'Mental Health Review Board' to review detention orders and order 'planned discharge'.

Many of these proposals were consistent with the Irish government's 1995 White Paper, which proposed a 'new Mental Health Act' and openly acknowledged that the Mental Treatment Act 1945 did 'not fully comply with this country's obligations under international law' (Department of Health, 1995: p. 13):

> 'The changes in Irish law that are required to ensure full compliance with our obligations under the European Convention [of Human Rights, ECHR] include a redefinition of the criteria for detention of mentally disordered persons, the introduction of procedures to review the decision to detain a person in a psychiatric hospital by a body independent of both the person who took the decision to detain and of the executive, an automatic review of long-term detention, and the introduction of greater safeguards for the protection of detained persons' (p. 15).

For some decades before implementation of the Mental Health Act 2001, then, the process of reform in Ireland was largely driven by European and international influences and human rights concerns, as evidenced by the Irish government's concern, in 1995, to comply with the ECHR, and the Law Society's explicit reliance on the ECHR and United Nations Principles for the Protection of Persons with Mental Illness and the Improvement of Mental Health Care (United Nations, 1991) in their recommendations. This European dimension came even more urgently into focus when the lack of automatic review of detention under the Mental Treatment Act 1945 formed the focus of a landmark case in the European Court of Human Rights (Rutherdale, 1994).[71]

In this case, a detained patient pointed to the lack of an automatic, independent review of psychiatric detention in Ireland and, when the Irish Supreme Court stated that this was not unconstitutional, the applicant took the case to the European Court of Human Rights, to argue that it breached his rights under the ECHR. A 'friendly settlement' was reached in 2000, under which the Irish state noted its obligations under the ECHR and undertook to pay an agreed compensatory sum to the applicant. Most importantly, the Irish state noted that the applicant was the first individual to bring this important issue to the European Court of Human Rights and that his claim had been initiated prior to the publication of the Mental Health Bill 1999, which formed a key part of Ireland's defence.

The Mental Health Bill 1999 was actually the culmination of a lengthy process of reform that had begun long before this case (O'Neill, 2005: pp. 23–32), but was pursued with considerably greater urgency after the case was instigated in the Irish courts in 1994 and later in the European Court of

Human Rights. As a result, this case reinforced the ECHR as the key driver of reform of mental health law in Ireland, and the Mental Health Bill 1999 led, in due course, to the Mental Health Act 2001. Human rights standards, as reflected in the ECHR, continued to dominate this reform process to the very end, as concerns about the human rights of detained patients persisted even after the 2001 Act had passed through the Oireachtas (Irish Parliament) on 8 July 2001, and full implementation was awaited (Coulter, 2005; Owens, 2005; Kelly, 2006b). The Mental Health Act 2001 was finally fully implemented on 1 November 2006.

Before exploring the 2001 Act itself, it is worth noting that the issue of public safety was virtually absent from the debate that led to the new legislation in Ireland. This contrasts with the situation in England, where public safety was a key concept in the reform process (Chapter 2). This difference is probably attributable to the absence of any recent high-profile case of homicide involving a mentally ill individual in Ireland. Interestingly, the issues of human dignity and capabilities (Kelly, 2014b) did not play an appreciable role in the reform process in either jurisdiction (Ireland or England and Wales), possibly because both reform processes largely pre-dated the UN Convention on the Rights of Persons with Disabilities (CRPD), Article 1 of which places particular emphasis on dignity.

The Mental Health Act 2001

The Mental Health Act 2001, which replaced the Mental Treatment Act 1945, is chiefly concerned with two aspects of psychiatric services: involuntary detention and mechanisms for assuring standards of care (Kelly, 2002, 2007b; Keys, 2002; Kennedy, 2007a; Leahy, 2007; Ryan, 2010). The four key parts of the Act concern:

- preliminary and general matters
- involuntary admission of persons to approved centres
- independent review of detention
- consent to treatment.

Preliminary and general matters

The Mental Health Act 2001 defines 'mental disorder' to include:

> 'mental illness, severe dementia or significant intellectual disability [where] there is a serious likelihood of the person concerned causing immediate and serious harm to himself or herself or to other persons [or] the judgment of the person concerned is so impaired that failure to admit the person to an approved centre would be likely to lead to a serious deterioration in his or her condition or would prevent the administration of appropriate treatment that could be given only by such admission' (section 3(1)).[72]

It is also necessary that detention and treatment 'would be likely to benefit or alleviate the condition of that person to a material extent' (section 3(1)). More specifically, 'mental illness' is:

'A state of mind of a person which affects the person's thinking, perceiving, emotion or judgment and which seriously impairs the mental function of the person to the extent that he or she requires care or medical treatment in his or her own interest or in the interest of other persons' (section 3(2)).

'Severe dementia' is 'a deterioration of the brain of a person which significantly impairs the intellectual function of the person thereby affecting thought, comprehension and memory and which includes severe psychiatric or behavioural symptoms such as physical aggression'. 'Significant intellectual disability' is 'a state of arrested or incomplete development of mind of a person which includes significant impairment of intelligence and social functioning and abnormally aggressive or seriously irresponsible conduct on the part of the person'.

These definitions accord moderately well with clinical definitions. For example, the World Health Organization defines intellectual disability ('mental retardation') as a condition of arrested or incomplete development of the individual's mind, characterised by impairment of skills that becomes apparent during the developmental period and that contributes to the individual's level of intelligence (WHO, 1996a: p. 1). The Mental Health Act 2001 echoes much of this wording, but adds a requirement for 'abnormally aggressive or seriously irresponsible conduct' (section 3(2)). This reflects the fact that once an individual fulfils the definition of 'significant intellectual disability', a form of mental disorder under section 3, that individual may become subject to detention under the legislation. The Mental Health Act 2007 introduced a similar requirement in England and Wales, where an individual with learning (intellectual) disability 'shall not be considered by reason of that disability' to be suffering from mental disorder 'unless that disability is associated with abnormally aggressive or seriously irresponsible conduct on his part' (section 2(2)).

Overall, however, the definitions in Ireland's Mental Health Act 2001 are closer to those in the original Mental Health Act 1983 in England and Wales than to the Mental Health Act 2007: the 1983 Act defined 'mental disorder' as 'mental illness, arrested or incomplete development of mind, psychopathic disorder and any other disorder or disability of mind' (section 1(2)), which is quite similar to Ireland's 2001 Act. The Mental Health Act 2007, however, removed these four categories in England and Wales, and redefined 'mental disorder' as 'any disorder or disability of the mind' (section 1(2)). While these changes were in line with recommendations of the Richardson Committee (Department of Health, 1999) and the Mental Health Act Commission (2003: pp. 85–86), they contrast with developments in Ireland, where the 2001 Act introduced detailed definitions of mental disorder and various other terms for the first time in Ireland.

Moreover, an individual cannot be detained under Ireland's 2001 Act solely on the grounds that they are 'suffering from a personality disorder' (section 8(2)), whereas in England and Wales, although the Mental Health Act 2007 removed the 1983 Act's requirement for 'abnormally aggressive or seriously irresponsible conduct' for a diagnosis of 'psychopathic disorder' (section 1(2)), detention can still occur when 'it is necessary for the health or safety of the patient or for the protection of other persons that he should receive such treatment' (section 3(2)(c)). This is a significant point of contrast between the jurisdictions.

Involuntary admission of persons to approved centres

Under Ireland's Mental Health Act 2001, an individual can be involuntarily admitted to an 'approved centre' (i.e. registered psychiatric in-patient facility) on the grounds that the individual is suffering from a 'mental disorder' (section 8(1)); a person cannot be so admitted solely on the grounds that the person '(a) is suffering from a personality disorder, (b) is socially deviant, or (c) is addicted to drugs or intoxicants' (section 8(2)). The Act does not provide a definition of 'socially deviant'.

An application for involuntary admission can be made by a spouse, relative, 'authorised officer' (section 9(8)), member of the Garda Síochána (police force) or, in circumstances where no one in these categories can be found, anyone else, subject to certain conditions (section 9(2)). In all cases, the applicant must have observed the individual within 48 hours of making the application (section 9(4)).

The next step involves examination of the individual by a registered medical practitioner (e.g. general practitioner) (sections 10(2) and 10(5)). Following this recommendation, the individual can be conveyed to the approved centre (section 13(1)) with the assistance of staff of the approved centre, if needed (section 13(2)). If 'there is a serious likelihood of the person concerned causing immediate and serious harm to himself or herself or to other persons', the Garda Síochána can enter the person's dwelling by force and ensure the removal of the person to the approved centre (sections 12 and 13).

At the approved centre, a consultant psychiatrist 'shall, as soon as may be, carry out an examination of the person' and either (a) complete an 'admission order' if 'he or she is satisfied that the person is suffering from a mental disorder' or (b) refuse to make such an order (section 14(1)). The patient cannot be detained for more than 24 hours without such an examination taking place and such an order being made or refused. If an admission order is made, it authorises 'the reception, detention and treatment of the patient concerned and shall remain in force for a period of 21 days' (section 15(1)); this period may be extended by a 'renewal order' for a period of up to 3 months (section 15(2));[73] this may be further extended by a period of up to 6 months; and each further extension can be for a period of up to 12 months (section 15(3)).[74]

Following the completion of an involuntary admission order, the consultant psychiatrist must inform the Mental Health Commission of the order and the Commission shall then (a) refer the matter to a mental health tribunal, (b) assign a legal representative to the patient, 'unless he or she proposes to engage one' and (c) direct that an independent psychiatrist examine the patient, interview the patient's consultant psychiatrist and review the patient's records (section 17(1)). Within 21 days of an involuntary admission, a mental health tribunal shall review the detention of the patient (see below).

Regarding treatment of physical as opposed to mental illness, the 2001 Act permits the clinical director to arrange for the transfer of a patient 'detained in that centre for treatment to a hospital or other place and for his or her detention there for that purpose' and the 'detention of a patient in a hospital or other place under this section shall be deemed for the purposes of this Act to be detention in the centre from which he or she was transferred' (section 22(1)).[75]

Regarding voluntary patients, the 2001 Act states that, when a voluntary patient 'indicates at any time that he or she wishes to leave the approved centre', a staff member may, if 'of opinion that the person is suffering from a mental disorder', detain the person for up to 24 hours (section 23(1)).[76] During this period, the consultant psychiatrist responsible for the care of the patient 'shall either discharge the person or arrange for him or her to be examined by another consultant psychiatrist' (section 24(1)) and, if that second psychiatrist 'is satisfied that the person is suffering from a mental disorder, he or she shall issue a certificate in writing' to that effect (section 24(2)(a)); then, the consultant psychiatrist responsible for the care of the patient can make a 21-day admission order (section 24(3)), which will be subject to review by a mental health tribunal within 21 days (section 24(4)).

Independent review of detention

The Mental Health Act 2001 made provision for the appointment of a 'Mental Health Commission', one of the functions of which is to appoint mental health tribunals 'to determine such matter or matters as may be referred to [them] by the Commission' (section 48(1)). One of the chief functions of tribunals is to review involuntary detention orders. Each tribunal comprises three members, including one consultant psychiatrist, one barrister or solicitor (of no fewer than 7 years' experience) and one other person, known as the lay member (section 48(3)). Decisions are made by majority voting (section 48(4)).

The Commission directs that an independent psychiatrist examines each detained patient, interviews the patient's consultant psychiatrist and reviews the patient's records. Then, within 21 days of an involuntary admission, a mental health tribunal reviews the detention and, 'if satisfied that the patient is suffering from a mental disorder' and that appropriate procedure has been followed, 'shall [...] affirm the order'; if the tribunal is not so satisfied, the tribunal 'shall [...] revoke the order and direct that the patient be discharged from the approved centre concerned' (section 18(1)). Similarly for renewal orders, a tribunal review must be held within 21 days of the making of the renewal order.[77] These changes are strongly protective of the patient's right to liberty and support patient dignity by facilitating exercise of specific capabilities in appealing detention orders.

Grounds for appeal of tribunal decisions are, however, limited: the patient 'may appeal to the Circuit Court against a decision of a tribunal to affirm an order made in respect of him or her on the grounds that he or she is not suffering from a mental disorder' (section 19(1)), i.e. there is no possibility of appeal to the Circuit Court on other grounds (e.g. procedural aberrations) (Mills, 2004). Following an appeal in the Circuit Court, the patient may, if they wish, appeal to the High Court, but not on grounds related to whether or not they suffer from a mental disorder; a patient may appeal to the High Court solely 'on a point of law' (section 19(16)). These restrictions appear significant, and it is notable (and concerning) that the burden of proof lies with the patient in the Circuit Court.

Consent to treatment

The Mental Health Act 2001 specifies that 'the consent of a [detained] patient shall be required for treatment' except where the patient is incapable of providing consent and the treating psychiatrist believes that treatment 'is necessary to safeguard the life of the patient, to restore his or her health, to alleviate his or her condition, or to relieve his or her suffering' (section 57(1)).

Psychosurgery can be carried out only if the (detained) patient consents in writing and surgery is authorised by a mental health tribunal (section 58(1)). For detained patients, electroconvulsive therapy (ECT) may be administered only if either (a) the patient consents in writing (section 59(1)(a)), or (b), for a patient 'unable or unwilling' to provide consent, the treatment is approved by the treating consultant psychiatrist and one other psychiatrist (section 59(1)(b)). Similarly, if 'medicine has been administered to a [detained] patient for the purposes of ameliorating his or her mental disorder for a continuous period of 3 months, the administration of that medication shall not be continued' unless either (a) the patient consents in writing, or (b) for a patient 'unable or unwilling' to provide consent, the treatment is approved by the treating consultant psychiatrist and one other psychiatrist (section 60).

Human rights implications

The Mental Health Act 2001 introduced several important changes to Irish mental health law. The High Court recognises that these changes are important in terms of human rights:

'These provisions are exacting and complex. They were designed, however, by the Oireachtas [Irish parliament] in order to replace the situation whereby it was potentially possible for a person to be certified and detained in a mental hospital and then forgotten. The need for periodic review and renewal, and the independent examination of these conditions is not a mere bureaucratic layer grafted on to the previous law for the treatment of those who are seriously ill and a danger to themselves and others: it is an essential component of the duty of society to maintain the balance between the protection of its interests and the rights of those who are apparently mentally ill'.[78]

Prior to the 2001 Act, myriad concerns were expressed about the Irish psychiatric service's apparent unreadiness for the legislation, including issues related to an apparent lack of resources (Barnes, 2006a; Shannon, 2006a; Wrigley, 2006), potential effects of mental health tribunals on therapeutic relationships (Whelan, 2004), legal representation for psychiatrists at tribunals (McGuinness, 2006), staffing of tribunals (O'Brien, 2006), disagreements about indemnity (McGuinness, 2005), rates of payment for psychiatrists at tribunals (Vize, 2005) and unclearness about responsibility for harm to patients resulting from lack of resources for implementing the new legislation (Ó Cionnaith, 2006). Psychiatrists expressed particular concern about the potential effects of adversarial tribunals on the therapeutic alliance with the patients concerned, increased administrative activity and potential for the legislation disproportionately to divert resources from voluntary to involuntary patient services (Ganter et al, 2005; Kelly & Lenihan, 2006).

In 2005, before full implementation of the Act, the Irish College of Psychiatrists stated that the absence of funding to implement the legislation in a timely fashion had serious implications in terms of human rights for both current and future patients, whose mental health services might be curtailed in order to divert resources to the implementation of the new legislation:

> 'This is a human rights issue. People are entitled to the increased safeguards which are central to the Act – and it is imperative that people already attending should not have their services curtailed so that the Act can be implemented' (Ganter, 2005: p. 26).

Following considerable discussion, some additional resources were made available for mental health services, including extra consultant psychiatrist posts and extra funds (Barnes, 2006b), and the final elements of the legislation (relating chiefly to tribunals) were implemented on 1 November 2006. In the first 11 months following full implementation, approximately 12% of involuntary admission and renewal orders examined by tribunals were revoked (McGuinness, 2007a). There is no systematic information available about the precise reasons for revocation (e.g. procedural aberrations, absence of mental disorder) because the Mental Health Commission does not record detailed reasons for the decisions of mental health tribunals. The Commission did, however, outline the cost of tribunals in 2007: at that time, each tribunal cost £2675 (€3377), including £1044 (€1319) for the patient's legal representative (Barnes, 2007).

Two years after full implementation, it was apparent that the 2001 Act had brought both challenges and benefits to Irish mental health services

(Kelly, 2009b; Ní Mhaoláin & Kelly, 2009). Some of the challenges related to the role of general practitioners in involuntary admissions, timing of tribunals, conduct of some patients' legal representatives, availability of reports by independent psychiatrists prior to tribunals and increased workloads reported by psychiatrists (Lynch, 2007; McGuinness, 2007b; O'Reilly, 2007; Baker, 2009; Jabbar et al, 2010). Notwithstanding these reported problems, 73% of psychiatrists reported that the legislation had resulted in greater protection for the rights of involuntary patients (O'Donoghue & Moran, 2009).

The precise effects of the legislation in relation to human rights can be considered under six specific headings:

- mental health tribunals for patients currently detained
- civil proceedings in the Circuit Court and High Court
- mental health tribunals for discharged patients
- mental capacity in relation to voluntary patients
- the Mental Health Act 2008
- paternalism.

Mental health tribunals for patients currently detained

The introduction of mental health tribunals to review all detention orders brings Irish legislation into greater accordance with the ECHR, which states that:

> 'Everyone who is deprived of his liberty by arrest or detention shall be entitled to take proceedings by which the lawfulness of his detention shall be decided speedily by a court and his release ordered if the detention is not lawful' (Article 5(4)).

In judgments to date, the European Court of Human Rights has found that delays of 55 days[79] and 24 days[80] are excessive, suggesting that a maximum delay of 2–3 weeks is likely to be acceptable, in the absence of specific requests by the patient for deferral (e.g. in order to seek independent medical opinion) (Bartlett et al, 2007: pp. 66–67). In Ireland, the 2001 Act requires that the Mental Health Commission arranges an independent medical examination prior to a tribunal review, and that tribunal reviews are held within 21 days of the signing of an order.

In 2007, however, it was reported that the Commission tended to schedule tribunal reviews for as late as possible in the 21 day period in order to minimise costs (McGuinness, 2007c); i.e. the review was scheduled for day 20 or 21, in the hope that the psychiatrist would by then have revoked the detention order, thus removing the need for a review at that time (although the individual could still request a tribunal at a later date). This practice was criticised by the Department of Health and Children (2007: p. 24). In 2008, the Mental Health Commission (2008: p. 88) stated that it was now 'fully committed to arranging the mental health tribunal hearing as early as possible'.

113

Before affirming an admission or renewal order, the mental health tribunal must be 'satisfied that the patient is suffering from a mental disorder' (section 18(1)(a)) and that appropriate procedures were followed in making the order. If there was a failure to follow procedures, the tribunal can still affirm the order provided that 'the failure does not affect the substance of the order and does not constitute an injustice' (section 18(1)(a)(ii)). This provision allows tribunals to overlook certain procedural anomalies, but it is not clear to what extent such discretionary powers are used by tribunals as no systematic record of tribunal reasoning is made public.

There is more evidence on this point available from the courts, which hear appeals. In *Z v Khattak and Anor*,[81] for example, there was a series of concerns regarding the procedures followed during an involuntary admission, including the following:

(a) the police took the individual in question into custody under section 12 of the 2001 Act, which requires that, following such detention, a member of the police force 'shall make an application forthwith in a form specified by the Commission to a registered medical practitioner for a recommendation' (section 12(2)); the police did not make such an application, and instead an application was signed by the patient's brother (under section 9);

(b) the subsequent 'examination' carried out by a general practitioner comprised a 'chat' of 10 minutes duration during which both parties smoked cigarettes at the rear of a police station; in the High Court, the general practitioner stated that he was not familiar with the definition of 'examination' in the 2001 Act and 'was not even aware of what a mental state examination might entail';

(c) a 'delay of seven and a half hours' occurred between the arrival of the individual in question at the approved centre and the examination by the consultant psychiatrist; the patient submitted to the High Court that this did not accord with the requirement that 'a consultant psychiatrist on the staff of the approved centre shall, as soon as may be, carry out an examination' (section 14(1)), although under the Act the individual can be detained at the approved centre for up to 24 hours for the purpose of such an examination (section 14(2));

(d) the detention order, when completed, was not sent to the Mental Health Commission within the 24-hour time limit required by the Act (section 16(1)); the order was faxed approximately 45 hours after completion.

Having considered the matter in some detail, the High Court: (a) stated that 'even though a somewhat unusual sequence of events occurred by the adoption of the [section] 9 procedure instead of continuing the procedures under [section] 12, there was nothing impermissible in what was done'; (b) expressed 'a certain disquiet' about the manner of the general practitioner's 'examination', but stated that 'this complaint does not invalidate the applicant's detention';[82] (c) stated that the Act did not require that the consultant psychiatrist 'should immediately drop whatever he was doing [...] and attend immediately or forthwith', provided the examination was performed within 24 hours; and (d), in relation to the failure to send the detention order to the Mental Health Commission within 24 hours, stated that 'while there has been a breach of a technical requirement in this regard, it has not affected any right of the applicant in any fundamental way or at all'.

Evidence from the High Court, including this case, clearly indicates a willingness at that level to overlook 'technical' concerns (such as failure to submit forms to the Commission within time limits), but, regrettably, there is no mechanism to assess similar precedents at the level of tribunals, which are held 'in private' (section 49(9)). Greater openness about tribunal reasoning, without breaking confidentiality, would undoubtedly enhance the protections offered by the tribunal system, not only in Ireland, but elsewhere too (Smith & Caple, 2014).

Civil proceedings in the Circuit Court and High Court

Under the Mental Health Act 2001, detained patients have automatic access to mental health tribunal reviews, in which the burden of proof lies on the detaining authority to demonstrate that the patient has a mental disorder and is lawfully detained (section 18). The patient can appeal against detention in the Circuit Court, although only on the grounds of not having a mental disorder (section 19(1)). In the Circuit Court, however, the burden of proof lies on the patient:

'On appeal to it under subsection (1), the Circuit Court shall:
  (a) unless it is shown by the patient to the satisfaction of the Court that he or she is not suffering from a mental disorder, by order affirm the order, or
  (b) if it is so shown as aforesaid, by order revoke the order' (section 19(4)).

If the detained patient wishes to appeal to the High Court, they can make such an appeal only on a point of law, and not in relation to the Circuit Court's decision regarding whether or not they have a mental disorder (section 19(16)). The 2001 Act also states:

'No civil proceedings shall be instituted in respect of an act purporting to have been done in pursuance of this Act save by leave of the High Court and such leave shall not be refused unless the High Court is satisfied:
  (a) that the proceedings are frivolous or vexatious, or
  (b) that there are no reasonable grounds for contending that the person against whom the proceedings are brought acted in bad faith or without reasonable care' (section 73(1)).

Compared with the Mental Treatment Act 1945, the 2001 Act reversed the onus of proof for initiating High Court proceedings: under the 2001 Act, the detaining authority must demonstrate that 'there are no reasonable grounds for contending that [it] acted in bad faith or without reasonable care' (section 73(1)), whereas under the 1945 Act, the patient had to demonstrate to the High Court that there were 'substantial grounds for contending' that the detaining authority 'acted in bad faith or without reasonable care' (section 260(1)).

Overall, the Mental Health Act 2001 broadened and clarified avenues of legal redress for individuals who object to their detention in psychiatric facilities (Ryan, 2010: pp. 96–98). In a Circuit Court appeal, however, the burden of proof still lies with the patient to demonstrate that they do not have a mental disorder (Shannon, 2006b; Whelan, 2008). The European Court of Human Rights has previously ruled that section 64 of the Mental Health (Scotland) Act 1984, which placed the burden of proof on the patient in an appeal against detention, was incompatible with the ECHR (Article 5(4)).[83] In 2007, a detained patient in Ireland instigated judicial proceedings in the High Court arguing that the fact that the burden of proof lies with the patient in Circuit Court appeals was incompatible with the ECHR.[84] As required under Ireland's European Convention on Human Rights Act 2003 (section 4), the High Court took account of relevant European case law, including, most notably, *Hutchison Reid v UK*.[85] The High Court concluded that the burden of proof must not lie with the patient in a first instance review of detention (i.e. to a mental health tribunal), but that this did not apply to courts of further appeal (i.e. the Circuit Court).[86]

Notwithstanding this judgment, an interim report produced by the Steering Group on the Review of the Mental Health Act 2001 (2012: p. 29) recommended that the 2001 Act should be revised so that the onus of proof does not fall on the patient in the Circuit Court, thus further protecting the patient's right to liberty.

Mental health tribunal reviews for discharged patients

If a detained patient has their detention order revoked by the treating psychiatrist prior to a mental health tribunal review, the review is cancelled and another 'shall not be held unless the patient indicates by notice in writing addressed to the Commission within 14 days of his or her discharge that he or she wishes such a review to be held' (section 28(5)). If the individual requests such a review, it shall be held in accordance with usual tribunal procedures for patients who are currently detained but 'with any necessary modifications'.

The specific purposes of tribunal reviews are to determine whether or not: (a) correct procedure was followed in instigating the detention, and (b) 'the patient is suffering from a mental disorder' on the day of the review (section 18(1)(a)).[87] If the review occurs following discharge, the procedural question (a) can be examined just as it is for a patient who is still detained at the time of the review (through examining documents, witnesses, etc.). The clinical question (b), however, is still phrased in the present tense, suggesting that the tribunal must determine whether or not 'the patient is suffering from a mental disorder' on the day that it sits, even though the individual in question is no longer a 'patient' within the meaning of the Act (section 2) and it is likely that no parties will argue that the individual still has a mental disorder, because the individual has already been discharged (Eldergill, 2008: p. 37).

The High Court has placed considerable emphasis on the use of the present tense in the phrase 'the patient is suffering from a mental disorder' (section 18(1)(a)).[88] When a patient who is discharged prior to tribunal review requests and has a review, and then wishes to appeal to the Circuit Court, the High Court has ruled that there is no statutory justification for such an appeal to be heard, because the only ground for such appeal is that the patient '*is* not suffering from a mental disorder' (emphasis added) (section 19(1)). In the case of the already discharged patient, the issue of whether or not the individual had a mental disorder at time of detention is a historical one and therefore does not represent grounds for appeal to the Circuit Court, which are 'that he or she *is* not suffering from a mental disorder' (emphasis added). On this basis, although a patient discharged prior to a tribunal review can later have a review on request, they cannot appeal its decision to the Circuit Court (and nor is it entirely clear what the tribunal is deciding).

Mental capacity in relation to voluntary patients

The Mental Health Act 2001 defines 'voluntary patient' as 'a person receiving care and treatment in an approved centre who is not the subject of an admission order or a renewal order' (section 2(1)). Throughout the remainder of the Act, the term 'patient' is used to mean a patient detained in accordance with the Act and not a voluntary patient. This definition of 'voluntary patient' is a broad one and does not make any reference to mental capacity. It can therefore include individuals who are not detained, but lack mental capacity (e.g. a patient admitted voluntarily in the first instance who loses mental capacity during their admission).

The High Court has supported this highly paternalistic definition of voluntary patient, stating that it 'was cast in the wide terms used in order to provide for the variety of circumstances wherein a person is in an approved centre receiving care and treatment, but not subject to an admission order or a renewal order, including [...] where a detention pursuant to an admission order or a renewal order breaks down, but where the patient is suffering from a mental disorder and receiving care and treatment'.[89] This position was upheld by the Supreme Court (Shannon, 2006b; Madden, 2009b).[90] As a result, while the 2001 Act explicitly outlines the requirements if involuntary patients are to be regarded as having capacity,[91] it does not require that voluntary patients have mental capacity in order to become voluntary patients in the first instance.

The Steering Group on the Review of the Mental Health Act 2001 (2012: p. 22) emphasised the need for supported decision-making structures for voluntary psychiatric in-patients with fluctuating capacity, and suggested that relevant measures be included in proposed mental capacity legislation, but it did not provide specific proposals to amend the definition of 'voluntary patient'. As a result, the current situation is that, in the absence of dedicated capacity legislation being implemented, individuals without capacity may be *de facto* deprived of their liberty without the protections of effective capacity or mental health legislation (Eldergill, 2008: p. 26), similar to the situation outlined in *Bournewood*,[92] which was incompatible with the ECHR (Eastman & Peay, 1998; Morris, 1999).

The Mental Health Act 2008

The Mental Health Act 2008 was a piece of emergency legislation enacted in response to a specific problem that emerged under the Mental Health Act 2001. In October 2008, an involuntary patient ('SM') engaged in judicial review proceedings in the High Court to appeal the decision of a tribunal to affirm a 12-month renewal order. According to SM and her psychiatrist, SM's detention was largely attributable to a lack of appropriate hostel accommodation in which she could be treated in a less restrictive environment (Cummings & O'Conor, 2009).[93] The section of the Mental Health Act 2001 governing 12-month renewal orders reads as follows:

> 'The period referred to in *subsection (1)* may be further extended by order made by the consultant psychiatrist concerned for a period not exceeding 6 months beginning on the expiration of the renewal order made by the psychiatrist under *subsection (2)* and thereafter may be further extended by order made by the psychiatrist for periods each of which does not exceed 12 months' (section 15(3)).

During initial submissions, the judge raised an issue regarding the duration of SM's renewal order (Cummings & O'Conor, 2009). Specifically, the judge pointed out that the renewal form designed by the Mental Health Commission used a 'tick box' system that did not permit the consultant psychiatrist to make a renewal order for any specified period less than 12 months; i.e. the renewal order could only be made out for 12 months in the first instance, although it could subsequently be revoked before 12 months had elapsed. This, in the view of the judge, appeared inconsistent with the 2001 Act, which stated that the renewal order 'may be further extended by order made by the psychiatrist for periods each of which does not exceed 12 months' (section 15(3)) (Carolan, 2008*a*).

After the judge had made these remarks, SM successfully applied to amend her proceedings to incorporate the judge's observations (Coulter, 2008). Having listened to arguments, the judge, on 17 October 2008, reserved his decision, which he did not deliver until 2 weeks later, on 31 October 2008 (Carolan, 2008*b*). It is of note that the Attorney General and Human Rights Commission were notice parties to these proceedings and, during the 2-week period between the judge reserving and delivering his decision, a piece of emergency legislation was passed by the Oireachtas (Parliament), titled the Mental Health Act 2008 (Collins, 2008).

The Mental Health Act 2008 stated that any renewal orders that might be deemed to be without a basis in law under the Mental Health Act 2001 for the reason suggested by the judge would be deemed lawful under the Mental Health Act 2008 and would be deemed (retrospectively) to have been lawful all along (section 3(1)). Such renewal orders would remain in force until:

'(a) the expiration of 5 working days immediately following the passing of this Act,

(b) a replacement renewal order is made to replace the unexpired renewal order, or

(c) the expiration of the last day of the maximum period concerned specified in section 15(2) or (3) of the Act of 2001 by which it extended or further extended the period referred to in section 15(1) of that Act, whichever occurs first' (section 3(2)).

On this basis, even if the judge were to rule that SM's renewal order was without legal basis under the 2001 Act, all other patients detained on such orders would remain legally detained for 5 working days under the Mental Health Act 2008, during which time the detaining authority could instigate a replacement renewal order or discharge the patient. On 31 October 2008, the day after the Mental Health Act 2008 was hurriedly signed into law, the judge duly ruled that SM's detention was without legal basis for the reason he had suggested at the outset. Some hours earlier, however, the Mental Health Act 2008 had become law and, over the subsequent 5 working days, an estimated 209 patients who were detained on pre-existing (flawed) renewal orders became the subject of replacement renewal orders (Cummings & O'Conor, 2009) that permitted the consultant psychiatrist to specify a precise period of detention and were, thus, consistent with the Mental Health Act 2001 (section 15).

The only exception to the provisions of the Mental Health Act 2008 were individuals who had already instigated proceedings in respect of this matter prior to the enactment of the Mental Health Act 2008, i.e. SM (section 7(2)). Even in the case of SM, however, the judge did not order her immediate release; owing to the fact that SM was clearly mentally ill and in need of treatment, the judge placed a stay of 4 weeks on his order for her release, so as to allow appropriate arrangements to be made (Carolan, 2008b). This decision was not without precedent: in February 2007, the High Court ruled that a particular detention was unlawful but noted that no parties contested the fact that the individual in question had a mental disorder; thus, to protect the individual's welfare, the High Court ordered that the applicant be released 7 hours after the Court's order was made, so as to facilitate immediate readmission under the Mental Health Act 2001 (Nolan, 2008: p. 177).[94]

It is estimated that the Mental Health Act 2008 resulted in the continued detention of 209 patients for up to 5 working days; completion of 209 replacement renewal orders during those 5 working days; and subsequent examination of these 209 replacement renewal orders by 209 mental health tribunals within 21 days. The resultant cost of the Mental Health Act 2008 was estimated at £786 942 (€993 377) (Cummings & O'Conor, 2009), excluding the costs of the judicial review process itself and the indirect costs of tribunals, which amount to double the direct costs (Blumenthal & Wessely, 1994). If that sum had been spent providing accommodation for SM, the lack of which had formed the original, hastily abandoned focus of her proceedings, SM could have been accommodated in an appropriate hostel for 370 years (Cummings & O'Conor, 2009).

Overall, the Mental Health Act 2008 was an emergency measure clearly intended pre-emptively to address a likely High Court ruling that might have resulted in the immediate release of 209 detained patients. Despite the 2008 Act's effectiveness in preventing the release of these mentally ill individuals owing to a poorly worded form, the initial substantive issue in this case (an alleged deficiency in resources) remained unaddressed and, paradoxically, the entire episode commanded a substantial opportunity cost in terms of diversion of state resources from the provision of care to the resolution of 'teething problems' with the 2001 Act (Whelan, 2008).

The Mental Health Act 2008, and the manner of its implementation, also raises the issue of paternalism. When delivering judgment on the case of SM, on the day after the 2008 Act had been rushed through Parliament, the judge stated that he had only learned of the emergency legislation in the newspapers (Carolan, 2008b; Coulter, 2008). The neatness of this sequence of events may, on the one hand, reflect the wisdom of having the Attorney General as a notice party to the proceedings, but may also, on the other hand, reflect the persistence of an arguably excessively paternalistic approach to people with mental illness. This is considered next.

Paternalism

Although the Mental Health Act 2001 opened up the possibility of greater observance of human rights and personal dignity, interpretation of the Act by Irish Courts, and the enactment of the Mental Health Act 2008, arguably demonstrate evidence of a paternalistic approach to people with mental illness similar to that in evidence under the Mental Treatment Act 1945 (Craven, 2009). The High Court made this explicit:

> 'In my opinion having regard to the nature and purpose of the Act of 2001 as expressed in its preamble and indeed throughout its provisions, it is appropriate that it is regarded in the same way as the Mental Treatment Act of 1945, as of a paternal character, clearly intended for the care and custody of persons suffering from mental disorder'.[95]

The Supreme Court agrees that interpretation of the 2001 Act 'must be informed by the overall scheme and paternalistic intent of the legislation',[96] as exemplified by the Act's requirement that the 'best interests of the person shall be the principal consideration with due regard being given to the interests of other persons' (section 4(1)). The High Court has stated that this section 'infuses the entire of the legislation with an interpretative purpose'.[97]

Several cases in the High and Supreme Courts have supported a paternalistic approach, especially when the actions are presented as taken in the best interests of the patient (Craven, 2009).[98] In *FW v Dept. of Psychiatry James Connolly Memorial Hospital*, a consultant psychiatrist had realised that a specific patient ('FW') was unlawfully detained, when it emerged that FW had issued proceedings against her husband (who had applied for her detention under the Mental Health Act 2001) under Ireland's Domestic Violence Act 1996.[99] The psychiatrist immediately advised the patient that she was free to go, but when the patient, some time later, chose to leave, staff of the hospital had speedily arranged that members of the police force were present at the door of the hospital to take her into custody and commence new involuntary detention proceedings at once. The patient challenged this detention in the High Court on the grounds that she had 'never been released in reality from an admitted unlawful detention'.[100] The High Court noted that the actions of the hospital were motivated by concern for the patient:

> 'I consider the action of [the consultant psychiatrist] and her staff to be highly creditable in the circumstances. Dealing with a very difficult situation, their predominant interest was the care and safety of the applicant. Their action ensured as best they could that when the applicant did leave their care, she did not depart into the night with no arrangements to ensure her safety and well-being. The actions of [the consultant psychiatrist] and her staff and those of the Gardaí at [the] Garda Station may well have prevented a tragic outcome to the day's event'.[100]

Notwithstanding this interpretation of the legislation in this and several other judgments,[101] there are still limits on the extent to which the legislation, even when interpreted paternalistically, permits the High Court or mental health tribunals to overlook non-compliance with the precise requirements of the Act (Casey *et al*, 2010). According to the High Court:

> 'It is to be borne in mind that [section] 4 requires that where decisions are made under the Act concerning the care and treatment of person, the best interest of the person is to be the principle [*sic*] consideration. This requirement applies to Mental Health Tribunals who must consider the validity or otherwise of Renewal Order or Admission Orders.
> In my opinion the best interests of a person suffering from a mental disorder are secured by a faithful observance of and compliance with the statutory safeguards put into the 2001 Act, by the Oireachtas. That together with the restriction in [section] 18(1)(a)(ii) mean that only those failures of compliance which are of an insubstantial nature and do not cause injustice can be excused by a Mental Health Tribunal'.[102]

Regrettably, it is not possible to establish the extent to which tribunals overlook such aberrations 'of an insubstantial nature' or, indeed, act in a paternalistic fashion, owing to the fact that the Mental Health Commission does not collect detailed data on reasons underlying tribunal decisions. At least some tribunal chairpersons, however, agree with the Courts that the legislation requires a paternalistic approach, and recommend that tribunals should be inquisitorial rather than adversarial in nature (Lee, 2008).

Notwithstanding such views, there is now significant evidence that at least some tribunals are adversarial and have significantly negative effects on the doctor–patient relationship (Department of Health and Children, 2007: p. 24; Jabbar *et al*, 2010). This is, broadly, inconsistent with the intention of the legislators that the 'best interests of the person shall be the principal consideration' in all decisions made under the 2001 Act (section 4(1)) and the generally paternalistic interpretations of the High and Supreme Courts (Craven, 2009).

The issue of paternalism is a complex one in Irish law. Whelan, for example, points to an international move away from paternalism towards autonomy (in, for example, the CRPD), but suggests that the Irish courts have not yet engaged with such debate in relation to the Mental Health Act 2001 (Whelan, 2009: p. 28). Kennedy (2012), an Irish professor of forensic psychiatry, argues that criticism of alleged paternalism 'arises from a mistaken translation of the legal Latin term *parens patriae*, the common law principle that the State (*patriae*), has parental (*parens*) obligations to care for the vulnerable amongst its citizens', as enshrined in the Constitution. He continues:

> 'Far from being a patriarchal instrument of oppression, *parens patriae* (the paternalistic interpretation of legislation regarding the vulnerable and incapacitated) is a means for the judiciary to hold the executive to some limited welfare obligations towards vulnerable citizens, in the absence of a comprehensive health and welfare system for all'.

Notwithstanding these arguments, the interim report of the Steering Group on the Review of the Mental Health Act 2001 stated that 'paternalism is incompatible with such a rights-based approach and accordingly the Act should be refocused away from "best interests" in order to enhance patient autonomy' (Steering Group on the Review of the Mental Health Act 2001, 2012: p. 11).[103]

Report of the Expert Group on the Review of the Mental Health Act 2001 (2015)

The interim report of the Steering Group on the Review of the Mental Health Act 2001 that was published in June 2012 informed the work of the subsequent Expert Group on the Review of the Mental Health Act 2001. The latter group met 13 times between September 2012 and September 2014, and published its report on 5 March 2015.[104]

The report of the Expert Group (Expert Group on the Review of the Mental Health Act 2001, 2015) presents 165 recommendations relating to virtually all areas of the Act.[105] Overall, it recommends that 'insofar as practicable, a rights based approach should be adopted throughout any revised mental health legislation' (p. 15) and that the principle of 'best interests' (Mental Health Act 2001: section 4(1)) should be replaced by:

'the following list of guiding principles of equal importance [to] be specified in the new law':

a. The enjoyment of the highest attainable standard of mental health, with the person's own understanding of his or her mental health being given due respect
b. Autonomy and self determination
c. Dignity (there should be a presumption that the patient is the person best placed to determine what promotes/compromises his or her own dignity)
d. Bodily integrity
e. Least restrictive care' (p. 15).

The report recommends that the definition of 'mental disorder' in the 2001 Act (section 3) should be removed and the Act should no longer provide definitions for 'severe dementia' or 'significant intellectual disability'. Instead, 'mental illness' should be redefined as 'a complex and changeable condition where the state of mind of a person affects the person's thinking, perceiving, emotion or judgement and seriously impairs the mental function of the person to the extent that he or she requires treatment' (p. 17). This is similar, although not identical, to the redefinition of 'mental disorder' in the Mental Health Act 2007 in England and Wales, which removed the four categories outlined in the 1983 Act and redefined 'mental disorder' as 'any disorder or disability of the mind' (section 1(2)).

Criteria for involuntary admission

The Expert Group report recommends new criteria for involuntary admission as follows:

'a. The individual is suffering from mental illness of a nature or degree of severity, which makes it necessary for him or her to receive treatment in an approved centre which cannot be given in the community;
b. It is immediately necessary for the protection of life of the person, for protection from a serious and imminent threat to the health of the person, or for the protection of other persons that he or she should receive such treatment, and it cannot be provided unless he or she is detained in an approved centre under the Act; and
c. The reception, detention and treatment of the person concerned in an approved centre would be likely to benefit the condition of that person to a material extent' (Expert Group on the Review of the Mental Health Act 2001, 2015: p. 22).

The report recommends defining treatment to include 'treatment to all patients admitted to or detained in an approved centre' (i.e. not just involuntary patients) and 'ancillary tests required for the purposes of safeguarding life, ameliorating the condition, restoring health or relieving suffering'; in addition, 'the provision of safety and/or a safe environment alone does not constitute treatment' (p. 18).

123

With regard to exclusions from detention, the 2001 Act states that a person cannot be involuntarily admitted 'by reason only of the fact that the person: (a) is suffering from a personality disorder, (b) is socially deviant, or (c) is addicted to drugs or intoxicants' (section 8(2)). The Expert Group Report recommends adding '(d) has an intellectual disability' (p. 23) to this list, consistent with the elimination of 'significant intellectual disability' as a category of 'mental disorder' (p. 17) and in furtherance of the principles of the CRPD (United Nations, 2006). A person with intellectual disability could be detained only if they fulfilled the revised definition of 'mental illness' and the other proposed detention criteria.

Voluntary and 'intermediate' patients

In light of various court decisions regarding the definition of 'voluntary patient' in the 2001 Act,[106] which does not require capacity (section 2), the Expert Group Report places considerable emphasis on assessing capacity, when indicated, before voluntary admission:

> 'If following the capacity assessment, it is deemed that a person has capacity to admit themselves, a voluntary admission may proceed. If it is deemed that they need support to understand, to make or to convey their decision, that support must be provided to assist in the voluntary admission process. If it is deemed that they do not have capacity in relation to this decision, and the person has a mental illness, they may only be admitted on an involuntary basis, provided they satisfy all the criteria for detention. A person who lacks capacity and has a mental illness, but does not fulfil the criteria for detention, may in specified circumstances be admitted as an "intermediate" patient' (Expert Group on the Review of the Mental Health Act 2001, 2015: pp. 27–28).

On this basis, 'a voluntary patient should be defined as a person who has the capacity (with support if required) to make a decision regarding admission to an approved centre and who, where the person retains capacity, formally gives his/her informed consent to such admission, and subsequent continuation of voluntary inpatient status and treatment on an ongoing basis as required' (p. 30).

It is proposed that a 'new category of patient', termed an 'intermediate' patient, should be introduced, comprising patients who do 'not have the capacity to consent to [voluntary] admission and equally do not fulfil the criteria for involuntary detention' (p. 33). These patients would not be detained, but would have the review mechanisms and protections of a detained person. For such patients, a mental health tribunal would focus on the question of capacity.

The involuntary admission process

Regarding the involuntary admission process, the Expert Group Report proposes that 'there should be a more expanded and active role for authorised officers' (Expert Group on the Review of the Mental Health Act

2001, 2015: p. 36), who 'after consultation with family/carers where possible and appropriate, make the decision on whether or not an application for involuntary admission of the person should be made' (p. 37). The Report recommends that 'an Authorised Officer should be the person to sign all applications for involuntary admission to an approved centre (this also includes change of patient status in an approved centre from voluntary to involuntary [...]). This will have the effect of reducing the burden on families/carers in these difficult circumstances and reducing the involvement of Gardaí in the admission process' (p. 37). 'An application by an Authorised Officer to involuntarily admit a person to an approved centre shall remain in force for 7 days from the time of the first application' (p. 37) and will need to be supported by a 'recommendation', completed by a registered medical practitioner within 24 hours (pp. 35, 38).

If a person is taken into custody by the Gardaí with a view to involuntary admission, the initial assessment 'should take place as soon as possible after the person is taken into custody' and in any case within 24 hours; and there should be a second 24-hour period in which the registered medical practitioner must carry out their assessment (p. 37). These measures are designed to minimise the time that mentally ill persons spend in police custody.

Following completion of the application (by the authorised officer) and recommendation (by a registered medical practitioner), and within 24 hours of the person's arrival at the in-patient facility, the involuntary admission 'must be certified by a consultant psychiatrist after examination of the patient and following consultation with at least one other mental health professional of a different discipline that is and/or will be involved in the treatment of the person in the approved centre. The opinion of that other mental health professional should be officially recorded' (p. 39). This requirement broadens multidisciplinary input to the decision-making process, but still leaves the final decision with the consultant psychiatrist.

If medical or surgical treatment is urgently required before arrival at the psychiatric in-patient facility (e.g. following overdose or injury), 'the patient may first be treated in an emergency department, hospital or clinic', but the '24-hour timeframe for the admission process to the approved centre should commence on arrival at the emergency department, hospital or clinic as though it was the approved centre named in the application and the appropriate assessment and the making of an order should be done within that timeframe' (p. 41). This provision ensures that medical and surgical care is provided as appropriate, but not at the expense of psychiatric care.

If psychiatric treatment is urgently required before the consultant psychiatrist can see the patient to certify the detention order, it can be provided if 'the consultant psychiatrist, after consultation (to be officially recorded) with another health care professional is of the opinion that it is necessary in emergency circumstances. [...] Emergency in this situation means that the treatment is deemed immediately necessary, that the person's actual behaviour is injurious to self or others and no other safe option is available' (p. 41).

Other proposed revisions

The Expert Group Report also makes various recommendations regarding mental health tribunals, including renaming them 'mental health review boards' (Expert Group on the Review of the Mental Health Act 2001, 2015: p. 47) (Box 4.1). The recommendations regarding oversight are especially welcome, particularly that regarding publication of review board decisions in anonymised form to allow the Mental Health Commission to oversee the integrity of the review board process.

Box 4.1 Changes to mental health tribunals ('mental health review boards') in Ireland proposed by the Expert Group on the Review of the Mental Health Act 2001

Title and power

- Mental health tribunals should be renamed 'mental health review boards'.
- Although decisions about the nature and content of treatment should remain within the remit of the multidisciplinary mental health team, review boards should have the authority to establish whether there is an individual care plan in place and whether it is compliant with the law.
- Review boards should also establish that the views of the patient as well as those of the multidisciplinary team were sought in the development of the care plan.

Timing

- The patient's detention must be reviewed by a review board no later than 14 days after the making of the admission order or the renewal order concerned (as opposed to the current 21 days).

Composition

- There should be no change in the current make up of review boards at this stage. The question of having a one-person review board should be re-examined in any future review of the mental health legislation.
- Review board members must continue to be clearly separate from the original decision maker and those conducting the independent multidisciplinary assessment for the review board.
- The 'other person' appointed to the review board should be known as the 'community member', and the person appointed to this role should not be or ever have been a medical practitioner, nurse or mental health professional, barrister or solicitor in Ireland or in another jurisdiction.

Attendance

- Patients should have a legal right to have a review board hearing deferred for specified periods (two periods of 14 days) if that is their wish. The deferral would have to be sought through the patient's legal representative.

(continued)

(Box 4.1 continued)

- The following individuals must attend the hearing: the patient's legal representative and the responsible treating clinician.
- The following individuals may attend the hearing: the patient, who must always have a right to attend the review board; the patient's advocate, at the invitation of the patient exercising their right to such support; the independent psychiatrist who undertook pre-review board assessment, if the review board so requests; and the author of the psychosocial report or, if they are unable to attend, another member of the multidisciplinary team on their behalf if the review board so requests.
- It should be a matter for the review board to decide who else should attend the hearing (other than the absolute right to attend of the patient, their legal representative and their advocate, if the patient so requests).

Role of the independent psychiatrist

- The patient's detention must be subject to an assessment report by an independent psychiatrist with input (to be officially recorded) from another mental health professional of a different discipline to be carried out within 5–7 days of the review board hearing.
- The range of mental health professionals whom the independent psychiatrist must consult for a section 17 assessment should be specified.
- A member of the multidisciplinary team from the approved centre who is registered with the appropriate professional regulatory body (i.e. CORU,[107] Nursing and Midwifery Board or Medical Council) should carry out a psychosocial report in the same time frame as that recommended for the independent psychiatrist's report. This report should concentrate on the non-medical aspects of the patient's circumstances.

Oversight

- The revised legislation should provide for the oversight of the integrity of the process of review boards by the Mental Health Commission to ensure that they operate in line with best practice.
- Information in relation to decisions of review boards should be published in anonymised form (to ensure patient confidentiality), thus allowing decisions to be available for the Mental Health Commission and/or the public to view.

(Adapted from: Expert Group on the Review of the Mental Health Act 2001, 2015: pp. 47–49)

Various other recommended changes in the Report relate to:

- mandatory multidisciplinary consultation for renewal orders (p. 50);
- reducing the maximum duration of a third renewal order from 12 to 6 months (p. 50);
- reducing periods of 'absence with leave' to a maximum of 14 days (p. 51);
- removing the onus of proof from the patient in Circuit Court appeals (p. 53);
- altering the procedure for detaining voluntary in-patients who fulfil detention criteria, so that it is essentially the same as that for detaining individuals from the community (with slight modifications to permit

holding power for up to 24 hours initially and to make it no longer necessary for a voluntary in-patient to request to leave to invoke this process) (pp. 55–56);

- requiring informed consent for the treatment of voluntary patients (p. 59) and mandatory multidisciplinary involvement in treatment decisions for involuntary patients who lack capacity (p. 60);
- limiting administration of involuntary treatment (including medication and ECT) to detained patients who lack capacity (i.e. no longer permitting involuntary treatment of capable 'unwilling' persons) (pp. 61–63);
- requiring a second opinion within 21 days (as opposed to the current 3 months) for administration of medication to detained patients who lack capacity, and requiring that such medication be 'of therapeutic material benefit to the patient' (p. 63);
- various measures relating to provision of information to patients (pp. 64–65) and care plans, which must be examined by mental health review boards (pp. 65–67; Box 4.1).

Other measures in the Report relate to inspections of mental health services (to include community facilities) (pp. 74–76), children (pp. 67–74) and advance healthcare directives (the last can be overruled under certain circumstances in the case of detained patients, but such overrulings must be notified to the Inspector of Mental Health Services within 3 days) (pp. 76–79).

Overall, the 165 recommendations presented in the report of the Expert Group on the Review of the Mental Health Act 2001 reflect the most recent advice on legislative change provided to the Irish government. To date, the only legislative initiative to follow the report is the passage of the Mental Health (Amendment) Act 2015 by the Oireachtas in December 2015. Subject to a commencement order, this Act removes the 'unwilling' criterion from sections 59 and 60 of the Mental Health Act 2001, with the result that ECT or medication (beyond 3 months) can be administered without consent only to detained patients who are 'unable' to consent (i.e. lack mental capacity).

Overall assessment

The Mental Health Act 2001 introduced many important changes to Irish mental health law, most notably in relation to involuntary admission procedures and independent reviews of involuntary detention orders. A majority of stakeholders in mental health services (patients, service providers and others) believe that the 2001 Act has helped protect human rights (Mental Health Commission, 2008: p. 69; O'Donoghue & Moran, 2009). More specifically, it resulted in: the removal of indefinite detention orders that existed under the Mental Treatment Act 1945; new involuntary admission procedures; automatic, independent review of detention orders by mental health tribunals; free legal representation and independent psychiatric opinions for patients prior to tribunals; and establishment of the Mental Health Commission to oversee implementation of the Act and standards of care. Many of these changes promote human rights, enhance dignity and advance patients' autonomous exercise of their capabilities, especially in relation to appealing against involuntary detention orders.

The implementation of the 2001 Act, and its subsequent case law have, however, raised a series of human rights issues. Some of these stem from: the absence of systematic data collection about tribunal decisions, which leads to uncertainty about reasons for revocations (e.g. procedural aberrations, absence of mental disorder); unclearness regarding the extent to which procedural aberrations are overlooked by tribunals; and an absence of cumulative tribunal 'case law' to guide tribunal decisions. There are also restrictions on the acceptable grounds for civil proceedings in the Circuit and High Courts, and the burden of proof lies with the patient in the Circuit Court (although there is now a proposal to change this).

Other human rights concerns stem from unclearness about the precise matters at issue in tribunal reviews for discharged patients and the legal definition of voluntary patient, which does not include a requirement for capacity; this, too, has been highlighted as an area in need of reform. The hurried enactment of the Mental Health Act 2008, which stemmed from a poorly worded statutory form, raised a number of specific issues, including the retrospective declaration that detentions based on flawed forms had been lawful all along and would remain so for 5 days. Finally, there is evidence of paternalism in the implementation and interpretation of the 2001 Act by the Courts, raising the matter of the balance between individual autonomy and exercise of capabilities on the one hand and the obligation on the state to protect the vulnerable on the other.

Overall, measures introduced in the Mental Health Act 2001 still hold strong potential to protect specific rights (e.g. the right to liberty), enhance patient dignity and promote the exercise of specific capabilities (e.g. challenging involuntary detention). As in England and Wales, however, these potential benefits are accompanied by significant limitations and caveats. Critically, there is evidence of arguably excessive emphasis on paternalism and welfare-based concerns in the implementation and interpretation of Ireland's 2001 Act, and it is not yet clear whether or not this trend is proportionate to the intrinsically paternalistic nature of much clinical practice and welfare-based concerns outlined in the Irish Constitution.

In resource terms, there are significant opportunity costs associated with the legislation, including increased workloads for medical staff and decreased time spent with patients, owing to increased administrative activities and attendance at tribunal reviews and court proceedings (McGuinness, 2007d; Baker, 2009; Jabbar et al, 2010). As a result, although there is significant agreement that the Act has enhanced protections of the right to liberty for detained individuals (O'Donoghue & Moran, 2009), there is little evidence that it has enhanced the quality of psychiatric services, and some evidence that the resource and opportunity costs of the legislation may even have eroded observance of 'the right to treatment' (Fitzsimons, 2007; O'Donoghue & Moran, 2009; Jabbar et al, 2010). This has significant implications in terms of effective treatment of mental illness, which would support patient dignity (Kelly, 2014b,c), and, as a result, limits the extent to which the legislation supports patients in the autonomous exercise of their capabilities.

The likely direction of future reforms in Ireland was indicated by the interim report of the Steering Group on the Review of the Mental Health Act 2001 in 2012, which stated that 'paternalism is incompatible with such a rights-based approach and accordingly the Act should be refocused away from "best interests" in order to enhance patient autonomy' (Steering Group on the Review of the Mental Health Act 2001, 2012: p. 11).

The proposed elimination of the principle of 'best interests' in the subsequent report of the Expert Group on the Review of the Mental Health Act 2001 is consistent with this interim recommendation, but contrasts sharply with recent developments in neighbouring jurisdictions (Kelly, 2015c). In Northern Ireland, for example, the Mental Capacity Bill 2015 (which fuses mental health legislation and capacity legislation into a single bill) specifies that when 'an act is done [or] decision is made for or on behalf of a person who is 16 or over and lacks capacity [it] must be done, or the decision must be made, in the person's best interests' (sections 2(1) and 2(2)). The 2015 Bill goes on to specify that determinations of what is in a person's (P's) 'best interests' should not be based on age, appearance or anything else that might lead to 'unjustified assumptions' (section 7(2)). The 'person making the determination [must] so far as practicable, encourage and help P to participate as fully as possible in the determination of what would be in P's best interests' (section 7(5)) and 'have special regard to (so far as they are reasonably ascertainable): (a) P's past and present wishes and feelings (and, in particular, any relevant written statement made by P when P had capacity); (b) the beliefs and values that would be likely to influence P's decision if P had capacity; and (c) the other factors that P would be likely to consider if able to do so' (section 7(6)).

In England and Wales, the Mental Health Act 2007 introduced 'patient wellbeing and safety' as a principle (section 8) and the Mental Health (Care and Treatment) (Scotland) Act 2003 includes 'the importance of providing the maximum benefit to the patient' (section 1(3)(f)) in its principles. By comparison, the Irish recommendation to remove 'best interests' would diminish the importance accorded to the idea that deprivation of liberty must be reciprocated by clear evidence of benefit to the patient in all related treatment and management decisions. This would be a regrettable omission and it is not a minor issue. The history of psychiatry is replete with examples of various actors (state, private, medical) taking actions that were societally convenient, but of questionable benefit to the mentally ill (Shorter, 1997; Scull, 2005, 2015). A clear requirement for benefit to the patient is a critical element in any mental health legislation that seeks genuinely to protect rights and to focus public, professional and political attention on the need to provide services that are effective, efficient, beneficial and empowering for patients. If the patient's best interests are not at the heart of decision-making, then whose interests will be served?

Against this background, considerable importance will attach to the interpretation of the new principle proposed in 2015 by the Expert Group: 'the enjoyment of the highest attainable standard of mental health, with the person's own understanding of his or her mental health being given due respect' (Expert Group on the Review of the Mental Health Act 2001, 2015: p. 15).

When questioned in the Dáil Éireann (Parliament's House of Deputies) in 2005 about resource problems as the 2001 Act was being initially rolled out (2001–2006), the government minister with responsibility for mental health responded that 'a constant reiteration and repetition about the problems in the mental health service is becoming a bit tiresome to many organisations'. Much good work is being done (O'Malley, 2005). 'Tiresome' as these issues may be, they are likely to come into increasing focus in future years owing not only to pressure resulting from delays in implementing Ireland's 2006 mental health policy, 'A Vision for Change' (Expert Group on Mental Health Policy, 2006; Guruswamy & Kelly, 2006), but also international pressure resulting from Ireland's public commitment to the WHO's Mental Health Declaration for Europe and Mental Health Action Plan for Europe (WHO Ministers of Health of Member States, 2005a,b), both of which emphasise the importance of adequate resourcing of mental health services (Mudiwa, 2005) and the need for services to benefit patients.

In addition, the WHO has made specific and robust recommendations in relation to mental health law in individual states (WHO, 1996b), placing a strong and welcome emphasis on the civil, political, economic and social rights of people with mental illness (WHO, 2005). Ireland's legislation accords with these standards in part but not in full, with particular deficits relating to economic and social rights (Kelly, 2011). Most concerningly, however, the Irish legislation, and the link it draws between 'mental disorder' and involuntary detention, still accords poorly with the CRPD, which specifies that 'the existence of a disability shall in no case justify a deprivation of liberty' (Article 14(1)(b)) (see Chapter 1). As a result, if certain persons with mental disorder (e.g. those sufficiently ill to be detained) fit the UN definition of 'persons with disabilities', then Ireland's Mental Health Act 2001 violates this CRPD requirement, as does mental health legislation in England, Wales, Northern Ireland and Scotland (Bennett, 2014; Kelly 2014a).

CHAPTER 5

The challenges of reform: Scotland

This chapter begins with an overview of the Mental Health (Care and Treatment) (Scotland) Act 2003, which governs involuntary admission and treatment in Scotland. It is not intended as an exhaustive analysis of the content of the legislation or a 'how to' manual for practitioners, but rather as the basis for a consideration and analysis of recent mental health legislative reform in Scotland, with particular emphasis on human rights. Rather than assuming an approach rooted primarily in case law, this chapter focuses instead on the process of legislative reform, and examines not only the 2003 Act but also the *Limited Review of the Mental Health (Care and Treatment) (Scotland) Act 2003* (Scottish Government Review Group, 2009) (the McManus Review) and the subsequent Mental Health (Scotland) Act 2015, which received Royal Assent on 4 August 2015. The chapter concludes with a consideration of the challenges of reform of mental health legislation in Scotland, and identifies themes or trends that may be transferrable to other jurisdictions, such as England, Wales, Northern Ireland and Ireland.

The Mental Health (Care and Treatment) (Scotland) Act 2003

Involuntary admission and treatment in Scotland is largely regulated by the Mental Health (Care and Treatment) (Scotland) Act 2003, which was significantly shaped by the report of the Millan Committee (2001), titled *New Directions: Report on the Review of the Mental Health (Scotland) Act 1984.* The key principles proposed by the Millan Committee are outlined in Box 5.1 and these, along with various specific recommendations, had a significant influence on the drafting of the 2003 Act.

The 2003 Act can be usefully examined from a human rights perspective under the following headings:

- principles and definition of 'mental disorder'
- duties of various state actors

Box 5.1 Summary of principles for Scottish mental health legislation proposed by the Millan Committee

1   Non-discrimination
Whenever possible, people with mental disorder should retain the same entitlements and rights as those with other health needs.

2   Equality
All powers under the 2003 Act should be exercised without any direct or indirect discrimination on the grounds of physical disability, age, gender, sexual orientation, race, colour, language, religion, or national, ethnic or social origin.

3   Respect for diversity
Patients should receive care, treatment and support in a fashion that respects their individual qualities, abilities and diverse backgrounds and properly takes account of their age, gender, sexual orientation, ethnic group and social, cultural and religious background.

4   Reciprocity
Where society imposes an obligation on a person to comply with a programme of treatment and care, it should impose a parallel obligation on the health and social care authorities to provide appropriate services, including ongoing care following discharge from compulsion.

5   Informal care
Care, treatment and support should be provided to people with mental disorder without recourse to compulsion, wherever possible.

6   Participation
Patients should be fully involved, to the extent permitted by their individual capacity, in all aspects of their assessment, care, treatment and support. Account should be taken of their past and present wishes, so far as these can be ascertained. Patients should be provided with all the information necessary to enable them to participate fully. All information should be provided in a fashion which makes it most likely to be understood.

7   Respect for carers
Those who provide care to patients on an informal basis should receive respect for their experience and role, receive appropriate advice and information, and have their needs and views taken into account.

8   Least restrictive alternative
Patients should be provided with any necessary care, treatment and support both in the least invasive manner and in the least restrictive manner and environment compatible with the delivery of effective and safe care, taking account of the safety of others, where appropriate.

9   Benefit
Any intervention under the Act should be likely to produce a benefit for the patient which cannot reasonably be achieved other than by this intervention.

10   Child welfare
For children with a mental disorder, the child's welfare should be paramount in any interventions imposed on the child under this Act.

(Adapted from Millan Committee, 2001: pp. 23–24)

- emergency detention
- short-term detention
- compulsory treatment orders
- the Mental Health Tribunal for Scotland
- treatments for detained patients
- various other provisions.

Principles and definition of 'mental disorder'

The Mental Health (Care and Treatment) (Scotland) Act 2003 makes it clear that when a person is taking action under the Act (e.g. treating a patient, instigating detention), he or she 'shall' have regard to certain principles, which merit quoting in full. These are:

'(a) the present and past wishes and feelings of the patient which are relevant to the discharge of the function;
(b) the views of:
   (i) the patient's named person;[108]
   (ii) any carer of the patient;
   (iii) any guardian of the patient; and
   (iv) any welfare attorney of the patient,
   which are relevant to the discharge of the function;
(c) the importance of the patient participating as fully as possible in the discharge of the function;
(d) the importance of providing such information and support to the patient as is necessary to enable the patient to participate in accordance with paragraph (c) above;
(e) the range of options available in the patient's case;
(f) the importance of providing the maximum benefit to the patient;
(g) the need to ensure that, unless it can be shown that it is justified in the circumstances, the patient is not treated in a way that is less favourable than the way in which a person who is not a patient might be treated in a comparable situation;
(h) the patient's abilities, background and characteristics, including, without prejudice to that generality, the patient's age, sex, sexual orientation, religious persuasion, racial origin, cultural and linguistic background and membership of any ethnic group' (section 1(3)).

Having had regard to the above, 'the person shall discharge the function in the manner that appears to the person to be the manner that involves the minimum restriction on the freedom of the patient that is necessary in the circumstances' (section 1(4)). In addition, in matters 'other than the making of a decision about medical treatment', the person shall have regard to '(a) the needs and circumstances of any carer of the patient which are relevant to the discharge of the function and of which the person is aware; and (b) the importance of providing such information to any carer of the patient as might assist the carer to care for the patient' (section 1(5)).

If the actions taken under the Act concern detention or compulsory treatment, 'the person who is discharging the function shall have regard to the importance of the provision of appropriate services to the person who is, or has been, subject to the certificate or order concerned (including, without prejudice to that generality, the provision of continuing care when the person is no longer subject to the certificate or order)' (section 6).

There are some exemptions from these principles. People (i.e. decision makers) exempt from this requirement include: '(a) the patient; (b) the patient's named person; (c) the patient's primary carer; (d) a person providing independent advocacy services to the patient under section 259 of this Act; (e) the patient's legal representative; (f) a curator *ad litem* appointed by the Tribunal in respect of the patient; (g) a guardian of the patient; or (h) a welfare attorney of the patient' (section 1(7)). In addition, these principles do not apply 'in relation to a patient who is under the age of 18 years' (section 2(1)); in such cases, 'the person shall discharge the function in the manner that appears to the person to be the manner that best secures the welfare of the patient' (section 2(4)), although the decision maker 'shall have regard to' the principles outlined in section 1(3), the matters outlined in sections 1(5) (circumstances of carers) and 1(6) (provision of services), and the principle of least necessary restriction (section 2(5)(c)).

Overall, these principles combine respect for the present and past wishes of the patient, patient participation in decision-making in so far as feasible, and the principle of least restriction. It is also important that the needs and circumstances of family members are explicitly acknowledged, as well as the need for continued provision of services in cases where detention and compulsory treatment are involved. Taken together, these principles are broadly supportive of patient autonomy and participation in care, as well as optimising protection of the right to liberty. It is especially noteworthy that the Act specifies that all functions shall be exercised 'in a manner that encourages equal opportunities and in particular the observance of the equal opportunity requirements' (section 3(2)).

The Act defines 'mental disorder' as any:

'(a) mental illness;
(b) personality disorder; or
(c) learning disability, however caused or manifested' (section 328(1)),

and adds that:

'a person is not mentally disordered by reason only of any of the following:

(a) sexual orientation;
(b) sexual deviancy;
(c) transsexualism;
(d) transvestism;
(e) dependence on, or use of, alcohol or drugs;
(f) behaviour that causes, or is likely to cause, harassment, alarm or distress to any other person;
(g) acting as no prudent person would act' (section 328(2)).

This definition contrasts in certain respects with the definition in Ireland, which specifies that a diagnosis of personality disorder is not sufficient to meet the relevant 'mental disorder' detention criterion (Mental Health Act 2001: section 8(2)(a)). In this respect, the Scottish definition is more similar to that in England and Wales, where personality disorder is not excluded and 'mental disorder' is simply 'any disorder or disability of the mind' (section 1(2)). Interestingly, the Mental Health Act 2007 in England and Wales (section 1) repealed the 1983 Act's exclusion relating to 'immoral conduct [or] sexual deviancy' (see Chapter 2) and, while this change may reflect the unlikeliness of anyone being diagnosed as mentally disordered on such a basis today, it nonetheless means that it is no longer explicitly unlawful (under mental health legislation) to do so in England and Wales, although it is in Scotland.

Duties of various state actors

The 2003 Act provides for the continuation of the Mental Welfare Commission for Scotland (section 4), the general duties of which include monitoring the operation of the Act, promoting best practice (section 5) and reporting on the operation of the Act (section 6). The Commission also has duties to bring various matters to the attention of government (sections 7 and 8), give advice (section 9), publish information and guidance (section 10), carry out investigations (sections 11 and 12), visit patients (section 13), interview patients or others as indicated (section 14), authorise medical examinations (section 15), authorise inspection of records (section 16), produce an annual report (section 18) and generate relevant statistical information (section 19). These functions are all extremely important in supporting a governance framework that facilitates sharing information, quality improvement and accountability; as such, all of these functions are critical, systems-level factors in protecting and promoting the rights of the mentally ill.[109]

Part 3 of the 2003 Act establishes the 'Mental Health Tribunal for Scotland' (section 21(1)) to 'discharge such functions as are conferred on it by virtue of this Act' (section 21(2)) (see below). Part 4 outlines duties of health boards and the State Hospitals Board for Scotland that relate to maintaining a list of 'approved medical practitioners' (section 22), 'provision of services and accommodation for certain patients under 18' (section 23) and 'provision of services and accommodation for certain mothers with post-natal depression' (section 24).

Local authorities are accorded certain duties in relation to the 'provision of services' to certain patients. For example, the local authority:

'(a) shall:
    (i) provide, for persons who are not in hospital and who have or have had a mental disorder, services which provide care and support; or
    (ii) secure the provision of such services for such persons; and
(b) may:
    (i) provide such services for persons who are in hospital and who have or have had a mental disorder; or
    (ii) secure the provision of such services for such persons' (section 25(1)).

Such services 'shall be designed to: minimise the effect of the mental disorder on such persons; and give such persons the opportunity to lead lives which are as normal as possible' (section 25(2)). In this context, 'care and support' includes 'residential accommodation' and 'personal care and personal support', although not 'nursing care' (section 25(3)).

The local authority shall also provide 'assistance with travel' (section 27) and 'services to promote well-being and social development', including '(a) social, cultural and recreational activities; (b) training for such of those persons as are over school age; and (c) assistance for such of those persons as are over school age in obtaining and in undertaking employment' (section 26(2)). Local authorities also have responsibilities to appoint 'mental health officers' (section 32) and to inquire into cases that present cause for concern (sections 33–35), such as persons who appear to have a mental disorder but may be subject to ill-treatment or neglect (section 33(2)(a)) or are 'living alone or without care' (section 33(2)(c)(1)).

Overall, these are interesting and important provisions that place considerable responsibilities and power in the hands of local authorities in Scotland. These provisions are, however, highly consistent with the social model of disability outlined in the Convention on the Rights of Persons with Disabilities (CRPD) (preamble (e)) and, if observed, have substantial potential to advance the rights of people with mental illness in a meaningful fashion by increasing social integration and protecting from ill-treatment and neglect.

Emergency detention

'Emergency detention' allows 'someone to be detained in hospital for up to 72 hours where hospital admission is required urgently to allow the person's condition to be assessed' (Scottish Executive, 2005; p. 4). This can occur if 'a medical practitioner carries out a medical examination of a patient' (section 36(1)(a)) and:

- 'considers that it is likely' (section 36(3)(b)): '(a) that the patient has a mental disorder; and (b) that, because of the mental disorder, the patient's ability to make decisions about the provision of medical treatment is significantly impaired' (section 36(4));
- 'is satisfied' (section 36(3)(c)): '(a) that it is necessary as a matter of urgency to detain the patient in hospital for the purpose of determining what medical treatment requires to be provided to the patient; (b) that if the patient were not detained in hospital there would be a significant risk: (i) to the health, safety or welfare of the patient; or (ii) to the safety of any other person; and (c) that making arrangements with a view to the grant of a short-term detention certificate would involve undesirable delay' (section 36(5)); and
- 'has consulted a mental health officer and that mental health officer has consented to the grant of an emergency detention certificate' (section 36(3)(d)), if practicable (section 36(6)).

An emergency detention certificate (section 36(1)) authorises: '(a) the removal, before the expiry of the period of 72 hours beginning with the granting of the emergency detention certificate, of the patient to a hospital or to a different hospital; and (b) the detention of the patient in hospital for the period of 72 hours' (section 36(8)). The 'hospital managers' then have responsibilities to arrange 'for an approved medical practitioner to carry out a medical examination of the patient' (section 38(2)) and inform, among others, the patient's 'nearest relative'[110] (section 38(4)). If the approved medical practitioner feels that conditions for detention are not met or that detention is no longer necessary, he or she 'shall revoke the certificate' (section 39).

During the period of emergency detention, the patient's responsible medical officer can suspend the authority to detain for a given period of time (section 41(1)) and this suspension may be subject to whatever conditions the responsible medical officer believes necessary: '(a) in the interests of the patient; or (b) for the protection of any other person' (section 41(3)). This suspension may be revoked for similar reasons (section 42).

The Act also contains detailed provisions relating to 'entry, removal and detention powers' (Part 19), which govern 'entry to premises' (section 292), 'removal to place of safety' (sections 293–298 and 300) and 'nurse's power to detain pending medical examination' (section 299).

Overall, these measures can result in emergency involuntary detention and, in due course, involuntary treatment. Having a 'mental disorder' is a key element in these criteria and, as a result, these provisions appear to violate the CRPD, which specifies that 'the existence of a disability shall in no case justify a deprivation of liberty' (Article 14(1)(b)). More specifically, if certain persons with mental disorders (e.g. some people with chronic schizophrenia) fit the UN definition of 'persons with disabilities' (Article 1), then this provision violates Article 14, as does mental health legislation in England, Wales and Ireland (Bennett, 2014; Kelly, 2014a) (see Chapter 1). The same applies to Scottish provisions relating to short-term detention and compulsory treatment orders, which are considered next.

Short-term detention

Short-term detention allows 'someone to be detained in hospital for up to 28 days' and it can 'only take place where it is recommended by a specially trained doctor (a psychiatrist) and agreed by a mental health officer' (Scottish Executive, 2005; p. 4). More specifically, a short-term detention certificate may be granted if an approved medical practitioner carries out a medical examination (section 44(1)(a)) and considers that it is likely (section 44(3)(b)):

'(a) that the patient has a mental disorder;
(b) that, because of the mental disorder, the patient's ability to make decisions about the provision of medical treatment is significantly impaired;

(c) that it is necessary to detain the patient in hospital for the purpose of:
    (i) determining what medical treatment should be given to the patient; or
    (ii) giving medical treatment to the patient;
(d) that if the patient were not detained in hospital there would be a significant risk (i) to the health, safety or welfare of the patient; or (ii) to the safety of any other person; and
(e) that the granting of a short-term detention certificate is necessary' (section 44(4)).[111]

A mental health officer must agree to the granting of the certificate (section 44(3)(d)), but must first:

'(a) interview the patient;
(b) ascertain the name and address of the patient's named person;
(c) inform the patient of the availability of independent advocacy services under section 259 of this Act; and
(d) take appropriate steps to ensure that the patient has the opportunity of making use of those services' (section 45(1)).

If steps (a) or (b) are impracticable (section 45(2)), the mental health officer must document relevant efforts (section 45(3)). On the certificate itself, the medical practitioner must specify their reasons for believing that relevant criteria are fulfilled (section 44(9)(a)) and, before granting the certificate, must, if practicable (section 44(11)), 'consult the patient's named person' and have regard to that person's views (section 44(10)). Once granted, the certificate authorises:

'(a) the removal, before the expiry of the period of 3 days beginning with the granting of the short-term detention certificate, of the patient to a hospital or to a different hospital;
(b) the detention of the patient in hospital for the period of 28 days beginning with:
    (i) if, immediately before the certificate is granted, the patient is not in hospital, the beginning of the day on which admission under authority of the certificate of the patient to hospital first takes place;
    (ii) if, immediately before the certificate is granted, the patient is in hospital, the beginning of the day on which the certificate is granted;
(c) the giving to the patient, in accordance with Part 16 of this Act, of medical treatment' (section 44(5)).

Once the certificate is provided to the hospital managers, they must notify '(a) the patient; (b) the patient's named person; (c) any guardian of the patient; and (d) any welfare attorney of the patient' (section 46(2)) and, within 7 days, the Mental Health Tribunal and the Mental Welfare Commission for Scotland (section 46(3)). The certificate may be extended following medical examination (section 47(1)(b)) if clinical criteria (section 44(4)(a)–(d)) are still met (section 47(2)(b)(i)) and consideration is given to whether, 'because of a change in the mental health of the patient, an application should be made under section 63 of this Act for a compulsory treatment order' (section 47(2)(b)(ii)) and it is not possible to make such an application within the time frame of the initial short-term detention certificate (section 47(3)(b)).

Such an 'extension certificate' requires the consent of a mental health officer (section 47(3)(c)), if practicable (section 47(6)), and, once granted, authorises '(a) the detention in hospital of the patient for the period of 3 days beginning with the expiry of the period for which the short-term detention certificate authorises the detention of the patient in hospital; and (b) the giving to the patient, in accordance with Part 16 of this Act, of medical treatment' (section 47(4)).

While a short-term detention certificate is in force, the patient's responsible medical officer 'shall, from time to time, consider' whether or not the patient still fulfils relevant criteria (section 44(4) (a)–(d)) and 'whether it continues to be necessary for the detention in hospital of the patient to be authorised by the certificate' (section 49(1)); if these conditions are no longer met, the responsible medical officer must revoke the certificate (section 49(2)).

While the certificate is in force, the patient or the patient's named person may apply to the Mental Health Tribunal for its revocation (section 50(1)) and, after appropriate representations and examination of evidence (section 50(2)), the Tribunal may revoke the certificate if relevant conditions are not met (section 50(4)). A short-term detention certificate may also be suspended for a period subject to conditions (section 53(3)), which may include 'that, during the period specified in the certificate, the patient be kept in the charge of a person authorised in writing for the purpose by the responsible medical officer' (section 53(4)(a)).

Overall, these measures ensure that short-term detention is based on objective medical expertise,[112] there is opportunity to appeal the detention to the Tribunal and treatment is given only when certain conditions are fulfilled (Part 16). Importantly, these provisions allow treatment to be administered during an often critical period and they also recognise the uncertainty inherent in the early stages of the diagnostic process: to authorise a short-term detention certificate the approved medical practitioner must just consider 'that it is *likely*' (section 44(3) (b)) (emphasis added) that the patient has a mental disorder (section 44(4)). This contrasts with the situation in, for example, Ireland, where the Mental Health Act 2001 requires a definitive decision about whether or not the patient has a 'mental disorder' at the very outset (section 14(1) (a)); the Scottish requirement is more realistic and pragmatic than the Irish one.

Compulsory treatment orders

A 'mental health officer shall apply to the Tribunal' for a compulsory treatment order (section 57(1)) if 'two medical practitioners carry out medical examinations of the patient in accordance with the requirements of section 58 of this Act' (section 57(2)) and both are 'satisfied:

'(a) that the patient has a mental disorder;
 (b) that medical treatment which would be likely to:

      (i)   prevent the mental disorder worsening; or

      (ii) alleviate any of the symptoms, or effects, of the disorder, is available for the patient;

(c) that if the patient were not provided with such medical treatment there would be a significant risk (i) to the health, safety or welfare of the patient; or (ii) to the safety of any other person;

(d) that because of the mental disorder the patient's ability to make decisions about the provision of such medical treatment is significantly impaired; and

(e) that the making of a compulsory treatment order is necessary' (section 57(3)).[113]

The medical practitioners must specify the reasons for their opinions (section 57(4)(b)), the symptoms and effects of the mental disorder (section 57(4)(d)) and measures that should be authorised by the order (section 57(4)(e)), among other matters. These two medical examinations must be performed within 5 days of each other (section 58(3)) and by 'approved medical practitioners' (section 58(2)(a)), although the patient's own general practitioner may perform one of the examinations (even if he or she is not an approved medical practitioner) (section 58(4)).

When making an application for a compulsory treatment order, the mental health officer 'shall': identify the patient's named person (section 59); interview the patient (section 61(2)(a)), if practicable (section 61(3)); provide relevant information and notification to various parties (section 61(2)(b)–(d)); prepare a report (section 61(2)(e) and (4)); and compile a 'proposed care plan', following consultation (section 62).

When all of this is completed, the mental health officer can apply to the Tribunal for a compulsory treatment order, submitting the reports by the medical practitioners, the mental health officer's report and the proposed care plan (section 63(3)). The Tribunal shall then afford the patient and various others (section 64(3)) 'the opportunity: (a) of making representations (whether orally or in writing); and (b) of leading, or producing, evidence' (section 64(2)).

After this, the Tribunal may refuse the application (section 64(4)(b)) or:

'(a) [...] make an order:

      (i)   authorising, for the period of 6 months beginning with the day on which the order is made, such of the measures mentioned in section 66(1) of this Act[114] as may be specified in the order;

      (ii) specifying such medical treatment, community care services, relevant services, other treatment, care or service as the Tribunal considers appropriate [...];

      (iii) recording (by reference to the appropriate paragraph (or paragraphs) of the definition of 'mental disorder' in section 328(1) of this Act) the type (or types) of mental disorder that the patient has; and

      (iv) if the order does not authorise the detention of the patient in hospital, specifying the name of the hospital the managers of which are to have responsibility for appointing the patient's responsible medical officer' (section 64(4)(a)).

The Tribunal can only make such an order if satisfied:

'(a) that the patient has a mental disorder;
(b) that medical treatment which would be likely to:
   (i) prevent the mental disorder worsening; or
   (ii) alleviate any of the symptoms, or effects, of the disorder, is available for the patient;
(c) that if the patient were not provided with such medical treatment there would be a significant risk (i) to the health, safety or welfare of the patient; or (ii) to the safety of any other person;
(d) that because of the mental disorder the patient's ability to make decisions about the provision of such medical treatment is significantly impaired;
(e) that the making of a compulsory treatment order in respect of the patient is necessary; and
(f) where the Tribunal does not consider it necessary for the patient to be detained in hospital, such other conditions as may be specified in regulations' (section 64(5)).

The Tribunal may also make an 'interim compulsory treatment order' for up to 28 days (section 65(2)). The short-term detention order may be extended by 5 days, during which period the patient remains detained and the Tribunal can 'determine whether an interim compulsory treatment order should be made' (section 69(a)). If an interim compulsory treatment order is made, the responsible medical officer must monitor whether or not the order is still necessary (section 72(1)) and revoke it if indicated (section 72(2)); the Mental Welfare Commission may also revoke such an order (section 73(2)).

Once a compulsory treatment order is made, the patient's responsible medical officer must prepare a 'care plan' (section 76(1)) and keep the patient under review, to ensure that conditions for detention are still met (section 80), revoking the order if they are not (section 80(3)).

Within 2 months of the scheduled expiration of the order, the responsible medical officer must perform a mandatory review of the patient (section 77) and either revoke the order (section 79(2)) or 'give notice to the mental health officer that the responsible medical officer is proposing to make a determination under section 86 of this Act extending the order' (section 84(2)). The mental health officer must then: interview the patient (section 85(2)(a)), if practicable (section 85(3)); inform the patient of the proposed extension and of their rights (section 85(2)(b)); and inform the responsible medical officer of his or her (i.e. the mental health officer's) opinion (section 85(d)). Once this is done, the responsible medical officer will submit a 'record' of his or her opinion and consultations to the Tribunal (section 87(2)), proposing to extend the order for either 6 months (in the first instance) or 12 months (for subsequent extensions) (section 88(4)). The responsible medical officer may also propose to vary the measures specified in the order, on the basis of the patient's needs (section 93).

If a patient who is under a compulsory treatment order fails to attend for medical treatment, the responsible medical officer, with the agreement of a mental health officer (section 112(2)), 'may take, or may cause a person authorised for the purpose by the responsible medical officer to take, the patient into custody and convey the patient: (a) to the place the patient is required to attend by the attendance requirement; or (b) to any hospital' (section 112(3)) to receive treatment (section 112(4)) for up to 6 hours (section 112(5)).

If the patient is generally non-compliant with an order (despite reasonable opportunity to comply) and 'it is reasonably likely that there would be a significant deterioration in the patient's mental health' if non-compliance continued (section 113(2)(c)), or if the matter is urgent and likely to lead to deterioration (section 113(3)), the 'patient's responsible medical officer may take, or may cause a person authorised for the purpose by the responsible medical officer to take, the patient into custody and convey the patient to a hospital' (section 113(4). There, the patient may be detained for up to 72 hours (section 113(5)); an appropriate examination must be performed (section 113(6)); and the responsible medical officer may 'grant a certificate authorising the continued detention in hospital of the patient for the period of 28 days' (section 114(2)), once a mental health officer agrees (section 114(3)(b)). If practicable, the responsible medical officer should consult the patient's named person before granting such an order (section 114(4)). An interim compulsory treatment order may also be considered (section 115), and either order can be examined and revoked by the Tribunal following application from the patient or his or her nearest person (section 120(2)).

Overall, these measures permit the granting of a compulsory treatment order under which specified treatments can be given. It is interesting that this can occur on either an in-patient or an out-patient basis: this contrasts with the primacy given to the location of treatment in, for example, Ireland's Mental Health Act 2001, which makes no specific provision for involuntary community treatment (although section 26 leave is sometimes used in that fashion) (Bainbridge et al, 2014). In England and Wales, there are detailed provisions for supervised community treatment separate from provisions for involuntary in-patient treatment (see Chapter 2). Finally, it is worth repeating that the Scottish provisions for compulsory treatment orders, like those for emergency detention and short-term detention (see above), appear to violate the CRPD, which specifies that 'the existence of a disability shall in no case justify a deprivation of liberty' (Article 14(1)(b)).

The Mental Health Tribunal for Scotland

The composition and nature of the Mental Health Tribunal for Scotland are outlined in Schedule 2 of the 2003 Act, which governs membership of the Tribunal (Part 1), organisation and administration (Part 2), procedure (Part 3) (which can be governed by rules to be made by the Scottish Ministers (section 10(1))), and provision of 'reports, information etc' (Part 4).

In practice, the Tribunal has a variety of important roles relating to detention orders, including refusing, modifying or granting compulsory treatment orders (section 64(4)). In addition, following a responsible medical officer's application for an extension of such an order, the Tribunal must review the application if it indicates a change in the type of mental disorder (section 101(2)(a)(i)), the mental health officer disagrees with it (section 101(2)(a)(ii)) or the Tribunal has not considered the case within the past 2 years (section 101(2)(b)). The Tribunal, having afforded the patient and relevant parties 'the opportunity: (a) of making representations (whether orally or in writing); and (b) of leading, or producing, evidence' (section 102(2)), may then revoke, modify or confirm the order (section 102(1)).

The responsible medical officer may also refer a case to the Tribunal (section 96(3)) 'if it appears to the responsible medical officer that any recorded matter specified in the compulsory treatment order is not being provided', following consultation with the mental health officer, among others (section 96(2)). The patient or their named person may also apply to the Tribunal, seeking revocation of a determination to extend a compulsory treatment order (section 99), revocation of a compulsory treatment order (section 100(2)(a)) or variation to the measures in the order (section 100(2)(b)), but not within the first 3 months of the order (section 100(4)). The Tribunal may refuse, modify or confirm such applications (section 103).

The Act also contains provisions for 'application to Tribunal in relation to unlawful detention' (section 291) and appeals (Part 22), including appeals 'against certain decisions of the Tribunal' (e.g. refusals to revoke certain orders), which can be made to the 'sheriff principal' (section 320); appeals against decisions of the sheriff principal can, in turn, be made to the Court of Session (section 321). Appeals against certain other decisions of the Tribunal (e.g. to revoke certain orders) can be made to the Court of Session (section 322), and there are various procedures and regulations to be observed (sections 323–324).

Overall, the tribunals system provides patients with opportunity to challenge their detention and a clear path of appeal, without the kinds of severe restrictions on appeals seen in other jurisdictions, such as Ireland, where a patient can appeal to the Circuit Court only on the grounds of not having a mental disorder (Mental Health Act 2001: section 19(1)) and can appeal to the High Court only on a point of law, and not in relation to whether or not they have a mental disorder (section 19(16)). In Scotland, given that the legal structure of the Tribunal and the subsequent appeals appears solid in theory, the extent to which it protects rights in practice is clearly heavily dependent on how it operates on the ground.

In this context, it is interesting that one research study, *An Exploration of the Early Operation of the Mental Health Tribunal for Scotland* (Dobbie *et al*, 2009), reported that 'there was consensus that the new system had improved patients' experiences, and reflected the guiding principles by being fairer for patients than the Sheriff Court system; more patient focused' (i.e. 'friendly, open and accountable') and 'more participatory, allowing patients to feel that they were listened to (even if they do not agree with the final decision) and to have a voice' (p. 64). There was, however concern that:

'• It can be very upsetting for patients and families to hear the evidence presented and have their mental ill health discussed in front of strangers.
• The new system may have a damaging impact on the therapeutic relationship between a patient and their psychiatrist/MHO [mental health officer], especially if they are giving evidence to support a CTO [compulsory treatment order] that the patient does not want.
• Some venues were criticised as being inappropriate for hearings; for example, insufficient or non-existent private space for families and for patients to talk to their solicitor' (p. 64).

The report concluded by providing various recommendations for improvements to the tribunals system, relating to 'improving systems for monitoring and audit' (p. 66); 'improving systems for the submission and processing of CTO applications'; 'specific roles' at the Tribunal (p. 67); 'dealing with the consequences of the legal/evidential nature of the tribunals'; 'training'; and various other matters. What is notable about these recommendations is that the majority relate to making the Tribunal more user friendly and comprehensible, rather than changing the fundamental nature of its tasks or decisions. This is a salutary reminder of the importance of process in reviewing decisions to deprive individuals of their liberty, and the need to ensure that tribunal hearings are seen to be efficient, transparent and fair.

Treatments for detained patients
Psychosurgery and other treatments specified in the same category

Scotland's 2003 Act outlines detailed regulations governing a range of different forms of treatment for detained patients. Psychosurgery (and other treatments specified in the same category) (section 234(2)) can be given to a patient 'capable of consenting' only if a designated medical practitioner (section 233) who is not the patient's responsible medical officer certifies in writing that: 'the patient is capable of consenting to the treatment; the patient consents in writing to the treatment; and having regard to the likelihood of its alleviating, or preventing a deterioration in, the patient's condition, it is in the patient's best interests that the treatment should be given to the patient' (section 235(2)).

In addition, 'two other persons (not being medical practitioners) appointed by the Mental Welfare Commission for the purposes of this subsection [must] certify in writing that: the patient is capable of consenting to the treatment; and the patient consents in writing to the treatment' (section 235(3)). Such treatment can only be given to a patient 'incapable of consenting' if:

• 'the patient does not resist or object to the treatment' (section 236(1)(b));
• 'a designated medical practitioner who is not the patient's responsible medical officer certifies in writing that: (a) the patient is incapable of consenting to the treatment; (b) the patient does not object to the treatment; and (c) having regard to the likelihood of its alleviating,

or preventing a deterioration in, the patient's condition, it is in the patient's best interests that the treatment should be given to the patient' (section 236(2));

- 'two persons (not being medical practitioners) appointed by the Commission for the purposes of this subsection certify in writing that: (a) the patient is incapable of consenting to the treatment; and (b) the patient does not object to the treatment' (section 236(3)); and
- 'on the application of the patient's responsible medical officer, the Court of Session has made an order declaring that the treatment may lawfully be given' (section 236(4)); such an order may be granted only if the Court 'is satisfied that: (a) having regard to the likelihood of its alleviating, or preventing a deterioration in, the patient's condition, it is in the patient's best interests that the treatment should be given to the patient; and (b) the patient does not object to the treatment' (section 236(5)).

Electroconvulsive therapy (ECT) (and other treatments specified in the same category)

Electroconvulsive therapy (ECT) (and other treatments specified in the same category) (section 237(3)) can be given to a patient 'capable of consenting and not refusing consent' only if 'the patient's responsible medical officer or a designated medical practitioner certifies in writing that: (a) the patient is capable of consenting to the treatment; (b) the patient consents in writing to the treatment; (c) the giving of medical treatment to the patient is authorised by virtue of this Act or the [Criminal Procedure (Scotland) Act 1995]; and (d) having regard to the likelihood of its alleviating, or preventing a deterioration in, the patient's condition, it is in the patient's best interests that the treatment should be given' (section 238(1)).

Such treatment can be given to a patient 'incapable of consenting' only if 'a designated medical practitioner who is not the patient's responsible medical officer certifies in writing that: (a) the patient is incapable of understanding the nature, purpose and likely effects of the treatment; (b) the giving of medical treatment to the patient is authorised by virtue of this Act or the [Criminal Procedure (Scotland) Act 1995]; and (c) having regard to the likelihood of its alleviating, or preventing a deterioration in, the patient's condition, it is in the patient's best interests that the treatment should be given' (section 239(1)). If 'the patient resists or objects to the treatment' the designated medical practitioner must certify that: '(a) the patient resists or objects to the treatment; but (b) it is necessary to give the treatment to the patient' (section 239(2)) for specific, urgent reasons (section 243(3)(a)–(c)).

Other treatments

Other regulations are outlined for various other treatments, including: '(a) any medicine (other than the surgical implantation of hormones) given for the purpose of reducing sex drive; (b) any other medicine; (c) provision, without the consent of the patient and by artificial means, of nutrition to the patient; and (d) such other types of treatment as may be specified in regulations for the purposes of this section' (section 240(3)). These treatments can be given to a patient 'capable of consenting and not refusing consent' only if 'the patient's responsible medical officer or a designated medical practitioner certifies in writing that: (a) the patient is capable of consenting to the treatment; (b) the patient consents in writing to the treatment; (c) the giving of medical treatment to the patient is authorised by virtue of this Act or the [Criminal Procedure (Scotland) Act 1995]; and (d) having regard to the likelihood of its alleviating, or preventing a deterioration in, the patient's condition, it is in the patient's best interests that the treatment should be given' (section 238 (1)).

Such treatments can be given to a patient 'refusing consent or incapable of consenting' only if 'a designated medical practitioner who is not the patient's responsible medical officer certifies in writing that: (a) the patient: (i) does not consent to the treatment; or (ii) is incapable of consenting to the treatment; (b) the giving of medical treatment to the patient is authorised by virtue of this Act or the [Criminal Procedure (Scotland) Act 1995]; and (c) having regard to the likelihood of its alleviating, or preventing a deterioration in, the patient's condition, it is in the patient's best interests that the treatment should be given' (section 241(1)). If the patient 'does not consent to the treatment' (section 241(1)(a)(i)), 'the designated medical practitioner shall: (a) if the reason for refusal of consent is known, have regard to the reason for the refusal; and (b) if the designated medical practitioner is of the opinion that the treatment should be given, include in any certificate [...] a statement of the reason for that opinion' (section 241(2)). If the patient is not in hospital, this section 'does not authorise the giving of medical treatment by force to the patient' (section 241(4)).

For other treatments (not mentioned in sections 234, 237 or 240), consent of the patient is required (section 242(3)), but if the patient does not consent (section 242(4)(a)(i)), 'consents otherwise than in writing' (section 242(4)(a)(ii)) or 'is incapable of consenting' (section 242(4)(b)), the medical treatment can be given if:

- the 'responsible medical officer determines that it is in the patient's best interests that the treatment be given' after 'having regard' to the reasons for the patient not consenting (if appropriate); the views of the patient and his or her named person; any advance statement; and 'the likelihood of the treatment's alleviating, or preventing a deterioration in, the patient's condition' (section 242(5)(a);
- 'in the case of a patient subject to an assessment order, an approved medical practitioner who is not the patient's responsible medical officer determines, after having regard to the matters mentioned [above], that it is in the patient's best interests that the treatment be given' (section 242(5)(b)); and

- 'the treatment is given by, or under the direction of, the patient's responsible medical officer' (section 242(5)(c)).

The reasons for these decisions must be recorded (section 242(5)(d) and (e)) and, again, if the patient is not in hospital, this section 'does not authorise the giving of medical treatment by force to the patient' (section 242(6)).

Urgent medical treatment

'Urgent medical treatment' may be given to a detained patient who does not consent or is incapable of consenting (section 243(2)) if its purpose includes any of the following:

'(a) saving the patient's life;
(b) preventing serious deterioration in the patient's condition;
(c) alleviating serious suffering on the part of the patient; and
(d) preventing the patient from:
(i) behaving violently; or
(ii) being a danger to the patient or to others' (section 243(3)).

This provision authorises the giving of medical treatment: '(a) for a purpose mentioned in any of paragraphs (b) to (d)' (above) 'only if the treatment is not likely to entail unfavourable, and irreversible, physical or psychological consequences' (section 243(4)(a)) and '(b) for a purpose mentioned in paragraph (c) or (d)' (above) 'only if the treatment does not entail significant physical hazard to the patient' (section 243(4)(b)). This provision does not authorise the giving of ECT if the patient is capable of consenting but does not consent to the treatment (section 243(5)). Treatment under this provision must be notified to the Mental Welfare Commission within 7 days (section 243(6)).

Such treatment certificates should not be granted without consulting with the patient, their named person and other relevant parties (section 245(3)), where practicable (section 245(4)).

Summary

Overall, these measures outline specific requirements for involuntary treatment to occur, with some treatments (e.g. psychosurgery, ECT) attracting particular safeguards. This reflects a broadly balanced approach to involuntary treatment, and ensures that all treatments are available to all patients, regardless of decision-making capacity; this is highly compliant with the CRPD, which requires that parties 'provide persons with disabilities with the same range, quality and standard of free or affordable health care and programmes as provided to other persons' (Article 25(a)). In the case of ECT, the National Institute for Health and Care Excellence (2010) recommends ECT for 'rapid and short-term improvement of severe symptoms after an adequate trial of other treatment options has proven ineffective and/or when the condition is considered to be potentially life-threatening, in individuals with, severe depressive illness, catatonia, or a prolonged or severe manic episode' (p. 5). The Scottish legislation ensures that persons with mental disorders, who may have impaired decision-making capacity, have access to this and all other treatments that are available to everyone else, as required by the CRPD.

Various other provisions

The Mental Health (Care and Treatment) (Scotland) Act 2003 presents various other provisions relating to transfers to other hospitals (Part 7, Chapter 6), suspension of measures authorising detention (Part 7, Chapter 7) and assessment of needs (for community care services etc.) (Part 14). In addition, once a compulsory order is made in relation to a patient (section 232), the mental health officer must, within 21 days, prepare a social circumstances report on the patient (section 231(1)), unless they feel that such a report would 'serve little, or no, practical purpose' (section 231(2)). In the latter case, the mental health officer must record their reasons for such a decision (section 231(2)(b)(i)) and send a copy to the patient's responsible medical officer and to the Mental Welfare Commission (section 231(2)(b)(ii)).

There are also extensive provisions relating to advocacy (section 259), including a provision that 'every person with a mental disorder shall have a right of access to independent advocacy' (section 259(1)); 'provision of information to patient' (section 260); 'provision of assistance to patient with communication difficulties' (section 261); 'access to medical practitioner for purposes of medical examination' (section 262); 'inspection of records by medical practitioner' (section 263); 'education of persons who have mental disorder' (section 277); and 'payments to persons in hospital to meet personal expenses' (section 288). Many of these measures are significantly supportive of patient dignity and autonomy in the often undignifying setting of psychiatric hospitals, and certain measures (such as those relating to advocacy and education) appear particularly helpful in optimising the exercise of patients' capabilities in such settings (Seedhouse & Gallagher, 2002).

As regards the more detailed implementation of the 2003 Act in practice, the Scottish Ministers 'shall […] draw up, give effect to and publish' Codes of Practice governing various functions under the legislation (section 274(1)) and 'any person discharging functions by virtue of this Act shall have regard (so far as they are applicable to the discharge of those functions by that person) to the provisions of any Code of Practice' (section 274(4)). It is to be hoped that such Codes are accorded equal or even greater importance than those relating to England and Wales, where the House of Lords, although it tolerated a specific violation of a particular Code,[115] went to great lengths to emphasise the importance of the Code, stating that it always carries substantial weight and should be considered with great care. Although the Code is not a binding instruction it is more than mere advice; departures from the Code should be rare and reasons for such departures should be spelled out clearly and logically in each case (see Chapter 2).

In Scotland, the 2003 Act contains interesting provisions regarding advance statements. It defines an 'advance statement' as one that specifies '(a) the ways the person making it wishes to be treated for mental disorder; (b) the ways the person wishes not to be so treated, in the event of the person's becoming mentally disordered and the person's ability to make decisions [being consequently] significantly impaired' (section 275(1)). Such a statement must comply with specific conditions (e.g. the person must have had capacity when they made the advance statement) (section 275(2)). If the Tribunal is satisfied that relevant conditions have been met, it shall 'have regard to the wishes specified' (section 276(1)), as shall any 'person giving medical treatment authorised by virtue of this Act or the [Criminal Procedure (Scotland) Act 1995]' (section 276(3)) and any 'designated medical practitioner' (section 276(4)). If any of these parties violates an advance statement (section 276(7)), they must: record in writing the circumstances in which the advance statement was violated and the reasons why (section 276(8)(a)); supply a copy of that record to relevant parties, including the person who made the advance statement (section 276(8)(b)); and place a copy of that record with the person's medical records (section 276(8)(c)). Although this does not accord absolute importance to the advance statement, it does create a strong requirement that it be considered.

As regards the European Convention on Human Rights (ECHR) 'right to respect for private and family life' (Article 8), the 2003 Act presents detailed provisions regarding 'communications' with detained patients, including that a 'postal packet' that a 'specified person' seeks to post may be withheld 'by the managers of the hospital in which the specified person is detained' if, among other requirements, 'the managers of the hospital consider that the postal packet is likely: (i) to cause distress to the person in question or any other person who is not on the staff of the hospital; or (ii) to cause danger to any person' (section 281(3)(b)). A similar condition can apply to the 'specified person' receiving a 'postal packet' (section 281(6)). Withholding the contents of such packages is subject to specific and detailed regulations (sections 281–283), as are the use of telephones by 'certain persons detained in hospital' (sections 284 and 285) and general measures required for 'safety and security in hospitals' (e.g. searches, restrictions, prohibitions, surveillance) (section 286).

Overall, these provisions appear to reflect a delicate balance between the need for autonomy and the ECHR 'right to respect for private and family life' (Article 8) on the one hand, and the need for security on the other, similar to that established in various cases in England and Wales.[116] Provided that such powers are not used arbitrarily, appropriate codes are observed, use is proportionate to demonstrated need, and there is a mechanism for complaint or appeal, these powers do not necessarily represent unjustified violations of rights.

Other provisions in the 2003 Act govern research (section 279), cross-border transfers (sections 289–290), measures that can be taken if a patient absconds (Part 20), offences (e.g. non-consensual sexual acts) (Part 21), the power to prescribe the form and use of documents (section 325) and orders, regulations and rules (section 326). The Act also contains extensive provisions relating to criminal proceedings involving mentally disordered persons (Part 8), compulsion orders and restriction orders (Parts 9 and 10), hospital directions and transfer for treatment directions (Part 11), transfers of patients (Part 12), suspension of relevant measures (Part 13) and 'detention in conditions of excessive security' (e.g. state hospitals) (sections 264–273); these measures are beyond the scope of this book, which focuses on civil rather than criminal or forensic matters.

The McManus Review

Background

Overall, the Mental Health (Care and Treatment) (Scotland) Act 2003 demonstrates significant similarities with mental health legislation in England, Wales, Ireland and Northern Ireland, but also various points of contrast. In Scotland, it is particularly notable that:

- The principles of the 2003 Act clearly reflect respect for the wishes of the patient, patient participation in decision-making and the principle of least restriction, as well as acknowledging circumstances of family members and the need for continued provision of services; these are very positive features of the legislation.

- Although the 2003 Act's definition of 'mental disorder' (section 328) accords moderately well with the definitions of the other jurisdictions, it contrasts in certain respects with those of Ireland (which excludes personality disorder) and England and Wales (which no longer explicitly excludes 'immoral conduct [or] sexual deviancy'); nonetheless, the Scottish definition is, overall, as clear and user-friendly as can probably be achieved in primary legislation.

- The roles that the 2003 Act accords to the Mental Welfare Commission for Scotland (Part 2) are critically important in supporting high standards, as are those accorded to the Mental Health Tribunal for Scotland (Part 3) and local authorities, especially in relation to provision of services (sections 25–27) that give patients 'the opportunity to lead lives which are as normal as possible' (section 25(2)). This is highly consistent with the CRPD and, if observed, should help protect and promote the rights and dignity of persons with mental illness; it also contrasts with certain other jurisdictions, such as Ireland, where mental health legislation contains no such provisions ensuring services.

- The 2003 Act's provisions relating to emergency detention (Part 5), short-term detention (Part 6) and compulsory treatment orders (Part 7) also have significant merits. For example, they are clear; the emergency detention and short-term detention procedures recognise that definitive diagnosis of 'mental disorder' may not be possible in the initial stages of the process (sections 36(3)(b) and 44(3)(b)); and treatment is both permitted in certain circumstances and subject to various specific requirements (sections 44(5)(c)). All three detention procedures, however, link involuntary detention and treatment with 'mental disorder', thus apparently violating the CRPD requirement that 'the existence of a disability shall in no case justify a deprivation of liberty' (Article 14(1)(b)); this is also the case in England, Wales, Ireland and Northern Ireland (Bennett, 2014; Kelly, 2014a).

- Provisions relating to the Mental Health Tribunal (Schedule 2) in Scotland appear to be a significant advance on previous arrangements, although there is probably still scope for procedural improvements (Dobbie *et al*, 2009), as is likely always to be the case for such hearings.

- Provisions relating to treatment (Part 16), too, appear to strike a reasonable balance between protections for detained patients and ensuring that all patients have access to the same range of treatments, regardless of their level of decision-making capacity; this is highly compliant with the CRPD (Article 25(a)).

- Other important and generally progressive measures in the 2003 Act relate to advocacy (section 259), provision of information (section 260), provision of assistance to patients with communication difficulties (section 261), education (section 277), Codes of Practice (section 274), advance statements (sections 275 and 276) and regulations governing communications and security (sections 281–286), which appear generally consistent with the ECHR 'right to respect for private and family life' (Article 8), once they are implemented in a reasonable and accountable fashion.

Following the introduction of the 2003 Act (Thomson, 2005), various concerns were expressed by different groups, relating, *inter alia*, to the extent to which the new legislation truly supported the principle of least restriction (Bennett & Mitchell, 2007), patients' lack of knowledge about advance statements (Foy *et al*, 2007), a lack of information about place-of-safety legislation (section 297) (Macaskill *et al*, 2011) and concern about the extent to which the legislation (in conjunction with other initiatives) had truly assisted with the provision of age-appropriate services for children and adolescents (Latimer, 2009). One 'before-and-after' study reported that the 2003 Act resulted in fewer patients being detained, but those that were detained were more likely to progress to longer-term detention (Smith & White, 2007). Overall, however, detained patients remained in hospital for shorter periods, the new power to enforce medication in the community having possibly helped reduce the length of detention in hospital.

Carswell *et al* (2007) studied psychiatrists' views and experiences of the 2003 Act and found that 12% believed that patient care had improved as a result of the Act; 65% believed that informal patients' care had suffered; 52% did not believe that the Mental Health Tribunal was better than the previous court system; and 59% felt that their out-of-hours workload had increased. In a later survey, Donaldson *et al* (2008) reported that 53% of respondents were now reasonably satisfied with the Act; 51% would choose it in preference to the previous Act; and 89% felt that their daytime workload had increased. While overall satisfaction had, therefore, improved, concerns were expressed in relation to bureaucratic and time-consuming paperwork, issues relating to the organisation and inflexibility of reviews before the Tribunal, the number of interim orders granted (necessitating further full Tribunal hearings with new panels) and various other matters (e.g. cost).

The Review

Against this background, the Scottish Government instituted a 'limited review' of the Mental Health (Care and Treatment) (Scotland) Act 2003, which was presented to the Scottish Ministers in March 2009 (Scottish Government Review Group, 2009). This focused, incisive report is known as the McManus Review as the Review Group was chaired by Jim McManus, Professor of Criminal Justice at Glasgow Caledonian University. The Review Group's terms of reference were:

'• To consider the operation of the processes in respect of the civil provisions of the Act in the context of the ten Millan Principles [Box 5.1] and advise on changes that should be made to improve the efficiency of the operation of the Act and the experience of patients;
• To advise on other minor amendments to the Act to resolve technical or other issues as provided to the Review Group by the Scottish Government to consider; and
• To report to the Minister for Public Health with recommendations following appropriate engagement with those with an interest in the operation of the Act' (Scottish Government Review Group, 2009: p. 4).

The Review Group engaged in a process of consultation and review, concentrating 'initially on five main areas of the Act's operation about which concerns had been raised: named persons, advance statements, medical examinations for compulsory treatment orders, tribunals and suspension of detention' (p. 5). The Review Group's final recommendations can be considered under the following six headings:

• advance statements
• independent advocacy
• named persons
• medical matters
• the tribunals system
• other issues

Advance statements

The Review Group noted that advance statements were introduced 'to improve patient participation' in treatment decisions but that 'the take-up of them has not been as high as expected' (p. 8). Reasons provided for the low uptake are summarised in Box 5.2.

153

Box 5.2 Reasons for low uptake of advance statements under the Mental Health (Care and Treatment) (Scotland) Act 2003

'• Most persons have never heard of advance statements and, even if they have, they do not think they would ever be relevant to them.

• People do not know how to go about making an advance statement, who they can have as a witness, and what to do with the document once they have drawn it up.

• Service users recognise that when they are unwell they need medical treatment and trust those who may provide this treatment to provide only appropriate treatment.

• When in recovery, many service users find it hard to contemplate being unwell again and are not ready to prepare for that eventuality.

• People do not believe that any regard will be had to their statement when it may be needed […].

• There is some confusion about the difference and similarity among advance statements, living wills and personal statements. This results in people entering irrelevant matters in their advance statements, which should only deal with treatments for mental disorder.'

(Scottish Government Review Group, 2009: pp. 8–9)

It is particularly interesting that some of those consulted told the Review Group that they felt their advance statement would be ignored, although this does not appear to be the case in practice:

'People do not believe that any regard will be had to their statement if the time comes when it may be needed. They stress that it can be overridden and feel it is therefore useless. In practice, however, figures from the Mental Welfare Commission show that the vast majority of advance statements are adhered to and very few overridden. (The Commission's Annual Report for 2007–08 recorded 13 actual overrides in the whole year)' (Scottish Government Review Group, 2009: p. 8).

Having considered the matter in some detail, the Review Group recommended: clarifying what can be included in advance statements; increasing awareness of advance statements; making it easier to make a valid advance statement; extending the range of witnesses and clarifying their role; highlighting the fact that few advance statements are over-ridden; and requiring 'responsible medical officers to review regularly any treatment in conflict with an advance statement and provide a written record of efforts made to address the person's stated wishes' (p. 9).

The Review Group also recommended creating a central register of advance statements, with copies also retained in medical records, noting that the Mental Welfare Commission had indicated that it would be prepared to hold such a register (p. 9). These are all important and useful provisions, aimed at realising in practice the potential that advance statements offer for greater patient autonomy and participation in clinical decision-making. What they require are, for the most part, non-legislative changes that optimise the potential of existing legal arrangements, rather than fundamental alterations to the law.

Independent advocacy

The Review Group noted that the Mental Health (Care and Treatment) (Scotland) Act 2003 (section 259) gives every person with a mental disorder a right to independent advocacy, placing a duty on NHS Boards and local authorities in collaboration to ensure the availability of independent advocacy services:

> 'It is particularly helpful for people who are at risk of being mistreated or ignored, or who wish to negotiate a change in their care, or are facing a period of crisis. Advocacy can be used by people with physical or mental disorders, or by people who simply feel overwhelmed and confused by institutions and care, or by their carers. It can be difficult, for a number of reasons, for service users to speak up for themselves. Advocacy can give a route by which this may be achieved' (Scottish Government Review Group, 2009: p. 10).

Notwithstanding these potential benefits of independent advocacy, the Review Group identified several problems with the existing advocacy service, including uneven availability in certain areas, a perceived focus of advocacy services on involuntary rather than voluntary patients, confusion about roles, certain advocates allegedly pursuing their own agendas rather than the patient's wishes, lack of clarity regarding how to complain about an advocate, specific difficulties with advocacy for certain groups (e.g. children, Black and minority ethnic patients) and issues relating to collective rather than individual advocacy.

Against this background, the Review Group recommended that the government ensure that advocacy services are fully available and funded across Scotland; failures to provide adequate advocacy should be reported to the Mental Welfare Commission; independent advocacy services should work in accordance with the Scottish Independent Advocacy Alliance Principles and Standards and Code of Practice; carers should have access to advocacy; application of the Code of Practice should be monitored; and NHS Boards and local authorities should support the development of collective advocacy groups in their own areas. As with the measures relating to advance statements, most of these recommendations involve better implementation of existing legislative provisions rather than amendments to the legislation itself (although some legislative change would be needed too).

Named persons

The Review Group noted various problems with the 'nearest relative' system (under the Mental Health (Scotland) Act 1984) and that the Millan

Committee (2001) had recommended that patients should be able to appoint a 'named person' with the right to:

'•   Require an assessment of the service user's needs;
•   Be notified and consulted if compulsory measures were being considered;
•   Be heard at the tribunal in any proceedings about the use of compulsion; and
•   Appeal against the use of compulsory measures' (Scottish Government Review Group, 2009: p. 13).

Against this background, the Mental Health (Care and Treatment) (Scotland) Act 2003 gave the patient the right to appoint a named person who: receives various notices and should be consulted during the compulsion process (if practicable); can appeal against compulsory orders (except emergency certificates) and various other matters; receives copies of papers presented to the Mental Health Tribunal; and has free legal representation.

From the perspective of economic and social rights, including the right to treatment, the named person also has one other critically important right:

'This is the right to request that the local authority and/or the NHS Board make a formal assessment of a service user's needs for social care or health services. (The service user and primary carer also have this right.) If the authorities refuse the request, they must give their reasons. It can sometimes be difficult to access help when necessary and this is a way of ensuring that a service user's needs receive proper consideration' (Scottish Government Review Group, 2009: p. 14).

The Review Group was informed of various issues relating to the named person in practice, including: misunderstandings and complexities about the role (which may lead to conflict with the patient); a need for named persons to be informed that they have been nominated as such; variable uptake among patients; concern among patients that nominating someone as a named person places additional burden on that person; patients' difficulties getting sensitive Tribunal information withheld from named persons (especially important in light of the patient's right to respect for private and family life under Article 8 of the ECHR); and the fact that a young person under 16 years of age cannot nominate a named person because the role is assumed by their parents (or person with parental responsibilities).

Following a highly detailed, lucid consideration of these issues, the Review Group made several recommendations, the most significant of which are summarised in Box 5.3.

These recommendations are extremely interesting from a human rights perspective. Some of the them (e.g. patients should have a named person only if they have appointed one) reflect a clear recognition of the right to autonomy, while others (e.g. the responsible medical officer should have a statutory obligation to consult the named person about the final care plan) reflect a clear recognition of welfare-based concerns. Overall, however, these recommendations strike a good balance between the patient's rights to liberty and autonomy, and the right to treatment, especially in situations where the patient may temporarily lack capacity to articulate adequately their own needs and protect adequately their own rights.

Medical matters

The Review Group devoted attention to a range of medical matters that had arisen since implementation of the 2003 Act. With regard to 'medical

---

Box 5.3 Summarised recommendations of the McManus Review relating to the role of named persons under the Mental Health (Care and Treatment) (Scotland) Act 2003

- Patients should have a named person only if they have appointed one.
- If a patient is unable to appoint a named person, their primary carer (or the nearest relative) should have an automatic right to appeal against orders, extension of orders and hospital transfers, but should not act as named person.
- If a patient who has not appointed a named person is unable to appoint one but has not signed a document expressing a wish not to have one, anyone with an interest should be able to apply to be appointed as a named person.
- In addition to its power to appoint a curator *ad litem*, the Mental Health Tribunal should be able to appoint a safeguarder if a patient has no lawyer, independent advocate or named person.
- There should be a nationwide publicity campaign about the role and function of the named person.
- Special efforts should be made by mental health service providers to encourage patients to consider appointing a named person as early as possible and during recovery.
- The form appointing the named person should require the written consent of the named person. The form should also contain a box setting out the consequences of appointing a named person, including the sharing of confidential information.
- Named persons should continue to have the powers they enjoy under the Mental Health (Care and Treatment) (Scotland) Act 2003, but should also receive notification from the police if the patient is taken to a place of safety.
- A mental health officer making an application for a compulsory treatment order should have a statutory duty to consult with the named person about the proposed care plan. In addition, the responsible medical officer should have a statutory obligation to consult the named person about the final care plan.
- A young person under the age of 16 who has adequate understanding of the consequences of appointing a named person should be able to do so.
- The Scottish Government should draw up a Code of Practice for named persons, covering matters such as confidentiality.

(Adapted from: Scottish Government Review Group, 2009: pp. 26–27)

---

examinations for compulsory treatment orders', the Review Group heard that only about 50% of second medical reports for compulsory treatment orders were provided by general practitioners; there were various problems with general practitioners' reports (e.g. perceived unfamiliarity with legislative requirements); and the requirements to ensure the independence of approved medical practitioners who provided a second report were 'difficult to comply with, especially in rural areas distant from other hospitals' (Scottish Government Review Group, 2009: p. 28).

The Review Group proposed that an application for a compulsory treatment order should continue to be accompanied by two medical reports, but that one should be prepared by the patient's own general practitioner. This general practitioner should have 'a duty to give a view on the approved medical practitioner's report', and 'in exceptional circumstances set out in regulations, the general practitioner's report may be provided by a second approved medical practitioner. When a general practitioner's report is not submitted to a mental health tribunal, there should be a requirement for the relevant NHS Board to notify the Mental Welfare Commission' (p. 31).

The Review Group also proposed that a medical examination to extend a compulsory treatment order 'in a hospital run by an independent healthcare provider must be made by an approved medical practitioner independent of that service' (p. 32), as was already the case for the initial application for a compulsory treatment order in such a hospital. This is an important provision and one that could usefully be applied in other jurisdictions, such as Ireland, where a second opinion to detain a voluntary patient (in any hospital, public or private) need not be independent (Mental Health Act 2001: section 24).

With regard to suspension of hospital detention under compulsory treatment orders, the Review Group noted that current provisions, 'although well intentioned, are inflexible and difficult to manage and have resulted in the development of excessively bureaucratic systems to count up the number of days a patient has had his or her detention requirement suspended. There has also been confusion over the calculation of the time limits' (Scottish Government Review Group, 2009: p. 35). The Review Group recommended that for brief periods out of hospital (not overnight), suspension should be authorised by the responsible medical officer and recorded in the case notes, but should not count towards any cumulative limit. For overnight and longer periods, 'the responsible medical officer would complete a suspension certificate. Such certificates could cumulatively authorise up to 200 overnight periods out of hospital in any 12 month period' although, following a tribunal hearing, this limit could, if appropriate, 'be "reset" and up to a further 200 overnight stays could be authorised by the responsible medical officer' (p. 36).

The Review Group did not recommend a change to the 2003 Act's section 238 requirement for written consent for treatments mentioned in sections 237(3) (e.g. ECT) and 240(3) ('treatments given over a period of time'), but suggested that, 'in situations where a patient refuses to sign but does indicate verbal consent [...] an opinion from a designated medical practitioner should be sought' (p. 37).

The Review Group also noted that there was 'widespread confusion about the purpose, content and format of care plans' (p. 37) and recommended that 'the Scottish Government should, by regulations, provide a template' for the care plan (under section 76) with a recommended time frame for completion, and that the template should (a) 'reflect the proposed care plan currently incorporated as Part 3 of the initial compulsory treatment order application' (section 63); (b) 'incorporate a guidance note that its content should reflect the overarching care plan inclusive of the care, support and treatment delivered to the individual by a range of disciplines and agencies'; (c) 'conclude with a section noting those consulted in its compilation, and to whom it has been circulated and when'; and (d) 'include the option to attach the CEL 13 care plan (enhanced care programme approach care plan)', where appropriate (pp. 38–39).

All of these changes seek to clarify and streamline care in accordance with the 2003 Act, although the requirement for involvement of the patient's own general practitioner may present logistical difficulties in certain circumstances, and the over-formalisation of care plans may limit flexibility in the delivery of care.

The tribunals system

The Review Group readily recognised that the setting up of a tribunals system (the Mental Health Tribunal for Scotland) under the 2003 Act had been a generally positive development, but also heard about specific problems with tribunal hearings, including, most notably:

- the large number of cases (over 50%) that require more than one hearing to reach a conclusion (i.e. the problem of multiple hearings)
- a perception of excessive formality and legality at some tribunal hearings
- the availability, quality and style of legal representation' (Scottish Government Review Group, 2009: p. 41).

The Review Group considered each of these problems separately and in some detail before settling on specific recommendations for each. With regard to 'the problem of multiple hearings', the Review Group suggested that:

- the time limit of 5 working days within which to arrange a hearing (once an application has been made within the 28-day period) (section 68(2)(a)) be extended to 10 working days, to allow for 'more proactive and effective case management' (p. 47) and give all parties more time to prepare for the hearing;
- where this additional 5-day period is used, the maximum period of time permitted for extension of interim compulsory treatment orders should be reduced by 5 working days from the present maximum of 56 days (p. 50) (section 65(3));

- patients who want to appoint a solicitor should be encouraged to do so at the earliest opportunity (p. 50);
- the mental health officer should give a copy of the application for a compulsory treatment order to the patient and/or the patient's solicitor at the same time as it is sent to the tribunal office (p. 50);
- the tribunals service should prepare codes of conduct for tribunal members and curators *ad litem*;
- 'where an interim order is proposed for a short period in order to allow for some specified action to be taken on behalf of the patient, the tribunal should be able to grant an interim order if the conditions for the order "appear to be met" [...], subject to a time limit of a maximum of 28 days' (p. 50).

In relation to 'excessive formality and legality', the Review Group emphasised the importance of training in tribunal skills, convenors assuming a flexible approach, reconsidering the use of voice recorders (if helpful) and the importance of venues being suited to their purpose (with access to water, toilets, waiting facilities, etc.). In addition, 'a Code of Conduct should be prepared by the Law Society of Scotland for legal representatives' and 'the preferred standards already contained within the Memorandum of Understanding [between the Tribunal service and health boards throughout Scotland] should be retained and maintained, but greater emphasis should be placed on ensuring that those preferred standards are met' (p. 56). None of these measures appeared to require adjustment of legislation, but all required the implementation of existing provisions in a more reliable, equitable and reasonable fashion.

The Review Group also addressed the issue of 'availability, quality and style of legal representation', suggesting that mental health law should be taught at undergraduate and postgraduate levels; in-service courses should be offered to solicitors to provide training in relation to mental health care and Tribunal skills; and 'consideration should be given as to how to encourage more solicitors to become involved in this particular area of law' (p. 59). It was also recommended that Tribunal members should be trained in relation to independent advocacy; professional interpretation services should be available as needed; and appeals relating to detention orders (e.g. section 44) should be dealt with promptly, within reasonable, defined time frames.

Other issues

The Review Group provided comments in relation to a number of other matters in addition to the above, many of which (again) relate to more efficient and orderly performance of various tasks already enshrined in the 2003 Act and its associated rules and Codes of Practice. In relation to 'reference to Mental Welfare Commission', for example, the Review Group noted:

'While there is currently no bar on the tribunal making a reference to the Mental Welfare Commission where it appears to the tribunal that the Commission's involvement might improve a service user's care or treatment, the Mental Health Tribunal for Scotland (Practice and Procedure) (No. 2) Rules 2005 make no mention of this option. We propose that specific mention is made in the Tribunal Rules to the Tribunal's right to make a reference to the Commission' (Scottish Government Review Group, 2009: p. 72).

The Review Group also recommended that there should be a review of the use of restraint and force; certificates under Part 16 ('medical treatment') should have an expiry date; the inclusion of learning (intellectual) disability in the Act should be reviewed; and issues relating to inspections should be re-examined, noting that 'recent research on service users' levels of satisfaction with mental health services directly correlates those levels with the physical state of hospital premises' (p. 75).

Summary

Overall, many of the recommendations of the McManus Review centred on more efficient, accountable implementation of existing legislative and regulatory provisions, especially as they relate to increasing awareness and effectiveness of advance statements; enhancing independent advocacy services; increasing awareness of, and participation in, the named person system; introducing regulations in relation to care plans (e.g. a template); encouraging patients to engage solicitors for hearings before a mental health review tribunal and improving sharing of information; introducing a code of conduct for tribunal members; reducing formality and legality at tribunal hearings, and improving facilities; enhancing training for participants at tribunal hearings, especially convenors; and considering further change in relation to the use of restraint and force, the status of learning (intellectual) disability within the Act, and monitoring standards.

Some of the Report's other recommendations appeared to require varying degrees of legislative change, including its recommendations to create a central register of advance statements; specific changes to the named person system; increased involvement of the patient's own general practitioner in applying for a compulsory treatment order; that a medical examination to extend a compulsory treatment order in a hospital run by an independent healthcare provider must be made by an approved medical practitioner independent of that service; revising and clarifying time frames for suspensions of hospital detention; and altering time frames for tribunal hearings, in order to facilitate better participation and hopefully reduce multiple hearings.

Mental Health (Scotland) Act 2015

Against the background of the McManus Review, the Mental Health (Scotland) Bill 2014 was introduced in June 2014, accompanied by

Explanatory Notes, a Policy Memorandum and a Delegated Powers Memorandum (Scottish Parliament, 2014*a,b,c*). The 2014 Explanatory Notes were clear about the purpose of the Bill:

> 'The Bill's overarching objective is to help people with a mental disorder to access effective treatment quickly and easily. The on-going monitoring to which the Mental Health (Care and Treatment) (Scotland) Act 2003 ('the 2003 Act') was subject to identified some aspects of the legislation which were not operating as efficiently and effectively as had been intended. To address these matters this Bill amends provisions within the 2003 Act and some related provisions in the Criminal Procedure (Scotland) Act 1995 ("the 1995 Act")' (Scottish Parliament, 2014*a*: para. 3).

The 2014 Bill led, in due course, to the Mental Health (Scotland) Act 2015, which received Royal Assent on 4 August 2015. The present discussion focuses on civil mental health legislation as it relates to adults with mental disorders, so the 2015 Act's amendments to the 2003 Act that relate to this area are of greatest interest. As the 2014 Policy Memorandum noted, 'in 2008, the Scottish Government [...] instituted a limited review of the civil provisions of the 2003 Act under the chairmanship of Professor Jim McManus and the Review Group reported back in March 2009' (Scottish Parliament, 2014*b*: para. 4). As a result, the recommendations of the McManus Review formed the basis for the new Act, which is considered next.

Objectives of the Mental Health (Scotland) Act 2015

Following the McManus Review, the Scottish Government noted that 'some recommendations would require primary legislation to amend the 2003 Act before they could be implemented. These recommendations related to advance statements, named persons, medical examinations, suspension of detention and multiple hearings at Mental Health Tribunal' (Scottish Parliament, 2014*b*: para. 5).

More broadly, the 2014 Policy Memorandum noted that the 'overarching approach of the 2003 Act is to ensure that the law and practice relating to mental health should be driven by a set of principles, particularly minimum interference in peoples' liberty and the maximum involvement of service users in any treatment' (Scottish Parliament, 2014*b*: para. 14). Consistent with this, and with the McManus Review, the primary objective of Part 1 of the 2014 Bill, which related to the 2003 Act, was:

> 'To improve the efficiency and effectiveness of the mental health system in Scotland by implementing the changes the Scottish Government said it would bring forward following on from the McManus Review; to provide a better system for the review of conditions of security to which patients are subject by adjusting the provisions which allow the Tribunal to consider, on application, whether a patient is being detained in conditions of excessive security, and make a number of technical and drafting amendments to improve the legislative framework' (para. 15).

Specific provisions of the Mental Health (Scotland) Act 2015

Sections 1, 2 and 3 of the 2015 Act concern the procedure for compulsory treatment. Section 1 provides that if a mental health tribunal is making a compulsory treatment order or interim compulsory treatment order, and the patient subject to the order has been detained in hospital under a short-term detention certificate or an extension certificate, then the 6-month period (for a compulsory treatment order) or 56 days (for an interim compulsory treatment order) must be reduced by the length of time the patient has been detained under section 47(4)(a) ('extension of detention pending application for compulsory treatment order') or section 68(2)(a) ('extension of short-term detention pending determination of application') of the 2003 Act. This measure aims 'to preserve the principle of least restriction' (Scottish Parliament, 2014b: para. 20).

Section 87 of the 2003 Act sets out the steps that responsible medical officers must take if they determined that a compulsory treatment order is to be extended without change: they must prepare a record setting out the reasons for the determination and whether the mental health officer agrees, disagrees or has not expressed a opinion (Scottish Parliament, 2015: para. 11).

Section 2 of the 2015 Act sets out new duties for mental health officers if a tribunal hearing is required (under section 101(2)(a) of the 2003 Act) to review the determination, i.e. if the determination states that there is a difference between the type of mental disorder that the patient has and that recorded in the original compulsory treatment order, or the mental health officer disagrees with the determination or has not expressed a opinion (Scottish Parliament, 2015: para. 13). This is an ostensibly reasonable measure, albeit one that increases administrative burden, with consequent opportunity costs.

Section 3 of the 2015 Act facilitates hospital transfers for patients subject to interim compulsory treatment orders (as well as compulsory treatment orders). Section 3 concerns section 113(5) of the 2003 Act, which governs the possible 72-hour detention of a patient who is generally non-compliant with a compulsory treatment order. Section 4 proposes that such a patient cannot also be subject to emergency detention in hospital. This is because 'a patient subject to detention under section 113(5) is already within a detention regime and the Scottish Government considers it is that regime which should govern any subsequent detention which follows immediately on that detention' (Scottish Parliament, 2014b: para. 31). Section 5 makes similar provision for a patient detained on a short-term detention order (section 44). Sections 4 and 5 also make various changes to notification procedures related to these processes.

Section 7 states that, if an emergency detention order is granted for a patient who is already on a compulsion order or interim compulsory treatment order, measures authorised by the latter two orders cease for the duration of the emergency detention order (with the exception of medical treatment in accordance with Part 16); this is consistent with the pre-existing position regarding compulsory treatment orders (section 43). Section 8 makes similar provision for when a short-term detention certificate is granted for such a patient. These measures will hopefully add clarity to these complex situations. Section 9 contains various measures regarding 'suspension of detention for certain purposes' generally aimed at increasing clarity and efficiency.

Section 10 concerns 'maximum suspension of particular measures'. It amends section 127 of the 2003 Act by providing that:

> 'the maximum period of suspension of detention for a [compulsory treatment order] may not exceed 200 days in a 12 month period; however, any period of suspension authorised by the [responsible medical officer] of 8 hours or less is not to be counted towards that total. For the purpose of calculation, any period of more than 8 hours and less than 24 hours is counted as one day towards the total period' (Scottish Parliament, 2015: para. 35).

Section 11 'allows emergency detention orders, short-term detention orders, interim compulsory treatment orders and compulsory treatment orders to authorise detention in a specified hospital unit [as opposed to 'hospital']. It also makes clear that a mental health officer's proposed care plan under section 62 of the 2003 Act may propose that a patient is detained in a specified hospital unit' (Scottish Parliament, 2015: para. 41). Similar amendments are made regarding transfer of prisoners (section 12) and transfer of certain patients within hospitals (section 13).

Sections 14 to 18 of the 2015 Act concern 'orders regarding level of security' in order 'to provide an effective right of appeal against a perceived level of excessive security for certain patients who are held out with the state hospital, to ensure as far as possible the principle of least restriction is upheld' (Scottish Parliament, 2014b: para. 58). Section 14, for example, amends sections 264 and 268 of the 2003 Act to introduce 'a new requirement for a report by a medical practitioner to accompany an application to the Tribunal under those sections for an order declaring that a patient is being detained in conditions of excessive security and requiring the health board to identify a hospital in which the patient could be detained in appropriate conditions. The report must state that, in the practitioner's opinion, the test set out in regulations is met in relation to the patient, and set out the reasons for that opinion' (Scottish Parliament, 2015: para. 50).

Section 16 removes references to 'qualifying' in respect of patients who may appeal under the section. Instead, any patient in a 'qualifying hospital' (defined under new section 271A) can appeal (Scottish Parliament, 2015: para. 55).

Section 19 creates a requirement that a mental health officer must notify the Mental Welfare Commission of the decision of the sheriff or justice of the peace when an application for a removal order is made under Part 19 of the 2003 Act. This is possibly a quite important provision, especially as 'the making of a removal order is a significant event as it can authorise detention for up to 7 days' and 'the absence of a duty to notify the Commission means that the Commission cannot consider whether to apply to make an application to the sheriff under section 295' (for 'recall or variation of removal order') (Scottish Parliament, 2014b: para. 70).

Section 20 of the 2015 Act clarifies that the time for which a nurse can detain a voluntary patient pending medical examination (section 299 of the 2003 Act) is 3 hours; this, too, appears reasonable and pragmatic, balancing the need to make careful assessments about clinical need with the right to liberty (although 3 hours is still a short period).

Section 21 modifies certain aspects of tribunal reviews for patients subject to compulsory treatment orders or compulsion and restriction orders. For example, 'Section 101 of the 2003 Act ensures that the Tribunal reviews a compulsory treatment order (CTO) at least once every 2 years. It does this by requiring a review to be carried out where, during the relevant 2-year period, the Tribunal has not been required to review the CTO by virtue of subsection (2)(a) and none of the following references or applications have been made to the Tribunal; namely, a reference under section 92 or 95 by a responsible medical officer or an application under section 99 or 100 by the patient or patient's named person' (Scottish Parliament, 2015: para. 67). Section 21 of the 2015 Act requires 'that an order has to be reviewed under section 101 if a reference or application under sections 92, 95, 99 or 100 has not been determined by the Tribunal, rather than the requirement being based upon when a reference or application has been made' (para. 69).

Section 22 'repeals section 251 and 253 [of the 2003 Act, concerning the patient's named person] so that the carer or relative does not become a named person by virtue of those sections if the patient does not nominate a named person. Therefore a patient aged 16 or over will only have a named person if they choose one' (Scottish Parliament, 2015: para. 72).

Under section 251 of the 2003 Act, an individual could be appointed as a named person without consenting to the role, although they could later decline to act. Section 23 of the 2015 Act 'makes provision for a person to be appointed as a named person by virtue of section 250 or 257, only if he or she has agreed to act as the person's named person and signed a docket to that effect' (Scottish Parliament, 2015: para. 73).

Section 24 of the 2015 Act 'repeals the Tribunal's power upon application to appoint a named person where no such person exists' (Scottish Parliament, 2014b: para. 90) as this was 'considered to breach the policy intention that a person should only have a named person if he or she wanted one and had appointed one as the need for trust between a person and his or her named person was considered an essential element of the role by virtually all respondents' (para. 91). Section 24 'makes provision for the Tribunal to remove an existing person if they are considered inappropriate to act as a named person and, if the individual appearing before the Tribunal is under 16, substitute another person to act as named person' (Scottish Parliament, 2015: para. 75). This would, however, leave certain patients without the benefits of a named person. Section 25 'makes provision about who will have the ability to act in relation to a patient, over the age of 16, who does not have a named person and who is incapable in relation to a decision about whether to make a decision to initiate an appeal or application' (para. 76).

Section 26 of the 2015 Act concerns advance statements and requires health boards to place a copy of any advance statement or document withdrawing a statement with the person's medical records and to send certain information to the Mental Welfare Commission. It also places a duty on the Commission to enter this information in a register to be maintained by the it and details who may inspect the register (Scottish Parliament, 2015: paras 80–82). This is consistent with the McManus Review, which recommended creating 'a central register of advance statements, with copies also retained in medical records' (Scottish Government Review Group, 2009: p. 9).

Also consistent with the McManus Review, section 28 of the 2015 Act requires 'assistance to be given to aid communication at examinations as well as to patients detained in hospital' (Scottish Parliament, 2014b: para. 99). More specifically, 'if the subject of a medical examination has difficulty in communicating or generally communicates in a language other than English, all reasonable steps must be taken to make arrangements to ensure [that they] can communicate during the examination. A written record must be made of the steps taken to facilitate this' (Scottish Parliament, 2015: para. 85).

Section 29 concerns 'conflicts of interest to be avoided' for medical examinations and section 30 adds any guardian or welfare attorney to the list of persons to be consulted in certain circumstances. Section 31 expands the pre-existing 'duty on health boards to provide services and accommodation for certain mothers with post-natal depression' (in section 24 of the 2003 Act) by also including mothers with mental disorders other than post-natal depression, and such interventions must 'be beneficial to the wellbeing of the child' (Scottish Parliament, 2015: para. 90). This is a progressive and sensible change.

The 2015 Act also presents provisions relating to 'cross-border transfers and absconding patients' (sections 32 and 33), 'arrangements for treatment of prisoners' (sections 34 and 35), 'provision of information by the Commission' (section 36), 'review of deaths of patients in hospital for treatment' (section 37), 'criminal cases' (Part 2) and 'victims' rights' (Part 3).

The challenges of reform

The process of reform of mental health legislation in Scotland is extremely interesting for several reasons. First, it demonstrates that significant reform, when it occurs, need not necessarily be root-and-branch reform, but can achieve significant and quite subtle change through amendments to existing measures. In relation to overarching principles, for example the McManus Review noted that:

'It is interesting to note that no-one raised any issue with the ten Millan principles [Box 5.1] throughout this process. Indeed, all during our consultation process, we heard nothing but praise for the principles, and it was clear that they are constantly in use for assessing whether the system is delivering what was intended. Several persons with whom we spoke suggested that the principles should be given more force in law. While it was accepted that this would pose great difficulties for the courts in interpretation, and thus for the operation of the system, it was agreed that there should be a clearer statement of the need for the principles to be observed in all matters relating to mental health, and not only in those areas governed by the Act' (Scottish Government Review Group, 2009: p. 5).

As a result, the magnitude and nature of the legislative reform process in Scotland is quite similar to the magnitude and nature of reforms introduced by the Mental Health Act 2007 in England and Wales, which amended the 1983 Act but did not replace it or even, arguably, fundamentally alter its nature. The current reform in Ireland is also a process of amendment rather than reinvention. All of these processes, in Scotland, England and Wales, and Ireland, however, contrast sharply with the current reform process in Northern Ireland, where an ambitious root-and-branch reform of a very fundamental nature is underway (see Chapter 3).

Second, the Scottish experience demonstrates that it is possible to achieve a significant degree of consensus during the process of reform not only in relation to fundamental principles (see above), but also in relation to other, more specific matters. As the McManus Review noted: 'there were no marked differences in opinions among those with different roles in the mental health system, and substantial agreement on many of the issues we raised' (Scottish Government Review Group, 2009: p. 6). As a result, the McManus Review significantly shaped the 2015 Act. While discussion and debate are a constant and, arguably, essential part of public discourse about mental health in virtually all jurisdictions, as evidenced in England and Wales in the report of the Richardson Committee (Department of Health, 1999), the Scottish experience demonstrates that is also possible to achieve a considerable degree of agreement on key issues, so as hopefully to optimise support for change and genuine reform on the ground.

Third, and possibly most important, the Scottish reform experience demonstrates that not all reform processes that seek to improve the functioning and effects of mental health legislation with a view to protecting rights require legislative change; much can be achieved through operating existing legislative provisions more effectively, comprehensively and transparently:

'Many of the changes we now recommend can be achieved without legislative action. Indeed, the Mental Health Tribunal for Scotland, which has cooperated fully with this review, is already undertaking organisational changes to address some of the issues we have raised. But some of our recommendations will require changes to the Act or the Rules. All recommendations are made in order to bolster delivery of the ten Millan principles' (Scottish Government Review Group, 2009: p. 7).

In these important respects, the process of legislative reform in Scotland is both instructive and interesting. Most especially, it underlines the importance of non-legislative factors in protecting and promoting the rights of people with mental illness. This fundamental issue is considered in greater depth in Chapters 6 and 7.

With respect to reforms that did require legislative change, the Mental Health (Scotland) Act 2015 introduces several of relevance to human rights and patient dignity, including clarity regarding the priority to be accorded to overlapping detention orders; various measures regarding suspension of detention (increasing efficiency and adding clarity to periods of suspension); clarifying rights of appeal against apparently excessive levels of security; requiring that a mental health officer must notify the Mental Welfare Commission when a decision regarding a removal order is made; clarifying the time for which a nurse can detain a voluntary patient pending medical examination (balancing the right to medical care with the right to liberty); various measures regarding the patient's named person; creating a central register of advance statements to be held by the Commission (although regulations regarding access will need to be implemented); increasing assistance to aid communication (e.g. for patients who communicate generally in a language other than English); and broadening the duty on health boards to provide services and accommodation for mothers not only with post-natal depression but also with other mental disorders.

These are generally positive and progressive changes that are consistent with international human rights standards (WHO, 2005), albeit that certain aspects of the Scottish legislation differ significantly from legislation in other jurisdictions: Irish mental health legislation, for example, has no equivalent of the 'named person' in Scottish legislation,[117] 'nearest relative' in England and Wales,[118] or 'nominated person' in Northern Ireland.[119]

There are, in addition, certain specific issues that still give cause for concern about the reform process in Scotland, including, not least, the 6-year lag between the McManus Review and the 2015 Act. Specific provisions of the 2015 Act are also cause for concern. For example, section 24 'makes provision for the Tribunal to remove an existing person if they are considered inappropriate to act as a named person and, if the individual appearing before the Tribunal is under 16, substitute another person to act as named person' (Scottish Parliament, 2015: para. 75). These matters require careful thought, especially in relation to respecting the views of older children in these areas.

Notwithstanding these issues, it still appears that the Scottish process of reform largely succeeds in striking delicate balances between legislative and non-legislative measures to promote rights and between the right to liberty and the right to access health services and treatment in a safe,

---

Box 5.4 'Seven themes for mental health' in the Mental Health Strategy for Scotland, 2012–2015.

1 Working more effectively with families and carers
2 Embedding more peer-to-peer work and support
3 Increasing the support for self-management and self-help approaches
4 Extending the anti-stigma agenda forward to include further work on discrimination
5 Focusing on the rights of those with mental illness
6 Developing the outcomes approach to include personal, social and clinical outcomes
7 Ensuring that we use new technology effectively as a mechanism for providing information and delivering evidence-based services

(Scottish Government, 2012)

---

accountable fashion. This emphasis on rights is consistent with the Mental Health Strategy for Scotland, 2012–2015 (Scottish Government, 2012), which outlined 'seven themes for mental health', including 'focusing on the rights of those with mental illness' (Box 5.4). On the basis of this chapter's consideration of the process of legal reform in Scotland, this clearly includes a right to access health services and treatment. The Revised Explanatory Notes accompanying the 2015 Bill as it evolved were explicit on this point, emphasising that 'the Bill's overarching objective is to help people with a mental disorder to access effective treatment quickly and easily' (Scottish Parliament, 2015: para. 4). This contrasts with the apparent legislative priorities in other jurisdictions, such as Ireland, which centre almost exclusively on involuntary detention and treatment (see Chapter 4).

This clear recognition of the centrality of mental health legislation in facilitating access to treatment in Scotland is greatly to be welcomed, not least because it supports the general idea of a legally definable right to access health services and treatment, as suggested in various declarations of human rights. The Universal Declaration of Human Rights (United Nations, 1948), for example, states that:

'Everyone has the right to a standard of living adequate for the health and well-being of himself and of his family, including food, clothing, housing and medical care and necessary social services, and the right to security in the event of unemployment, sickness, disability, widowhood, old age or other lack of livelihood in circumstances beyond his control' (Article 25(1)).

With regard to mental disorder in particular, the UN's Principles for the Protection of Persons with Mental Illness and the Improvement of Mental Health Care (United Nations, 1991) state that all people are entitled to receive the best mental healthcare available and to be treated with humanity and respect, and there shall be no discrimination on the

169

grounds of mental illness. In essence, persons with mental illness have the same rights to medical and social care as all other people. More recently, the CRPD (United Nations, 2006) was equally, if not more, emphatic on that point.

Against this background, it is interesting and progressive that the process of legislative review in Scotland articulates that the purpose of the 2015 Act is to secure timely access to mental health services. It is also notable that the issue of public safety was not accorded the degree of attention in the McManus Review (Scottish Government Review Group, 2009) that it received in the report of the Richardson Committee in England and Wales (Department of Health, 1999). In this respect, the Scottish reform process is similar to the Irish one, where the issue of public safety was virtually absent from the debate, possibly owing to the absence of any recent high-profile case of homicide involving a mentally ill individual in Ireland (Chapter 4).

Overall, however, one of the key messages articulated throughout the process of legislative reform in Scotland, which is transferable to other jurisdictions, is the importance of non-legislative factors in protecting and promoting the rights of the mentally ill. This fundamental issue is considered in greater detail in Chapters 6 and 7.

CHAPTER 6

Structural violence, power and mental illness

The preceding four chapters in this book have examined the extent to which mental health legislation in England and Wales (Chapter 2), Northern Ireland (Chapter 3), Ireland (Chapter 4) and Scotland (Chapter 5) protect and promote human rights, and how processes of reform in each jurisdiction shed light on different ways of using mental health legislation to advance the rights of people with mental illness.

This chapter returns more explicitly to broader themes explored in Chapter 1, which examined the relationship between human rights and mental illness. It considers the relevance of the European Convention on Human Rights (ECHR) (which has arguably produced the greatest shift in thinking in this area to date), as well as the UN Principles for the Protection of Persons with Mental Illness and the Improvement of Mental Health Care (United Nations, 1991) and Convention on the Rights of Persons with Disabilities (CRPD) (United Nations, 2006), especially in relation to economic and social rights, and avoidance of discrimination and stigma.

It is, in particular, the CRPD's expansive vision of rights that informs the approach of this chapter and the following one. Indeed, continued improvement of mental health legislation is clearly necessary to protect and promote certain rights of the mentally ill, and current legislation increasingly does so quite well in areas of traditional concern (i.e. involuntary detention and treatment), at least in certain jurisdictions (Kelly, 2011). As a result, the greatest progress is now likely to be made by focusing on mechanisms other than mental health legislation for protecting and promoting other rights that are often infringed among people with mental illness, such as economic and social rights, and assuring access to an adequate standard of care for voluntary and involuntary patients.

The CRPD is especially strong on this point, requiring signatory states 'to promote, protect and ensure the full and equal enjoyment of all human rights and fundamental freedoms by all persons with disabilities, and to promote respect for their inherent dignity' (Article 1). This requirement for strong, assertive action to promote rights (and not just avoid impinging them) permeates the entire CRPD, and provides patients, advocates

171

and carers with a fresh and solid basis for more assertive action for the protection of rights not only in the legal sphere, but also in the realms of social advocacy and political activism.

Against this background, this chapter examines the extent to which people with mental illness truly enjoy full exercise of various rights in broader society and reasons underpinning the apparent systematic neglect or violation of so many rights in this population. More specifically, the next section invokes the concept of 'structural violence' (Farmer, 2003) to describe the cumulative effects of adverse social, economic and political forces which, along with the stigma of mental illness, impair access to psychiatric and social services among people with mental illness, and amplify the effects of mental illness in the lives of sufferers and their families (Kelly, 2005). The example of schizophrenia is used to demonstrate the overarching social and economic factors that contribute to the exclusion of many people with mental illness from full participation in civic and social life, constraining them to live lives shaped by stigma, isolation, homelessness and denial of rights. The subsequent section (Power and mental illness) suggests reasons why, despite the relatively high prevalence of mental illness, the rights and legitimate needs of the mentally ill continue to be neglected, and persons with mental illness do not appear to wield sufficient political power to rectify this situation, even in countries with ostensibly democratic political systems. Finally, broad measures to improve this situation are suggested towards the end of this chapter and, more explicitly for clinicians, in Chapter 7.

Structural violence and mental illness

'Structural violence' comprises forces such as poverty, racism, socio-economic inequality and discrimination, which necessarily have an influence on people's health (Farmer, 1999). While the term has its origins in the Liberation theology of Latin America (Galtung, 1969), the concept has been more recently applied to medical and public health issues, including, for example, the spread of HIV/AIDS in Haiti (Farmer, 2003) and the epidemic of tuberculosis in prisons in the former USSR (Keshavjee & Becerra, 2000). In both cases, it is argued that the spread and population impact of these illnesses are related, at least in part, to the social, economic and political forces that shape both the landscape of risk for developing the illness and the context in which healthcare is provided. More specifically, Farmer (1997) identified several socially conditioned factors that increased rates of transmission of HIV/AIDS among women in Haiti. These include: socially determined patterns of gender inequality, reflected in male-dominated control of material resources such as land and property; traditional and non-traditional patterns of sexual union, which increase the chances that sexually transmitted pathogens will be shared among three or more persons; the high prevalence of sexually transmitted diseases and a lack of access to treatment facilities among the poor; the absence of public health interventions; and continued political violence, which undermines the stability of healthcare systems and hinders the development of preventive programmes. These powerful social, economic and political factors not only affect patterns of susceptibility and exposure to illness (Kreiger *et al*, 1993), but also limit the effectiveness of healthcare systems and reduce access to services, especially among the poor (Farmer, 2003).

The next section explores the relevance of structural violence in the context of mental illness, using schizophrenia as an example, acknowledging the clinical features and current understanding of the biological basis for the illness, but also examining the social and political factors relevant to its clinical features, and summarising the adverse social circumstances associated with schizophrenia, including social exclusion, homelessness and violations of human rights (Kelly, 2005). In large part, these phenomena are not integral elements of the illness itself, but are attributable to the ways in which schizophrenia is patterned, interpreted and treated by societies, resulting in denial of rights, denial of opportunity and broad-based social exclusion.

Clinical and biological dimensions of schizophrenia

Schizophrenia is a common, disabling mental illness with a morbid lifetime risk of about 1% (Jablensky, 1997; van Os & Kapur, 2009; Howes & Murray, 2014). It is estimated that there are 15 new cases of schizophrenia per 100 000 population per year in Western Europe – an incidence equal to that of type 1 diabetes (EURODIAB ACE Study Group, 2000). Schizophrenia is characterised by a range of symptoms related to thinking, emotion, behaviour and judgement, as outlined in the International Classification of Mental and Behavioural Disorders (ICD-10) (World Health Organization, 1992) and the Diagnostic and Statistical Manual of Mental Disorders (DSM-5) (American Psychiatric Association, 2013).

Schizophrenia has far-reaching effects on the lives of patients and their families. Life expectancy is considerably reduced in people with the illness compared with the general population (Brown, 1997): on average, men with schizophrenia die 15 years earlier, and women 12 years earlier, than the rest of the population, and this is not accounted for by unnatural deaths (Crump *et al*, 2013). Although most individuals with schizophrenia do survive until middle age, it has long been recognised that the illness is associated with greatly reduced social interaction (Leary *et al*, 1991; Armijo *et al*, 2013; Lavelle *et al*, 2014) and reduced rates of marriage and reproduction (Lane *et al*, 1995; Rocca *et al*, 2014).

In addition, because schizophrenia tends to occur in early adult life it can affect education and professional progression, and substantially reduces the likelihood of maintaining full employment (Harding *et al*, 1987; Schennach *et al*, 2012). One study of 295 people with chronic schizophrenia found that two-thirds of participants were unemployed; 13.6% were involved in full-time work/study; 9.8% were involved in part-time work/study; and 4.4% were engaged in work/study under 50% of the time (Üçok *et al*, 2012).

The issue of employment is a key one. As the Scottish Government points out in its Mental Health Strategy for Scotland, 2012–2015:

> 'We know that being in the right work is good for a person's health and improves their quality of life and wellbeing. This is also true for people with a mental or physical health condition. Remaining in, or returning to work quickly, aids recovery and more people gain health benefits from being in work than are negatively affected by it [Waddell *et al*, 2008]. However, people with mental illness are less likely to be engaged in work than the general population or those with other health conditions with one review identifying that 79% of people with serious, long-term mental health problems are not in employment [Riddell *et al*, 2005]. Improving and increasing access to employment for those with mental illness is challenging, but necessary and achievable.
>
> [...]
>
> There is an evidence base that shows that, with the right kind of help, people with serious mental health problems can successfully get and keep work. This applies irrespective of individual characteristics such as clinical history or previous employment. A Cochrane systematic review found that those with severe mental illness who received supported employment were two or three times more likely to be in competitive employment at 12 months [Crowther *et al*, 2001]' (Scottish Government, 2012: pp. 44–45).

At societal level, the economic costs of schizophrenia are substantial. Direct costs include the provision of healthcare, social services and accommodation. Indirect costs reflect the impact of patients' reduced earning power on the national economy. In 2000, the annual cost of schizophrenia to the USA was estimated at US$40 billion (£23.8 billion) – three times as much as the US space programme (Torrey, 2001). In 2002, the overall cost of schizophrenia in the USA was estimated at US$62.7 billion (£37.4 billion), comprising US$22.7 billion (£13.5 billion) in direct healthcare costs (broken down into US$7.0 billion (£4.2 billion) in out-patient costs, US$5.0 billion (£3.0 billion) for medication, US$2.8 billion (£1.7 billion) for in-patient care and $8.0 billion (£4.8 billion) for long-term care); US$7.6 billion (£4.5 billion) in direct non-healthcare costs (e.g. living-cost offsets); and US$32.4 billion (£19.3 billion) in indirect costs (Wu *et al*, 2005).

In England, the estimated total societal cost of schizophrenia in 2004–2005 was £6.7 billion, comprising £2 billion in direct costs of treatment and care and nearly £4.7 billion in indirect costs (Mangalore & Knapp, 2007). In Ireland, the cost of mental health problems in 2006 exceeded €3 billion (£2.4 billion), or 2% of gross national product (O'Shea & Kennelly, 2008). This figure includes over €1 billion (£0.8 billion) for health and social care, and over €2 billion (£1.6 billion) in lost economic output, comprising €1044.6 million (£835.0 million) due to non- and under-employment, €207 million (£165.5 million) due to premature mortality and €751.1 million (£600.4 million) due to unpaid work. The cost of schizophrenia alone in Ireland was €460.6 million (£368.2 million) in 2006 (Behan *et al*, 2008).

The true cost of schizophrenia, however, can only be described in human terms – in a reduced quality of life, limited opportunity for personal development, ongoing morbidity and increased mortality, as well as the stress and suffering of family members and carers.

The biological underpinnings of schizophrenia are not fully known. It is likely that the illness results from a complex interaction of inherited genetic predispositions, disruptions to nervous system development before birth, and further causative and contributory factors acting in adolescence and early adulthood. One particularly convincing model implicates: developmental alterations as a result of variant genes; early insults to the brain, and childhood adversity (which may sensitise the dopamine system); social adversity (which may bias cognitive schema used to interpret experiences); subsequent stress, which may result in dysregulated dopamine release, leading to misattribution of salience to stimuli, which are, in turn, misinterpreted by biased cognitive processes; and further stress resulting from hallucination and paranoia, eventually resulting in hardwiring of psychotic beliefs by repeated dopamine dysregulation (Howes & Murray, 2014).

Despite clear evidence of such a biological basis for the illness, however, there is also considerable evidence that the individual's social and personal environment have a substantial impact on many aspects of schizophrenia. In particular, there is evidence that: socioeconomic group has a significant effect on the clinical features of the illness, such as duration of untreated illness and age at presentation to health services; schizophrenia is associated with a particularly high rate of homelessness; migration is associated with increased rates of schizophrenia; and schizophrenia, along with other mental illnesses, is associated with widespread and systematic denial of human rights, including increased risk of imprisonment. These matters are considered next, each in turn.

Schizophrenia and socioeconomic group

In 1939, Faris & Dunham (1939) found that schizophrenia was more common in areas of cultural and economic impoverishment, suggesting that the illness occurs more commonly in lower socioeconomic groups. Subsequent research, however, does not provide consistent support for this link: although Croudace et al (2000) found a similarly increased risk of schizophrenia in lower socioeconomic groups, this was not replicated by either a large birth cohort study from Finland (Mäkikyrö et al, 1997) or a case–control study from Ireland (Mulvany et al, 2001).

An alternative explanation for the link observed by Faris & Dunham is that, rather than schizophrenia being a consequence of belonging to a lower socioeconomic group, belonging to a lower socioeconomic group may be a consequence of schizophrenia. This model was soon supported by several studies showing that 'downward social drift' may be the result of ongoing symptoms of schizophrenia or repeated hospital admissions, leading to impaired ability to hold down a job and to sustain rented accommodation (Eaton, 1980).

In addition to schizophrenia affecting socioeconomic group, it now appears that socioeconomic group may have significant effects on other clinical features of the illness. For example, individuals from lower socioeconomic groups tend to present with schizophrenia at an earlier age than those from higher socioeconomic groups (Mulvany *et al*, 2001); this is a particularly significant association because early age at first presentation is generally associated with more severe forms of the illness (Bellino *et al*, 2004). There is also long-standing evidence that individuals from lower socioeconomic groups tend to have a longer duration of untreated psychosis before first presentation to healthcare services (Clarke *et al*, 1999) and, again, long duration of untreated illness is, for the most part, associated with more severe illness and poor treatment outcomes (Addington *et al*, 2004; Kline & Schiffman, 2014; Penttilä *et al*, 2014).

Taken together, these findings suggest that individuals from lower socioeconomic groups have an earlier onset of schizophrenia and/or develop a more severe form of the illness. The relatively late presentation to healthcare services may also be attributable to increased tolerance towards symptoms in lower socioeconomic groups, differential attendance at primary care centres, or reduced access to secondary health services.

Schizophrenia and homelessness

Multiple studies have demonstrated that homeless populations have increased rates of mental illness compared with the general population (George *et al*, 1991; Holohan, 2000; O'Carroll & O'Reilly, 2008). One study by Teesson *et al* (2004) found that the 1-year prevalence of schizophrenia in the homeless population in Australia was 23% among men and 46% among women. Overall, it appears likely that the prevalence of schizophrenia among homeless persons is around 11% (range 4–16%) (Auquier *et al*, 2013), which is considerably higher than the (approximately) 1% life-time prevalence of schizophrenia in the general population (Jablensky, 1997; van Os & Kapur, 2009; Howes & Murray, 2014). The management of schizophrenia in homeless people is particularly challenging because they are often the most difficult to engage with treatment and are especially vulnerable owing to their homelessness (Auquier *et al*, 2013).

Homelessness is, however, by no means the invariable accompaniment of schizophrenia (Hankonen *et al*, 1999). Rates of mental illness in the homeless population vary considerably between countries: high-income welfare states, in particular, have relatively low rates of homelessness among the mentally ill (Melle *et al*, 2000). Moreover, homelessness is not randomly distributed among people with mental illness. One study in the USA found that homelessness was associated with greater severity of symptoms, younger age at first hospital admission and the presence of substance misuse (Opler *et al*, 2001).

The association between homelessness and substance misuse is now supported by multiple studies (Dixon, 1999; D'Amore *et al*, 2001; O'Carroll & O'Reilly, 2008). This association has implications for both the assessment of healthcare needs and the delivery of services, as substance misuse is significantly associated with aggression and violence in first-episode psychosis (Foley *et al*, 2005); and among individuals with schizophrenia, those who misuse drugs are more likely to engage in aggressive or violent acts than are those who do not (Steadman *et al*, 1998; Fleischman *et al*, 2014).

A comorbid diagnosis of substance misuse also increases the likelihood that an individual with schizophrenia will be the victim of crime (Hiday *et al*, 1999). The problems presented by the combination of schizophrenia and substance misuse is an example of 'syndemics', the synergistic interaction of two coexistent diseases and the resultant excess burden of disease (Singer & Clair, 2003). This is further compounded by the fact that homeless individuals also tend to have an excess of physical health problems (Martens, 2001; O'Carroll & O'Reilly, 2008).

There is intriguing and disturbing evidence to suggest that homelessness among the mentally ill constitutes a somewhat different phenomenon than homelessness among the population without mental illness. Susser *et al* (1991) found that homelessness among the mentally ill in the USA was not associated with many of the risk factors for homelessness in the general population, including male gender, Black race and alcohol misuse. In addition, individuals with severe mental illness such as schizophrenia may encounter particular problems accessing community care services following discharge from hospital (Melzer *et al*, 1991) and additional difficulties adapting to housing following prolonged periods of homelessness. All of these problems substantially complicate the process of reintegration into society (Yanos *et al*, 2004).

Consequently, interventions aimed at addressing homelessness among individuals with severe mental illness may need to address a range of needs that differ, at least in some respects, from the needs of homeless individuals without mental illness. Indeed, Silva *et al* (2013) suggest that, despite the good intentions of public health workers, some policies and practices inadvertently further disadvantage already marginalised populations, compounding their problems. They suggest that ways to overcome this include public consultation with marginalised persons, teaching of ethics and philosophy of science in public health training, and increased health equity impact assessments. Their position is supported by disturbing evidence that during Ireland's economic boom in the early 2000s, the proportion of homeless people with mental illness in Dublin actually increased rather than decreased (O'Carroll & O'Reilly, 2008), emphasising the need for specially designed policies to address the needs of this particularly disadvantaged, vulnerable and neglected group.

Such specially designed policies would also be highly consistent with Article 19 of the CRPD, which requires signatory states to:

'recognize the equal right of all persons with disabilities to live in the community, with choices equal to others, and [to] take effective and appropriate measures to facilitate full enjoyment by persons with disabilities of this right and their full inclusion and participation in the community, including by ensuring that:

(a) Persons with disabilities have the opportunity to choose their place of residence and where and with whom they live on an equal basis with others and are not obliged to live in a particular living arrangement;
(b) Persons with disabilities have access to a range of in-home, residential and other community support services, including personal assistance necessary to support living and inclusion in the community, and to prevent isolation or segregation from the community;
(c) Community services and facilities for the general population are available on an equal basis to persons with disabilities and are responsive to their needs'.

Schizophrenia and migration

As mentioned earlier, in his studies of HIV/AIDS in Haiti, Farmer (1997, 2003) identified several social, economic and political factors that structure the overall risk for these illnesses. These factors include gender inequalities, patterns of sexual interaction, prevailing economic conditions, patterns of social change and ongoing political violence. There is a remarkable paucity of robust studies that examine the relevance of similar sociopolitical factors in relation to schizophrenia. The one exception is migration, for which there is a significant literature (Bhugra & Jones, 2001; Cantor-Graae & Selten, 2005; Howes & Murray, 2014).

Increasing rates of transnational migration have been one of the defining features of recent decades and there is consistent evidence that migration has significant effects on both physical and mental health (Gavin *et al*, 2001; Thomas & Gideon, 2013). Egyptian and Asian immigrants into the UK, for example, have increased rates of bulimia and anorexia nervosa (Bhugra & Jones, 2001), and many migrant groups show high levels of depression, suicidal thoughts and self-harm (Nazroo, 1997; Al-Maskari *et al*, 2011). Asylum seekers present particular challenges to mental health services as they come from a wide variety of cultural backgrounds and have sharply diminished social support. Many have experienced human rights abuse, torture or displacement in their homeland and, on arrival in the host country, may face confinement in detention centres, enforced dispersal and ongoing discrimination (Silove *et al*, 2000). The rate of post-traumatic stress among refugees is ten times that in the general population (Lavik *et al*, 1996; Crumlish & O'Rourke, 2010).

Schizophrenia is also more common among migrants, with research work in the 1990s demonstrating a fourfold increase in risk among certain groups of migrants to The Netherlands compared with the native population (Selten *et al*, 1997) and a sixfold increase among African–Caribbeans living in the UK (Harrison, 1990). Overall, the totality of studies to date indicates that the relative risk of schizophrenia is 2.7 in first-generation migrants and

4.5 in the second generation, with an overall relative risk of 2.9. This risk is greater among migrants from low- and middle-income ('developing') as opposed to high-income ('developed') countries (relative risk: 3.3) (Cantor-Graae & Selten, 2005).

This increased rate of schizophrenia is difficult to explain because the incidence of schizophrenia is not increased in migrants' countries of origin (Hickling & Rodgers-Johnson, 1995) and migrants do not appear to have increased exposure to known biological risk factors for the illness, such as obstetric complications (Hutchinson *et al*, 1997). It is notable, however, that the increase in risk of schizophrenia among migrants shows a powerful inverse relation to the size of the migrant group in the host country: the smaller the migrant group, the larger the increase in risk of schizophrenia (Boydell *et al*, 2001). This supports the idea that the migrant effect on risk of schizophrenia may be attributable to an altered stress response, possibly associated with being part of a minority group and exposed to discrimination (Howes & Murray, 2014). At the present level of biological understanding of schizophrenia, this is a finding that lends itself more readily to psychosocial explanations than to biological ones, although it should be noted that the aetiological relevance of socio-environmental factors remains extremely difficult to explore, not least because relationships may be bidirectional (e.g. social isolation may be a risk factor for illness, but may also be a result of illness or premorbid personality). Nonetheless, the concept of 'social capital' has been evoked to explain the relationship between risk of psychosis and size of migrant group.

The concept of social capital was independently invented at least six times throughout the 20th century alone (Putnam, 2000; Field, 2003). In essence, 'social capital' comprises the informal networks and norms that enable collective action and hold communities and societies together. It is fundamentally rooted in two central elements: the existence of community networks that are based on trust and the use of these networks to enable community action.

There is a significant accumulation of research evidence demonstrating that high social capital is associated with good mental health. In the early 2000s, Weitzman & Kawachi (2000) reported that students from US college campuses with higher-than-average social capital (measured as average time spent volunteering in the previous 30 days, aggregated to campus level) had a 26% lower individual risk for binge drinking than their peers at colleges with lower social capital. McCulloch (2001) studied how individuals' perceptions of social capital were related to health outcomes, and found that people in the lowest categories of social capital had increased psychiatric morbidity. These data suggest that social capital at group level (or perceived social capital at individual level) may have a beneficial effect on mental health. In addition, across Europe there is an inverse relationship between social trust and national suicide rates (i.e. the higher the social trust, the lower the suicide rate), after controlling for gender, age, marriage rates, standardised income and reported sadness (Kelly *et al*, 2009).

In relation to schizophrenia, Boydell *et al* (2002) used aggregated responses from a community questionnaire as an indicator of social cohesion and found an inverse association between perceived social cohesion and the incidence of psychosis in south London. This is consistent with the idea that the increased risk of psychosis in migrants may be related, at least in part, to reduced social capital in smaller migrant groups (Boydell *et al*, 2001). Moreover, social capital may be related not only to the incidence of mental illness, but also to ways in which individuals with mental illness are treated: Rosenheck *et al* (2001), for example, found that areas with high social capital offered better housing to homeless mentally ill people. Social factors may also be relevant to outcome: the International Pilot Study of Schizophrenia conducted by the World Health Organization (WHO) (1973) indicated that the core symptoms of schizophrenia were remarkably consistent across all of the countries involved in the study, but there were considerable variations in outcome, with low- and middle-income countries showing better outcomes than high-income ones. Although largely unexplained, this observation may be related, at least in part, to higher levels of social integration in certain low- and middle-income countries.

The link between social factors and schizophrenia may also be related, at least in part, to the observed link between urbanicity and increased risk of the illness, as evidenced by higher rates of schizophrenia and psychosis-like phenomena in individuals born, brought up or living in urban areas (Pedersen & Mortensen, 2001; Sundquist *et al*, 2004; Kelly *et al*, 2010). Urbanicity, which appears to have a synergistic relationship with family risk of psychosis (van Os *et al*, 2003), may be a proxy for a number of different biological or psychosocial factors, including social isolation and social inequality (van Os *et al*, 2000). These factors may be particularly relevant to the increased risk of psychosis experienced by smaller migrant groups living in urban areas, although Sundquist *et al* (2004) found that urbanicity at birth retained a significant association with schizophrenia even after controlling for migrant status (Kelly *et al*, 2010).

Overall, the link between migration and schizophrenia is strong, incompletely explained and provides further evidence of the social construction of at least some of the risk for schizophrenia and its resultant disability.

Schizophrenia and imprisonment

Forensic psychiatry is a branch of psychiatry concerned with the recognition and treatment of mental illness in the context of offending behaviour, often in the setting of prisons. Individuals with mental illness are grossly overrepresented in prison populations (Fazel & Danesh, 2002). One study of 109 samples totalling 33 588 prisoners across 24 countries showed that 3.6% of male prisoners and 3.9% of female prisoners had psychosis, including schizophrenia (Fazel & Seewald, 2012). In addition, 10.2% of male prisoners and 14.1% of female prisoners had major depression, with rates of depression among prisoners rising in the USA over time. Among young offenders (aged 16 to 20 years), 23% were at ultra-high risk of psychosis (Flynn et al, 2012).

A number of possible explanations for this phenomenon have been presented. In the first instance, there is evidence that individuals with serious mental illness are more likely to engage in certain offences than individuals without mental illness (Hodgins, 1992; Hodgins et al, 2014), even though, when considered at societal level, the proportion of violence attributable to schizophrenia is relatively small (Walsh et al, 2001).

Other factors also act to increase rates of imprisonment among the mentally ill, and are likely of greater magnitude. For example, people with mental illness are more likely than those without to be arrested in similar circumstances, and remand is more likely even when lesser offending is associated with mental illness (Taylor & Gunn, 1984; Teplin, 1984; Huxter, 2013). Another explanation relates to deinstitutionalisation (closure of long-stay psychiatric hospitals) and an inverse relationship between accommodation in psychiatric hospitals and imprisonment rates (Torrey, 1995; Markowitz, 2006; Kelly, 2007c). It is also noteworthy that rates of arrest are higher among individuals with schizophrenia who misuse substances compared with those who do not (Morgan et al, 2013).

Sixteen years ago, Gunn (2000) argued that the trend towards committal to prison rather than admission to hospital in this population was most likely related to administrative and social factors, including the enduring stigma of mental illness, economic considerations on the part of policy makers and broader changes in sociopolitical attitudes.

More recently, Torrey (2013), in an especially vivid and compelling examination of experiences of the mentally ill in the USA, argued that changes in mental health services there, including the closure of psychiatric institutions, resulted not in better care located in communities, but in neglect, underfunded treatment programmes and higher rates of community violence. At least one-third of the homeless are seriously mentally ill, he argued, and prisons are now grossly overcrowded, chiefly because people with serious mental illness constitute some 20% of prisoners.

In summary, the accumulated evidence regarding mental illness and imprisonment now clearly demonstrates extraordinarily high rates of mental illness among prisoners, which is most likely attributable, at least in part, to prevailing social and political factors, rather than factors related to the epidemiology or clinical features of the illnesses themselves. Interestingly, from a historical perspective, there is substantial evidence that society has always tended to place individuals with mental illness in some form of detention, ranging from the small, private asylums of the 18th century to the large-scale, public 'mental institutions' of the 19th and 20th centuries (Shorter, 1997), although this appears to have worsened, especially in relation to prisons, in recent decades (Torrey, 2013).

Rather than reflecting an absolute increase in overall rates of detention, however, recent trends probably demonstrate a shift in relation to the place of detention, from psychiatric hospitals to prisons (Kelly, 2007c). This development raises many specific concerns, including denial of liberty in circumstances where a person without mental illness would not be denied their liberty, potential violation of the right to treatment in prison settings, and the persistence of alarmingly high rates of self-harm and suicide in custody (Shaw *et al*, 2004; Duthé *et al*, 2013; Hawton *et al*, 2014).

The effects of structural violence

Overall, then, despite clear evidence of a substantial biological basis to schizophrenia (van Os & Kapur, 2009; Howes & Murray, 2014), there is compelling evidence that social, economic and political factors play a large role in shaping the genesis, presentation, features, management and outcome of the illness. The adverse effects of these social, economic and political factors and practices, along with the enduring stigma of mental illness (Byrne, 1999, 2000; Barczyk, 2015), constitute a form of structural violence that acts to impair access to psychiatric care and social services, and amplifies the effects of schizophrenia in the lives of sufferers, their families and carers. As a result of these overarching social and economic circumstances, individuals with schizophrenia are often systematically excluded from full participation in civic and social life, and constrained to live lives that are shaped, in large part, by stigma, isolation, homelessness and denial of basic rights.

The concept of structural violence provides an especially useful framework within which to examine the relationships between schizophrenia and these various social, economic and political factors. Structural violence represents a broader concept than the more traditional idea of social exclusion, which may, of course, be a result of structural violence and also relate to risk of illness. Structural violence is explicitly concerned with the broader social, economic and political forces that shape both the landscape of risk for illness and the context in which illnesses develop and are treated (Farmer, 1999). The concept of structural violence also focuses attention on the effects of societal factors in relation to such illness and helps identify those aspects of aetiology that are best addressed at societal level, by acknowledging the influence of broader sociopolitical factors on health and healthcare systems (Kelly, 2005, 2012).

The relative importance of various factors that contribute to structural violence may vary between illnesses and between individuals. Farmer (2003) is critical of overly reductionist analyses of the relationship between structural violence and human suffering, and demonstrates that explanations based solely on gender, ethnicity or cultural differences fail adequately to explain the phenomena associated with structural violence. In the context of schizophrenia, evidence to support the relevance of structural violence can be drawn from the literature on socioeconomic groupings, homelessness, migration and forensic psychiatry, suggesting that each of these components plays a role in structural violence in this population. This list, however, is unlikely to be exhaustive. Moreover, Sen (2003) argues that the best way to approach the study of structural violence is through 'real-life' examples that examine the experiences of affected individuals. Such an approach is likely to inform future studies of the 'lived experience' of structural violence in the context of schizophrenia and is also likely to assist in developing a more fine-grained understanding of structural violence in this group.

Other areas for future study include the possible confounding effects of cultural relativism in the medical–anthropological approach to structural violence (Hatch, 1983) and further consideration of the ways in which structural violence can be integrated with existing biological and psycho-social understandings of illnesses such as schizophrenia. There is a particular need for further research into the relationships between genetic risk and socio-environmental factors in schizophrenia, especially in light of long-standing evidence of significant gene–environment interactions in a range of psychiatric disorders, including, for example, compelling evidence that specific genetic factors moderate the effect of stressful life events in producing symptoms of depression (Caspi *et al*, 2003). Similar studies may now be possible in relation to schizophrenia, especially given recent advances in genetic knowledge about the illness (Schizophrenia Working Group of the Psychiatric Genomics Consortium, 2014), and would help integrate apparent social and psychological risk factors with genetic understandings.

It is interesting to note that factors constituting structural violence against people with mental illness (i.e. socioeconomic factors and non-clinical determinants of homelessness, migration and imprisonment) are not substantively related to matters explicitly addressed in mental health legislation or any of the legislative issues discussed in Chapters 2, 3, 4 and 5 of this book. This is because civil mental health legislation in the jurisdictions examined is chiefly concerned with involuntary admission and treatment, i.e. protection of the right to liberty rather than any other rights. This contrasts with the broader conceptualisation of rights reflected in the CRPD and by the WHO (2005). While it is notable that legislation in England, Wales and Ireland (Kelly, 2011), as well as Northern Ireland (Chapter 3) and Scotland (Chapter 5), is now largely compliant with WHO standards in these areas of traditional concern in mental health (i.e. involuntary admission and treatment), it still does not present the broad assurances of rights, including economic and social rights, as suggested by the WHO (2005) and as suggested by the concept of structural violence.

An approach to policy and services, and indeed legislation, informed by an awareness of structural violence offers the tools and opportunities to remedy these deficits through deeper and broader understanding of the factors contributing to systematic violation of the rights and dignity of people with mental illness. Attempts to address the needs of homeless mentally ill people provide a good example of the opportunities and challenges involved. In this context, an approach informed by structural

183

violence focuses on interventions developed with an awareness of broader administrative, social and political factors contributing to the problem. These factors include, for example, systematic discrimination and difficulties experienced by the mentally ill in the contexts of employment (Harding *et al*, 1987; Schennach, *et al*, 2012) and accommodation (Yanos *et al*, 2004; Auquier *et al*, 2013), and a failure to structure medical and social services in such a way as to facilitate access by people with mental illness (Melzer *et al*, 1991; Whiteford *et al*, 2014).

Against this background, Min *et al* (2004) attempted to improve use of medical and social services through broad-based 'case management services' for the homeless mentally ill and found that, above all else, use of vocational and psychosocial rehabilitation services (rather than more traditional medical interventions) was associated with reduced rates of homelessness. In a similar vein, Pollio *et al* (2003) demonstrated that helping individuals with mental illness to access cross-sector services optimises outcomes in a range of domains, including physical health, mental health and accommodation – all of which may be impaired in schizophrenia.

Whiteford *et al* (2014), in an especially compelling study of system-level, intersectoral links between the mental health and non-clinical support sectors, identified multiple, non-core clinical areas for potential improvement, including better inter-agency coordination; optimising attitudes, knowledge and skills mixes; service co-location; blended-funding models; and ensuring that integration strategies are implemented as planned. As with the studies by Min *et al* (2004) and Pollio *et al* (2003), the work of Whiteford *et al* (2014) addressed factors that relate to the administrative and social contexts in which services are provided to people with mental illness (e.g. structure of services, access protocols, availability of resources), rather than biologically based innovations or changes in core clinical aspects of treatment.

At a broader, sociopolitical level, the predicament of the homeless mentally ill may further benefit from a more assertive rights-based approach on the part of patients, carers, advocates, healthcare professionals and legislators. As discussed in Chapter 1, the human rights of people with mental illness were clearly outlined in 1991 in the UN's Principles for the Protection of Persons with Mental Illness and the Improvement of Mental Health Care (United Nations, 1991) (Box 1.1) and in the CRPD, although, as with most statements of rights, these principles do not have the status of 'hard law', so there is no absolute obligation to use them to define a minimum standard of care (Harding, 2000; United Nations, 2006). Nonetheless, they can usefully inform developments in policy and legislation in individual countries (Kelly, 2001) and are compelling tools with which to shape mental health policy and practice in both legislative and extra-legislative spheres (WHO, 2013). In this way, these principles provide a powerful language and set of concepts with which to challenge the underlying assumptions of discriminatory care paradigms and the structural violence that perpetuates homelessness among people with mental illness.

In the first instance, however, there is a strong need to recognise and further explore the role of socio-environmental and sociopolitical factors in the development and outcome of schizophrenia and other mental illnesses. Such an approach needs to be underpinned by enhanced aetiological models that elucidate the interactions between genetic risk and social environment and can better inform biopsychosocial approaches to management (Gabbard & Kay, 2001; WHO, 2001). The greatest challenge in relating structural violence to mental illness is probably the conceptual one: acknowledging that social, economic and political structures have a substantial impact on the development and outcome of mental illnesses such as schizophrenia, and recognising that these phenomena constitute a form of systematic and unrelenting violence against the mentally ill. The lessons of history are not promising (Shorter, 1997), but the constant search for ways to improve the lives of society's disadvantaged is a fundamental characteristic of civilisation – and the process can usefully start by recognising and remedying the adverse effects of society itself.

Another useful step is to develop an understanding of why, despite the numbers affected by mental illness, their human rights and legitimate needs continue to be neglected, structural violence persists and they do not appear to wield proportionate political power sufficient to rectify this situation, even in countries with ostensibly democratic political systems. This issue is considered next, along with suggestions about how to improve the situation. Suggestions for measures to improve human rights and promote social justice in clinical practice, designed more explicitly for clinicians, are presented in Chapter 7.

Power and mental illness

Up to one in four individuals meet the diagnostic criteria for an anxiety, mood, impulse control and/or substance use disorder in any given year (Kessler et al, 2005). More severe mental illness is relatively less common, but by no means uncommon: the approximate lifetime prevalence of bipolar affective disorder is between 1 and 2% (Bebbington & Ramana, 1995; Merikangas et al, 2007) and that of schizophrenia is 1% (Jablensky, 1997; van Os & Kapur, 2009; Howes & Murray, 2014). Despite this prevalence, mental health services remain poorly funded (Carlisle, 2003; Torrey, 2013), mental illness remains poorly understood (Byrne, 2000; Arboleda-Flórez, 2003; Barczyk, 2015) and the mentally ill, especially those with severe, recurring disorders, are constrained to live lives that are shaped, in large part, by social isolation, reduced employment prospects, ongoing stigma and the denial of basic rights (Kelly, 2005, 2007c). Even mental health legislation, developed and implemented in countries that are ostensibly democratic, such as England, Wales (Chapter 2), Northern

Ireland (Chapter 3), Ireland (Chapter 4) and Scotland (Chapter 5), fails to address key deficits relating to human rights (Kelly, 2011).

This combination of circumstances raises fundamental questions in relation to power and freedom as experienced by individuals with mental illness: if so many people are affected by mental illness, why do such social discrimination, denial of rights and service deficiencies persist? If so many are affected, why is mental illness consistently associated with such erosion of power, freedom and rights, and exclusion from full participation in civic and social life? Why do the mentally ill appear not to wield the political power to remedy this situation that their numbers suggest they should command?

In the past, discussions of freedom and power in relation to mental illness have tended to focus largely on the role of mental health professionals in allegedly denying certain individuals the right to liberty by confining them in psychiatric institutions and administering psychiatric treatments against their will (Szasz, 2002). Certainly, involuntary admission to public hospitals, private asylums and various psychiatric facilities has been a consistent and often concerning feature in the history of psychiatry (Shorter, 1997). In addition, although there is clear evidence that involuntary admission is associated with clinical factors such as severe symptoms (Figuerdo et al, 2000; Hustoft et al, 2013) and reduced insight (Kelly et al, 2004), there is also evidence that it is associated with factors that are less related to the core illness, such as aggression (Foley et al, 2005; Hustoft et al, 2013), contact with police, not living in one's own house or flat, being unmarried, having a lower level of education, being on social benefits and having had less contact with psychiatric services before admission (Hustoft et al, 2013).

Notwithstanding the importance and complexity of these apparent determinants of involuntary admission status, this section of the book is not primarily concerned with power, freedom and rights as they relate to involuntary detention of the mentally ill; these were explored in some detail in Chapters 2, 3, 4 and 5, focusing on mental health legislation in the relevant jurisdictions. Instead, this chapter and the final chapter of this book build further on the idea of broader structural violence against people with mental illness (see above), arguing that commentaries that focus exclusively on legislation relating to involuntary admission fail to acknowledge the larger, subtler and more powerful ways in which the freedom and power of the mentally ill are defined and undermined by a range of other factors, some but not all of which are illness related (Kelly, 2006a). These factors include the structure of power in contemporary societies, the ways in which societies interpret and treat mental illness and, to a much lesser extent, the effects of mental illness itself.

The sociological underpinnings of this situation can be usefully examined through the theory of power outlined by Lukes (2005) and the theory of interest groups outlined by Olson (1965, 1982). The next section explores how both theories shed light on the ways in which a society's responses to mental illness affect the power, freedom and rights of the mentally ill and perpetuate a 'power gap' that limits the opportunities for the mentally ill to participate fully in shaping the societies in which they live. It then outlines possible ways to address this power gap, including approaches based on explicitly rights-based perspectives, approaches based on enhancing direct political participation, and other approaches, including increasing democratic accountability, further developing mental health legislation and adapting the concept of 'soft power' to strengthen forums for the identification and articulation of the concerns of people with mental illness.

Three dimensions of power

Lukes (2005) describes a three-dimensional view of power. The first dimension concerns observable decision-making behaviour in societies, especially when this involves deciding between contested policy options, i.e. how decisions are taken and conflicts resolved (Dahl, 1961). The second dimension concerns the determination of which issues or options are presented to decision makers, i.e. how it is decided which issues are included on the decision-making agenda and which issues are not (Bachrach & Baratz, 1970). This dimension also encompasses the determination of the range of policy options that are considered as possible responses to issues on the political agenda. The third dimension concerns the forces that determine what needs people recognise themselves as having, i.e. how they decide what their own needs are (Lukes, 2005). This third dimension, then, concerns forces that affect individual's perception, cognition and self-view in such a way as to: (a) shape the needs they perceive themselves as having; (b) determine the demands and requests they make of themselves, others and society; and (c) determine, at least in part, which issues may start to reach the political agenda. For individuals with mental illness, the experiences of all three dimensions of power may be affected not only by mental illness itself, but also (arguably more powerfully) by the way that societies pattern, interpret and respond to mental illness (Kelly, 2006a).

Mental illness, interest groups and the first dimension of power

The first dimension of power concerns observable decision-making behaviour in societies, especially when this involves deciding between contested policy options (Dahl, 1961; Lukes, 2005). In democratic societies, many policy decisions appear to result from the actions or preferences of a number of different groups, and the term 'polyarchy' has been used to describe contemporary 'government by many groups' (Dahl, 1972). These groups may include government bodies, quasi-autonomous institutions, interest groups, trade unions, churches and voluntary organisations.

Individuals with mental illness and their carers have a long history of support group and interest group formation, e.g. Mind (www.mind.org.uk) and SANE (www.sane.org.uk) in the UK, SHINE (www.shineonline.ie) in Ireland and the National Alliance on Mental Illness (NAMI; www.nami.org) in the USA. Despite such activism, social discrimination and service deficiencies persist, and mental illness is still associated with significant social exclusion. One explanation for this apparent paradox is presented by Olson (1965, 1982). Olson outlines a primarily economic analysis of an individual's decision to join an interest group, in which (a) the cost of membership is balanced against (b) the perceived probability that the individual's joining will make a difference to the outcome, multiplied by (c) the value of the ultimate outcome (e.g. better representation of the interests of the mentally ill), plus (d) any additional economic benefits of membership for the individual (e.g. members' discounts in shops). The probability that an individual joining the interest group will make a significant difference to the ultimate outcome is generally seen as inversely proportional to the size of the group, i.e. individuals tend to believe that they will make a bigger difference to small rather than large groups.

In the case of mental health interest groups, there is often no direct monetary cost of membership (factor (a) above), but membership can involve devoting time to group activities, so there may be significant non-monetary and opportunity costs. Similarly, there tend to be few obvious economic benefits of membership for the individual (factor (d)), but there may be significant non-monetary benefits in terms of informal support and networking.

Mental illness is, however, relatively common: as already mentioned, around one in four individuals meet the diagnostic criteria for an anxiety, mood, impulse control and/or substance use disorder in any given year (Kessler *et al*, 2005), although this figure is based on the case-seeking methodology of the US National Comorbidity Study, so not all individuals who fulfil diagnostic criteria would necessarily regard themselves as ill and not all would have serious, recurring disorders. Nonetheless, epidemiological data consistently show that even serious, recurring mental illness is by no means uncommon (see above). In addition, such illnesses affect not only the individual with the illness, but also family, friends and carers, especially in the context of serious, recurring disorders. Given this relatively high prevalence of the 'interest' of mental illness (even for serious, recurring disorders), the limiting factor on the size of the interest group is likely to be the perceived probability that the individual's joining will make a difference to the outcome (factor (b)). Olson's theory suggests that an interest group reflecting an interest with such a wide distribution will tend to be smaller in size than the prevalence of the interest suggests it should be, i.e. it will be disproportionately small.

This is not to suggest that mental health interest groups are necessarily ineffective: there are many effective interest groups in this field, providing vital supports and services to a range of stakeholders. Olson's theory simply suggests that such interest groups, though they may appear to be large, powerful and effective at their present size, are not quite as large, powerful and effective as the prevalence of the interest in the community initially suggests they might be, given that the interest at issue is so widely shared. This, in turn, suggests that their impact on policy-making will not be proportionate to the true distribution of the interest in the broader population. This is plainly the case with mental illness.

Mental illness, structural violence and the second dimension of power

The second dimension of power concerns the determination of which issues are presented to decision makers and which policy options are presented as possible responses to these issues (Bachrach & Baratz, 1970; Lukes, 2005). From this perspective, the persistence of social discrimination and deficiencies in mental health services is linked, at least in part, to the exclusion of individuals with mental illness from social and political decision-making processes and a subsequent lack of emphasis on mental health at policy levels. This systematic exclusion of people with mental illness from full participation in civic and social life forms a key element of the structural violence perpetrated against them (Kelly, 2005).

Even in the case of a mental illness such as schizophrenia, which has a substantial biological basis (van Os & Kapur, 2009; Howes & Murray, 2014), there is evidence that some of the disability associated with the illness is related, at least in part, to social and political factors, including the effects of socioeconomic group on clinical features of the illness, social and administrative factors contributing to increased homelessness, the relationship between migration and increased rates of schizophrenia, and disproportionately high rates of imprisonment of individuals with mental illness, especially those with psychosis (see above).

These links demonstrate that social, economic and political forces act to marginalise and stigmatise those with mental illness in society and reduce their opportunities to participate fully in societal and political decision-making processes. This systematic exclusion results in: (a) a lack of emphasis on mental health issues on social and political agendas at all levels; (b) the subsequent exclusion of the mentally ill from full participation in political life; and (c) ongoing governmental failure effectively to address deficiencies in health and social services for people with mental illness.

The second dimension of power refers not only to determination of which issues reach the sociopolitical agenda, but also determination of the range of policy options that are considered as possible responses (Lukes, 2005). Bachrach & Baratz (1970) describe this process in terms of 'decision-making' and 'non-decision-making', where the latter refers to the effective suppression of certain policy options that might threaten entrenched societal or political interests. This is not a new phenomenon: in 1972, Crenson demonstrated how the issue of air pollution was kept off the political agenda in one city in the USA, thus severely limiting the articulation of the full range of possible responses to this issue (Crenson, 1972).

A similar process of exclusion of people with mental illness from agenda-setting and decision-making may help explain the persistence of the power gap experienced by the mentally ill. This exclusion may be both mediated and compounded by institutional structures and procedures that produce a 'mobilisation of bias' (Bachrach & Baratz, 1970) and act as 'filters' to exclude certain problems from the political agenda and exclude certain options from consideration as solutions. A similar process has been described in relation to the subordination of women in the USA in the 1950s and the dominance of the assumptions of corporate capitalism in the 1980s (Block, 1987); the presence of analogous institutional filters and an undoubted mobilisation of bias against people with mental illness helps explain why some of the possible remedies for the power gap (below) have not been implemented and often do not even feature on decision-making agendas.

Mental illness, agency and the third dimension of power

The third dimension of power concerns the forces that determine what needs people recognise themselves as having (Lukes, 2005). For any individual, recognising one's own needs is a complex process that depends on a range of cognitive, perceptual, social and political processes. Given these myriad influences, the concept of individual agency is central to the recognition of one's true needs. Sen (1999), in particular, highlights the role of individual agency in addressing deprivation, enhancing participatory democracy and driving societal development in both 'developed' and 'developing' countries. Sen (1999) emphasises that freedom is both a means and a goal of development and that individual agency is central to both freedom and development.

The erosion of individual agency in individuals with mental illness, and thus the erosion of their articulation of their own needs, may be a subtle, multidimensional phenomenon, attributable to a range of factors, including: (a) the symptoms of the mental illness itself; (b) the absence of effective mental healthcare systems; (c) an absence of knowledge about alternative systems; and (d) societal attitudes to mental illness.

First, the symptoms of mental illness are many and varied, and can include changes in mood (e.g. depression), cognitive symptoms (e.g. difficulties with reasoning) and perceptual disturbances (e.g. hallucinations) (Sims, 1995; Casey & Kelly, 2007). For the majority of individuals with mental illness, however, the illness tends to be mild (40.4%) or moderate (37.3%) (Kessler *et al*, 2005) and may not be of sufficient severity to have a lasting effect on their perception of their needs. Moreover, the most common symptoms are those of anxiety, and symptoms such as delusions and hallucinations tend to be concentrated among a smaller proportion of individuals who may have more than one mental illness at any given time (Kessler *et al*, 2005). For this minority of individuals, however, enduring symptoms may have significant effects on individual agency, and the development of advocacy services forms a critical component of service provision for this group (Rosenman *et al*, 2000; Kelly, 2001).

Second, the absence of effective mental healthcare erodes individual agency and limits the ability of individuals with mental illness to achieve other forms of freedom. Sen (1999) emphasises that services such as effective healthcare (like freedom) represent both a means and a goal of societal development and argues that the absence of effective healthcare is a significant 'unfreedom' that obstructs full participation in social and political life. There is ample evidence that effective mental healthcare is not being delivered in many countries around the world (WHO, 2013), resulting in significant unfreedoms for the mentally ill.

In 2001 the WHO devoted its World Health Report to the theme 'Mental Health: New Understanding, New Hope' and emphasised that many individuals do not receive the mental healthcare they need, and that services in many countries are underdeveloped, oversubscribed and do not reflect the mental health needs of the populations they aim to serve (WHO, 2001). In 2013, the WHO confirmed, in its Mental Health Action Plan: 2013–2020, that between 76 and 85% of people with serious mental illness in low- and middle-income countries still receive no treatment; in high-income countries, that figure is a still shocking 35–50% (WHO, 2013). This intolerable situation allows the symptoms of untreated, treatable mental illness to further disable individuals, erode their autonomy at fundamental levels, and substantially limit their achievement and enjoyment of important freedoms.

Third, limited knowledge of alternative systems also plays a role in the erosion of individual agency in individuals with mental illness. Lukes (2005) emphasises that the third dimension of power relates to the shaping of individuals' perceptions of their own needs and the idea that the current order of things is fixed and immutable, i.e. that present circumstances represent the only possible option. This situation can arise when individuals are unaware of alternatives to the present state of affairs, or are simply accustomed to accepting current circumstances without question. In the case of mental illness, individuals may simply accept that present levels of psychiatric care and social provision are not amenable to change, or they may be satisfied with minor fluctuations in the existing order of things rather than substantive reform. In this context, there is a particular role for international support and advocacy groups that can collectively articulate alternatives to existing systems and engage in political and social debate about the relative merits of different options for future service development.

Fourth, for individuals with serious, recurring mental illness, recognition and articulation of alternative systems may be further hampered by general societal attitudes and stigma associated with mental ill health (Byrne, 1999; Arboleda-Flórez, 2003; Barczyk, 2015). A stigma is defined as a mark of shame or discredit, and the stigma associated with mental illness often relates to a poor understanding or limited experience of matters related to mental health and illness (Goffman, 1963; Byrne, 2000). There is strong evidence that negative societal attitudes and stigma about mental illness have negative effects on the physical and mental health of the mentally ill, and can have a deleterious effect on help-seeking behaviour (Miller & Major, 2000; Arboleda-Flórez, 2003; Clement et al, 2015.

191

In terms of power, negative societal attitudes and stigma may perpetuate a belief that individuals with mental illness are unable or unwilling to participate fully in the political process. Such negative attitudes can also shape the ways in which mental illness is interpreted and treated at a societal level, and can shape societal value systems that (explicitly and implicitly) inform the judgements individuals make about their own needs. In these ways, societal attitudes towards mental illness can erode the third dimension of power in individuals experiencing mental health problems, reducing their ability to recognise and articulate their own needs and reducing their awareness of possible alternative systems for meeting such needs as they do identify.

Example: mental illness and the second dimension of power in China

The primary purpose of this section is to examine the ways in which mental illness and society's responses to it erode the power and freedom of the mentally ill. Regrettably, it is beyond the scope of this book to provide detailed, comparative examples of the ways the lives of people with mental illness are affected by these factors in a range of contrasting political and social settings in different countries. For the purposes of illustration, however, it is useful to explore specific aspects of the second dimension of power as it applies to individuals with mental illness in the People's Republic of China.

China is a useful example in this context because there has been long-standing concern about alleged abuses of human rights in mental health settings in that country (Munro, 2000, 2002, 2006; Branigan, 2010). More generally, too, China has become the subject of increased international attention in relation to human rights issues in recent years, and is currently undergoing a period of sustained social, economic and political transformation, which presents a unique opportunity for reform.

The second dimension of power concerns the determination of which issues appear on agendas for decision makers and which policy options are presented as possible responses to these issues (Bachrach & Baratz, 1970; Lukes, 2005). Despite long-standing external concern about human rights in mental health settings in China (Munro, 2002; Branigan, 2010), this matter remained largely absent from political and decision-making agendas for many decades, owing chiefly to a lack of voice and lack of power among the mentally ill and their families. Recent decades, however, saw increased external and internal recognition of these issues, as evidenced by the concerns of both the Global Initiative on Psychiatry (www.gip-global.org) and the World Psychiatric Association (www.wpanet.org), among others.

In 2012, there was significant progress when China passed a mental health law aiming to prevent people from being involuntarily detained and treated in psychiatric facilities, standardising mental health services, requiring general hospitals to set up special out-patient clinics or provide counselling, and calling for the training of more doctors in mental healthcare (Associated Press, 2012). While multiple factors undoubtedly played a role in these developments, and there is still more work to be done in terms of implementation, it is noteworthy that this increased recognition of the rights of the mentally ill has, at the very least, coincided with increased pressure for accountability and democratic reform in Chinese public life in general, as well as increased (albeit still limited) press freedom and increased (albeit still limited) recognition of broader human rights issues in China; i.e. improvement in relation to the human rights of the mentally ill occurred in the context of pressure to change broader political, societal and contextual factors, which also necessarily affected the situation of the mentally ill.

The second dimension of power, however, concerns not only the inclusion of specific issues on the decision-making agenda, but also the presentation of possible policy responses to them. This aspect of the second dimension of power is likely to present significant challenges in China. These challenges may stem from the process of professional acculturation in mental health professions and the persistence of fear emanating from China's institutional and political past (Munro, 2000). In addition, it is clear that the issues involved in China are ultimately more complex than a simple lack of democracy and this broader range of issues requires further study.

In principle, however, a process of multi-level democratisation is likely to help in strengthening individual agency among those affected by mental illness in China and in generating policy options for improvement of mental health services. In addition, the development of greater social and political freedoms in other domains (e.g. local democracy initiatives, enhanced press freedom) may create the environment needed to address the fundamental patterns of structural violence and consolidate progressive change: as Sen (1999) points out, there are strong interconnections between social, political and economic freedoms, and factors that affect one form of freedom are likely also to have an impact on others.

In these ways, an analysis of the second dimension of power as it applies to people with mental illness in China can help both to (a) explain the exclusion of mental health issues from agendas for decision-making and action, and (b) identify possible approaches to resolving these issues, chiefly based on strengthening individual agency among the mentally ill and deepening other forms of freedom throughout Chinese society, with consequent benefit in terms of mental health and human rights. Other approaches to addressing the power gap experienced by people with mental illness are outlined next.

Addressing the power gap

The persistent erosion of power and freedom experienced by individuals with mental illness has resulted in a significant power gap, whereby their needs are grossly underrepresented on both societal and political agendas. As a result, the rights of the mentally ill are persistently undermined by a collection of social and political arrangements that limit not only the extent

193

of present freedoms, but also the potential to achieve further freedoms through social and political systems.

There are several possible approaches to resolving these problems. All of these approaches find their roots in the enhancement of individual agency among the mentally ill, and all approaches are interlinked. For purposes of presentation, potential solutions can be grouped into three broad categories: (a) approaches taking explicitly rights-based perspectives; (b) approaches based on enhancing direct political participation; and (c) other approaches, including increasing democratic accountability, developing mental health legislation and adapting the concept of 'soft power' to strengthen forums for the identification and articulation of the concerns of people with mental illness.

Human rights approaches

The rights and freedoms of the mentally ill, including those admitted to hospital on an involuntary basis, are outlined in the UN's Principles for the Protection of Persons with Mental Illness and the Improvement of Mental Health Care (United Nations, 1991) (Box 1.1) and the CRPD (United Nations, 2006). Despite their emphasis on protecting the social and civil rights of individuals with mental illness, however, there are significant problems with implementing these declarations. As discussed in Chapter 1, there is no binding legal obligation on UN member states to use these principles to define a minimum standard of care (Harding, 2000). Thus, notwithstanding the contents of these declarations, allegations of the denial of human rights in mental health settings are still likely to present cause for ongoing concern in certain parts of the world: whereas allegations of the political abuse of psychiatry throughout the 1970s and 1980s tended to focus on the USSR (Bloch & Reddaway, 1977, 1985), in recent times increased attention has been paid to alleged abuses of psychiatry in China (Munro, 2006; Branigan, 2010). Although there are recent signs of significant change (Associated Press, 2012; see also pp. 192–193 above), greater awareness of these issues among all stakeholders continues to play a critical role in identifying and eliminating human rights abuses, improving standards of care and sustaining positive change.

Overall, from a rights-based perspective, the power gap experienced by people with mental illness could be addressed, at least in part, by promoting and facilitating greater adherence to the principles outlined in the UN declarations, as well as other relevant legislation such as the Human Rights Act 1998 in the UK (Bindman et al, 2003). Some jurisdictions are actively bringing national legislation into line with these international standards, especially over the past decade (Mental Health Commission, 2005), but the pace of change varies significantly between countries. Additional measures that might enhance the pace of reform include: (a) the strengthening of advocacy, empowerment and guardianship processes, especially advocacy services based on patients' needs and best interests, in addition to more traditional rights-based advocacy (Rosenman et al, 2000); and (b) increased emphasis on multi-level governance and accountability throughout mental health services (James *et al*, 2005), with specific emphasis on quality improvement initiatives in mental health and social services for the mentally ill and their families (WHO, 2001, 2013). Many of these matters are already being addressed in various ways through mental health legislation in England, Wales (Chapter 2), Northern Ireland (Chapter 3), Ireland (Chapter 4) and Scotland (Chapter 5).

Political participation

Another approach to resolving the power gap experienced by individuals with mental illness is based on increasing their involvement in the myriad processes of societal governance, political choice and democratic participation. This might usefully involve (a) improving voting rates among the mentally ill and (b) promoting the formation of more effective interest groups.

There is, in general, a paucity of data about rates and patterns of voting among individuals with mental illness and those secondarily affected by such illness (e.g. family, friends, carers) (Kelly, 2014*e*). This is explained, at least in part, by the fact that the lives of most individuals with mental illness are not solely defined by the illness, so there may not be a direct or readily detectable link between mental illness and voting choices. Nonetheless, evidence suggests that, in the absence of dementia or cognitive impairment (Ott *et al*, 2003), the voting patterns of individuals with mental illness tend to differ somewhat, though not irrationally, from voting patterns of the overall population (Melamed *et al*, 1997*a,b*; Bullenkamp & Voges, 2004), with a general tendency towards the liberal side of the political spectrum (Howard & Anthony, 1977; Bullenkamp & Voges, 2004).

One study, for example, found that out-patients with enduring mental illness in Germany were more likely to vote for left-wing parties compared with the general population (Bullenkamp & Voges, 2004), suggesting that the political choices of the mentally ill reflect a set of priorities that is different from that of the overall population. Another study, conducted in Israel, identified smaller differences in voting preferences among in-patients with mental illness than among the general population (Melamed *et al*, 1997*a*), but in Canada the proportions of votes cast in psychiatric hospitals for various political parties were virtually the same as in the surrounding areas (Valentine & Turner, 1989). Interestingly, there is evidence that psychiatric in-patients are particularly well-informed voters (Bhopal *et al*, 1988; Jaychuk & Manchanda, 1991) and a majority report positive subjective feelings following voting, including a sense of responsibility, belonging to the general community and pride (Melamed *et al*, 2007). Nonetheless, voting rates among psychiatric in-patients can be as low as 10% (Siddique & Lee, 2014) or 3% (Humphreys & Chiswick, 1993).

In a notably progressive initiative in Ireland, patients at the Central Mental Hospital (Ireland's only in-patient forensic psychiatry facility) voted for the first time in general elections in 2007, following a European

Court of Human Rights ruling in 2005 (O'Brien, 2007). Voting took place in the same way as voting at any other polling station and was overseen by the county sheriff. Voter turnout was high, at 75% (Kennedy, 2007b). Two years later, turnout at the Central Mental Hospital remained high in the European and local elections, and on the eve of the poll, three election candidates attended a question and answer session for detained patients in the hospital (Houston, 2009).

Clearly, individuals directly or indirectly affected by mental illness represent an extremely large political constituency – a constituency that political organisations rarely address during campaigns. One reason for this may be a perception among politicians that individuals with enduring mental illness do not vote; failure to vote among the mentally ill, however, is likely to be attributable, at least in part, to remediable secondary correlates of mental illness (e.g. homelessness), lack of knowledge (McIntyre et al, 2012) or administrative problems (Humphreys & Chiswick, 1993), rather than primary symptoms of mental illness itself. In Israel, for example, the most common reason for in-patients with mental disorder not voting is that they do not have identity cards (Melamed et al, 2013).

The relevance of contributory factors such as this demonstrates that the systematic disenfranchisement of individuals with mental illness represents a problem that is, to a significant extent, remediable. This situation can be addressed not only by patients themselves, but also by advocacy services and other stakeholders through: (a) improved staff awareness of patients' voting rights (Rees, 2010); (b) provision of relevant information to patients, especially in-patients (McIntyre et al, 2012); (c) where indicated, assessments of voting capacity, using standardised, proven tools such as the Competency Assessment Tool for Voting (CAT-V) (Appelbaum et al, 2005; Raad et al, 2009); and (d) voter-registration programmes; all of these ((a)–(d)) have important roles to play in the re-enfranchisement process (Nash, 2002; Lawn et al, 2014).

Another reason for the relatively low profile of mental health issues in political debate may relate to an apparent political consensus about mental health policy, for example a consensus that traditional services need to be expanded or that custodial approaches are needed for safety reasons (Warner, 2004). Alternatively, the manufacture of such a faux consensus may simply be a way to avoid debating the challenging social and political issues raised by mental illness. In either case, it is unlikely that any apparent political consensus on such a complex matter is an accurate reflection of a true social consensus, and it is only by repeatedly raising issues related to mental health that real political debate can evolve.

A second approach to enhancing political participation involves the formation of more effective interest groups. From the perspective of the interest group, possible ways to achieve this include: (a) reducing the cost of individual membership (e.g. reducing travelling times by holding more local meetings); (b) outlining more clearly the ways in which an individual's joining will make a difference (i.e. emphasising the need for each individual to add their voice to the group); (c) outlining more clearly the value of the ultimate outcome to the individual and society (i.e. the benefits of greater awareness of mental health issues at local, national and international policy levels); and (d) emphasising the additional individual benefits of membership (e.g. highlighting 'process benefits' such as informal networking). Many successful interest groups already engage in these strategies to optimise membership levels. An alternative or additional strategy involves the formation of numerous smaller interest groups, which may represent individuals with specific disorders, rather than the very broad category of 'mental illness'; an example is the National Eating Disorders Association in the UK (www.nationaleatingdisorders.org). This might help optimise the balance between group size and the benefits of membership.

Other approaches

Strategies aimed at reducing the power gap experienced by individuals with mental illness are likely to be most effective when they are based on research into roles and functions of power and freedom in the context of mental illness. Researchers can approach these matters at multiple levels, including: (a) the individual level, examining issues of power in the traditional therapeutic relationship between mental health professional and the patient (Guggenbühl-Craig, 1971; Cutcliffe & Happell, 2009); (b) the local level, examining local service provision and issues of quality, accountability and governance (James *et al*, 2005); and (c) national and international levels, examining national health and social policy, protection of human rights by legislation, and globalised or transnational dimensions of mental healthcare (WHO, 2001, 2013; Kelly, 2003; Eaton *et al*, 2014*a*,*b*).

Various critical movements within psychiatry during the 1960s and 1970s were concerned with many of these issues, especially as they related to power, although the writings of Thomas Szasz (1960, 1961) and R. D. Laing (1960), among others, provided an ideological rather than data-based response to them. In the 1990s, however, the emergence of novel and arguably less unified forms of activism, along with advances in biological psychiatry, undercut at least some of the arguments of these movements (Dain, 1994). Some of these matters may be addressed, at least in part, through the emergence of schools of 'critical psychiatry' and 'post-psychiatry' (Thomas & Bracken, 2004).

Particular problems arise, however, when researching or addressing issues related to the third dimension of power, i.e. identifying the forces that determine what needs people recognise themselves as having (Lukes, 2005). For individuals with mental illness, this process may be especially challenging, owing to the primary effects of mental illness as well as the ways in which that illness is patterned, interpreted and treated by society (Kelly, 2005, 2007*c*). In this context, the development of national mental health legislation has a particular role to play, not only through the protection of human rights and enhancement of service-level accountability, but also through mental health tribunals to review each case of involuntary detention (Kelly, 2002, 2011; Whelan, 2004; Sarker & Adshead, 2005). Correctly designed and conducted, tribunals may not only identify issues related to the process of detention itself, but may also reveal other latent issues or concerns that affected individuals may have difficulty recognising in themselves or expressing to others (Carney, 2012; Smith & Caple, 2014). The tribunal process can, then, facilitate exploration of the third dimension of power, strengthen individual agency and enhance the social and political freedoms of persons with mental illness (Sen, 1999).

Psychiatric and social care are, of course, always delivered in a particular sociopolitical setting and it is possible that larger-scale changes in this sociopolitical context could also have a beneficial effect on both freedom and power, as experienced by individuals with mental illness. Interestingly, there is evidence that individuals with mental illness cope well with large-scale political and societal change (Priebe & Broker, 2000), provided that appropriate medical and psychiatric support are available throughout (Axer et al, 1992).

The precise sociopolitical circumstances that optimise mental health have yet to be identified, but it appears that level of democracy is important for both mental health (Wise & Sainsbury, 2007) and the freedoms and social conditions experienced by individuals with mental and physical illness. Sen (1999), for example, argues that no famine has ever occurred in a country with a functioning democracy. In the context of alleged human rights abuses in mental health settings, it is notable that neither of the two countries that have been the subjects of most attention, the USSR (Bloch & Reddaway, 1985) and the People's Republic of China (Munro, 2000, 2002, 2006), was characterised by either a strong democracy or a particularly strong free press during the periods in question. Of course, the issues involved in both countries were ultimately more complex than a simple lack of democracy, and while this broader range of issues requires further study, it is notable that improvements in China coincided with increased media and press scrutiny, and increased international focus on human rights (Branigan, 2010; Associated Press, 2012).

The development of greater democratic accountability is, however, a complex, multilayered process. Traditional methods include the development of more democratic processes for decision-making at local and national levels (corresponding to the first dimension of power) and of greater flexibility in terms of social and political agendas, often characterised by enhanced participatory democracy at multiple levels, and the emergence of a strong free press (corresponding to the second dimension of power). For individuals with mental illness, however, the third dimension of power may present particular challenges, and reform may need to involve enhancement of overall levels of mental health services, development and revision of national mental health legislation, and adaptation of the principles of 'soft power' (Nye, 2004), which would involve: (a) providing public education about mental illness; (b) persuading citizens that mental health issues are important for all sectors of society; and (c) providing a forum for individuals with mental illness to describe and articulate their own concerns about their psychiatric, social and political situations.

Advocacy has a particular role to play both in strengthening the context in which legislative reform takes place and in developing more assertive and participatory forms of treatment for mental illness (Edd *et al*, 2005; Lustig, 2012). There is a strong role for mental health legislation in this area. In England and Wales, for example, the Mental Health Act 2007 introduced the requirement that the 'appropriate national authority shall make such arrangements as it considers reasonable to enable persons ("independent mental health advocates") to be available to help qualifying patients' (section 30(2)). Such help 'should, so far as practicable, be provided by a person who is independent of any person who is professionally concerned with the patient's medical treatment' and can relate to a range of matters, including details of mental health legislation, medical treatment, 'rights which may be exercised under this Act by or in relation to [the patient]' and 'help (by way of representation or otherwise) in exercising those rights' (see Chapter 2). Other examples have been provided in previous chapters.

Advocacy plays a critical role in shaping societal attitudes towards various illnesses and disabilities. Groups such as Disability Rights UK (disabilityrightsuk.org) have made remarkable progress in shaping public attitudes towards disability, and cancer advocacy groups have helped transform cancer from a deeply stigmatising illness in the 1950s into a better understood and better funded condition today (Lerner, 2005). In the case of cancer, these changes in societal attitudes have been accompanied by improved understanding of the scientific basis of the illness and improved forms of treatment for many cancers. Similar advances in the field of psychiatry, combined with advocacy programmes for the mentally ill, such as those of Mind (www.mind.org.uk) in the UK, can help achieve and sustain such changes in relation to mental health.

Conclusions

This chapter has moved well beyond matters explicitly addressed in mental health legislation in England and Wales (Chapter 2), Northern Ireland (Chapter 3), Ireland (Chapter 4) and Scotland (Chapter 5), beyond the ways in which such legislation protects and promotes the human rights of the mentally ill, and beyond the ways in which processes of mental health legislative reform in each jurisdiction shed light on the further use of such legislation to protect and promote rights. Building on these analyses, this chapter returned to some of the broader themes explored in Chapter 1, looking at the relationship between human rights and mental illness in wider social and political contexts, as reflected in the UN Principles for the

Protection of Persons with Mental Illness and the Improvement of Mental Health Care (United Nations, 1991) (Box 1.1) and the CRPD (United Nations, 2006), which commit signatory states to a range of protections and promotion of human rights within a very broad societal framework.

In this context, the concept of 'structural violence' (Farmer, 2003) was invoked to describe the cumulative effects of adverse social, economic and societal forces which, along with the social stigma of mental illness, impair access to psychiatric and social services among people with mental illness and amplify the effects of illness in the lives of sufferers and their families (Kelly, 2005, 2007c). As a result of these overarching social and economic factors, many of the mentally ill are systematically excluded from full participation in civic and social life and are constrained to live lives shaped by stigma, isolation, homelessness, imprisonment, social dislocation and denial of rights. Rights-based mental health legislation is not necessarily the only, or even the best, way to address key aspects of this situation, which relates in large part to broader social justice and denial of rights, rather than just denial of liberty.

This chapter argues that the enhancement of individual agency is central to efforts to address the 'power gap' experienced by the mentally ill. This can be achieved, at least in part, through a combination of: (a) rights-based approaches; (b) approaches based on enhancing direct political participation (e.g. voter registration, formation of more effective interest groups); and (c) additional approaches, including increasing accountability throughout services, recognising the effects of sociopolitical change on the context of care and adapting the concept of 'soft power' to strengthen advocacy programmes. Dismantling institutional filters (Block, 1987) and reversing the 'mobilisation of bias' against the mentally ill (Bachrach & Baratz, 1970) present particular challenges not only in terms of political reform, but also in terms of reforming societal attitudes that provide critical support to prevailing political and institutional assumptions and procedures.

This process of reform is certainly a complex one, but it is also both urgent and important, and requires commitment not only from mental health patients, but also from advocacy groups, service providers, policy makers and political decision makers. In the absence of such commitment, individuals with enduring mental illness will continue to experience lives that are shaped, in large part, by socioeconomic discrimination, denial of human rights, and denial of social, political and economic freedoms routinely enjoyed by individuals without mental illness. This situation reflects a profound imbalance of power that is unworthy of any democratic state.

Mental health legislation has a key role to play in remedying this situation, but so too do the conceptual shifts and policy measures outlined in this chapter, many of which map more readily onto the right to dignity rather than the more focused rights more commonly protected by mental health legislation (e.g. the right to liberty) (Kelly, 2014b).[120] In the complicated setting of mental healthcare, it is clearly essential that this vital right, liberty, is protected, through appropriate regulation and monitoring of involuntary detention and treatment, among other matters. Increasingly, however, mental health legislation in certain jurisdictions protects this right with sophistication and flexibility, thanks, in large part, to the ECHR (Kelly, 2011), as outlined in preceding chapters of this book.

An exclusive focus on the right to liberty alone, however, clearly fails to address or even acknowledge the broader range of social injustices and denials of rights commonly experienced by people with enduring mental illness (Kelly, 2007a). The approach outlined in this chapter takes a much broader and essentially sociological or political perspective strongly to heart, and the next, final chapter in this book continues this theme, looking more closely at steps that clinicians can take to help achieve social justice for the mentally ill, protect rights and effect meaningful change, through mental health legislation, mental health practice and various other areas of endeavour.

CHAPTER 7

Conclusions: fighting for rights

This chapter draws together arguments, discussions and conclusions from preceding chapters and suggests ways to promote rights in clinical practice, with particular emphasis on achieving social justice for the mentally ill, their families and all who are affected by mental illness.

Arguments, themes, comparisons

Mental illness has long been associated with denial of human rights, especially denial of liberty and dignity. Although the 1700s and 1800s saw significantly increased emphasis on, and restatements of, key ideas about justice and human rights in general, the experiences of many individuals with mental illness during this period remained bleak, characterised by chronic neglect, social exclusion, and denial of agency and dignity in large, overcrowded institutions.

A detailed statement of rights specific to the mentally ill eventually appeared in the form of the United Nations' (UN's) Principles for the Protection of Persons with Mental Illness and the Improvement of Mental Health Care (United Nations, 1991), but it is the European Convention on Human Rights (ECHR), which came into force in 1953, that has produced the greatest shift in thinking, with a series of judgments that strongly re-emphasise various protections for the rights of individuals detained under mental health legislation, especially in relation to humane conditions in therapeutic settings and prompt, effective reviews.

The ECHR was given 'further effect' with its incorporation into national legislation in the UK (Human Rights Act 1998) and Ireland (European Convention on Human Rights Act 2003). As a result, it is now clear that there is a positive obligation on public bodies (at least in the UK and Ireland) to promote rights, and this appears to have particularly broad implications for mental health services, although this responsibility has yet to be fully delineated and operationalised satisfactorily.

In 2005, the World Health Organization (WHO) set out a 'Checklist for Mental Health Legislation', detailing human rights standards that need to be met in each jurisdiction (WHO, 2005). Concerningly, mental health legislation in England, Wales and Ireland fails to meet many of these standards, chiefly (but not exclusively) in areas relating to promoting rights, voluntary patients (especially non-protesting, incapacitous patients), protection of vulnerable groups and emergency treatment (Kelly, 2011). In both jurisdictions, however, mechanisms other than mental health law (e.g. policy) may meet some of the WHO requirements, although some of the requirements clearly remain challenging.

Perhaps the greatest challenges, however, stem from the UN Convention on the Rights of Persons with Disabilities (CRPD; United Nations, 2006), which states that 'the existence of a disability shall in no case justify a deprivation of liberty' (Article 14(1)(b)) and requires that states take strong, assertive action to promote rights and not just avoid impinging them. Some of the challenges presented by these statements of rights, and especially the ECHR, are reflected in the revision process that led to the Mental Health Act 2007 in England and Wales.

England and Wales

The Mental Health Act 2007 in England and Wales (which amended the 1983 Act) was largely motivated by the twin concerns of public safety and human rights, the latter because cases brought before the courts since the Human Rights Act 1998 had raised important issues relating to, for example, the burden of proof in mental health tribunals, respect for private and family life (ECHR, Article 8) and the power of tribunals to release patients. This contrasts significantly with the position in Ireland, where the theme of public safety was (and remains) essentially absent from public discussion about mental health law: in Ireland, human rights dominate public debate on this matter single-handedly.

Notwithstanding these matters, the 2007 legislation in England and Wales made a number of important changes with the potential to advance the dignity and human rights of detained patients. Key changes include revising and simplifying the definition of 'mental disorder' and replacing the 'treatability test' of the 1983 Act with a requirement that 'appropriate medical treatment is available'. The 2007 legislation also introduced significant expansions of professional roles, although it remains unclear to what extent these have been implemented in practice, and whether or not renewal orders made without the involvement of medical doctors meet the requirement for objective medical evidence for involuntary admission. The expansion of professional roles in England and Wales also goes further than analogous suggestions in Ireland, which would require only that the consultant psychiatrist consult a mental health professional of another discipline at various points in the involuntary admission and treatment process, but final decisions would still lie with the psychiatrist.

In England and Wales, the 2007 Act also improved patients' control over selection of their 'nearest relative'; simplified supervised community treatment procedures; introduced new safeguards for electroconvulsive therapy (ECT) for detained patients; and further restricted the grounds on which emergency ECT can be administered. All of this helps further protect patient's rights, including their right to treatment. Finally, the 2007 Act introduced automatic referral to a mental health tribunal for patients admitted for assessment and established a system of independent mental health advocates (although not all patients qualify).

Overall, the changes introduced by the 2007 Act present a mixture of increased protections for certain human rights, specific measures that support patient dignity and capabilities, and other measures that are clearly paternalistic in tone and content. Notwithstanding the concern about paternalism, the legislation demonstrated strong overall potential to advance rights. It is less clear, however, to what extent these changes are being implemented in practice; for example, the expansion of professional roles is clearly taking a considerable time to bed down.

In addition, it remains a real concern that the 2007 Act increased the stigma associated with mental illness owing to its focus on risk of violence (Batty, 2008). It is also concerning that, as noted by the Mental Health Alliance (2006) and King's Fund (2008), by redefining mental disorder and removing the treatability test, the 2007 Act could permit clinicians to detain some patients who would not have been detained under the unamended 1983 Act. Further, it has been correctly observed that, although the 2007 legislation updated and improved the 1983 Act, it did not represent a root-and-branch review of the legislation (King's Fund, 2008).

Northern Ireland

The same certainly cannot be said of the situation in Northern Ireland, where, in contrast to the Mental Health Act 2007 in England and Wales, the Northern Ireland Mental Capacity Bill 2015 proposes a genuinely complex and potentially progressive shift from the current legislative position. Northern Ireland's Mental Capacity Bill 2015 presents a range of interesting provisions relating to the treatment of individuals with impaired mental capacity. While its overarching principles have much in common with other jurisdictions (e.g. a presumption of capacity), the Northern Irish Bill is notable for its welcome, pragmatic emphasis on best interests, which echoes provision in the Republic of Ireland, although there are recent suggestions to remove 'best interests' from the Irish legislation.

Overall, most of the measures in Northern Ireland's 2015 Bill have modest potential to protect and promote human rights; for example, the elimination of distinction between those who are mentally ill and those who have reduced capacity for other reasons, enunciation of clear overarching principles, a robust 'lasting powers of attorney' system, revised rights of review, clear criteria for deciding who lacks capacity and how compulsion is to be authorised, and strong measures relating to nominated persons, independent advocates and second opinions.

There are, however, certain human rights concerns, too, most notably that linking deprivation of liberty with 'an impairment of, or a disturbance in the functioning of, the mind or brain' (section 3(1)) complies poorly with the CRPD requirement that 'the existence of a disability shall in no case justify a deprivation of liberty' (Article 14(1)(b)) – although it is very difficult to see how this requirement of the CRPD can ever be met, as long as mental health or capacity legislation permits any form of detention (Kelly, 2014a). In addition, the 2015 Bill states that 'nothing in this Act permits a decision on any of the following matters to be made on behalf of a person' (e.g. family relationships and voting rights) (sections 273 and 274) and these exclusions, while pragmatic and similar to those in other jurisdictions, comply poorly with the CRPD requirement that persons with disability 'enjoy legal capacity on an equal basis with others in *all* aspects of life' (emphasis added) (Article 12(2)). These issues are evident not only in Northern Ireland but also, to varying degrees, in England, Wales, Ireland and Scotland. Dawson (2015) argues persuasively for a more realistic approach to interpreting the CRPD in this context.

In the final analysis, Northern Ireland's 2015 Bill appears genuinely 'ground-breaking' (Department of Health, Social Services and Public Safety in Northern Ireland & Northern Ireland Department of Justice, 2014: p. 35) in one way only: it fuses mental health legislation and mental capacity legislation into a single Bill. Such a 'fusion law' will hopefully help to shift focus away from risk of harm as the central criterion for involuntary treatment and thus facilitate earlier intervention in mental illness, uniform application of criminal law, reduced discrimination and application of consistent ethical principles across medical law (Dawson & Szmukler, 2006). Potential demerits of the fusion approach include: an absence of research on the reliability of emergency capacity assessments; the possibility that more people with mental disorders who retain capacity might be imprisoned rather than receiving mental healthcare; a possible move away from a decision-specific model of capacity (Bartlett & Sandland, 2014); and the idea that repeatedly treating individuals just to the point where they regain capacity and then leaving them to fend for themselves could have negative outcomes (Maden, 2007).

Although such a fusion law certainly appears to have potential merits, it remains the case that none of the more detailed, specific measures presented in Northern Ireland's 2015 Bill appears especially 'ground-breaking' in itself, so it is difficult to argue that simply integrating mental health and capacity legislation into a single document really reflects a 'ground-breaking' step forward, especially when the 2015 Bill explicitly extends mental health-style legislation into areas and circumstances where the use of compulsion may already occur in dubious legal circumstances (e.g. nursing homes), but where the extraordinarily extensive measures outlined in the 2015 Bill are likely to be relatively new. This may have the merit of bringing transparency to certain practices, but it remains a fact that these measures include powers to force individuals to accept treatment not only in psychiatric hospitals, but also in other establishments and community settings, even to the point of determining where a person may or may not live. The evidence base for the effectiveness of such extensive compulsory community powers is decidedly unclear (Burns *et al*, 2013).

Finally, through its strong emphasis on decision-making capacity, the 2015 Bill requires that impairment of decision-making capacity is a mandatory prerequisite for any compulsory intervention in relation to any person, including a person with mental illness. This contrasts sharply with the view of Richardson Committee in England and Wales, which found that only a 'small minority' of those consulted believed that 'a mental health act should authorise treatment in the absence of consent only for those who lack capacity' and 'a much larger body of opinion which was prepared to accept the overriding of a capable refusal in a health provision on grounds of public safety in certain circumstances' (Department of Health, 1999: p. 19). By way of contrast, the 2015 Bill in Northern Ireland places impaired decision-making capacity at the heart of all compulsory interventions.

Ireland

This also contrasts with the position in the Ireland, where the Mental Health Act 2001 introduced many important changes to Irish mental health law and a majority of stakeholders believe it has genuinely helped to protect human rights (Mental Health Commission, 2008: p. 69; O'Donoghue & Moran, 2009). More specifically, it resulted in: the removal of indefinite detention orders that existed under the Mental Treatment Act 1945; new involuntary admission procedures; automatic, independent review of detention orders by mental health tribunals; free legal representation and independent psychiatric opinions for patients prior to tribunal hearings; and establishment of the Mental Health Commission. Many of these changes promote human rights, enhance dignity and advance patients' autonomous exercise of capabilities.

Specific human rights issues have, however, arisen, some of which stem from: the absence of detailed data collection about decisions of mental health tribunals, leading to uncertainty about reasons for revocations (e.g. procedural aberrations, absence of mental disorder); unclearness regarding the extent to which procedural aberrations are overlooked; and an absence of cumulative tribunal 'case law'. There are also restrictions on the acceptable grounds for civil proceedings in the Circuit and High Courts, and the fact that the burden of proof lies with the patient in the Circuit Court.

Other human rights concerns stem from unclearness about the precise matters at issue in tribunals for discharged patients and the legal definition of voluntary patient, which does not include a requirement for capacity. The hurried enactment of the Mental Health Act 2008, which stemmed from a poorly worded statutory form, raised a number of issues, including the retrospective declaration that detentions based on flawed forms had been lawful all along and would remain so for the first 5 days. Finally, there is significant evidence of paternalism in the implementation and interpretation of the 2001 Act, especially by the Courts, raising the issue of the balance between individual autonomy and exercise of capabilities on the one hand and the constitutional obligation on the Irish state to protect the vulnerable on the other.

Overall, measures introduced in the Mental Health Act 2001 hold strong potential to protect specific rights (e.g. right to liberty), enhance patient dignity and promote the exercise of specific capabilities (e.g. challenging involuntary detention). As in other jurisdictions, however, these potential benefits are accompanied by significant limitations and caveats. In resource terms, there are also opportunity costs associated with the legislation, including increased workloads for medical staff and decreased time spent with patients, owing to increased administrative activities and attendance at tribunals and court proceedings (McGuinness, 2007d; Baker, 2009; Jabbar et al, 2010). As a result, while there is significant agreement that the Act has enhanced protections of the right to liberty for detained individuals (O'Donoghue & Moran, 2009), there is little evidence that it has enhanced the quality of psychiatric services (Fitzsimons, 2007; O'Donoghue & Moran, 2009; Jabbar et al, 2010). This situation has significant implications in terms of effective treatment of mental illness which would support patient dignity and, as a result, limits the extent to which the legislation supports patients' autonomous exercise of capabilities and the right to treatment.

Scotland

The proposed elimination of the principle of best interests from mental health legislation in Ireland contrasts sharply with developments in neighbouring jurisdictions, and would diminish the importance accorded to the idea that deprivation of liberty must be reciprocated by clear evidence of benefit to the patient. This leads to an interesting comparison with the position in Scotland, where the Mental Health (Care and Treatment) (Scotland) Act 2003 was, when introduced, a notably progressive piece of legislation and still clearly reflects respect for the wishes of the patient, alongside best interests. It also emphasises patient participation in decision-making and the principle of least restriction, as well as acknowledging circumstances of family members and need for mental health services. Its definition of 'mental disorder' accords moderately well with those of the other jurisdictions (although there are points of contrast) and, in terms of quality assurance, the roles accorded to the Mental Welfare Commission for Scotland, the Mental Health Tribunal for Scotland and local authorities are clearly critical for supporting high standards.

The 2003 Act's provisions relating to involuntary detention are clear (if somewhat complex) and often notably pragmatic; for 'emergency' and 'short-term' detention, for example, the Act sensibly recognises that definitive diagnosis may be impossible in the initial stages and also permits treatment, subject to various requirements (this contrasts with Ireland). Despite these merits, these detention procedures probably violate the CRPD (Article 14(1)(b)) by linking detention and treatment with 'mental disorder'. Nonetheless, these treatment provisions still appear to strike a reasonable balance between protection of rights and ensuring that all patients have access to the same range of treatments regardless of their level of decision-making capacity, consistent with the CRPD (Article 25(a)).

In 2009, the McManus Review of the operation of the 2003 Act (Scottish Government Review Group, 2009) made a series of recommendations, many of which of centred on more efficient, accountable implementation of existing provisions rather than fundamental change. Against this background, the Mental Health (Scotland) Act 2015 (which received Royal Assent in August 2015) presented several legislative changes of relevance to human rights and patient dignity, including: clarity regarding the priority to be accorded to overlapping detention orders; various measures regarding suspension of detention (increasing efficiency and adding clarity to periods of suspension); clarifying rights of appeal against apparently excessive levels of security; requiring that a mental health officer must notify the Mental Welfare Commission when a decision regarding a removal order is made; clarifying the time for which a nurse can detain a voluntary patient for medical examination (balancing the right to medical care with the right to liberty); various measures regarding the patient's 'named person'; creating a central register of advance statements to be held by the Commission (although regulations regarding access will need to be implemented); increasing assistance to aid communication (e.g. for patients who communicate generally in a language other than English); and broadening the duty on health boards to provide services and accommodation for mothers not only with post-natal depression, but also with other mental disorders.

Overall, the Scottish reform process demonstrates several interesting themes, including that: (a) significant reform, when it occurs, need not necessarily be root-and-branch reform, but can achieve important and quite subtle change though amendments to existing measures; (b) during the process of reform it is possible to achieve a significant degree of consensus on both fundamental principles and more specific matters, which hopefully will optimise implementation of change; and (c) not all reform processes that seek to improve the functioning and effects of mental health legislation with a view to protecting rights require legislative change: much can be achieved through operating existing provisions more effectively, comprehensively and transparently.

In addition, the spirit of the Mental Health (Scotland) Act 2015 is highly consistent with the emphasis on rights in the Mental Health Strategy for Scotland, 2012–2015 (Scottish Government, 2012), especially given that the Explanatory Notes to the 2015 Bill that culminated in the Act stated emphatically that 'the Bill's overarching objective is to help people with a mental disorder to access effective treatment quickly and easily' (Scottish Parliament, 2015: paragraph 4). This statement supports the general idea of a legally definable right to treatment, consistent with the Universal Declaration of Human Rights (United Nations, 1948; Article 25(1)), the UN's Principles for the Protection of Persons with Mental Illness and the Improvement of Mental Health Care (United Nations, 1991) and the CRPD's requirement that 'States Parties [i.e. signatory states] shall take all appropriate measures to ensure access for persons with disabilities to health services that are gender-sensitive, including health-related rehabilitation [and] provide persons with disabilities with the same range, quality and standard of free or affordable health care and programmes as provided to other persons' (United Nations, 2006: Article 25). This is further underpinned by the 2003 Act's requirement that local authorities provide services designed to give persons with mental disorder 'the opportunity to lead lives which are as normal as possible' (section 25(2)(b)), which is also highly consistent with the CRPD and notably progressive in tone.

Summary

Overall, mental health legislation in all of the jurisdictions examined demonstrates strong emphasis on several key themes: treatment for mental illness, involuntary admission based on a combination of mental illness and risk (the precise balance between the two varying between jurisdictions), protection of the right to liberty (albeit with a shared position that this right may be qualified at times) and mental capacity (albeit that impaired mental capacity is a stronger prerequisite for any involuntary intervention in Northern Ireland than elsewhere). Most of all, however, the four jurisdictions find their greatest common ground in the fact that they protect certain human rights (especially the right to liberty) quite well in areas of traditional concern in mental healthcare (i.e. involuntary detention and treatment), but are less effective protecting rights in other areas (e.g. economic and social rights) (Kelly, 2011). As a result, the greatest progress is now likely to be made by focusing on mechanisms other than mental health legislation for protecting and promoting other rights that are often infringed among the mentally ill, such as economic and social rights, and assuring access to an adequate standard of care for voluntary and involuntary patients. This is where the idea of 'structural violence' is useful and constructive (Farmer, 1999, 2003).

Structural violence

In Chapter 6 of this book, schizophrenia was used as an example to demonstrate that, despite clear evidence of a substantial biological basis to the illness, social, economic and political factors play a large role in shaping its genesis, presentation, features, management and outcome. The adverse effects of these social, economic and political factors and practices, along with enduring stigma about mental illness, constitute a form of structural violence that acts to impair access to psychiatric care and social services, and amplifies the effects of schizophrenia in the lives of sufferers, their families and carers (Kelly, 2005). As a result of these overarching social and economic circumstances, individuals with schizophrenia are often systematically excluded from full participation in civic and social life, constrained to live lives that are shaped, in large part, by stigma, isolation, homelessness and denial of basic rights.

The sociological underpinnings of this situation are analysed using the theory of power outlined by Lukes (2005) and the theory of interest groups outlined by Olson (1965, 1982), and Chapter 6 argues that the enhancement of individual agency is central to efforts to address this 'power gap' experienced by people with mental illness (Kelly, 2006a).

Solutions are likely to involve a combination of: (a) rights-based approaches (e.g. strengthened advocacy, empowerment and guardianship processes, and increased emphasis on multi-level governance in mental health services, all informed by rights); (b) approaches based on enhancing direct political participation (e.g. voter registration, formation of more effective interest groups); and (c) additional approaches, including increasing accountability throughout services, recognising the effects of sociopolitical change on the context of care and adapting the concept of 'soft power' to strengthen advocacy programmes. Dismantling institutional filters and reversing the 'mobilisation of bias' against the mentally ill (Bachrach & Baratz, 1970) present particular challenges not only in terms of political reform, but also in terms of reforming societal attitudes that provide critical support to prevailing political and institutional assumptions and procedures relating to people with mental illness.

Mental health legislation has a key role to play in remedying this situation, but so too do the conceptual shifts and policy measures outlined in Chapter 6, many of which map more readily onto the right to dignity rather than the specific rights more commonly protected by mental health legislation (e.g. the right to liberty). As in many other areas of life, much activity and potential for progress in this area of mental illness are located in the realm between coercive law and complete freedom, in the sphere of social activity and activism (Kimball, 2014). An exclusive focus on legislative protection of the right to liberty alone, then, will clearly fail to address or even acknowledge the broader range of social injustices and denials of rights commonly experienced by people with mental illness in this broader sphere. Social and political solutions are required to address these broader denials of rights, as is the dedication and work of practising clinicians, who are in a unique position to take positive steps to help achieve social justice for the mentally ill, protect rights and effect meaningful change. Some of these steps are considered next.

Promoting rights and social justice

As previous chapters have discussed, issues relating to human rights are a staple feature of psychiatric practice. They arise in relation to virtually every area of practice, ranging from involuntary treatment to decisions about deployment of scarce resources, from neglect of the social rights of the mentally ill to reports of active abuse of rights and 'political psychiatry' in various parts of the world, such as Russia (van Voren, 2014) and the Czech Republic, the only country in the EU without an official mental health policy in 2014 (Allen, 2014). The concluding section of this book outlines key ways in which clinicians can protect and promote the human rights of people with mental illness through clinical practice, mental health service management, social engagement and international activism (Kelly, 2015*d*), in addition to the measures already outlined in Chapter 6 for political empowerment of the mentally ill (e.g. advocacy, voter registration, formation of more effective interest groups).

Clearly, the first step for clinicians is to become familiar with the human rights frameworks of the ECHR, WHO, UN and CRPD (Chapter 1), in terms of both their specific provisions and the values they seek to promote, as explored throughout this book. Familiarity with national mental health legislation is also essential (Chapters 2–5), but it is a key message of this book that observance of rights stretches well beyond legislative measures (Chapter 6) and into the realms of social and political activism (Eaton *et al*, 2014*a,b*). In this broader context, the materials and discussions presented in this book can be usefully supplemented by the five books relating to human rights and psychiatry listed in Box 7.1.

In terms of day-to-day clinical practice, it is clear that observance of the values and measures outlined in the UDHR, ECHR, CRPD and national mental health legislation requires a dynamic balance between support and autonomy, and this balance may vary over time, especially (but not exclusively) among persons with mental disorder (Minkowitz, 2010). To help operationalise these concepts in clinical practice, it is useful to re-emphasise that the concept of dignity is central to all rights and there is arguably no human right that is unconnected with dignity (Feldman, 2002; Osiatyński, 2009). The centrality of dignity is consistent with the emphasis that the UDHR and CRPD both place on 'inherent dignity', and provides an excellent foundational principle to guide the protection and promotion of human rights in psychiatric practice (Seedhouse & Gallagher, 2002; Kelly, 2014*b*).

It is also useful to bear in mind that dignity has both subjective and objective dimensions, and there is a dynamic interplay between the two in psychiatry, as is the case in other areas of life (Beyleveld & Brownsword, 2001; Feldman, 2002; Kelly, 2014*b*). Against this background, there are four key domains in which mental health practitioners can work to improve both objective and subjective dimensions of dignity among people with mental illness and their families and carers:

- day-to-day clinical practice
- mental health service management
- social engagement
- international activism.

Day-to-day clinical practice

The key way in which psychiatrists protect and promote human rights in clinical settings is by providing high-quality, evidence-based mental

---

Box 7.1 Five key books relating to human rights and psychiatry

Bartlett, P. & Sandland, R. (2014) *Mental Health Law: Policy and Practice* (4th edn). Oxford University Press

This text provides a superb guide to mental health law in practice, with plenty of references to recent cases and new legislation, especially in England and Wales, although its discussions and conclusions have broad international applicability.

Dudley, M., Silove, D. & Gale, F. (eds) (2012) *Mental Health and Human Rights: Vision, Praxis, and Courage*. Oxford University Press

This interesting, diverse volume includes contributions looking at culture and context in human rights, the relevance of genes and biology, political abuses of psychiatry, the pharmaceutical industry, vulnerable groups, rights in poorly resourced settings, and the challenges of global mental health and human rights.

McSherry, B. & Weller, P. (eds) (2010) *Rethinking Rights-Based Mental Health Laws*. Hart Publishing

The book presents a series of provocative and thoughtful essays on human rights and mental health law from a range of international perspectives. It includes contributions on the limits of rights-based approaches, the CRPD, compulsory out-patient treatment and human rights outside the 'first world'.

Gostin, L., Bartlett, P., Fennell. P., *et al* (eds) (2010) *Principles of Mental Health Law and Policy*. Oxford University Press

This is a detailed, comprehensive and important book, not least because the authors clearly recognise the links between mental health law and policy which together shape mental health services and, in significant part, the observance or denial of rights among the mentally ill.

Bartlett, P., Lewis, O. & Thorold, O. (2007) *Mental Disability and the European Convention on Human Rights.* Martinus Nijhoff Publishers

This text focuses on the ECHR and related case law in the context of mental disability, but is also an extremely valuable example of lucid thinking about rights, not only in the context of healthcare, but also in the context of broader community participation. As a result, many of the discussions throughout the book are of increasing relevance as experience with the CRPD grows internationally.

healthcare that reduces patients' symptoms, increases capabilities, enhances dignity and thus promotes rights. There is strong evidence that medications commonly used in psychiatry are as effective as those used in general medicine (Leucht *et al*, 2012) and there are growing, convincing evidence bases for myriad psychological therapies (Gabbard *et al*, 2007). Using these therapies wisely, judiciously and as indicated makes a strong contribution to enhancing patients' individual agency and promoting their rights.

That is not to say that routine clinical practice is necessarily sufficient in itself to promote patients' rights, but rather that providing care that is evidence based and effective is probably the most important contribution psychiatrists routinely make to increasing dignity and enjoyment of rights – and it is a vital contribution (Kelly, 2014*b*). Familiarity with national mental health legislation is a key element of this, and there are excellent guides available for the Mental Capacity Act 2005 (Brindle *et al*, 2015) and the Mental Health Act 1983, as amended in 2007, in England and Wales (Zigmond, 2016) to assist with this task. Multidisciplinary teamwork is also critical, recognising that recovery depends on diverse inputs that address social needs as well as psychological and medical ones (Gabbard & Kay, 2001). All of these measures in and of themselves help protect patients' rights in important and enduring ways, and help articulate key clinical values, such as compassion (Cox & Gray, 2014), in broader healthcare contexts.

Mental health service management

Psychiatrists are commonly involved in determining specific aspects of the management of mental health services and these, too, are key determinants of the circumstances in which patients construct and experience their recoveries. The circumstances in which services are provided are especially important determinants of the promotion or undermining of dignity, and Shotton & Seedhouse (1998) directly link loss of dignity with the extent to which circumstances prevent exercise of capabilities. In this context, they articulate various levels of loss of dignity, including trivial loss (when dignity is easily restored), serious loss (when substantial effort is required to restore dignity) and devastating loss (when it is impossible to regain dignity without help). An awareness of these possibilities can usefully inform clinicians' involvement in service planning and delivery, with particular emphasis on issues relating to loss of dignity in institutional and other psychiatric settings (Shannon, 2014),

More specifically, creating appropriate circumstances to support dignity involves developing an awareness of the importance of respect, weighing the balance between independence and dependence, and promoting the individual's own priorities and interests (Cashmore, 2014), in the context of staff practices, clinical environments, debates about equitable distribution of resources (Campbell, 2014) and various other aspects of organising care (Gallagher & Seedhouse, 2002). For psychiatrists, this approach supports the importance of involvement in service management that promotes improved circumstances for patients by offering mental health facilities of an adequate standard, developing staffing and rostering practices that recognise patient as well as staff realities, and ensuring patient involvement in service redevelopments and governance.

Social engagement

Mental illness and recovery are experienced in specific social contexts and these circumstances invariably play important roles in recovery and reintegration processes following episodes of mental disorder. Poor people are likely to develop mental disorders at earlier ages and have longer durations of untreated illness than more affluent peers (Kelly, 2005; 2006a). People with mental disorders are at increased risk of underemployment and homelessness, and more likely than those without mental disorders to be arrested in similar circumstances. These adverse societal factors, combined with the stigma of mental illness, constitute a form of 'structural violence' that amplifies the effects of mental disorders in the lives of sufferers and their families (Chapter 6), and effectively excludes many from full participation in civic and social life (Kelly, 2014c).

Against this background, there is a clear role for psychiatry in social advocacy for the mentally ill. This is likely to involve at least some of the measures outlined in Chapter 6 for political empowerment of individuals with mental illness (e.g. advocacy, voter registration, formation of more effective interest groups). The CRPD is of great assistance in this regard, owing to its welcome articulation of the rights of persons with disabilities in the broader social context, rather than just in the context of healthcare. The CRPD is thus a powerful tool with which to advocate for better, more equitable treatment of people with mental disorder not just in healthcare settings, but also in terms of social care, as well as broader acceptance and genuine integration in society.

A growing awareness of the importance of public mental health is another welcome recognition of the role of contextual factors in recovery from mental disorder and maintaining mental wellness (Eaton, 2012). There are clear, compelling roles for psychiatrists in these areas, especially in relation to social advocacy for their patients and ongoing programmes to address stigma, which remains a persistent problem for people with mental illness in most parts of the world (Dinos, 2014; Gergel, 2014; Howe et al, 2014).

International activism

Global inequality is easily the greatest single social and human rights issue of our time (Jacoby, 2014; Piketty, 2014) and global health inequality is the greatest single bioethical issue. This is as true in mental health as it is in other areas of medicine, if not more so. The WHO points out that, although 14% of the global burden of disease is attributable to mental, neurological and substance use disorders, most of the people affected (up to 75% in many low-income countries) do not have access to the treatment they need.[121] This is a truly global problem, and while the human rights issues commonly discussed in high-income countries (often relating to involuntary admission and treatment) certainly merit attention and remedy, the greatest human rights issue at global level is lack of access to care, rather than protection from it (Kelly, 2014c; Tuffrey-Wijne & Hollins, 2014).

In this context, issues of discrimination, exclusion from care, denial of agency and lack of social security are key factors in determining the kinds of lives that persons with mental disorder lead in many parts of the world (Kelly, 2005; Callard et al, 2012; Lamichhane, 2014). An international perspective is essential if mental health workers are to appreciate the nature and extent of these challenges and seek possible solutions (EU, UN, etc.) at transnational levels. In the area of mental health law, for example, there are diverse and contrasting developments in various jurisdictions: in Ireland, for example, it was recently proposed that 'dignity' should become the overarching principle of mental health legislation (Kelly, 2014b), whereas in Northern Ireland the Mental Capacity Bill 2015 suggests merging mental health and capacity legislation into a single act, thus increasing compliance with the CRPD but also, intriguingly, retaining 'best interests' as the overarching principle, in apparent (paradoxical) violation of the CRPD (Chapter 3). These diverse approaches merit study with a view to their applicability or adaptation elsewhere.

This book has focused on England and Wales, Northern Ireland, Ireland and Scotland, but equally interesting developments are occurring in other jurisdictions around the world: Callard et al (2012) provide valuable examples of initiatives and practices in countries such as New Zealand, India and Indonesia. An awareness of this global dimension to human rights in mental illness can both stimulate global activism at transnational level and enhance advocacy and protection of rights at local or national level. Box 7.2 presents specific resources and indicates ways of becoming involved.

An awareness of the global context also highlights the fact that, while protecting the right to liberty is a crucial first step in protecting and promoting the rights of the mentally ill, there are many other rights in need of protection too, most of which are substantially shaped by social, economic and political realities. All of these issues require solutions based not just in the clinic, but in the arenas of political advocacy, economic reform and campaigns for global social justice (Chapter 6).

The measures required include not only good-quality clinical care (which is clearly essential), but also better mental health service management, renewed social advocacy and engagement, and international activism, as well as steps to promote the empowerment of people with mental illness and their families, including formation of more effective interest groups, voter registration and broader political activism. In the words of the

---

Box 7.2   Five free online resources relating to human rights and psychiatry

The website of Human Rights in Mental Health – Federation Global Initiative on Psychiatry (FGIP) (www.gip-global.org) is an excellent resource for clinicians interested in human rights in psychiatry. The FGIP is an international non-profit foundation founded in 1980 as the International Association on the Political Use of Psychiatry. It actively supports the development of mental health services in low- and middle-income countries and seeks to bring about structural reforms, by working at grass-roots level with local partners and at governmental level with politicians and policy makers. The website provides a guide to the foundation's activities, access to publications and reports, and much more.

The World Health Organization (WHO) website has an excellent section devoted to mental health (www.who.int/mental_health/en). This portal provides access to a wealth of WHO resources relating to mental health policy, mental health in emergencies and, in particular, the 'WHO Mental Health Gap Action Programme' (mhGAP), which aims at scaling up services for mental, neurological and substance use disorders, especially in low- and middle-income countries.

The *WHO Resource Book on Mental Health, Human Rights and Legislation* (WHO, 2005) is available in its entirety online, free of charge (www.who.int/mental_health/ policy/legislation/Resource%20Book_Eng2_WEB_07%20%282%29.pdf). This is the most detailed set of human rights standards for mental health legislation published to date and includes a 'Checklist for Mental Health Legislation', detailing specific human rights standards which, according to the WHO, need to be met in each jurisdiction.

The United Nations (UN) Enable website (www.un.org/disabilities) is the official website of the Secretariat for the Convention on the Rights of Persons with Disabilities (CRPD) in the Division for Social Policy and Development of the Department of Economic and Social Affairs at the UN Secretariat. The website provides public information on topics related to disability, updates on the work of the UN for persons with disabilities, and provides a wealth of information about the CRPD, including its full text, dates of signature and ratification by various countries, and myriad other resources.

The website of the Royal College of Psychiatrists (www.rcpsych.ac.uk) has a section devoted to the College's Special Committee on Human Rights (www. rcpsych.ac.uk/workinpsychiatry/specialcommitteesofcouncil/humanrights.aspx). This site provides details of the committee's membership, a brief history, a statement of principles and purpose, and useful links to relevant legislation, articles and an especially useful guide to the UK legal system.

19th-century German pathologist, anthropologist and politician Rudolf Virchow (1821–1902): 'Medicine is a social science, and politics is nothing but medicine on a large scale' (Macleod & McCullough, 1994).

Aux barricades!

Notes

1   *HL v UK (Bournewood)* [2004] 40 EHRR 32. See also: *HM v Switzerland* [2004] 38 EHRR 17. In this case, HM resided in an unlocked area of an institution and, unlike HL, had continued contact with the outside world, so that the European Court of Human Rights ruled that there was no deprivation of liberty; HM also, later, consciously agreed to stay at this residence.

2   *Guzzardi v Italy* [1980] 3 EHRR 333. In this case, the patient was living at home subject to a curfew and limitation on geographical movements, and the European Court of Human Rights ruled that this represented detention under Article 5. See also: *Ashingdane v UK* [1985] 7 EHRR 528. In this case, there was a delay in the transfer of a detained individual from a high-security hospital to a local psychiatric hospital in which he would have likely enjoyed less severe circumstances of detention, but the European Court of Human Rights ruled that Article 5 concerned the fact of detention, and not the severity of the detention regime, so the delay in transfer did not represent a breach of Article 5 in this respect.

3   *Winterwerp v Netherlands* [1979] 2 EHRR 387. In this case, W, an individual with brain damage and schizophrenia, was detained in a psychiatric hospital under an emergency procedure following a theft, and later had the detention extended by a district court (supported by medical evidence); W later challenged his detention on various grounds, including the alleged absence of opportunity for him to challenge medical evidence. See also: *X v UK* [1981] 4 EHRR 188. In this case, the European Court of Human Rights noted that 'national authorities are better placed to evaluate the evidence adduced before them'; this is consistent with the Court's general reliance on national courts for the determination of facts and on medical doctors for medical opinions (such as the presence or absence of 'mental disorder').

4   *X v UK* [1981] 4 EHRR 188.

5   *X v UK* [1981] 4 EHRR 188. In this case, the only review of emergency detention available was the English habeas corpus procedure and the European Court of Human Rights ruled that this was sufficient to meet the requirements of Article 5(4) in the emergency situation.

6   The precise duration of an 'emergency' situation has not been determined by the Court; see: *Winterwerp v Netherlands* [1979] 2 EHRR 387 (in which the Court tolerated a 6-week emergency 'with hesitation'); see also: Bartlett *et al* (2007): p. 56.

7   *Hutchison Reid v UK* [2003] 37 EHRR 9. In this case, the applicant had a psychopathic disorder and national law stated that detention was warranted

only if medical treatment could alleviate or prevent deterioration of his condition; domestic courts determined that the availability of treatments that could alleviate symptoms or manifestations of the disorder (if not the disorder itself) was sufficient to justify detention, and the European Court of Human Rights upheld this decision.

8   *Van der Leer v Netherlands* [1990] 12 EHRR 567; *Ashingdane v UK* [1985] 7 EHRR 528; *Fox, Campbell and Hartley v UK* [1990] 13 EHRR 157.

9   *Aerts v Belgium* [1998] 29 EHRR 50. In this case, Aerts, who had substance misuse problems and borderline personality disorder, committed a serious assault and was detained under the Belgian Social Protection Act for treatment, but was sent to a prison, where therapeutic facilities were not available; the European Court of Human Rights concluded there had been a breach of Article 5(1)(e) owing to the non-availability of treatment in this setting.

10 *Herczegfalvy v Austria* [1991] 15 EHRR 437.

11 In *Nowicka v Poland* [2003] 1 FLR 417, the applicant was arrested on the order of a Polish District Court and placed in prison for the purpose of psychiatric examination; her daughter requested visiting rights and the District Court granted one visit per month; the European Court of Human Rights ruled that, although the detention could be considered to pursue legitimate aims, this restriction on visiting rights did not pursue, and was not proportionate to, any legitimate aim, and was therefore a breach of Article 8.

12 *Winterwerp v Netherlands* [1979] 2 EHRR 387. See also: *X v UK* [1981] 4 EHRR 188.

13 *Johnson v UK* [1997] 27 EHRR 296. In this case, the applicant was diagnosed with schizophrenia and personality disorder (later revised to 'drug-induced psychosis'), and although tribunals recommended phased discharge to a hostel, he remained detained in hospital for many years, despite medical opinion that he was no longer suffering from a mental disorder; the European Court of Human Rights found a violation of Article 5(1) owing to the indefinite deferral of release, but also noted that it may not be appropriate to 'order the immediate and absolute discharge of a person who is no longer suffering from the mental disorder which led to his confinement' but that such discharge might best occur in a phased fashion, subject to conditions.

14 *Kolanis v UK* [2006] 42 EHRR 12. In this case, the applicant was detained, but discharge was recommended by a mental health review tribunal provided that certain community conditions were met; these conditions were not met, the applicant was not discharged, and the applicant appealed against his continued detention; the European Court of Human Rights ruled that discharge was not appropriate in the absence of resources to meet the conditions under which discharge had been approved.

15 *Kolanis v UK* [2006] 42 EHRR 12. In this case, once the tribunal authorised discharge subject to certain conditions, the next date for tribunal review was 1 year later, which, the Court concluded, did not meet the requirement for 'promptness'.

16 See also: *Winterwerp v Netherlands* [1979] 2 EHRR 387. In this case, hearings held by the Dutch District and Regional Courts fulfilled the first two of these criteria but lacked 'judicial character': W had not been notified of various hearings and had not been afforded opportunity to question evidence against him.

17 *De Wilde, Ooms and Versyp v Belgium* [1972] 1 EHRR 438.

18 *HL v UK (Bournewood)* [2004] 40 EHRR 32.

19   *X v UK* [1981] 4 EHRR 188; discharge may, however, be delayed in order to ensure the safety of the patient or public; see *Johnson v UK* [1997] 27 EHRR 296.

20   *X v UK* [1981] 4 EHRR 188.

21   *Megyeri v Germany* [1992] 15 EHRR 584; see also: *Nikolova v Bulgaria* [2001] 31 EHRR 3; *Pereira v Portugal* [2003] 36 EHRR 49.

22   *E v Norway* [1990] 17 EHRR 30. In this case, E was transferred to a secure psychiatric setting on 21 July 1988; applied for a court hearing on 3 August 1988; and judgement was delivered on 27 September 1988.

23   *LR v France* [2002] Application No. 33395/96.

24   *TH v DPP* [2006] 3 IR 520.

25   *JF v DPP* [2005] 2 IR 174.

26   The Committee on the Rights of Persons with Disabilities examines reports on implementation of the CRPD submitted by UN member states. The Committee cannot legally enforce its recommendations or the provision of an overdue report, but reports are made public.

27   *X v UK* [1981] 4 EHRR 181.

28   *Winterwerp v Netherlands* [1979] 2 EHRR 387; *X v UK* [1981] 4 EHRR 188.

29   *R (H) v Mental Health Review Tribunal* [2002] EWHC 1522 (Admin), [2002] QB 1.

30   *R (M) v Secretary of State for Health* [2003] EWHC 1094 (Admin), [2003] 1 MHLR 88.

31   *R (N) v Ashworth Special Hospital Authority* [2001] EWHC 339 (Admin), [2001] HRLR 46.

32   *R (Munjaz) v Mersey Care NHS Trust* [2003] EWCA Civ 1036, [2004] QB 395.

33   *R (Munjaz) v Mersey Care NHS Trust* [2005] UKHL 58, [2006] 2 AC 148.

34   *Munjaz v UK* [2012] App no 2913/06 (ECHR, 17 July).

35   The European Court of Human Rights did, however, acknowledge that there may be circumstances in which further deprivation of a detained individual's residual liberty may engage Article 5 rights, in contrast to the position outlined in *R v Deputy Governor of Parkhurst Prison, ex parte Hague and Weldon* [1992] 1 AC 58. This ruling may have implications for advocates or lawyers challenging various specific additional restrictions placed on detained patients.

36   *R (D) v Secretary of State for the Home Department* [2002] EWHC 2805 (Admin), [2003] 1 WLR 1315; see also: *Benjamin v UK* (2002) 36 EHRR 1.

37   *R (KB) v Mental Health Review Tribunal* [2003] EWHC 193 (Admin), [2004] QB 936.

38   *R (C) v London South and West Region Mental Health Review Tribunal* [2001] EWCA Civ 1110, [2002] 1 WLR 176. In this case, automatically listing hearings to take place 8 weeks after application was deemed to be a breach of Article 5(4) of the ECHR as it did not permit flexibility in response to patient's circumstances.

39   *R (M) v Secretary of State for Health* [2003] EWHC 1094 (Admin), [2003] 1 MHLR 88.

40   *R (PS) v Responsible Medical Officer* [2003] EWHC 2335 (Admin).

41   *Hutchison Reid v UK* [2003] 37 EHRR 211. See also: Buchanan & Grounds (2011), Duggan (2011).

42   *Savage v South Essex Partnership NHS Foundation Trust* [2008] UKHL 74, [2010] EWHC 865 (QB).

43   *Rabone & Anor v Pennine Care NHS Trust* [2012] UKSC 2. See also: Bowcott (2012), Madden (2012).

44   *R (N) v Ashworth Special Hospital Authority* [2001] EWHC 339 (Admin), [2001] HRLR 46.

45 *Winterwerp v Netherlands* [1979] 2 EHRR 387.
46 *R (M) v Secretary of State for Health* [2003] EWHC 1094 (Admin), [2003] 1 MHLR 88.
47 *Johnson v UK* [1997] 27 EHRR 296.
48 *Winterwerp v Netherlands* [1979] 2 EHRR 387.
49 The House of Lords has found that this does not violate ECHR rights (*R (H) v Secretary of State for Health* [2005] UKHL 60, [2006] 1 AC 441).
50 *R (M) v Secretary of State for Health* [2003] EWHC 1094 (Admin); [2003] 1 MHLR 88.
51 *R (PS) v Responsible Medical Officer* [2003] EWHC 2335 (Admin).
52 *Hutchison Reid v UK* [2003] 37 EHRR 211.
53 Section 4 concerns 'admission for assessment in cases of emergency'; sections 5(2) and (4) concern making an 'application in respect of patient already in hospital'; section 135 concerns a 'warrant to search for and remove patients'; and section 136 concerns 'mentally disordered persons found in public places'.
54 *Winterwerp v Netherlands* [1979] 2 EHRR 387.
55 *HL v UK (Bournewood)* [2004] 40 EHRR 32.
56 'Psychiatrists welcome Northern Ireland announcement of world-first single capacity and mental health legislation' (www.rcpsych.ac.uk/mediacentre/pressreleasearchives/2009/annsinglecapacitymhlegislation.aspx). Accessed 26 November 2015.
57 This relates to 'compulsory admission to hospital and guardianship'.
58 This Convention contains various measures concerning legal and jurisdictional issues relating to 'the protection in international situations of adults who, by reason of an impairment or insufficiency of their personal faculties, are not in a position to protect their interests' (Convention on the International Protection of Adults: Preamble; see also: Hill, 2009). Schedule 9 of the 2015 Bill gives effect to the Convention in Northern Ireland and 'makes related provision as to the private international law of Northern Ireland' (section 272).
59 In England, the Supreme Court has confirmed that there are two key questions to ask in order to determine whether a deprivation of liberty has occurred (referred to by Lady Hale as the 'acid test'): Is the person subject to continuous supervision and control? *and* Is the person free to leave? (*P v Cheshire West and Chester Council & Anor, and P and Q v Surrey County Council* [2014] UKSC 19).
60 See: section 25(3) and Schedules 1 and 2. This requirement does not apply in an 'emergency' (section 24(3)); 'emergency' is defined in section 62.
61 As previously, it is necessary that 'before doing the act, D takes reasonable steps to establish whether P lacks capacity in relation to the matter' (section 9(1)(c)) and 'when doing the act, D reasonably believes: (i) that P lacks capacity in relation to the matter; and (ii) that it will be in P's best interests for the act to be done' (section 9(1)(d)).
62 There is, again, an exemption in 'an emergency' (section 22(3)).
63 The first extension, based on a medical report within the previous month and a statement from the 'responsible person' (e.g. an approved social worker), may extend the authorisation for 6 months (sections 37 and 39). Further extensions are for periods of 1 year, based on a medical report within the previous 2 months and a statement from the 'responsible person' (sections 38 and 39). In addition, the 'nominated person' (section 52) and 'independent advocate' (section 53) must be consulted and their views taken into account in making the report (section 43(3)). Overall, 'provided the criteria for authorisation

continue to be met, it will be possible to extend the original authorisation (initially for 6 months and then yearly thereafter) without the need for referral back to the panel' (DHSSPSNI & NIDoJ, 2014: p. 27).

64 Section 66(1): 'An act is done "despite" a reasonable objection from a person's nominated person if the nominated person: (a) has reasonably objected to the proposal to do the act; and (b) has not, by the time the act is done, withdrawn that objection (by any means)'.

65 Section 66(1): 'An act is resisted by a person if the doing of the act is secured by the use of force or a threat to use force'.

66 That is, if P is subject to compulsion under the legislation (section 23).

67 There is also a 'duty of HSC trust to notify the Attorney General' in certain circumstances (section 49).

68 Section 132(8): 'In this section "impairing condition" means a condition which is (or may be) attributable to, or which causes or contributes to (or may cause or contribute to), an impairment of, or a disturbance in the functioning of, the mind or brain'.

69 Part 10 ('Criminal justice') is beyond the scope of this book, as is Part 12 ('Children').

70 *R (Munjaz) v Mersey Care NHS Trust* [2005] UKHL 58, [2006] 2 AC 148.

71 *Croke v Smith* [1994] 3 IR 529; *Croke v Smith (No. 2)* [1998] 1 IR 101, *Croke v Ireland* [2000] ECHR 680.

72 The phrase 'serious likelihood' of harm has been interpreted by the High Court to represent a standard of proof of a high level of probability that is beyond the normal standard of proof in civil actions (i.e. more likely, or probable, to be true), but below the standard in criminal prosecution (i.e. beyond reasonable doubt); i.e. 'proof to a standard of a high level of likelihood as distinct from simply being more likely to be true' (*MR v Cathy Byrne, administrator, and Dr. Fidelma Flynn, clinical director, Sligo Mental Health Services, Ballytivnan, Co. Sligo* [2007] IEHC 73). In the same case, the meaning of the word 'serious' in the phrase 'immediate and serious harm' was interpreted as differing depending on whether the harm is directed at self or others: 'Clearly, the infliction of any physical injury on another could only be regarded as "serious" harm, while the infliction of a minor physical injury on the person themselves could be regarded as not "serious"'.

73 Each new period of detention begins on the expiry of the previous period, once the renewal order has been completed prior to the expiry of the previous order (*MD v Clinical Director of St Brendan's Hospital & Anor* [2007] IEHC 183); see also: Madden (2007).

74 Renewal orders should be completed by the consultant psychiatrist responsible for the care and treatment of the patient; more than one consultant psychiatrist may meet that description (e.g. if a detained patient is under the care of a consultant forensic psychiatrist in the Central Mental Hospital, Ireland's forensic psychiatry inpatient facility, but their catchment-area or usual psychiatrist is also involved in their treatment) (*JB v The Director of the Central Mental Hospital and Dr. Ronan Hearne and the Mental Health Commission and the Mental Health Tribunal* [2007] IEHC 201). See also: *MM v Clinical Director Central Mental Hospital* [2008] IESC 31; Madden (2008a).

75 Such transfers must be arranged by the clinical director, but the High Court found that, in cases of medical emergency, it would be 'manifestly absurd and contrary to the whole spirit and intention of the Act' to potentially jeopardise the health of a detained patient owing to the non-availability of the clinical

director to personally 'arrange' such transfer to a medical facility; other staff may do so under such circumstances (*Patrick McCreevy v The Medical Director of the Mater Misericordiae Hospital in the City of Dublin, and the Clinical Director of St. Aloysius Ward Psychiatric Unit of the Mater Misericordiae Hospital in the City of Dublin and the Health Service Executive and, by order, the Mental Health Tribunal* [2007] SS 1413).

76 The individual must *express a desire to leave* for this procedure to be invoked; other expressions of disagreement with treatment plans (e.g. declining medication) do not constitute grounds for detention under this section (*Q v St Patrick's Hospital* [2006] O'Higgins J, *ex tempore*, 21 December 2006).

77 The 21 days commence on the date of the *making* of the renewal order, even if it does not come into effect on that day (i.e. if it has been made some days in advance of the expiry of the existing detention order) (*AMC v St Lukes Hospital, Clonmel* [2007] IEHC 65).

78 *D Han v The President of the Circuit Court and Doctor Malcolm Garland and Doctor Richard Blennerhassett and Doctor Conor Farren and Professor Patrick McKeon and the Mental Health Commission and the Mental Health Tribunal* [2008] IEHC 160.

79 *E v Norway* (1990) 17 EHRR 30. In this case, E was transferred to a secure psychiatric setting on 21 July 1988; applied for a court hearing on 3 August 1988; and judgment was delivered on 27 September 1988.

80 *LR v France* [2002] Application No. 33395/96 (ECHR, 27 June 2002).

81 *Z v Khattak & Anor* [2008] IEHC 262.

82 The Mental Health Subcommittee of the Criminal Law Committee of the (Irish) Law Society subsequently noted that the judge had 'endorsed, less than overwhelmingly,' this mental state examination (Mental Health Subcommittee, 2009: p. 44).

83 *Hutchison Reid v UK* [2003] 37 EHRR 211.

84 *TS v Mental Health Tribunal, Ireland, The Attorney General, The Minister for Health and Children, The Mental Health Commission, Bola Oluwole and Ciaran Power* [2007] JR 1562.

85 *Hutchison Reid v UK* [2003] 37 EHRR 211.

86 *TS v Mental Health Tribunal, Ireland, The Attorney General, The Minister for Health and Children, The Mental Health Commission, Bola Oluwole and Ciaran Power* [2007] JR 1562. This is also the position held by the Department of Health and Children (2007: p. 16).

87 *T O'D. v Harry Kennedy & Ors* [2007] IEHC 129.

88 *D Han v The President of the Circuit Court and Doctor Malcolm Garland and Doctor Richard Blennerhassett and Doctor Conor Farren and Professor Patrick McKeon and the Mental Health Commission and the Mental Health Tribunal* [2008] IEHC 160.

89 *EH v Clinical Director of St. Vincent's Hospital & Ors* [2009] IEHC 69.

90 *EH v St. Vincent's Hospital & Ors* [2009] IESC 46.

91 Section 56: 'In this Part "consent", in relation to a patient, means consent obtained freely without threats or inducements, where: (a) the consultant psychiatrist responsible for the care and treatment of the patient is satisfied that the patient is capable of understanding the nature, purpose and likely effects of the proposed treatment; and (b) the consultant psychiatrist has given the patient adequate information, in a form and language that the patient can understand, on the nature, purpose and likely effects of the proposed treatment.'

92 *HL v UK (Bournewood)* [2004] 40 EHRR 761.

93   *SM v The Mental Health Commissioner, The Mental Health Tribunal, The Clinical Director of St Patrick's Hospital, Dublin, Attorney General and the Human Rights Commission* [2008] JR 749.

94   *JH v Vincent Russell, Clinical Director of Cavan General Hospital* [2007] unreported High Court judgment.

95   *MR v Cathy Byrne, administrator, and Dr. Fidelma Flynn, clinical director, Sligo Mental Health Services, Ballytivnan, Co. Sligo* [2007] IEHC 73.

96   *EH v St. Vincent's Hospital & Ors* [2009] IESC 46.

97   *T O'D. v Harry Kennedy & Ors* [2007] IEHC 129.

98   *PL v Clinical Director of St. Patricks University Hospital and Dr. Séamus Ó Ceallaigh* [2012] IEHC 15.

99   *FW v Dept. of Psychiatry James Connolly Memorial Hospital* [2008] IEHC 283. Although a spouse can make an application for involuntary admission, the term 'spouse', for this purpose, does not include a person 'in respect of whom an application or order has been made under the Domestic Violence Act, 1996' (Mental Health Act 2001: section 9(8)). See also: Madden (2008*b*).

100 *FW v Dept. of Psychiatry James Connolly Memorial Hospital* [2008] IEHC 283.

101 See, for example, *EH v St. Vincent's Hospital & Ors* [2009] IESC 46; *MR v Cathy Byrne, administrator, and Dr. Fidelma Flynn, clinical director, Sligo Mental Health Services, Ballytivnan, Co. Sligo* [2007] IEHC 73; *T O'D. v Harry Kennedy & Ors* [2007] IEHC 129.

102 *WQ v Mental Health Commission* [2007] IEHC 154; see also: *Q v St Patrick's Hospital* [2006] O'Higgins J, *ex tempore*, 21 December 2006.

103 See also: *FX v Clinical Director of the Central Mental Hospital* [2015] IEHC 190 (especially paragraphs 42–44 in relation to 'best interests' and applications to the High Court).

104 I was nominated to the Expert Group on the Review of the Mental Health Act 2001 by the College of Psychiatrists of Ireland and appointed to the group by Minister Kathleen Lynch, Minister for Primary Care, Social Care (Disabilities and Older People) and Mental Health, in 2012. I have written this book in a personal capacity, as a psychiatrist. The views expressed are mine and not necessarily those of the Expert Group on the Review of the Mental Health Act 2001, the College of Psychiatrists of Ireland or any other body or person.

105 This section of the book is largely an adapted version of Kelly (2015*b*).

106 *EH v Clinical Director of St. Vincent's Hospital & Ors* [2009] IEHC 69; *EH v St. Vincent's Hospital & Ors* [2009] IESC 46.

107 Ireland's multiprofession health regulator.

108 A person over the age of 16 years can nominate a named person, who can play various roles under the legislation (sections 250–253, 255–257).

109 See Schedule 1 of the 2003 Act for more details regarding the Mental Welfare Commission for Scotland.

110 The definition of 'nearest relative' is outlined in section 254.

111 'Subject to Regulation 3, the circumstances in which there is to be taken to be a conflict of interest in relation to the medical examination for the purposes of sections 44 (short-term detention in hospital) and 47 (extension of short-term detention in hospital) are where the approved medical practitioner is: (a) related to the patient in any degree specified in the Schedule; or (b) employed by or contracted to provide services in or to an independent health care service in which the patient will be detained if detention is authorised under either section 44 or, as the case may be, section 47' (The Mental Health (Conflict

of Interest) (Scotland) (No. 2) Regulations 2005, Para. 2). 'Notwithstanding Regulation 2, the circumstances in which there is not to be taken to be a conflict of interest in relation to the medical examination for the purposes of sections 44 and 47, are where failure by the approved medical practitioner to carry out the medical examination would result in a delay which would involve serious risk to the health, safety or welfare of the patient or to the safety of other persons' (Para. 3).

112 *Winterwerp v Netherlands* [1979] 2 EHRR 387.

113 'The circumstances in which there is to be taken to be a conflict of interest in relation to the medical examination for the purposes of section 58(5) (requirements for medical examinations relating to compulsory treatment orders) are where: (a) either medical practitioner is related to the patient in any degree specified in the Schedule; (b) the two medical practitioners are related to each other in any degree specified in the Schedule; (c) it is proposed that the compulsory treatment order should authorise the detention of the patient in an independent health care service and either medical practitioner is employed by or contracted to provide services in or to that independent health care service; or (d) it is proposed that the compulsory treatment order should authorise the detention of the patient in a hospital other than an independent health care service and both medical practitioners are employed by or contracted to provide services in or to that hospital' (The Mental Health (Conflict of Interest) (Scotland) (No. 2) Regulations 2005, Para. 4(1)). See also: Paras 4(2) and 5.

114 Section 66(1) concerns 'measures that may be authorised', including details of detention at a 'specified hospital', the giving of 'medical treatment', attendance for 'medical treatment' or 'community care services', a requirement to 'reside at a specified place' and a requirement to permit visits by, for example, the 'mental health officer' or 'responsible medical officer'.

115 *R (Munjaz) v Mersey Care NHS Trust* [2005] UKHL 58, [2006] 2 AC 148.

116 See, for example: *R (N) v Ashworth Special Hospital Authority* [2001] EWHC 339 (Admin), [2001] HRLR 46.

117 Mental Health (Care and Treatment) (Scotland) Act 2003, Part 17 (Chapter 1).

118 Mental Health Act 1983, sections 26–30.

119 Mental Capacity Bill (2015), Part 3.

120 The Mental Health (Care and Treatment) (Scotland) Act 2003 is a notable and progressive exception, as it explicitly requires local authorities to provide broad-based social services to certain patients; i.e. the local authority '(a) shall: (i) provide, for persons who are not in hospital and who have or have had a mental disorder, services which provide care and support; or (ii) secure the provision of such services for such persons; and (b) may: (i) provide such services for persons who are in hospital and who have or have had a mental disorder; or (ii) secure the provision of such services for such persons' (section 25(1)). Such services 'shall be designed to: (a) minimise the effect of the mental disorder on such persons; and (b) give such persons the opportunity to lead lives which are as normal as possible' (section 25(2)). In this context, 'care and support' includes 'residential accommodation' and 'personal care and personal support', although not 'nursing care' (section 25(3)).

121 'WHO Mental Health Gap Action Programme (mhGAP)' (www.who.int/mental_health/mhgap/en). Accessed 26 November 2015.

References

Adams, G. B. (1912) *The Origin of the English Constitution*. Yale University Press.

Addington, J., Van Mastrigt, S. & Addington, D. (2004) Duration of untreated psychosis. *Psychological Medicine*, **34**, 277–284.

Al-Maskari, F., Shah, S. M., Al-Sharhan, R., *et al* (2011) Prevalence of depression and suicidal behaviors among male migrant workers in United Arab Emirates. *Journal of Immigrant and Minority Health*, **13**, 1027–1032.

Ali, A. Y. (1989) *The Meaning of the Holy Qur'an*. Amana Publications.

Allen, S. (2014) Coercion and human rights in Czech psychiatry: a human rights perspective from MDAC. *Lancet Psychiatry*, **1**, 177–178.

American Psychiatric Association (2013) *Diagnostic and Statistical Manual of Mental Disorders (5th edn) (DSM-5)*. American Psychiatric Association.

Andrews, J. & Scull, A. (2002) *Customers and Patrons of the Mad-Trade: The Management of Lunacy in Eighteenth-Century London, with the Complete Text of John Munro's 1766 Case Book*. University of California Press.

Appelbaum, P. S., Bonnie, R. J. & Karlawish, J. H. (2005) The capacity to vote of persons with Alzheimer's disease. *American Journal of Psychiatry*, **162**, 2094–2100.

Arboleda-Flórez, J. (2003) Considerations on the stigma of mental illness. *Canadian Journal of Psychiatry*, **48**, 645–650.

Armijo, J., Méndez, E., Morales, R., *et al* (2013) Efficacy of community treatments for schizophrenia and other psychotic disorders: a literature review. *Frontiers in Psychiatry*, **4**, 116.

Associated Press (2012) China passes mental health law. *Guardian*, 26 October.

Auquier, P., Tinland, A., Fortanier, C., *et al* (2013) Toward meeting the needs of homeless people with schizophrenia: the validity of quality of life measurement. *PLoS One*, **8**, e79677.

Axer, H. A., Corrigan, P. W. & Liberman, R. P. (1992) Helping chronic psychiatric patients adjust to sociopolitical changes in Poland. *Psychiatry*, **55**, 207–213.

Bachrach, P. & Baratz, M. S. (1970) *Power and Poverty: Theory and Practice*. Oxford University Press.

Bacik, I. (2001) A human rights culture for Ireland? In *Towards a Culture of Human Rights in Ireland* (eds I. Bacik & S. Livingstone), pp. 1–45. Cork University Press in association with the Centre for Cross Border Studies (Armagh).

Bainbridge, E., Byrne, F., Hallahan, B., *et al* (2014) Clinical stability in the community associated with long-term approved leave under the Mental Health Act 2001. *Irish Journal of Psychological Medicine*, **31**, 143–148.

Baker, N. (2009) Psychiatrists seek to readmit patients released by tribunals. *Irish Examiner*, 7 April.

Bamford Review of Mental Health and Learning Disability (Northern Ireland) (2007a) *A Comprehensive Legislative Framework*. Department of Health, Social Services and Public Safety.

Bamford Review of Mental Health and Learning Disability (Northern Ireland) (2007*b*) *A Comprehensive Legislative Framework: Executive Summary*. Department of Health, Social Services and Public Safety.

Bamrah, J. S., Datta, S., Rahim, A., *et al* (2007) UK's Mental Health Bill. *Lancet*, **370**, 1029.

Barczyk, A. N. (2015) Relationship between the public's belief in recovery, level of mental illness stigma, and previous contact. *Community Mental Health Journal*, **51**, 38–47.

Barnes, J.-A. (2006*a*) Red-letter day for mental health? *Irish Medical News*, **41**, 4.

Barnes, J.-A. (2006*b*) Mental health chief confident HSE will meet legal obligations. *Irish Medical News*, **40**, 24.

Barnes, J.-A. (2007) Mental health tribunals cost €2.56m. *Irish Medical News*, **22**, 12.

Bartlett, P. (2012) The United Nations Convention on the Rights of Persons with Disabilities and mental health law. *Modern Law Review*, **75**, 752–778.

Bartlett, P. & McHale, J. (2003) Mental incapacity and mental health: the development of legal reform and the need for joined-up thinking. *Journal of Social Welfare and Family Law*, **25**, 313–324.

Bartlett, P. & Sandland, R. (2014) *Mental Health Law: Policy and Practice* (4th edn). Oxford University Press.

Bartlett, P., Lewis, O. & Thorold, O. (2007) *Mental Disability and the European Convention on Human Rights*. Martinus Nijhoff Publishers.

Batty, D. (2008) Law 'reinforced mental health stereotypes'. *Guardian*, 18 February.

Bebbington, P. & Ramana, R. (1995) The epidemiology of bipolar affective disorder. *Social Psychiatry and Psychiatric Epidemiology*, **30**, 279–292.

Behan, C., Kennelly, B. & O'Callaghan, E. (2008) The economic cost of schizophrenia in Ireland: a cost of illness study. *Irish Journal of Psychological Medicine*, **25**, 80–87.

Bellino, S., Rocca, P., Patria, L., *et al* (2004) Relationships of age at onset with clinical features and cognitive functions in a sample of schizophrenia patients. *Journal of Clinical Psychiatry*, **65**, 908–914.

Bennett, D. M. (2014) The UN Convention on the Rights of Persons with Disabilities and UK mental health legislation. *British Journal of Psychiatry*, **205**, 76–77.

Bennett, D. M. & Mitchell, K. M. (2007) Is the Mental Health (Care and Treatment) (Scotland) Act 2003 the least restrictive option? *Psychiatric Bulletin*, **31**, 194.

Bernstein, R. A., Manchester, R. A. & Weaver, L. A. (1980) The effect of visiting on psychiatric patients in a general hospital. *Community Mental Health Journal*, **16**, 235–240.

Beyleveld, D. & Brownsword, R. (2001) *Human Dignity in Bioethics and Biolaw*. Oxford University Press.

Bhopal, J. S., Meagher, J. B. & Soos, J. (1988) Political awareness of psychiatric patients. *Canadian Medical Association Journal*, **139**, 1033.

Bhugra, D. & Appleby, L. (2008) Mental illness, the law and rudeness. *Guardian*, 3 Nov.

Bhugra, D. & Jones, P. (2001) Migration and mental illness. *Advances in Psychiatric Treatment*, **7**, 216–222.

Bindman, J., Maingay, S. & Szmukler, G. (2003) The Human Rights Act and mental health legislation. *British Journal of Psychiatry*, **182**, 91–94.

Bloch, S. & Reddaway, P. (1977) *Russia's Political Hospitals: The Abuse of Psychiatry in the Soviet Union*. Victor Gollancz.

Bloch, S. & Reddaway, P. (1985) *Soviet Psychiatric Abuse: The Shadow Over World Psychiatry*. Westview Press.

Block, F. (1987) *Revising State Theory*. Temple University Press.

Bluglass, R. (1984) The origins of the Mental Health Act 1983: doctors in the house. *Bulletin of the Royal College of Psychiatrists*, **8**, 127–134.

Blumenthal, S. & Wessely, S. (1994) The cost of mental health review tribunals. *Psychiatric Bulletin*, **18**, 274–276.

Bowcott, O. (2012) Hospital breached duty of care to psychiatric patient, supreme court rules. *Guardian*, 8 February.

Bowen, P. (2007) *Blackstone's Guide to The Mental Health Act 2007*. Oxford University Press.

Boydell, J., Van Os, J., McKenzie, K., *et al* (2001) Incidence of schizophrenia in ethnic minorities in ecological study into interactions with environment. *BMJ*, **323**, 1336–1338.

Boydell, J., McKenzie, K., Van Os, J., *et al* (2002) The social causes of schizophrenia. *Schizophrenia Research*, **53** (suppl. 1), 264.

Branigan, T. (2010) China accused of holding woman in mental hospital for challenging officials. *Guardian*, 31 August.

Brindle, D. (2007) A new act, but mental health battles remain. *Guardian*, 11 July.

Brindle, N., Branton, T., Stansfield, A., *et al* (2015) *A Clinician's Brief Guide to the Mental Capacity Act* (2nd edn). RCPsych Publications.

Brown, S. (1997) Excess mortality in schizophrenia: a meta-analysis. *British Journal of Psychiatry*, **171**, 502–508.

Buchanan, A. & Grounds, A. (2011) Forensic psychiatry and public protection. *British Journal of Psychiatry*, **198**, 420–423.

Bugajski, J. (1987) *Czechoslovakia: Charter 77's Decade of Dissent*. Praeger Publishers.

Bullenkamp, J. & Voges, B. (2004) Voting preferences of outpatients with chronic mental illness in Germany. *Psychiatric Services*, **55**, 1440–1442.

Burns, T., Rugkåsa, J., Molodynski, A., *et al* (2013) Community treatment orders for patients with psychosis (OCTET): a randomised controlled trial. *Lancet*, **381**, 1627–1633.

Butcher, J. (2007) Controversial Mental Health Bill reaches the finishing line. *Lancet*, **370**, 117–118.

Byrne, P. (1999) Stigma of mental illness: changing minds, changing behaviour. *British Journal of Psychiatry*, **174**, 1–2.

Byrne, P. (2000) Stigma of mental illness and ways of diminishing it. *Advances in Psychiatric Treatment*, **6**, 65–72.

Callard, F., Sartorius, N., Arboleda-Flórez, J., *et al* (2012) *Mental Illness, Discrimination and the Law: Fighting for Social Justice*. Wiley-Blackwell.

Campbell, D. (2014) Mental health patients face postcode lottery, claims Labour. *Guardian*, 25 July.

Cantor-Graae, E. & Selten, J. P. (2005) Schizophrenia and migration: a meta-analysis and review. *American Journal of Psychiatry*, **162**, 12–24.

Carlisle, D. (2003) Dereliction of duty. *Health Service Journal*, **113**, 12–15.

Carney, T. (2012) Australian mental health tribunals – 'space' for rights, protection, treatment and governance? *International Journal of Law and Psychiatry*, **35**, 1–10.

Carolan, M. (2008*a*) Psychiatric patient takes case against involuntary detention in hospital. *Irish Times*, 16 October.

Carolan, M. (2008*b*) Woman's hospital detention ruled unlawful by court. *Irish Times*, 1 November.

Carswell, C., Donaldson, A. & Brown, K. (2007) Psychiatrists' views and experiences of the Mental Health (Care and Treatment) (Scotland) Act 2003. *Psychiatric Bulletin*, **31**, 83–85.

Casey, P. & Kelly, B. D. (2007) *Fish's Clinical Psychopathology: Signs and Symptoms in Psychiatry* (3rd edn). Gaskell.

Casey, P., Brady, P., Craven, C., *et al* (2010) *Psychiatry and the Law* (2nd edn). Blackhall Publishing.

Cashmore, P. (2014) Cruel intentions. *Guardian (G2)*, 28 July.

Caspi, A., Sugden, K., Moffitt, T. E., *et al* (2003) Influence of life stress on depression: moderation by a polymorphism in the 5-HTT gene. *Science*, **301**, 386–389.

Cassese, A. (1992) The General Assembly: historical perspective, 1945–1989. In *The United Nations and Human Rights: A Critical Appraisal* (ed P. Alston), pp. 25–54. Clarendon Press.

Chang, W. (1998) The Confucian theory of norms and human rights. In *Confucianism and Human Rights* (eds W. T. de Bary & T. Weimings), pp. 117–141. Columbia University Press.

Cicero, M. T. (54–51 BC) *De re publica*. Reprinted (1950) as *On the Commonwealth* (trans. G. Sabine & S. Smith). Bobbs-Merrill.

Clarke, M., Brown, S., McTigue, O., *et al* (1999) Duration of untreated psychosis in first episode schizophrenia and its relationship to premorbid functioning. *Schizophrenia Research*, **36** (suppl.), 38–39.

Clement, S., Schauman, O., Graham, T., *et al* (2015) What is the impact of mental health-related stigma on help-seeking? A systematic review of quantitative and qualitative studies. *Psychological Medicine*, **45**, 11–27.

Coid, J. W. (1994) The Christopher Clunis enquiry. *Psychiatric Bulletin*, **18**, 449–452.

Collins, S. (2008) Emergency mental health law rushed through Dáil. *Irish Times*, 31 October.

Committee on the Rights of Persons with Disabilities (2014) *General Comment No. 1 (2014): Article 12: Equal Recognition before the Law*. United Nations.

Cooney, T., O'Neill, O. (1996) *Psychiatric Detention: Civil Commitment in Ireland (Kritik 1)*. Baikonur.

Coulter, C. (2005) Legal rights of mental health sufferers ignored. *Irish Times*, 1 November.

Coulter, C. (2008) Government and judge combine to clear up loophole. *Irish Times*, 1 November.

Council of Europe (1950) *European Convention on Human Rights (Convention for the Protection of Human Rights and Fundamental Freedoms)*. Council of Europe.

Council of Europe (1977) *Recommendation (818) on the Situation of the Mentally Ill*. Council of Europe.

Council of Europe (1983) *Recommendation R(83)2 of the Committee of Ministers to Member States Concerning the Legal Protection of Persons Suffering from Mental Disorder Placed as Involuntary Patients*. Council of Europe.

Council of Europe (1994) *Recommendation 1235 on Psychiatry and Human Rights*. Council of Europe.

Council of Europe (2000a) *White Paper Regarding a Draft Recommendation on Legal Protection of Persons Suffering from Mental Disorder*. Council of Europe.

Council of Europe (2000b) *White Paper on the Protection of the Human Rights and Dignity of People Suffering from Mental Disorder*. Council of Europe.

Court, C. (1994) Clunis inquiry cites 'catalogue of failure'. *BMJ*, **308**, 613.

Cox, J. & Gray, A. (2014) The College reply to Francis misses the big question: a commentary on OP92. *Psychiatric Bulletin*, **38**, 152–153.

Craven, C. (2009) Signs of paternalist approach to the mentally ill persist. *Irish Times*, 27 July.

Crenson, M. A. (1972) *Unpolitics of Air Pollution*. Johns Hopkins University Press.

Croudace, T. J., Kayne, R., Jones, P. B., *et al* (2000) Non-linear relationship between an index of social deprivation, psychiatric admission prevalence and the incidence of psychosis. *Psychological Medicine*, **30**, 177–185.

Crowther, R., Marshall, M., Bond, G. R., *et al* (2001) Vocational rehabilitation for people with severe mental illness. *Cochrane Database of Systematic Reviews*, **2**, CD003080.

Crumlish, N. & O'Rourke, K. (2010) A systematic review of treatments for post-traumatic stress disorder among refugees and asylum-seekers. *Journal of Nervous and Mental Disease*, **198**, 237–251.

Crump, C., Winkleby, M. A., Sundquist, K., *et al* (2013) Comorbidities and mortality in persons with schizophrenia: a Swedish national cohort study. *American Journal of Psychiatry*, **170**, 324–333.

Cummings, E. & O'Conor, O. (2009) The SM Judgment and the Mental Health Act 2008. *Irish Medical Journal*, **7**, 234.

Curtice, M. J. R. (2009) Medical treatment under Part IV of the Mental Health Act 1983 and the Human Rights Act 1998: review of Article 3 and 8 case law. *Psychiatric Bulletin*, **33**, 111–115.

Cutcliffe, J. & Happell, B. (2009) Psychiatry, mental health nurses, and invisible power: exploring a perturbed relationship within contemporary mental health care. *International Journal of Mental Health Nursing*, **18**, 116–125.

Dahl, R. A. (1961) *Who Governs? Democracy and Power in an American City*. Yale University Press.

Dahl, R. A. (1972) *Polyarchy: Participation and Opposition*. Yale University Press.

Dain, N. (1994) Reflections on antipsychiatry and stigma in the history of American psychiatry. *Hospital and Community Psychiatry*, **45**, 1010–1014.

D'Amore, J., Hung, O., Chaing, W., *et al* (2001) The epidemiology of the homeless population and its impact on an urban emergency department. *Academic Emergency Medicine*, **8**, 1051–1055.

Dawson, J., (2015) A realistic approach to assessing mental health laws' compliance with the UNCRPD. *International Journal of Law and Psychiatry*, **40**, 70–79.

Dawson, J. & Szmukler, G. (2006) Fusion of mental health and incapacity legislation. *British Journal of Psychiatry*, **188**, 504–509.

Dawson, J. & Szmukler, G. (2007) Mental health and incapacity legislation: authors' reply. *British Journal of Psychiatry*, **190**, 177.

De Búrca, G. (2001) The drafting of the European Union Charter of Fundamental Rights. *European Law Review*, **26**, 126–138.

Department of Health (1995) *White Paper: A New Mental Health Act*. TSO (The Stationery Office).

Department of Health (1999) *Review of the Mental Health Act 1983*. Department of Health.

Department of Health (2008) *Code of Practice: Mental Health Act 1983*. TSO (The Stationery Office).

Department of Health (2012) *Post-Legislative Assessment of the Mental Health Act 2007 (Cmnd 8408)*. TSO (The Stationery Office).

Department of Health (2015) *Mental Health Act 1983: Code of Practice*. TSO (The Stationery Office).

Department of Health and Children (2007) *Review of the Operation of the Mental Health Act 2001*. Department of Health and Children.

Department of Health and Social Security (1975a) *Better Services for the Mentally Ill (Cmnd 6233)*. HMSO.

Department of Health and Social Security (1975b) *Review of the Mental Health Act 1959*. HMSO.

Department of Health and Social Security (1981a) *Care in the Community: A Consultative Document on Moving Resources for Care in England, Outlining a Continued Commitment to Community Care*. HMSO.

Department of Health and Social Security (1981b) *Reform of Mental Health Legislation*. HMSO.

Department of Health and Social Security (1983) *Mental Health (Hospital, Guardianship and Consent to Treatment) Regulations*. HMSO.

Department of Health and Social Security (2007) *Mental Health Act 2007 Explanatory Notes*. HMSO.

Department of Health, Social Services and Public Safety in Northern Ireland & Northern Ireland Department of Justice (2014) *Draft Mental Capacity Bill (NI): Consultation Document (May 2014)*. DHSSPSNI.

Dinos, S. (2014) Stigma creating stigma: a vicious circle. *Psychiatric Bulletin*, **38**, 145–147.

Division of Mental Health and Prevention of Substance Abuse (WHO) (1996) *Mental Health Care Law: Ten Basic Principles*. World Health Organization.

Dixon, L. (1999) Dual diagnosis of substance abuse in schizophrenia. *Schizophrenia Research*, **35** (suppl. 1), S93–S100.

Dobbie, F., Reid, S., Martin, C., *et al* (2009) *An Exploration of the Early Operation of the Mental Health Tribunal for Scotland*. Scottish Government/Social Research.

Dols, M. W. (1987) Insanity and its treatment in Islamic society. *Medical History*, **31**, 1–14.

Dols, M. W. (2007) Insanity in Islamic law. *Journal of Muslim Mental Health*, **2**, 81–99.

Donaldson, A., Carswell, C. & Brown, K. (2008) 1 Year on: how psychiatrists feel about the Mental Health (Care and Treatment) (Scotland) Act 2003. *Psychiatric Bulletin*, **32**, 464–466.

Donnelly, J. (1998) *International Human Rights* (2nd edn). Westview Press.

Dudley, M., Silove, D. & Gale, F. (eds) (2012) *Mental Health and Human Rights: Vision, Praxis, and Courage*. Oxford University Press.

Duggan, C. (2011) Dangerous and severe personality disorder. *British Journal of Psychiatry*, **198**, 431–433.

Duthé, G., Hazard, A., Kensey, A., *et al* (2013) Suicide among male prisoners in France: a prospective population-based study. *Forensic Science International*, **233**, 273–277.

Dyer, C. (2001) Ruling could free dozens of mentally ill offenders. *Guardian*, 29 March.

Dyer, J. A. T. (1996) Rehabilitation and Community Care. In *Companion to Psychiatric Studies* (5th edn) (eds R. E. Kendell & A. K. Zealley), pp. 927–941. Churchill Livingstone.

Eastman, E. & Peay, J. (1998) Bournewood: an indefensible gap in mental health law. *BMJ*, **317**, 94–95.

Eaton, W. W. (1980) *The Sociology of Mental Disorders*. Praeger.

Eaton, W. W. (ed.) (2012) *Public Mental Health*. Oxford University Press.

Eaton, J., DeSilva, M., Regan, M., *et al* (2014a) There is no wealth without mental health. *Lancet Psychiatry*, **1**, 252–253.

Eaton, J., Kakuma, R., Wright, A., *et al* (2014b) A position statement on mental health in the post-2015 development agenda. *International Journal of Mental Health Systems*, **8**, 28.

Edd, J. R., Fox, P. G. & Burns, K. (2005) Advocating for the rights of the mentally ill. *International Journal of Psychiatric Nursing Research*, **11**, 1211–1217.

Edmundson, W. (2004) *An Introduction to Rights*. Cambridge University Press.

El-Hai, J. (2005) *The Lobotomist: A Maverick Medical Genius and his Tragic Quest to Rid the World of Mental Illness*. John Wiley and Sons.

Eldergill, A. (2008) The best is the enemy of the good. *Journal of Mental Health Law*, **5**, 21–37.

EURODIAB ACE Study Group (2000) Variation and trends in incidence of childhood diabetes in Europe. *Lancet*, **355**, 873–876.

European Union (1992) Treaty on European Union. *Official Journal of the European Communities*, **C191**, article 1.

European Union (1997) Treaty of Amsterdam amending the Treaty of the European Union, the Treaties establishing the European Communities and certain related acts. *Official Journal of the European Communities*, **C340**, 1–144.

European Union (2000) Charter of Fundamental Rights of the European Union. *Official Journal of the European Communities*, **C364**, 1–22.

European Union (2008) Consolidated versions of the Treaty on European Union and the Treaty on the Functioning of the European Union. *Official Journal of the European Communities*, **C115**, 13–46.

Expert Group on Mental Health Policy (2006) *A Vision for Change*. The Stationery Office Dublin.

Expert Group on the Review of the Mental Health Act 2001 (2015) *Report of the Expert Group on the Review of the Mental Health Act 2001*. Department of Health.

Fadden, G., Bebbington, P. & Kuipers, L. (1987) The burden of care: the impact of functional psychiatric illness on the patient's family. *British Journal of Psychiatry*, **150**, 285–292.

Faris, R. B. & Dunham, H. W. (1939) *Mental Disorders in Urban Areas*. University of Chicago Press.

Farmer, P. (1997) Ethnography, social analysis, and the prevention of sexually transmitted HIV infections among poor women in Haiti. In *An Anthropology of Infectious Disease* (eds M. C. Inhorn & P. J. Brown), pp. 413–438. Gordon and Breach.

Farmer, P. (1999) Pathologies of power: rethinking health and human rights. *American Journal of Public Health*, **89**, 1486–1496.

Farmer, P. (2003) *Pathologies of Power*. University of California Press.

Fazel, S. & Danesh, J. (2002) Serious mental disorder in 23,000 prisoners: a systematic review of 62 surveys. *Lancet*, **359**, 545–550.

Fazel, S. & Seewald, K. (2012) Severe mental illness in 33 588 prisoners worldwide: systematic review and meta-regression analysis. *British Journal of Psychiatry*, **200**, 364–373.

Feldman, D. (2002) *Civil Liberties and Human Rights in England and Wales* (2nd edn). Oxford University Press.

Fennell, P. (2007) *Mental Health: The New Law*. Jordan Publishing.

Fenwick, H. (2007) *Civil Liberties and Human Rights* (4th edn). Routledge-Cavendish.

Field, J. (2003) *Social Capital*. Routledge.

Figuerdo, J. L., Gutirrez, M., Mosquera, F., *et al* (2000) Involuntary hospitalization in the first psychotic episodes: associated factors. *Actas Espanolas de Psiquiatria*, **28**, 275–278.

Finnane, P. (1981) *Insanity and the Insane in Post-Famine Ireland*. Croon Helm.

Fitzsimons, K. (2007) Right to treatment should not be forgotten in psychiatry. *Irish Medical News*, **45**, 4.

Fleischman, A., Werbeloff, N., Yoffe, R, *et al* (2014) Schizophrenia and violent crime: a population-based study. *Psychological Medicine*, **44**, 3051–3057.

Flynn, D., Smith, D., Quirke, L., *et al* (2012) Ultra high risk of psychosis on committal to a young offender prison: an unrecognised opportunity for early intervention. *BMC Psychiatry*, **12**, 100.

Foley, S., Kelly, B. D., Clarke, M., *et al* (2005) Incidence and clinical correlates of aggression and violence in patients with first episode psychosis. *Schizophrenia Research*, **72**, 161–168.

Forsythe, D. P. (1995) The UN and human rights at fifty: an incremental but incomplete revolution. *Global Governance*, **1**, 297–318.

Forsythe, D. P. (2000) *Human Rights in International Relations*. Cambridge University Press.

Foy, J., MacRae, A., Thom, A., *et al* (2007) Advance statements: survey of patients' views and understanding. *Psychiatric Bulletin*, **31**, 339–341.

Freeman, M. (2002) *Human Rights*. Polity Press.

Gabbard, G. O. & Kay, J. (2001) The fate of integrated treatment. *American Journal of Psychiatry*, **158**, 1956–1963.

Gabbard, G. O., Beck, J. S. & Holmes, J. (eds) (2007) *Oxford Textbook of Psychotherapy*. Oxford University Press.

Gallagher, A. & Seedhouse, D. (2002) Dignity in care: the views of patients and relatives. *Nursing Times*, **98**, 38–40.

Galtung, J. (1969) Violence, peace, and peace research. *Journal of Peace Research*, **6**, 167–191.

Ganter, K. (2005) Funding for Mental Health Act is a human rights issue. *Medicine Weekly*, **13**, 26.

Ganter, K., Daly, I. & Owens, J. (2005) Implementing the Mental Health Act 2001. *Irish Journal of Psychological Medicine*, **22**, 79–82.

Gavin, B. E., Kelly, B. D., Lane, A., *et al* (2001) The mental health of migrants. *Irish Medical Journal*, **94**, 229–230.

George, S. L., Shanks, N. J. & Westlake, L. (1991) Census of single homeless people in Sheffield. *BMJ*, **302**, 1387–1389.

Gergel, T. L. (2014) Too similar, too different: the paradoxical dualism of psychiatric stigma. *Psychiatric Bulletin*, **38**, 148–151.

Goffman, E. (1963) *Stigma: Notes on the Management of Spoiled Identity*. Prentice-Hall.

Goldman, H. H. (2000) Implementing the lessons of mental health service demonstrations: human rights issues. *Acta Psychiatrica Scandinavica Supplementum*, **399**, 51–54.

Gostin, L. O. (1975a) *A Human Condition: The Mental Health Act from 1959 to 1975* (Vol. 1). National Association for Mental Health (MIND).

Gostin, L. O. (1975b) A Human Condition: The Law Relating to Mentally Abnormal Offenders. *Observations, Analysis and Proposals for Reform* (Vol. 2). National Association for Mental Health (MIND).

Gostin, L. & Gable, L. (2004) The human rights of persons with mental disabilities: a global perspective on the application of human rights principles to mental health. *Maryland Law Review*, **63**, 20–121.

Gostin, L., Bartlett, P., Fennell, P., *et al* (2010) *Principles of Mental Health Law and Policy*. Oxford University Press.

Government of Ireland (1937) *Bunreacht na hÉireann (Constitution of Ireland)*. The Stationery Office Dublin.

Gray, J. (1986) *Liberalism*. Open University Press.

Guggenbühl-Craig, A. (1971) *Power in the Helping Professions*. Spring.

Gunn, J. (1981) Reform of mental health legislation. *BMJ*, **283**, 1487–1488.

Gunn, J. (2000) Future directions for treatment in forensic psychiatry. *British Journal of Psychiatry*, **176**, 332–338.

Guruswamy, S. & Kelly, B. D. (2006) A change of vision? Mental health policy. *Irish Medical Journal*, **99**, 164–166.

Hall, I. & Ali, A. (2009) Changes to the Mental Health and Mental Capacity Acts: implications for patients and professionals. *Psychiatric Bulletin*, **33**, 226–230.

231

Hallaran, W. S. (1810) *An Enquiry into the Causes Producing the Extraordinary Addition to the Number of Insane together with Extended Observations on the Cure of Insanity with Hints as to the Better Management of Public Asylums for Insane Persons.* Edwards and Savage.

Hankonen, T., Saarinen, S. & Salokangas, R. K. (1999) Deinstitutionalization and schizophrenia in Finland II: discharged patients and their psychosocial functioning. *Schizophrenia Bulletin*, **25**, 543–551.

Harding, T. W. (2000) Human rights law in the field of mental health: a critical review. *Acta Psychiatrica Scandinavica Supplementum*, **399**, 24–30.

Harding, C. M., Brooks, G. W., Ashikaga, T., *et al* (1987) The Vermount longitudinal study of persons with severe mental illness. II: Long-term outcome of subjects who retrospectively met DSM-III criteria for schizophrenia. *American Journal of Psychiatry*, **144**, 727–735.

Harrison, G. (1990) Searching for the causes of schizophrenia: the role of migrant studies. *Schizophrenia Bulletin*, **16**, 663–671.

Hatch, E. (1983) *Culture and Morality: The Relativity of Values in Anthropology.* Columbia University Press.

Havel, V. (2008) *To the Castle and Back.* Portobello Books.

Hawton, K., Linsell, L., Adeniji, T., *et al* (2014) Self-harm in prisons in England and Wales: an epidemiological study of prevalence, risk factors, clustering, and subsequent suicide. *Lancet*, **383**, 1147–1154.

Healy, D. (1996) Irish psychiatry in the twentieth century. In *150 Years of British Psychiatry. Volume II: The Aftermath* (eds H. Freeman & G. E. Berrios), pp. 268–291. Athlone Press.

Helfer, L. R. (2008) Redesigning the European Court of Human Rights: embeddedness as a deep structural principle of the European human rights regime. *European Journal of International Law*, **19**, 125–159.

Hervey, T. K. (2005) We don't see a connection: the 'right to health' in the EU Charter and European Social Charter. In *Social Rights in Europe* (eds G. de Búrca & B. de Witte), pp. 305–338. Oxford University Press.

Hickling, F. W. & Rodgers-Johnson, P. (1995) The incidence of first contact schizophrenia in Jamaica. *British Journal of Psychiatry*, **167**, 193–196.

Hiday, V. A., Swartz, M. S., Swanson, J. W., *et al* (1999) Criminal victimization of persons with severe mental illness. *Psychiatric Services*, **50**, 62–68.

Hill, D. (2009) I. The Hague Convention on the International Protection of Adults. *International and Comparative Law Quarterly*, **58**, 469–476.

Hodgins, S. (1992) Mental disorder, intellectual deficiency, and crime. *Archives of General Psychiatry*, **49**, 476–483.

Hodgins, S., Piatosa, M. J. & Schiffer, B. (2014) Violence among people with schizophrenia: phenotypes and neurobiology. *Current Topics in Behavioral Neurosciences*, **17**, 329–368.

Hogan, G. & Whyte, G. (2003) *J. M. Kelly: The Irish Constitution* (4th rev. edn). Tottel Publishing.

Holohan, T. W. (2000) Health and homelessness in Dublin. *Irish Medical Journal*, **93**, 41–43.

Houston, M. (2009) 60% turnout at hospital poll. *Irish Times*, 30 May.

Howard, G. & Anthony R. (1977) The right to vote and voting patterns of hospitalized psychiatric patients. *Psychiatric Quarterly*, **49**, 124–132.

Howe, L., Tickle, A. & Brown, I. (2014) 'Schizophrenia is a dirty word': service-users' experiences of receiving a diagnosis of schizophrenia. *Psychiatric Bulletin*, **38**, 154–158.

Howes, O. D. & Murray, R. M. (2014) Schizophrenia: an integrated sociodevelopmental-cognitive model. *Lancet*, **383**, 1677–1687.

Humphreys, M. & Chiswick, D. (1993) Getting psychiatric patients to the polls in the 1992 General Election. *Psychiatric Bulletin*, **17**, 18–19.

Hunt, L. (2007) *Inventing Human Rights: A History.* W. W. Norton.

Hustoft, K., Larsen, T. K., Auestad, B., *et al* (2013) Predictors of involuntary hospitalizations to acute psychiatry. *International Journal of Law and Psychiatry*, **36**, 136–143.

Hutchinson, G., Takei, N., Bhugra, D., *et al* (1997) Increased rate of psychosis among African-Caribbeans in Britain is not due to an excess of pregnancy and birth complications. *British Journal of Psychiatry*, **171**, 145–147.

Huxter, M. J. (2013) Prisons: the psychiatric institution of last resort? *Journal of Psychiatric and Mental Health Nursing*, **20**, 735–743.

Information Centre (2007) *In-patients Formally Detained in Hospitals Under the Mental Health Act 1983 and Other Legislation; 1995–96 to 2005–06*. Information Centre/Government Statistical Service.

Inspectors of Lunatics (1893) *The Forty-Second Report (With Appendices) of the Inspector of Lunatics (Ireland)*. Thom & Co. for HMSO.

Irish Human Rights Commission (2007) *Annual Report 2006*. Irish Human Rights Commission.

Ishay, M. R. (2004) *The History of Human Rights: From Ancient Times to the Globalization Era*. University of California Press.

Islamic Council (1981) *Universal Islamic Declaration of Human Rights*. Islamic Council.

Jabbar, F., Kelly, B. D. & Casey, P. (2010) National survey of psychiatrists' responses to implementation of the Mental Health Act 2001 in Ireland. *Irish Journal of Medical Science*, **179**, 291–294.

Jablensky, A. (1997) The 100-year epidemiology of schizophrenia. *Schizophrenia Research*, **28**, 111–128.

Jacoby, R. (2014) Something better than this. *Le Monde Diplomatique*, 12 August.

James, A., Kendall, T. & Worrall, A. (eds) (2005) *Clinical Governance in Mental Health and Learning Disability Services: A Practical Guide*. Gaskell.

Jaychuk, G. & Manchanda, R. (1991) Psychiatric patients and the federal election. *Canadian Journal of Psychiatry*, **36**, 124–125.

Joska, J. A. & Stein, D. J. (2008) Mood disorders. In *The American Psychiatric Publishing Textbook of Psychiatry* (5th edn) (eds R. E Hales, S. C. Yudofsky & G. O. Gabbard), pp. 457–503. American Psychiatric Publishing Inc.

Kelly, B. D. (2001) Mental health and human rights: challenges for a new millennium. *Irish Journal of Psychological Medicine*, **18**, 114–115.

Kelly, B. D. (2002) Viewpoint: the Mental Health Act 2001. *Irish Medical Journal*, **95**, 151–152.

Kelly, B. D. (2003) Globalisation and psychiatry. *Advances in Psychiatric Treatment*, **9**, 464–474.

Kelly, B. D. (2004*a*) Mental health policy in Ireland, 1984–2004: theory, overview and future directions. *Irish Journal of Psychological Medicine*, **21**, 61–68.

Kelly, B. D. (2004*b*) Mental illness in nineteenth century Ireland: a qualitative study of workhouse records. *Irish Journal of Medical Science*, **173**, 53–55.

Kelly, B. D. (2005) Structural violence and schizophrenia. *Social Science and Medicine*, **61**, 721–730.

Kelly, B. D. (2006*a*) The power gap: freedom, power and mental illness. *Social Science and Medicine*, **63**, 2118–2128.

Kelly, B. D. (2006*b*) Irish mental health law. *Irish Psychiatrist*, **7**, 29–30.

Kelly, B. D. (2007*a*) Social justice, human rights and mental illness. *Irish Journal of Psychological Medicine*, **24**, 3–4.

Kelly, B. D. (2007*b*) The Irish Mental Health Act 2001. *Psychiatric Bulletin*, **31**, 21–24.

Kelly, B. D. (2007*c*) Penrose's Law in Ireland: an ecological analysis of psychiatric inpatients and prisoners. *Irish Medical Journal*, **100**, 373–374.

Kelly, B. D. (2008*a*) Mental health law in Ireland, 1821–1902: building the asylums. *Medico-Legal Journal*, **76**, 19–25.

Kelly, B. D. (2008*b*) Mental health law in Ireland, 1945 to 2001: Reformation and renewal? *Medico-Legal Journal*, **76**, 65–72.

Kelly, B. D. (2008*c*) The Mental Treatment Act 1945 in Ireland: an historical enquiry. *History of Psychiatry*, **19**, 47–67.

Kelly, B. D. (2008*d*) The emerging mental health strategy of the European Union. *Health Policy*, **85**, 60–70.

Kelly, B. D. (2009*a*) Community treatment orders under the Mental Health Act 2007 in England and Wales: what are the lessons for Irish mental health legislation? *Medico-Legal Journal of Ireland*, **15**, 43–48.

Kelly, B. D. (2009*b*) The Mental Health Act 2001. *Irish Medical News*, **20**, 29.

Kelly, B. D. (2011) Mental health legislation and human rights in England, Wales and the Republic of Ireland. *International Journal of Law and Psychiatry*, **34**, 439–454.

Kelly, B. D. (2012) Mental illness and structural violence. *Irish Medical Journal*, **105**, 30.

Kelly, B. D. (2014a) An end to psychiatric detention? Implications of the United Nations Convention on the Rights of Persons with Disabilities. *British Journal of Psychiatry*, **204**, 174–175.

Kelly, B. D. (2014b) Dignity, human rights and the limits of mental health legislation. *Irish Journal of Psychological Medicine*, **31**, 75–81.

Kelly, B. D. (2014c) Rights of people with mental illness. *Lancet Psychiatry 2014*, **1**, e4.

Kelly, B. D. (2014d) Mental capacity and participation in research. *Irish Medical Times*, **18**, 20.

Kelly, B. D. (2014e) Voting and mental Illness: the silent constituency. *Irish Journal of Psychological Medicine*, **31**, 225–227.

Kelly, B. D. (2015a) The Assisted Decision-Making (Capacity) Bill 2013: content, commentary, controversy. *Irish Journal of Medical Science*, **184**, 31–46.

Kelly, B. D. (2015b) Revising, reforming, reframing: Report of the Expert Group on the Review of the Mental Health Act 2001 (2015). *Irish Journal of Psychological Medicine*, **32**, 161–166.

Kelly, B. D. (2015c) Best interests, mental capacity legislation and the UN Convention on the Rights of Persons with Disabilities. *BJPsych Advances*, **21**, 188–195.

Kelly, B. D. (2015d) Human rights in psychiatric practice: an overview for clinicians. *BJPsych Advances*, **21**, 54–62.

Kelly, B. D. & Lenihan, F. (2006) Attitudes towards the implementation of the Mental Health Act 2001. *Irish Journal of Psychological Medicine*, **23**, 82–84.

Kelly, B. D., Clarke, M., Browne, S., *et al* (2004) Clinical predictors of admission status in first episode schizophrenia. *European Psychiatry*, **19**, 67–71.

Kelly, B. D., Davoren, M., Mhaoláin, A. N., *et al* (2009) Social capital and suicide in 11 European countries: an ecological analysis. *Social Psychiatry and Psychiatric Epidemiology*, **44**, 971–977.

Kelly, B. D., O'Callaghan, E., Waddington, J. L., *et al* (2010) Schizophrenia and the city: A review of literature and prospective study of psychosis and urbanicity in Ireland. *Schizophrenia Research*, **116**, 75–89.

Kennedy, H. (2007a) *The Annotated Mental Health Acts*. Blackhall Publishing.

Kennedy, H. (2007b) The general election campaign. *Irish Times*, 23 May.

Kennedy, H. (2012) 'Libertarian' groupthink not helping mentally ill. *Irish Times*, 12 September.

Keshavjee, S. & Becerra, M. C. (2000) Disintegrating health services and resurgent tuberculosis in post-Soviet Tajikistan: an example of structural violence. *JAMA*, **283**, 1201.

Kessler, R. C., Chui, W. T., Demler, O., *et al* (2005) Prevalence, severity and comorbidity of 12-month DSM-IV disorders in the National Comorbidity Survey Replication. *Archives of General Psychiatry*, **62**, 617–627.

Keys, M. (2002) *Mental Health Act 2001 (Round Hall Annotated Legislation)*. Round Hall.

Kimball, R. (2014) Academic freedom fighter. *Wall Street Journal (Europe Edition)*, 5 August.

Kingdon, D., Jones, R., Lönnqvist, J. (2004) Protecting the human rights of people with mental disorder: new recommendations emerging from the Council of Europe. *British Journal of Psychiatry*, **185**, 277–279.

King's Fund (2008) *Briefing: Mental Health Act 2007*. The King's Fund.

Kisely, S. R. & Campbell, L. A. (2014) Compulsory community and involuntary outpatient treatment for people with severe mental disorders. *Cochrane Database of Systematic Reviews*, **12**,CD004408.

Kline, E. & Schiffman, J. (2014) Psychosis risk screening: a systematic review. *Schizophrenia Research*, **158**, 11–18.

Kreiger, N., Rowley, D., Herman, A., *et al* (1993) Racism, sexism, and social class: implications for studies of health, disease, and well-being. *American Journal of Preventive Medicine*, **9** (suppl. 6), 82–122.

Laing, J. M. (2003) Reforming mental health law and the ECHR: will the rights of mentally vulnerable adults be protected? *Journal of Social Welfare and Family Law*, **25**, 325–340.

Laing, J. M. (2012) The Mental Health Act: exploring the role of nurses. *British Journal of Nursing*, **21**, 234–238.

Laing, R. D. (1960) *The Divided Self: An Existential Study in Sanity and Madness*. Penguin.

Lamichhane, J. (2014) Strengthening civil and political rights of people with mental illness. *Lancet Psychiatry*, **1**, 173.

Lane, A., Byrne, M., Mulvany, F., *et al* (1995) Reproductive behaviour in schizophrenia relative to other mental disorders. *Acta Psychiatrica Scandinavica*, **91**, 222–228.

Latimer, K. (2009) Mental Health (Care and Treatment) (Scotland) Act 2003: impact on child and adolescent in-patient services. *Psychiatric Bulletin*, **33**, 69–71.

Lavelle, M., Healey, P. G. & McCabe, R. (2014) Nonverbal behavior during face-to-face social interaction in schizophrenia: a review. *Journal of Nervous and Mental Disease*, **202**, 47–54.

Lavik, N. J., Hauff E., Skrondal A., *et al* (1996) Mental disorder among refugees and the impact of persecution and exile: some findings from an out-patient population. *British Journal of Psychiatry*, **169**, 726–732.

Law Reform Committee (1999) *Mental Health: The Case for Reform*. The Law Society.

Lawn, S., McMillan, J., Comley, Z., *et al* (2014) Mental health recovery and voting: why being treated as a citizen matters and how we can do it. *Journal of Psychiatric and Mental Health Nursing*, **21**, 289–295.

Lawton-Smith, S., Dawson, J. & Burns, T. (2008) Community treatment orders are not a good thing. *British Journal of Psychiatry*, **193**, 96–100.

Leahy, T. (2007) Challenges with new mental health law. *Forum*, **24**, 14–15.

Leary, J., Johnstone, E. C. & Owens, D. C. (1991) Social outcome. *British Journal of Psychiatry*, **159** (suppl. 13), 13–20.

Lee, G. (2008) Far from the madding crowd. *Law Society Gazette*, **6**, 40–43.

Lenin, V. I. (1918) Reprinted (1964) as *Collected Works; Volume 26*. Progress Publishers.

Lerner, B. H. (2005) *Breast Cancer Wars: Hope, Fear, and the Pursuit of a Cure in Twentieth-Century America*. Oxford University Press.

Letsas, G. (2007) *A Theory of Interpretation of the European Convention on Human Rights*. Oxford University Press.

Leucht, S., Hierl, S., Kissling, W., *et al* (2012) Putting the efficacy of psychiatric and general medicine medication into perspective: review of meta-analyses. *British Journal of Psychiatry*, **200**, 97–106.

Locke, J. (1689) *A Letter Concerning Toleration*. Reprinted (1991) in *A Letter Concerning Toleration in Focus* (eds J. Horton & S. Mendus). Routledge.

Locke, J. (1690) Reprinted (1980) as *Second Treatise of Government* (ed. C. B. Macpherson). Hackett Publishing.

Lord Goldsmith Q.C. (2001) A charter of rights, freedoms and principles. *Common Market Law Review*, **38**, 1201–1216.

Lukes, S. (2005) *Power: A Radical View* (2nd edn). Palgrave Macmillan.

Lustig, S. (ed.) (2012) *Advocacy Strategies for Health and Mental Health Professionals: From Patients to Policies*. Springer Publishing.

Lynch, P. (2007) GPs in revolt over psychiatric admissions. *Irish Medical News*, **39**, 1.

Lyons, F. S. L. (1985) *Ireland Since the Famine*. Fontana.

Macaskill, A. M., Brodie, B. A. & Keil, B. (2011) Scottish place of safety legislation: local audit of Section 297 Mental Health (Care and Treatment) (Scotland) Act 2003. *The Psychiatrist*, **35**, 185–189.

MacBride, S. (1997) The imperatives of survival. In *Nobel Lectures: Peace, 1971–1980* (eds I. Abrams & T. Frängsmyr), pp. 86–101. World Scientific.

Macdonald, M. (1963) Natural rights. In *Philosophy, Politics and Society* (ed P. Laslett), pp. 35–55. Basil Blackwell.

Macleod, S. M. & McCullough, H. N. (1994) Social science education as a component of medical training. *Social Science and Medicine*, **39**, 1367–1373.

Madden, E. (2007) Involuntary detention found admissible in the High Court. *Irish Medical Times*, **28**, 20.

Madden, E. (2008*a*) Supreme Court rules on Mental Health Act. *Irish Medical Times*, **22**, 26.

Madden, E. (2008*b*) Judge commends action of hospital staff in detention. *Irish Medical Times*, **37**, 28.

Madden, E. (2009*a*) Section of Mental Health Act was unconstitutional. *Irish Medical Times*, **30**, 15.

Madden, E. (2009*b*) Supreme Court critical of case taken against St Vincent's Hospital. *Irish Medical Times*, **28**, 18.

Madden, E. (2012) Important UK Supreme Court decision on human rights. *Irish Medical Times*, **18**, 26.

Maden, A. (2007) Mental health and incapacity legislation. *British Journal of Psychiatry*, **190**, 176.

Mäkikyrö, T., Isohanni, M. & Moring, J. (1997) Is a child's risk of early onset schizophrenia increased in the highest social class? *Schizophrenia Research*, **23**, 245–252.

Mandelstam, M. (2005) *Community Care Practice and the Law* (3rd edn). Jessica Kingsley Publishers.

Mangalore, R. & Knapp, M. (2007) Cost of schizophrenia in England. *Journal of Mental Health Policy and Economics*, **10**, 23–41.

Markowitz, F. (2006) Psychiatric hospital capacity, homelessness, and crime and arrest rates. *Criminology*, **44**, 45–72.

Martens, W. H. (2001) A review of physical and mental health in homeless persons. *Public Health Reviews*, **29**, 13–33.

McCulloch, A. (2001) Social environments and health: a cross-sectional survey. *BMJ*, **323**, 208–209.

McGuinness, I. (2005) Consultants not to apply for mental health tribunal positions. *Irish Medical Times*, **10**, 1.

McGuinness, I. (2006) Tribunals to decide on legal representation. *Irish Medical Times*, **45**, 1.

McGuinness, I. (2007*a*) Tribunals revoke 12 per cent of detentions. *Irish Medical Times*, **43**, 3.

McGuinness, I. (2007*b*) Litany of failures. *Irish Medical News*, **6**, 1.

McGuinness, I. (2007*c*) Penny-pinching delays. *Irish Medical Times*, **25**, 1.

McGuinness, I. (2007*d*) More court appeals. *Irish Medical Times*, **24**, 3.

McHale, J. (2009) Fundamental Rights and Health Care. In *Health Systems Governance in Europe: The Role of EU Law and Policy* (eds E. Mossialos, G. Permanand, R. Baeten, *et al*), pp. 282–314. Cambridge University Press.

McHale, J., Fox, M., Gunn, M., *et al* (2007) *Health Care Law: Text and Materials* (2nd edn). Sweet and Maxwell.

McIntyre, J., Yelamanchili, V., Naz, S., *et al* (2012) Uptake and knowledge of voting rights by adult in-patients during the 2010 UK general election. *The Psychiatrist*, **36**, 126–130.

McSherry, B. & Weller, P. (eds) (2010) *Rethinking Rights-Based Mental Health Laws*. Hart Publishing.

Melamed, Y., Shamir, E., Solomon, Z. & Elizur, A. (1997*a*) Hospitalized mentally ill patients in Israel vote for the first time. *Israeli Journal of Psychiatry and Related Sciences*, **34**, 69–72.

Melamed, Y., Solomon, Z. & Elizur, A. (1997*b*) Voting by Israeli patients. *Psychiatric Services*, **48**, 1081.

Melamed, Y., Doron, A., Finkel, B., *et al* (2007) Israeli psychiatric inpatients go to the polls. *Journal of Nervous and Mental Disease*, **195**, 705–708.

Melamed, Y., Donsky, L., Oyffe, I., *et al* (2013) Voting of hospitalized and ambulatory patients with mental disorders in parliamentary elections. *Israel Journal of Psychiatry and Related Sciences*, **50**, 13–16.

Melle, I., Friis, S., Hauff, E. & Vaglum, P. (2000) Social functioning of patients with schizophrenia in high-income welfare societies. *Psychiatric Services*, **51**, 223–228.

Melzer, D., Hale, A. S., Malik, S. J., *et al* (1991) Community care for patients with schizophrenia one year after hospital discharge. *BMJ*, **303**, 1023–1026.

Menéndez, A. J. (2002) Chartering Europe: legal status and policy implications of the Charter of Fundamental Rights of the European Union. *Journal of Common Market Studies*, **40**, 471–490.

Mental Health Act Commission (2003) *Tenth Biennial Report 2001–2003: Placed Amongst Strangers*. TSO (The Stationery Office).

Mental Health Alliance (2006) *Mental Health Act 2007: Report Stage Briefing, House of Commons*. Mental Health Alliance (http://www.mentalhealthalliance.org.uk/pre2007/documents/Commons_Report_Stage_General_Briefing.pdf).

Mental Health Commission (2005) *Annual Report 2004*. Mental Health Commission.

Mental Health Commission (2008) *Report on the Operation of Part 2 of the Mental Health Act 2001*. Mental Health Commission.

Mental Health Commission (2009) *Rules Governing the Use of Seclusion and Mechanical Means of Bodily Restraint*. Mental Health Commission.

Mental Health Subcommittee (2009) Advising a mentally disordered client. *Law Society Gazette*, **103**, 44–45.

Merikangas, K. R., Akiskal, H. S., Angst, J., *et al* (2007) Lifetime and 12-month prevalence of bipolar spectrum disorder in the National Comorbidity Survey Replication. *Archives of General Psychiatry*, **64**, 543–552.

Michael, P. & Hirst, D. (1999) Establishing the 'rule of kindness': the foundation of the North Wales Lunatic Asylum, Denbeigh. In *Insanity Institutions and Society, 1800–1914: A Social History of Madness in Comparative Perspective* (eds J. Melling & B. Forsythe), pp. 159–179. Routledge.

Millan Committee (2001) *New Directions: Report on the Review of the Mental Health (Scotland) Act 1984*. Scottish Executive.

Miller, C. T. & Major, B. (2000) Coping with stigma and prejudice. In *The Social Psychology of Stigma* (eds T. F. Heatherton, R. E. Kleck, M. R. Hebl, *et al*), pp. 243–272. Guilford Press.

Mills, S. (2004) The Mental Health Act 2001. *Irish Psychiatrist*, **5**, 49–55.

Min, S. Y., Wong, Y. L. & Rothbard A. B. (2004) Outcomes of shelter use among homeless persons with serious mental illness. *Psychiatric Services*, **55**, 284–289.

Minkowitz, T. (2007) The United Nations Convention on the Rights of Persons with Disabilities and the right to be free from non-consensual psychiatric interventions. *Syracuse Journal of International Law and Commerce*, **34**, 405–428.

Minkowitz, T. (2010) Abolishing mental health laws to comply with the Convention on the Rights of Persons with Disabilities. In *Rethinking Rights-Based Mental Health Laws* (eds B. McSherry & P. Weller), pp. 151–177. Hart Publishing.

Mollica, R. F. (1983) From asylum to community: the threatened disintegration of public psychiatry. *New England Journal of Medicine*, **308**, 367–373.

Moncrieff, J. (2003) The politics of a new Mental Health Act. *British Journal of Psychiatry*, **183**, 8–9.

Morgan, V. A., Morgan, F., Valuri, G., *et al* (2013) A whole-of-population study of the prevalence and patterns of criminal offending in people with schizophrenia and other mental illness. *Psychological Medicine*, **43**, 1869–1880.

Morris, F. (1999) Mental health law after Bournewood: some legal and practical implications. *Journal of Mental Health Law*, February, 41–47.

Morsink, J. (1999) *The Universal Declaration of Human Rights: Origins, Drafting and Intent*. University of Pennsylvania Press.

Mudiwa, L. (2005) Ireland signs WHO declaration on mental health. *Medicine Weekly*, **3**, 18.

Mulholland, C. (2009) *A Socialist History of the NHS*. VDM Verlag.

Mullan, G. (2008) Incorporation of the ECHR into Irish law. In *Human Rights Law* (2nd edn) (eds B. Moriarity & E. Massa), pp. 69–81. Oxford University Press/Law Society of Ireland.

Mulvany, F., O'Callaghan, E., Takei, N. *et al* (2001) Effect of social class at birth on risk and presentation of schizophrenia. *BMJ*, **323**, 1398–1401.

Munro, R. (2000) Judicial psychiatry in China and its political abuses. *Columbia Journal of Asian Law*, **14**, 1–128.

Munro, R. (2002) *Dangerous Minds: Political Psychiatry in China Today and its Origins in the Mao Era*. Human Rights Watch & Geneva Initiative on Psychiatry.

Munro, R. (2006) *China's Psychiatric Inquisition: Dissent, Psychiatry and the Law in Post-1949 China*. Wildy, Simmonds and Hill Publishing.

Nash, M. (2002) Voting as a means of social inclusion for people with a mental illness. *Journal of Psychiatric and Mental Health Nursing*, **9**, 697–703.

National Institute for Health and Care Excellence(2010) *Update May 2010: Guidance on the Use of Electroconvulsive Therapy*. NICE (https://www.nice.org.uk/guidance/ta59/documents/ta59-electroconvulsive-therapy-ect-summary2).

Nazroo, J. (1997) *Ethnicity and Mental Health: Fourth National Survey of Ethnic Minorities*. Policy Studies Institute.

Neier, A. (2006) Social and economic rights: a critique. *Human Rights Brief*, **13**, 1–3.

NHS Information Centre for Health and Social Care (2011) *In-patients Formally Detained in Hospitals under the Mental Health Act 1983*. NHS/National Statistics.

Ní Mhaoláin, Á. & Kelly, B. D. (2009) Ireland's Mental Health Act 2001: where are we now? *Psychiatric Bulletin*, **33**, 161–164.

Nilforooshan, R., Amin, R. & Warner, J. (2009) Ethnicity and outcome of appeal after detention under the Mental Health Act 1983. *Psychiatric Bulletin*, **33**, 288–290.

Nimmagadda, S. & Jones, C. N. (2008) Consultant psychiatrists' knowledge of their role as representatives of the responsible authority at mental health review tribunals. *Psychiatric Bulletin*, **32**, 366–369.

Nolan, N. (2008) Case law on the MHA 2001: part 1. *Irish Psychiatrist*, **3**, 176–182.

Nussbaum, M. C. (1992) Human functioning and social justice: in defence of Aristotelian essentialism. *Political Theory*, **20**, 202–246.

Nussbaum, M. C. (2000) *Women and Human Development: The Capabilities Approach*. Cambridge University Press.

Nye, J. S. (2004) *Soft Power*. Public Affairs.

O'Brien, C. (2006) Reviews for mental patients in detention. *Irish Times*, 1 November.

O'Brien, C. (2007) 22 people vote at mental hospital. *Irish Times*, 22 May.

O'Carroll, A. & O'Reilly, F. (2008) Health of the homeless in Dublin: has anything changed in the context of Ireland's economic boom? *European Journal of Public Health*, **18**, 448–453.

Ó Cionnaith, F. (2006) Consultants not responsible for harm under Act. *Medicine Weekly*, **43**, 1.

O'Donoghue, B. & Moran, P. (2009) Consultant psychiatrists' experiences and attitudes following the introduction of the Mental Health Act 2001. *Irish Journal of Psychological Medicine*, **26**, 23–26.

Olson, M. (1965) *Logic of Collective Action*. Harvard University Press.

Olson, M. (1982) *The Rise and Decline of Nations*. Yale University Press.

O'Malley, T. (2005) Mental health services. *Dáil Éireann Debate*, **597**, 4 (10 February).

O'Neill, A.-M. (2005) *Irish Mental Health Law*. First Law.

Opler, L. A., White, L., Caton, C. L., *et al* (2001) Gender differences in the relationship of homelessness to symptom severity, substance abuse, and neuroleptic noncompliance in schizophrenia. *Journal of Nervous and Mental Diseases*, **189**, 449–456.

O'Reilly, B. (2007) Congratulations to IMT for raising the issues of mental health tribunals. *Irish Medical Times*, **14**, 19.

Organization of the Islamic Conference (1990) *Cairo Declaration on Human Rights in Islam*. Organization of the Islamic Conference.

O'Shea, E. & Kennelly, B. (2008) *The Economics of Mental Health Care in Ireland*. Mental Health Commission.

Osiatyński, W. (2009) *Human Rights and Their Limits*. Cambridge University Press.

O'Sullivan, D. (1998) The history of human rights across the regions: Universalism vs cultural relativism. *International Journal of Human Rights*, **2**, 22–48.

Ott, B. R., Heindel, W. C. & Papandonatos, G. D. (2003) A survey of voter participation by cognitively impaired elderly patients. *Neurology*, **60**, 1546–1548.

Owens, J. (2005) Mental health services crying out for reform. *Irish Times*, 21 November.

Oxleas NHS Foundation Trust (2013) *London's first non-medical Approved Clinician*. Oxleas NHS Foundation Trust (http://www.oxleas.nhs.uk/news/2013/5/londons-first-non-medical-appr/). Accessed 26 November 2015.

Paine, T. (1776) *Common Sense*. Reprinted (1953) in *Common sense, and other political writings*. Liberal Arts Press.

Paine, T. (1791) *Rights of Man*. Reprinted (1969) as *The Rights of Man*. Penguin.

Pearsall, J. & Trumble, B. (eds) (1996) *The Oxford English Reference Dictionary* (2nd edn). Oxford University Press.

Pedersen, C. B. & Mortensen, P. B. (2001) Evidence of a dose–response relationship between urbanicity during upbringing and schizophrenia risk. *Archives of General Psychiatry*, **58**, 1039–1046.

Penttilä, M., Jääskeläinen, E., Hirvonen, N., *et al* (2014) Duration of untreated psychosis as predictor of long-term outcome in schizophrenia: systematic review and meta-analysis. *British Journal of Psychiatry*, **205**, 88–94.

Perlin, M. L., Kanter, A. S., Treuthart, M. P., *et al* (2006a) *International Human Rights and Comparative Mental Disability Law*. Carolina Academic Press.

Perlin, M. L., Kanter, A. S., Treuthart, M. P., *et al* (2006b) *International Human Rights and Comparative Mental Disability Law: Documents Supplement*. Carolina Academic Press.

Phillips, P. & Nasr, S. J. (1983) Seclusion and restraint and prediction of violence. *American Journal of Psychiatry*, **140**, 229–232.

Piketty, T. (2014) *Capital in the Twenty-First Century*. Harvard University Press.

Pollio, D. E., North, C. S., Eyrich, K. M., *et al* (2003) Modelling service access in a homeless population. *Journal of Psychoactive Drugs*, **35**, 487–495.

Pollis, A. & Schwab, P. (1980) Human rights: a western construct with limited applicability. In *Human Rights: Cultural and Ideological Perspectives* (eds A. Pollis & P. Schwab), pp. 4–34. Praeger.

Porter R (2002) *Madness: A Brief History*. Oxford University Press.

Powell, G., Caan, W. & Crowe, M. (1994) What events precede violent incidents in psychiatric hospitals? *British Journal of Psychiatry*, **165**, 107–112.

Power, S. (2002) *A Problem from Hell: America and the Age of Genocide*. Basic Books.

Power, S. (2008) *Chasing the Flame: Sergio Vieira de Mello and the Fight to Save the World*. Penguin.

Pridmore, S. & Pasha, M. I. (2004) Psychiatry and Islam. *Australasian Psychiatry*, **12**, 380–385.

Priebe, S & Broker, M. (2000) Political change and course of schizophrenia in East Germany, 1984–1994. *Social Psychiatry and Psychiatric Epidemiology*, **35**, 255–258.

Prior, P. M. (2007) Mentally disordered offenders and the European Court of Human Rights. *International Journal of Law and Psychiatry*, **30**, 546–557.

Psychiatrist (1944) Insanity in Ireland. *The Bell*, **7**, 303–310.

Puta-Chekwe, C. & Flood, N. (2001) From division to integration: economic, social, and cultural rights as basic human rights. In *Giving Meaning to Economic Social and Cultural Rights* (eds I. Merali & V. Oosterveld), pp. 39–51. University of Pennsylvania Press.

Putnam, R. D. (2000) *Bowling Alone: The Collapse and Revival of American Community*. Simon and Schuster.

Raad, R., Karlawish, J. & Appelbaum, P. S. (2009) The capacity to vote of persons with serious mental illness. *Psychiatric Services*, **60**, 624–628.

Rapaport, J. & Manthorpe, J. (2008) Family matters: Developments concerning the role of the nearest relative and social worker under mental health law in England and Wales. *British Journal of Social Work*, **38**, 1115–1131.

Rees, G. (2010) Suffrage or suffering? Voting rights for psychiatric in-patients. *British Journal of Psychiatry*, **197**, 159.

Reynolds, J. (1992) *Grangegorman, Psychiatric Care in Dublin Since 1815*. Institute of Public Administration/Eastern Health Board.

Richards, F. & Dale, J. (2009) The Mental Health Act 1983 and incapacity: what general hospital doctors know. *Psychiatric Bulletin*, **33**, 176–178.

Richardson, G. (2005) The European convention and mental health law in England and Wales: moving beyond process? *International Journal of Law and Psychiatry*, **28**, 127–139.

239

Riddell, S., Banks, P. & Tinklin, T. (2005) *Disability and Employment in Scotland: A Review of the Evidence Base.* Scottish Executive.

Ritchie, J. H., Dick, D., Lingham, R. (1994) *The Report of the Inquiry into the Care and Treatment of Christopher Clunis.* HMSO.

Robins, J. (1986) *Fools and Mad: A History of the Insane in Ireland.* Institute of Public Administration.

Robinson, R. & Scott-Moncrieff, L. (2005) Making sense of Bournewood. *Journal of Mental Health Law,* May, 17–25.

Rocca, P., Montemagni, C., Zappia, S. *et al* (2014) Negative symptoms and everyday functioning in schizophrenia: a cross-sectional study in a real world-setting. *Psychiatry Research,* **218**, 284–289.

Roosevelt, F. D. (1941) The Four Freedoms (speech). Reprinted (2005) In *American Political Rhetoric: A Reader* (5th edn) (eds P. A. Lawler & R. M. Schaefer), pp. 357–360. Rowman and Littlefield.

Rosenheck, R., Morrissey, J., Lam, J., *et al* (2001) Service delivery and community: social capital, service systems integration, and outcomes among homeless persons with severe mental illness. *Health Services Research,* **36**, 691–710.

Rosenman, S., Korten, A. & Newman, L. (2000) Efficacy of continuing advocacy in involuntary treatment. *Psychiatric Services,* **51**, 1029–1033.

Rousseau, J.-J. (1762) *Du contrat social ou Principes du droit politique.* Reprinted (1973) as *The Social Contract and Discourses* (trans. & rev. G. D. H. Cole). J. M. Dent & Sons.

Royal College of Psychiatrists (2009) Psychiatrists welcome Northern Ireland announcement of world-first single capacity and mental health legislation. RCPsych (http://www.rcpsych.ac.uk/pressparliament/pressreleases2009/annsinglecapacitymhlegislation.aspx). Accessed 16 October 2015.

Royal Commission (1926) *Report of the Royal Commission on Lunacy and Mental Disorders* (Cmd. 2700). HMSO.

Royal Commission on the Law Relating to Mental Illness and Mental Deficiency (1957) *Royal Commission on the Law Relating to Mental Illness and Mental Deficiency 1954–1957: Report* (Cmnd 169). HMSO.

Rutherdale, A. (1994) Detention in mental hospital after 6 month period without new order invalid. *Irish Times,* 26 September.

Ryan, D. (2010) *The Mental Health Acts 2001–2009.* Blackhall Publishing.

Sarkar, S. P. & Adshead, G. (2005) Black robes and white coats: who will win the new mental health tribunals? *British Journal of Psychiatry,* **186**, 96–98.

Schennach, R., Musil, R., Möller, H. J. *et al* (2012) Functional outcomes in schizophrenia: employment status as a metric of treatment outcome. *Current Psychiatry Reports,* **14**, 229–236.

Schizophrenia Working Group of the Psychiatric Genomics Consortium (2014) Biological insights from 108 schizophrenia-associated genetic loci. *Nature,* **511**, 421–427.

Scottish Executive (2005) *The New Mental Health Act: What's It All About? A Short Introduction.* Scottish Executive.

Scottish Government (2012) *Mental Health Strategy for Scotland, 2012–2015.* The Scottish Government.

Scottish Government Review Group (2009) *Limited Review of the Mental Health (Care and Treatment) (Scotland) Act 2003: Report.* Scottish Government.

Scottish Parliament (2014a) *Mental Health (Scotland) Bill: Explanatory Notes (and Other Accompanying Documents).* APS Group Scotland.

Scottish Parliament (2014b) *Mental Health (Scotland) Bill: Policy Memorandum.* APS Group Scotland.

Scottish Parliament (2014c) *Mental Health (Scotland) Bill: Delegated Powers Memorandum.* APS Group Scotland.

Scottish Parliament (2015) *Mental Health (Scotland) Bill [As Amended at Stage 2]: Revised Explanatory Notes.* APS Group Scotland.

Scull, A. (2005) *The Most Solitary of Afflictions: Madness and Society in Britain, 1700–1900.* University Press.

Scull, A. (2015) *Madness in Civilization*. Thames and Hudson.

Seedhouse, D. & Gallagher, A. (2002) Clinical ethics: undignifying institutions. *Journal of Medical Ethics*, **28**, 368–372.

Select Committee on the Lunatic Poor in Ireland (1817) *Report from the Select Committee on the Lunatic Poor in Ireland with Minutes of Evidence Taken Before the Committee and an Appendix*. House of Commons.

Selten, J. P., Slaets, J. P. & Kahn, R. S. (1997) Schizophrenia in Surinamese and Dutch Antillean immigrants to The Netherlands. *Psychological Medicine*, **27**, 807–811.

Sen, A. (1999) *Development as Freedom*. Oxford University Press.

Sen, A. (2003) *Foreword*. In Pathologies of Power: Health, Human Rights, and the New War on the Poor (P. Farmer), p. xi–xviii. University of California Press.

Shannon, J. (2006a) Getting one's Act together. *Medicine Weekly*, **43**, 20.

Shannon, J. (2006b) Mental Health Act is in breach of human rights. *Medicine Weekly*, **45**, 1.

Shannon, J. (2014) Patient clothing 'breach of dignity' – MHC. *Irish Medical News*, **27**, 8.

Shaw, J., Baker, D., Hunt, I. M., *et al* (2004) Suicide by prisoners. *British Journal of Psychiatry*, **184**, 263–267.

Shorter, E. (1997) *A History of Psychiatry: From the Era of the Asylum to the Age of Prozac*. John Wiley and Sons.

Shotton, L. & Seedhouse, D. (1998) Practical dignity in caring. *Nursing Ethics*, **5**, 246–255.

Siddique, A. & Lee, A. (2014) A survey of voting practices in an acute psychiatric unit. *Irish Journal of Psychological Medicine*, **31**, 229–231.

Silove, D., Steel, Z. & Watters, C. (2000) Policies of deterrence and the mental health of asylum seekers. *JAMA*, **284**, 604–611.

Silva, D. S., Smith, M. J. & Upshur, R. E. (2013) Disadvantaging the disadvantaged: when public health policies and practices negatively affect marginalized populations. *Canadian Journal of Public Health*, **104**, e410–e412.

Sims, A. (1995) *Symptoms in the Mind: An Introduction to Descriptive Psychopathology* (2nd edn). Saunders.

Singer, M. & Clair, S. (2003) Syndemics and public health: reconceptualizing disease in bio-social context. *Medical Anthropology Quarterly*, **17**, 423–441.

Singh, D. K. & Moncrieff, J. (2009) Trends in mental health review tribunal and hospital managers' hearings in north-east London 1997–2007. *Psychiatric Bulletin*, **33**, 15–17.

Singh, S. P., Greenwood, N., White, S., *et al* (2007) Ethnicity and the Mental Health Act 1983. *British Journal of Psychiatry*, **191**, 99–105.

Smith, A. & Caple, A. (2014) Transparency in mental health: why mental health tribunals should be required to publish reasons. *Journal of Law and Medicine*, **21**, 942–956.

Smith, H. & White, T. (2007) Before and after: introduction of the Mental Health (Care and Treatment) (Scotland) Act 2003. *Psychiatric Bulletin*, **31**, 374–377.

Smith, R. K. M. (2007) *Textbook on International Human Rights* (3rd edn). Oxford University Press.

Spellman, J. (1998) Section 260 of the Mental Treatment Act, 1945 reviewed. *Medico-Legal Journal of Ireland*, **4**, 20–24.

Steadman, H. J., Mulvey, E. P., Monahan, J., *et al* (1998) Violence by people discharged from acute psychiatric inpatient facilities and by others in the same neighbourhoods. *Archives of General Psychiatry*, **55**, 393–401.

Steering Group on the Review of the Mental Health Act 2001 (2012) *Interim Report of the Steering Group on the Review of the Mental Health Act 2001*. Department of Health.

Sundquist, K., Frank, G. & Sundquist, J. (2004) Urbanisation and incidence of psychosis and depression: follow-up study of 4.4 million women and men in Sweden. *British Journal of Psychiatry*, **184**, 293–298.

Susser, E. S., Lin, S. P. & Conover, S. A. (1991) Risk factors for homelessness among patients admitted to a state mental hospital. *American Journal of Psychiatry*, **148**, 1659–1664.

Szasz, T. S. (1960) The myth of mental illness. *American Psychologist*, **15**, 113–118.

Szasz, T. (1961) *The Myth of Mental Illness: Foundations of a Theory of Personal Conduct*. Dell Publishing.

241

Szasz, T. (2002) *Liberation by Oppression*. Transaction.

Szmukler, G. (2000) Homicide enquiries. *Psychiatric Bulletin*, **24**, 6–10.

Szmukler, G., Daw, R. & Callard, F. (2014) Mental health law and the UN Convention on the Rights of Persons with Disabilities. *International Journal of Law and Psychiatry*, **37**, 245–252.

Taylor, P. J. & Gunn, J. (1984) Violence and psychosis. I. Risk of violence among psychotic men. *BMJ (Clinical Research Edition)*, **288**, 1945–1949.

Teesson, M., Hodder, T. & Buhrich, N. (2004) Psychiatric disorders in homeless men and women in inner Sydney. *Australian and New Zealand Journal of Psychiatry*, **38**, 162–168.

Teplin, L. A. (1984) Criminalizing mental disorder: the comparative arrest rate of the mentally ill. *American Psychologist*, **39**, 794–803.

Thomas, F. & Gideon, J. (eds) (2013) *Migration, Health and Inequality*. Zed Books.

Thomas, P. & Bracken, P. (2004) Critical psychiatry in practice. *Advances in Psychiatric Treatment*, **10**, 361–370.

Thompson, D. (1971) *The Early Chartists*. University of South Carolina Press.

Thomson, L. D. G. (2005) The Mental Health (Care and Treatment) (Scotland) Act 2003: civil legislation. *Psychiatric Bulletin*, **29**, 381–384.

Tomuschat, C. (2008) *Human Rights: Between Idealism and Realism* (2nd edn). Oxford University Press.

Torrey, E. F. (1995) Jails and prisons – America's new mental hospitals. *American Journal of Public Health*, **85**, 1611–1613.

Torrey, E. F. (2001) *Surviving Schizophrenia* (4th edn). Quill/HarperCollins.

Torrey, E. F. (2013) *American Psychosis: How the Federal Government Destroyed the Mental Illness Treatment System*. Oxford University Press.

Torrey, E. F. & Miller, J. (2001) *The Invisible Plague: The Rise of Mental Illness from 1750 to the Present*. Rutgers University Press.

Tuffrey-Wijne, I. & Hollins, S. (2014) Preventing 'deaths by indifference': identification of reasonable adjustments is key. *British Journal of Psychiatry*, **205**, 86–87.

Üçok, A., Gorwood, P., Karaday, G., et al (2012) Employment and its relationship with functionality and quality of life in patients with schizophrenia: EGOFORS Study. *European Psychiatry*, **6**, 422–425.

United Nations (1948) *Universal Declaration of Human Rights*. United Nations.

United Nations (1991) *Principles for the Protection of Persons with Mental Illness and the Improvement of Mental Health Care*. United Nations Secretariat Centre for Human Rights.

United Nations (2006) *Convention on the Rights of Persons with Disabilities*. United Nations.

Unsworth, C. (1987) *The Politics of Mental Health Legislation*. Clarendon Press.

US Bureau of the Census (1975) *Historical Statistics of the United States, Colonial Times to 1970 (Bicentennial Edition), Part 2*. Government Printing Office.

Valentine, M. B. & Turner, T. (1989) Political awareness of psychiatric patients. *Canadian Medical Association Journal*, **140**, 498.

Van Os, J. & Kapur, S. (2009) Schizophrenia. *Lancet*, **374**, 22–28.

Van Os, J., Driessen, G., Gunther, N., et al (2000) Neighbourhood variation in incidence of schizophrenia: evidence for person–environment interaction. *British Journal of Psychiatry*, **176**, 243–248.

Van Os, J., Hanssen, M., Bak, M., et al (2003) Do urbanicity and familial liability coparticipate in causing psychosis? *American Journal of Psychiatry*, **160**, 477–482.

Van Voren, R. (2014) Is there a resumption of political psychiatry in the former Soviet Union? *International Psychiatry*, **11**, 73–74.

Vize, E. (2005) Pay threat to psychiatrists over mental health tribunals. *Medicine Weekly*, **41**, 1.

Waddell, G., Burton A. K. & Kendall, N. A. S. (2008) *Vocational Rehabilitation: What Works, for Whom and When?* TSO (The Stationery Office).

Wadham, J., Mountfield, H., Edmundson, A., et al (2007) *Blackstone's Guide to The Human Rights Act 1998* (4th edn). Oxford University Press.

Walsh, D. & Daly, A. (2004) *Mental Illness in Ireland 1750–2002: Reflections on the Rise and Fall of Institutional Care*. Health Research Board.

Walsh, E., Buchanan, A. & Fahy, T. (2001) Violence and schizophrenia: examining the evidence. *British Journal of Psychiatry*, **180**, 490–495.

Walsh, O. (1999) 'The designs of providence': race, religion and Irish insanity. In *Insanity Institutions and Society, 1800–1914: A Social History of Madness in Comparative Perspective* (eds J. Melling & B. Forsythe), pp. 223–242. Routledge.

Warner, R. (2004) *Recovery from Schizophrenia: Pyschiatry and Political Economy* (3rd edn). Brunner-Routledge.

Weitzman, E. R. & Kawachi, I. (2000) Giving means receiving: the protective effect of social capital on binge drinking on college campuses. *American Journal of Public Health*, **90**, 1936–1939.

Welch, C. B. (1984) *Liberty and Utility: The French Idéologues and the Transformation of Liberalism*. Columbia University Press.

Welsh, S. F. & Keeling, A. (2013) The Deprivation of Liberty Safeguards. In *Mental Capacity Legislation: Principles and Practice* (eds R. Jacob, N. Gunn & A. Holland), pp. 78–95. RCPsych Publications.

Whelan, D. (2004) Mental health tribunals. *Medico-Legal Journal of Ireland*, **10**, 84–89.

Whelan, D. (2008) Legacy of unresolved legal issues on mental health. *Irish Times*, 4 November.

Whelan, D. (2009) *Mental Health: Law and Practice*. Round Hall.

Whiteford, H., McKeon, G., Harris, M., *et al* (2014) System-level intersectoral linkages between the mental health and non-clinical support sectors: a qualitative systematic review. *Australian and New Zealand Journal of Psychiatry*, **48**, 895–906.

Wicks, E. (2007) *Human Rights and Healthcare*. Hart Publishing.

Williamson, A. (1970) The beginnings of state care for the mentally ill in Ireland. *Economic and Social Review*, **10**, 280–291.

Wise, M. & Sainsbury, P. (2007) Democracy: the forgotten determinant of mental health. *Health Promotion Journal of Australia*, **18**, 177–183.

Wollstonecraft, M. (1792) *A Vindication of the Rights of Woman: With Strictures on Political and Moral Subjects*. Reprinted (1987) in *A Vindication of the Rights of Woman: Mary Wollstonecraft* (2nd edn) (ed. C. H. Poston). W. W. Norton.

World Health Organization (1973) *Report of the International Pilot Study of Schizophrenia*. WHO.

World Health Organization (1992) *The ICD-10 Classification of Mental and Behavioural Disorders*. WHO.

World Health Organization (1996a) *ICD-10 Guide for Mental Retardation*. WHO.

World Health Organization (1996b) *Mental Health Law: Ten Basic Principles*. WHO.

World Health Organization (2001) *The World Health Report 2001. Mental Health: New Understanding, New Hope*. WHO.

World Health Organization (2005) *WHO Resource Book on Mental Health, Human Rights and Legislation*. WHO.

World Health Organization (2013) *Mental Health Action Plan: 2013–2020*. WHO.

World Health Organization Ministers of Health of Member States (2005a) *Mental Health Declaration for Europe: Facing the Challenges, Building Solutions* (WHO European Ministerial Conference on Mental Health) (WHO EUR/04/5047810/6). WHO.

World Health Organization Ministers of Health of Member States (2005b) *Mental Health Action Plan for Europe: Facing the Challenges, Building Solutions* (WHO European Ministerial Conference on Mental Health) (WHO EUR/04/5047810/7). WHO.

Wrigley, M. (2006) A state of unpreparedness. *Irish Medical Times*, **40**, xi.

Wu, E. Q., Birnbaum, H. G., Shi, L., *et al* (2005) The economic burden of schizophrenia in the United States in 2002. *Journal of Clinical Psychiatry*, **9**, 1122–1129.

Yanos, P. T., Barrow, S. M. & Tsemberis, S. (2004) Community integration in the early phase of housing among homeless persons diagnosed with severe mental illness. *Community Mental Health Journal*, **40**, 133–150.

Zigmond, T. (2016) *A Clinician's Brief Guide to the Mental Health Act* (4th edn). RCPsych Publications.

Index

Compiled by Linda English